Early Education
DIRECTOR'S MANUAL

Early Education DIRECTOR'S MANUAL

Compiled by Debi Lydic

Revised and updated by Debbi Keeler and Leanne Leak

purposeful design®
p u b l i c a t i o n s
A Division of ACSI

Colorado Springs, Colorado

Purposeful Design Publications is the publishing division of the Association of Christian Schools International (ACSI) and is committed to the ministry of Christian school education, to enable Christian educators and schools worldwide to effectively prepare students for life. As the publisher of textbooks, trade books, and other educational resources within ACSI, Purposeful Design Publications strives to produce biblically sound materials that reflect Christian scholarship and stewardship and that address the identified needs of Christian schools around the world.

Unless otherwise identified, all Scripture quotations are taken from the Holy Bible, New International Version® (NIV®), © 1973, 1978, 1984 by International Bible Society. Used by permission of Zondervan Publishing House. All rights reserved.

Nutrition Activities for Children in chapter 11 is reprinted from Nutrition standards for child-care programs—Position of ADA, *Journal of the American Dietetic Association*, with permission of the American Dietetic Association.

Form 7.27 Beginnings Workshop is reprinted from King, Gratz, Scheuer, and Claffey, The ergonomics of child care: Conducting worksite analyses, *Work* 6:25–32, with permission from IOS Press.

Printed in the United States of America
16 15 14 13 12 11 10 09 08 07   1 2 3 4 5 6 7

Debi Lydic, Debbi Keeler, and Leanne Leak
    Early education director's manual
    ISBN 978-1-58331-038-0   Catalog #5150

Purposeful Design Publications
A Division of ACSI
PO Box 65130 • Colorado Springs, CO 80962-5130
Customer Service: 800/367-0798 • Website: www.acsi.org

Table of Contents

Chapter 2
PHILOSOPHY AND MISSION OF CHRISTIAN EARLY EDUCATION 27

Chapter 3
GOD'S DESIGN FOR GROWTH 37

Chapter 6
THE ROLE OF THE DIRECTOR 70

Chapter 7
SELECTING AND WORKING WITH STAFF 85

Chapter 8

Chapter 9
ESTABLISHING APPROPRIATE ENVIRONMENTS 149

Chapter 11
CARING FOR THE NEEDS OF CHILDREN 185

Whether traditional part-time or full-day weekday, all early education programs require strong qualified leaders in order to make a difference in the lives of the children and families they serve.

The leadership of an early education program is multifaceted. Directors must be educated and experienced in early childhood education and child development, but also in other subject areas such as budgeting, hiring practices, curriculum development, and especially coping with adult personalities.

However, in all the planning, preparation, and execution of the director's responsibilities, we must never forget the focus of the program: the children. In ACSI's 2001 *Preschool Director's Manual*, Debi Lydic wrote the following:

> One of the daily tasks on my checklist for the [early education] center's custodian is to remove all handprints from the windows, walls, and doors of our school. With a little window spray, all evidence of the day's happenings and of inquisitive little minds and bodies disappears.

> There are other "handprints" left around our center that even the strongest cleaning agent cannot wipe away so easily. The handprint left by the teacher who gently dries a child's tears. The handprint left by the director who gave up precious time to visit with a hurting parent. The handprint the teacher receives from a child's trusting smile. The handprint passed from teacher to teacher as they serve the Lord and one another. And, alas, every once in a while, there are some not-so-nice handprints. Like the handprint of an unkind work spoken in haste, or the handprint of impatience...not to mention the handprint of selfishness. They are all here, the marks of the good and the not so good.

> As administrators of Christian early childhood programs, we have the joy of molding and educating staff, parents, and children. We also have the challenge of conflict resolution, decision making, and problem solving. Knowing how to balance the roles of shepherd, servant, and steward is awesome, at times almost overwhelming. The joys and challenges bring us to our knees, trusting Christ to help us every moment of the day. The handprints we leave and receive along with the daily joys and challenges will last for eternity.

In this edition of the ACSI *Early Education Director's Manual*, two of ACSI's finest, Leanne Leak and Debbi Keeler, have updated the earlier work of Debi Lydic. It is the prayer of all of us that God, through "the works of his hands" which "are faithful and just" (Psalm 111:7) will leave such strong imprints on your heart that we will see His handprint on the children you serve.

Robin Stephenson
Director, Early Education Services
Association of Christian Schools International

GETTING STARTED

Chapter 1

"Let the little children come to me, and do not hinder them, for the kingdom of God belongs to such as these." (Mark 10:14)

Beginning the Process

Starting a new Christian early education program is a challenging but exciting adventure. The process is complex, but commitment to young children and their families justifies the time and effort it takes. Introducing Jesus to the heart of a child is one of the greatest experiences God has given His people. The care and education of young children is a serious responsibility, so it is essential for the sponsoring church or individual to feel the Lord's calling to the endeavor. Prayer and complete dependence on the Lord are important throughout the process.

■ Understanding the commitment

By establishing an early education program in your community, you are providing a valuable service to families in their important role as the primary educators of their children. Families will come to you in good faith, believing that you have a clear understanding of child development and that you will provide quality care and education in a loving Christian environment. Your center will be a significant asset both to the families you serve and to the community as a whole.

Entering into this process requires an understanding of the biblical perspective on educating children. Such a perspective should be the foundational reason for beginning a new program, and not any hope of financial gain. Churches, other organizations, and individuals should give serious thought to the start-up process, recognizing how large an investment in time, money, emotional effort, and professional resources will be required.

■ *Beginning with much prayer*

Before and during the planning process, you need to take time to seek the Lord's will. It is important to consider the availability of resources, to count the cost, and to pray about how to proceed. As you go forward, you should have clear signs from the Lord that your organization has developed the right plan at the right time. Beginning a program without the proper direction and support can be disastrous for you and the children you enroll. A shared vision among the program's founders is essential to establishing biblical priorities for the future.

■ *Taking on the likeness of Christ*

Throughout the process of opening an early education center, your goal should be to serve Christ by benefiting the children and families you will serve, and excellence should be your first priority. In this way you will be demonstrating the love that Christ had for little children and the high regard in which He held them. As you network with professionals and talk with community members, they should sense your genuine love for children and your desire to provide them with quality Christian early education.

■ *Benefits of the commitment*

In their book *Weekday Early Education Administrative Guide*, Bob Couch and Lois Gamble explain, "The purpose of the Christian weekday early education program is ministry that is consistent with the biblical philosophy and ministry of the church or school. A church extends its ministry by providing care, education, and growth opportunities for each child enrolled and by providing a program of outreach to the children's families." [1] Thus Christian early education programs benefit the sponsoring church or other organization as well as the family and the child. The church benefits through an outreach ministry to families and the community that meets real social, emotional, and spiritual needs. Additionally, unchurched families are often drawn to Christian early education programs because parents recognize that they are safe environments where their children will receive moral instruction and have opportunities for character development. These families may become open to the gospel as they develop trusting relationships at the early education center. The needs of families are met as early educators partner with them in caring for their children in a safe, nurturing environment. The children benefit through a well-rounded developmental program that encourages play experiences that foster growth in the spiritual, social, emotional, creative, cognitive, and physical areas of development. As children grow in these areas, they are gaining a foundation for all their future learning.

The Biblical Perspective on Educating Children

■ *Priority of children in the kingdom*

Several accounts in the Gospels show both the importance of young children to God and their place in His kingdom. The Gospel of Mark records an incident in which mothers were bringing their children to Jesus to have them blessed (10:13–16). The disciples shooed the children away, telling them not to bother Jesus. Children are often vulnerable to those who see them as a bother, as less significant than adults, with concerns that are less important. Providing quality care and instruction for young children requires a clear understanding of the priority they deserve to have in our society. Providing such care is a part of respecting the individual regardless of age or productive ability. Jesus' response to the disciples was clear. He was indignant with them and insisted that the children be allowed to come to Him.

Jesus went on to explain that the kingdom of God belongs to those who are like little children. The kingdom of God receives those who come to their heavenly Father in simple faith and trust. The Lord even goes as far as to say that we must all become like little children. The implications are significant for those of us who desire to care for them. In our understanding and nurturing of young children, we must learn from them and follow their cues. To do so involves specializing in the field of early education in order to properly respect children's value and uniqueness in every stage of their childhood. Jesus took the time to welcome children into His arms and to bless each one. As churches develop early education programs, they should take their cue from Jesus, modeling for their community love, respect, time, and investment in young lives.

■ Valuing the weak and vulnerable

It is common in our society to devalue the weak and vulnerable. Those not seen as productive adults are considered less important than others. Young children are treated as such in many homes and societies around the world. Again, Scripture speaks clearly about this distorted value system. In Mark 10:31, Jesus says, "But many who are first will be last, and the last first."

From this passage we see God's eternal value system, and we learn to adapt ours to His, placing great value on those who are weak and dependent. Awareness of weakness is humbling, but it allows for a refining process of acceptance of limitations, which can be a very redeeming quality. We need to value children who have special problems and needs rather than seeing them as an imposition on our time and energy as adults.

■ Partnering with the family

The investigation process for beginning a program must respect the primary role of the parents in educating their children. As early educators, we must constantly resist the temptation to think that we are replacing the parents with ourselves by taking on their children's education. From a biblical perspective we understand clearly the God-given role of parents and their constant involvement in the lives

and education of their children. In an early education program, our role is to support parents in promoting their children's development, both personally and educationally.

In some situations, parents may not fully embrace their God-given role. They may want the program staff to step in and take over to make up for their own inadequacy. It is essential to continually place the responsibility for the child with the parent. Early education programs should give a high priority to parent involvement and communication, and they should look to parents as a primary source of guidance and direction.

■ Putting priority on the process

We must consider the unique characteristics of early education programs and what their priorities must be. We see that a multifaceted approach to learning involves all six developmental areas: social, emotional, physical, creative, spiritual, and cognitive. Our priority is supporting the natural *process* of growth in each area as opposed to the *products* that result from the children's participation in our program. Early education programs emphasize the building blocks of growth in all the areas of development, the goal being a well-balanced child.

Sponsoring Agency

Before any persons or groups do detailed planning, they should be able to answer one question positively: Does the sponsoring congregation or school have a sense of mission about developing an early education program? Only if the answer is a resounding *yes* is it time to address such concerns as how to provide appropriate facilities. The sponsoring organization must be aware that the early education program will have an impact on its building and its other programs. Whether a new structure is built or an existing one remodeled, the center's presence will make an impact. For the sponsoring agency, the benefits of sharing the gospel, introducing sound

Christian education, and providing quality childcare must clearly outweigh any concerns about wear and tear on the facilities. Preschool/childcare programs in church settings often share the costs of custodial services, utilities, and playground equipment. The final arrangement should be presented in writing so that all parties concerned are aware of what was agreed upon.

In their book *Early Childhood Ministry and Your Church,* Kathleen Seaton and Linda Rothaar say, "A healthy congregation is one in which there is an awareness of the real needs in the community, respect and love for all people, and a gospel-driven drive to serve others." [2] Establishing and maintaining a Christian early education center is one way for a congregation to meet real needs in its community.

These are some questions the sponsoring agency must answer:

- How will the early education center affect our organization?
- What impact will the sharing of facilities have?
- Will the center be for church members only or for anyone in the community?
- Will church members receive discounts or other benefits?
- How will expenses, such as the cost of utilities, be divided?
- What inside space will be available to the center, such as classrooms, hallway bulletin boards, a kitchen, a reception area?
- What outside space will be available to the center, such as a playground and parking spaces?
- What arrangements can be made for evening meetings with staff and/or parents?
- What can be done if the church needs space for a large meeting or funeral during the early education program's hours?

Assessing the community need

Those who desire to start an early education program must determine right away whether one is needed. The following facts and statistics may help in determining the need:

- A significant number of mothers work outside the home. An Education Commission of the States report reveals that 65 percent of mothers with children under age six are in the labor force and 84 percent of children have participated in early care and learning programs. [3]

- According to the National Research Council, approximately 80 percent of children age five and younger with employed mothers are in a childcare arrangement with someone other than a parent for an average of almost forty hours a week. [4]

- Many young children are living in poverty and need high-quality programs to improve health conditions and prevent future academic failure.

- Research on the development of the brain and of human intelligence increasingly suggests that positive stimulation of the brain during the early years creates the foundation for a child's lifelong thinking, attitudes, and behavior. A stressful environment or one that lacks stimulation can impair healthy brain development.

Developing a study committee

You will want to establish a study committee to help determine the church and community needs. The committee members should be of such caliber that they could be the program's first early education board members. (See forms 1.1 Start-up Checklist and 1.5 Goals Worksheet.) You will want to research the answers to such questions as these:

- What are the needs of the community? (See form 1.2 Start-up Survey.)

- What are the characteristics (including economic status) of the community?
- What hours of operation would best meet children's and families' needs?
- What age groups in the community are underserved (infant, toddler, preschool, school age)?
- Are there children in the community who have special needs and whose need for early education services is unmet?
- How many early education programs already exist in your general area?
- How many of them are Christian programs?
- What are their tuition rates and hours of operation?
- What financial resources does the church have for financing a start-up and an ongoing program that meets the state standards?
- How will the program effectively share facility space with other church programs?
- Is the facility's condition good enough to create an attractive and well-appointed environment for young children?
- How will the early education program relate to the existing church ministries?
- What staff benefits will the program be able to support in order to hire qualified staff members?
- What are the city requirements for zoning, and will the location be approved?

■ Summarizing findings and making plans

It is recommended that, in addition to answering these and other questions, the study committee survey the church and the community for important information that will affect the direction of the program. The committee should provide a written summary of its findings to facilitate discussion and final approval for the process.

Legal steps should be taken to incorporate the new program as a part of the church corporation or as a private 501(c)3 nonprofit organization. Your community may have regulations that prohibit having childcare centers in certain areas, especially residential zones. You should check your local planning department regulations for such barriers before you invest money and move forward with your plans.

■ Obtaining wise counsel

The Christian community (both church and parents) must be made aware of the ministry of your new program. It is important to contact professionals in the church, those who can provide a financial base, and those who have the expertise needed to establish the program. Hiring a consultant with expertise in early education is essential, especially during the early planning stages. A professional early educator will assist you in establishing a program that is developmentally appropriate. Parents in your community will also need to be informed so that they can provide necessary support of several types: (1) prayer support, (2) student enrollment support, (3) financial support, (4) professional support.

■ Establishing ongoing leadership

The study committee should transition to an early education board soon after they have presented their research and have had the program approved. This new board will be instrumental in providing key leadership and will follow a decision-making process that will facilitate the program's development. Following are guidelines for creating the early education board:

- Pray for the Lord's guidance.
- Select people who have a heart for young children.
- Have a representation of parents who will have children in the program.
- Select people who have the time to commit to this new role and are able to attend early education events throughout the year.
- Select people with professional expertise that will be of value to the program.

- Select people who have a vision for Christian ministry and education.
- Acquire information from the ACSI order department on establishing a board.
- Send in an application for membership in ACSI and apply for individual board membership in the International Association of Christian School Board members (IACSB).

Hiring a Director

Hiring the director or lead teacher can be an exceptionally helpful step in developing an early education program. (See form 1.3 Interview Questions for Early Education Directors.) A qualified educator will save the organization both time and money by utilizing his or her expertise in the field of Christian early education. (See chapter 6 for more information on director qualifications.)

Licensing Requirements

In some places licensing guidelines are very general or even nonexistent. In other places they are quite stringent. The leaders of the new early education program will save time, effort, and headaches by becoming familiar with any legal requirements. If licensing is not required or if the requirements are minimal, using the information and guidelines in this manual and the *ACSI Preschool Accreditation Manual* can help to ensure a high-quality program. Before starting the program, leaders should check with any existing regulatory agency so as to avoid unnecessary problems later. Here are some questions to ask:

- What are the licensing requirements?
- What employee qualifications are mandated?
- What facility requirements are addressed?
- What additional insurance needs will there be?

Purpose of the Program
■ Philosophy and mission
Developing a philosophy of Christian early education is the starting point as you consider beginning

your program. (See form 1.4 School Description.) The philosophy will affect the type of program you develop. A clearly articulated statement of faith with an explanation of its relationship to your program is important, as parents will need to know your program's spiritual priorities. An understanding of how young children learn differently from those in K–12 programs will assist you in establishing a program that follows developmentally appropriate practices and is right for each stage of a child's growth.

Chapter 2 details how your program can develop written statements of faith, purpose, and philosophy. These statements will give you a clear direction as you set your goals and priorities, and they will assure prospective parents of your program's spiritual focus.

■ Services provided
Licensing requirements may be based on the planned hours of operation. Traditional programs typically offer preschool for three- and four-year-olds, usually in Monday-Wednesday-Friday classes and Tuesday-Thursday classes, for approximately two and a half hours a day. Today, early childhood education is offered in almost as many styles as there are programs.

Forming a clear idea of the services you are interested in providing will assist you in developing your overall plan. The information gathered in your needs assessment on community demographics and the scope of the program desired by the families you will serve will inform these decisions. As an organization you need to discuss whether you are interested in providing a full-day weekday program or a traditional part-time program. If it is a full-day program, how many meals will you provide for the children? Other support services such as parent education, screenings, and special-needs services are opportunities you will want to consider. Any services you offer should be consistent with your mission statement.

■ *Benefiting children vs. benefiting the organization*

Typically churches and organizations are initially attracted to starting new early education programs because of the perceived value that the programs will bring to the overall organization. This perceived value can include additional members, new sources of revenue, and outreach to the community. Much thought and prayer must be given in this area. Keep in mind that benefiting the children must have first priority, above any perceived value to the organization. Quality care must never be sacrificed for financial gain.

Financial Resources

■ *Start-up funds*

Fiscal responsibility is critical for those who would begin an early education program. Funds need to be allocated for finding an adequate facility or for bringing an existing one up to the required standard. Money must be put aside to purchase or supplement existing furniture, fixtures, equipment, teaching materials, and consumable supplies. Initial operating expenses include hiring staff, advertising, and managing until the center has a full enrollment. It is wise to set aside operating funds sufficient for three months as part of the new program's start-up costs. Early education programs usually open with a less-than-full enrollment and thus do not reach their financial potential in the first year. (For more on finances, see chapter 5, "Managing Finances.")

Start-up funds for beginning a program may come from a variety of sources, including the following:

- The sponsoring organization
- Loans taken out by members of the organization
- A mortgage on the church buildings
- Grants or funds made available by foundations or other private groups

- City, state, and federal assistance (Be aware that accepting public funds may limit a school's freedom to share Christ with the children.)

■ *Operating income*

The major funding for the center's program is likely to come from the parents. Before a new early education center is started, tuition costs for comparable programs should be researched. The school's main sources for operating funds are often these:

- Tuition charged to parents for the program
- Donations from supporters of the program
- Support allocated by the church

Realistic Expectations

■ *Takes time and planning*

Having realistic expectations can be an asset during this beginning process. Many organizations enter the process with a great deal of enthusiasm and a vision for the program's unfolding within a short time, but usually this vision does not become reality. Putting together a business plan, bringing the facility into compliance with state standards, and applying for a state license where required—these can take months. Typically the whole process takes a minimum of one to two years. Each program faces its own challenges, so the start-up process can vary significantly among different programs. As you complete the process, your priority should be taking the time to do things well.

■ *Start small*

It is always wise and realistic to start small. A center needs time to develop a reputation among families. It is common for programs not to be filled when they begin but to grow as they gain momentum and familiarity in the community. New programs may take up to three years to achieve a balanced budget and even longer to make a profit. Because early education programs are labor intensive, the potential for profit is limited. However, once a program becomes established, it is likely to become self-supporting, even profitable, particularly when it has an equitable shared-space agreement with the sponsoring agency. Larger programs (those with a hundred or more children) are more likely than others to become profitable over time. Keeping these facts in mind will help you be realistic regarding matters of revenue.

ACSI Membership and Accreditation

Membership in the Association of Christian Schools International is available to those early education programs that complete the membership application process. ACSI membership entitles your center to participate in such programs as conventions, conferences, and Early Education Equippers and to receive such services as accreditation, certification, and curriculum information and materials. Your ACSI regional office can provide you with information about membership.

Once an early education program has been established, its leaders will want to consider its becoming accredited. Accreditation is a means of recognizing educational institutions that meet prescribed standards as well as validating the integrity and quality of their programs. Achieving accreditation as an early education program ensures that, for your institution, excellence does indeed begin at the early childhood level. Besides confirming that standards of quality have been met, accreditation gives parents extra confidence in the program and helps the administration reevaluate the standards regularly and strive to maintain them. Several different accreditation programs have been designed for preschool/childcare programs. They all basically address the quality of the early education program and its appropriateness to the age of the children. By addressing the spiritual aspect of the center, ACSI goes one step beyond traditional accreditation programs.

It is important to note the difference between ACSI membership and ACSI accreditation. Membership entitles the center to participate in the many services and programs that the association provides. Accreditation is an opportunity available only to member schools. The application form is available from the ACSI regional office. Achieving accreditation is a challenging and rewarding process that requires hard work and the full participation of the center's administration, staff, and parents.

In Philippians 3:14, the apostle Paul challenges Christians to "press on toward the goal to win the prize for which God has called me heavenward in Christ Jesus." The Christian preschool/childcare center is also pressing on toward the goal of emulating Jesus Christ, a lifelong process that includes daily evaluation of what is being done and of how the program can become more effective in the lives of children, parents, and staff. The standards set by ACSI challenge the program to continue in the process of becoming the very best for the sake of the Lord Jesus Christ.

FORM 1.1

Start-up Checklist

Start-up Checklist

This checklist should be adapted to reflect your school's needs more accurately. Although it shows a nine-month process, the entire process may actually take nine to fifteen months.

First Month of Preparation

☐ 1. Select a committee from the school or church board to oversee the early education center's program and to become familiar with all licensing regulations. At this time, consider hiring a director familiar with early education programs.

☐ 2. The committee should develop a written philosophy for early childhood education (see chapter 2).

☐ 3. Decide on the space/facility available (see chapter 9). If you will be sharing a space, establish facility arrangements in a written agreement. If you are building or remodeling, find out about city and county building requirements and zoning permits.

Second and Third Months

☐ 4. Seek legal advice in drawing up papers for becoming incorporated as a separate corporation or for inclusion in an existing one.

☐ 5. Arrange for insurance coverage.

☐ 6. Select a name for the center, checking to assure that no existing center has the same name.

☐ 7. Prepare a budget. Keep it separate from that of any sponsoring organization in order to track gains and deficits accurately.

☐ 8. Institute licensing procedures if required by a city or state regulatory agency. This process will include a visit from the fire department.

Fourth, Fifth, and Sixth Months

☐ 9. Design a written job description for the early education director, and select a qualified candidate (see chapter 6).

☐ 10. Review personnel policies to incorporate certified staff into the current policies or to establish new policies (see chapter 4).

Seventh, Eighth, and Ninth Months

☐ 11. Review or establish job descriptions, contracts, and an employee handbook for all staff members (see chapter 7).

☐ 12. Advertise job openings, and interview potential staff members.

☐ 13. Prepare forms for recording children's information. You may need to find out about licensing regulations (see chapter 11).

☐ 14. Prepare an orientation and in-service training for new staff members.

☐ 15. Prepare a parent handbook to be given when children enroll (see chapter 12).

☐ 16. Develop publicity information about the center—brochures and advertisements to let the public know when enrollment will begin.

☐ 17. Order equipment and supplies. Additional materials may be acquired through donations, garage sales, and an "early education center shower."

☐ 18. Schedule an open house and a parent-orientation meeting.

 purposeful design · *Early Education* DIRECTOR'S MANUAL

FORM 1.2

Start-up Survey

At the present time *‹church/school name›* is considering starting an early education center. If you will answer the following questions, it will be helpful.

Are you attending church in this area? **Yes / No**

Which church? _____

Would you be interested in a Christian early education center? **Yes / No**
Comments _____

Do you feel an early education center is needed in this geographic area? **Yes / No**
Comments _____

Do you have 2- to 5-year-old children? **Yes / No**
How many? _____

Would you make use of an early education center in this area? **Yes / No**
Comments _____

What hours would you want a center to be available? _____

What do you expect from an early education program? _____

What would you want offered in an early education curriculum? _____

How many days per week and hours per day would you be interested in having your child attend? _____

Days a week:	Monday	Tuesday	Wednesday	Thursday	Friday
Hours a day:	Mornings	Afternoons	All day		

If you do not have children ages 2 to 5, do you feel an early education center would be a contribution to this area? **Yes / No**
Comments _____

Optional
Name: _____
Address: _____
Phone: _____

Thank you for taking the time to fill out this survey. If you do not have a church home, we invite you to visit us in the near future. Please call *‹local number›* for further information about our programs. We will also keep you informed about the opening of our Christian early education center.

 purposeful design · *Early Education* DIRECTOR'S MANUAL

FORM 1.3

Interview Questions for Early Education Directors

1. What is your philosophy of Christian early childhood education?

2. Describe the distinctions between Christian early childhood programs and secular ones.

3. How would you facilitate the integration of biblical principles into the children's daily activities?

4. How should Bible stories, Scripture, and prayer be incorporated into daily, weekly, and monthly planned experiences?

5. How can the Christian early education center serve families? What steps would you take to reach out to unchurched families and link them with the local church?

6. Describe the process of spiritual development in young children. What types of experiences do children need to develop a healthy concept of God? a healthy concept of self?

7. What attributes would you look for in young teachers?

8. How would you evaluate a potential applicant's spiritual maturity and preparation for teaching? What criteria are important in selecting teachers?

9. How would you promote the professional development of the teaching staff?

10. How would you encourage the spiritual development of the teaching staff?

11. What are your thoughts on teacher recruitment and retention?

12. How would you resolve conflict among the staff?

13. Describe the process of curriculum development.

14. Describe your relationship with your previous supervisors.

15. What is the role of parents in the Christian early education program?

16. How would you promote parents' involvement in the early education program?

17. How would you respond to parents' complaints?

18. What would you do to promote enrollment in the early education program?

19. What experience have you had in managing a budget?

20. How would you develop the early education program's facility?

21. Describe the role of the learning environment in the early education program curriculum.

22. How would you assess the children's development? How would you report the information to parents?

23. How would you maintain an effective working relationship with other ministries sharing your classrooms?

24. How would you employ written and verbal communication in building relationships with staff and parents?

25. How would you implement teacher evaluation?

purposeful design · *Early Education* DIRECTOR'S MANUAL

FORM 1.4

School Description

‹church/school name› Early Education Center

A Corporation

‹church/school name› Early Education Center is a nonprofit religious corporation in the State of *‹name of state›*. It is owned by the *‹church/school name›*, which is also a nonprofit religious corporation in *‹name of state›*.

‹church/school name› Early Education Center is licensed by the State of *‹name of state›* Department of Social/Human Services. *‹church/school name›* Early Education Center is a member of the Association of Christian Schools International.

The governing board of the early education center is composed of parents who have or have had children in the center and are members of *‹name of church›*. The *‹church/school name›* Early Education Center administration, with the advice and ratification of the governing board, originates and implements the policies that govern the center and the guidelines for its effective business operation.

Evangelical

The Bible curriculum centers on a systematic understanding of the events of the Old and New Testaments. The focus of the study is the Person and work of Jesus Christ. Jesus is presented as the Creator God (Genesis 1; John 1; Colossians 1), the Savior Redeemer (Isaiah 53; John; Acts; New Testament), the reigning King of kings and Lord of lords, the One whose return we momentarily expect.

Christ-Centered

‹church/school name› Early Education Center is a privately owned and operated evangelical Christian early education center. It is not parochial in its religious emphasis. The center's governing board, with the advice of the center's administration, has adopted a statement of faith that is consistent with the doctrinal statements of the National Association of Evangelicals and the Association of Christian Schools International. These doctrines are taught in the classroom, and they are the foundation of the entire curriculum.

Not Against, but For

We are not "against" public early education centers, but we are "for" private evangelical Christian early education. It is our conviction that parents should be given the option of sending their children to a private evangelical Christian early education center. We are privileged to make that option available to families within the radius of our campus.

Not Competition, but Excellence

Our motivation is not competition with public or private early education centers. Instead, our motivation is to achieve excellence in curriculum, biblical understanding, physical and motivational development, and social and emotional maturity by giving young children "room and time to grow."

purposeful design · *Early Education* DIRECTOR'S MANUAL

FORM 1.4

School Description (Continued)

Not in Place of, but in Support of, the Home and Church
We cannot take the place of the father and mother of the young child, and have no desire to do so. We cannot do what the parents will not do. Our objective is to firmly support and reinforce what the parents are already doing in the home. If the home is not Christ-centered and biblically based, then who and what we are in Christ may introduce Christ to the parents and family.

Not a Church, but an Early Education Center
We are not a five-day-a-week church. <church/school name> Early Education Center supports and reinforces what the family and church are doing. Our teachers must have made a personal profession of faith in the Lord Jesus Christ and must be active in a local church. The center's program is not designed to take the place of Sunday school, worship, or other phases of church life. If the center is viewed as having that purpose, we will be unable to accomplish our goal of supporting and reinforcing the life of both family and church.

Reasons for Being
An early education center must keep in clear focus its reasons for being. Ours are as follows:
1. To give children an opportunity, an atmosphere, and some assistance in growing
2. To give Christian families an early education center that stands for, supports, and reinforces the evangelical Christian worldview and way of life
3. To prepare children to "live in this world" but not "become a part of this world"
4. To take away from our society the "prime time" it has taken in our children's minds. (We are reclaiming their primary hours of learning so that Christ will be at the center of their learning experiences.)
5. To provide children an opportunity to develop special skills under the direction of teachers who love and honor Christ.

purposeful design

Early Education DIRECTOR'S MANUAL

FORM 1.5

Goals Worksheet

Goal	Tasks	Person Responsible	Timeline	Progress

purposeful design

Early Education

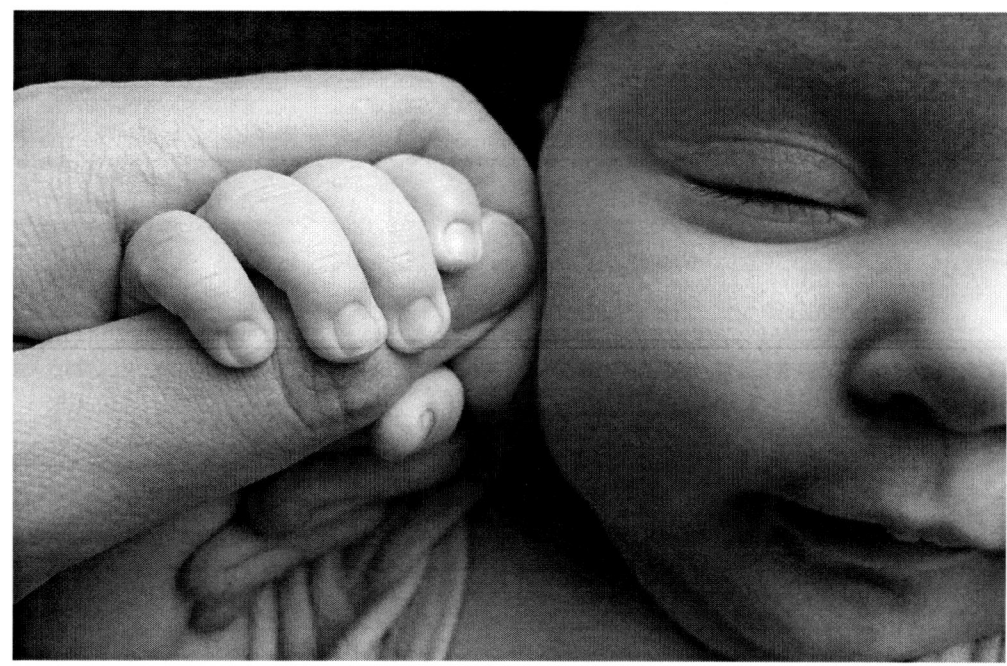

PHILOSOPHY AND MISSION OF CHRISTIAN EARLY EDUCATION

Chapter 2

Test everything. Hold on to the good. (1 Thessalonians 5:21)

Philosophy of Early Education

Every area of the early education program is affected by its philosophy of early childhood education. Any time the question "Why?" is asked and answered, the philosophy is revealed, whether the question concerns the content of the curriculum, the selection of teachers, the discipline procedures, or the fees charged. Every early education administrator must ask these questions: Why does our program exist? What is distinctive about it? What are its goals? How will we reach them? The answers will grow out of the program's philosophy.

A clearly articulated philosophy is crucial to the development and success of a Christian early education program. The philosophy documents express the values and beliefs that are the foundation of the program. These documents require careful thought and planning. The statements should be written in such a way that they can easily be applied to the content of the program through the curriculum and activities. Paul Kienel, founding president of ACSI, says this:

> Basic to the implementation of the Christian philosophy in the Christian school is the setting down in written form of a clearly articulated statement of its Christian philosophy, the result of its clear understanding of the biblical imperatives of its existence and the necessary integration of God's truth in every facet of its ministry.[1]

The primary distinctive of a Christian early education philosophy is that it is based on God's Word. It reflects biblical principles, includes scriptural references, and represents a thoroughly Christian view of life. The overall philosophy documents should include the following:

1. A statement of faith
2. Purpose statements (about mission, vision, and expected outcomes)
3. A Bible-based educational philosophy

Statement of Faith

The governing board will be responsible for adopting the statement of faith, or doctrinal statement, for the early education program. The statement of faith is the foundation of basic beliefs on which the philosophy, purpose, aims, policies, procedures, and programs will be built. While any two Christian early education programs are likely to differ in certain details of their theology, every program's statement of faith, being established and grounded in Holy Scripture, should contain the essence of the Christian faith. Because young children are limited in their ability to think abstractly, the doctrinal topics regularly mentioned in early education classrooms typically concern the basics of the Christian faith. The statement of faith should include appropriate Scripture references. Church-sponsored programs may be able to access their congregation's or denomination's faith statement.

■ *The ACSI statement of faith*

Early education programs that are not associated with a particular church or denomination may want to consider adopting ACSI's statement of faith:

1. We believe the Bible to be the inspired, the only infallible, authoritative, inerrant Word of God (2 Timothy 3:16, 2 Peter 1:21).

2. We believe there is one God, eternally existent in three persons—Father, Son, and Holy Spirit (Genesis 1:1, Matthew 28:19, John 10:30).

3. We believe in the deity of Christ (John 10:33), His virgin birth (Isaiah 7:14, Matthew 1:23, Luke 1:35), His sinless life (Hebrews 4:15, 7:26), His miracles (John 2:11), His vicarious and atoning death (1 Corinthians 15:3, Ephesians 1:7, Hebrews 2:9), His resurrection (John 11:25, 1 Corinthians 15:4), His ascension to the right hand of God (Mark 16:19), His personal return in power and glory (Acts 1:11, Revelation 19:11).

4. We believe in the absolute necessity of regeneration by the Holy Spirit for salvation because of the exceeding sinfulness of human nature; and that we are justified on the single ground of faith in the shed blood of Christ and that only by God's grace and through faith alone we are saved (John 3:16–19, 5:24, Romans 3:23, 5:8–9, Ephesians 2:8–10, Titus 3:5).

5. We believe in the resurrection of both the saved and the lost; those that are saved to the resurrection of life, and those that are lost to the resurrection of condemnation (John 5:28–29).

6. We believe in the spiritual unity of believers in our Lord Jesus Christ (Romans 8:9, 1 Corinthians 12:12–13, Galatians 3:26–28).

7. We believe in the present ministry of the Holy Spirit by whose indwelling the Christian is enabled to live a godly life (Romans 8:13–14, 1 Corinthians 3:16, 6:19–20, Ephesians 4:30, 5:18).

■ *Publishing the statement of faith*

Not every board will require all families enrolling in the early education program to believe in or agree with the statement of faith. However, every enrolling family should be aware that the center's curriculum, activities, and programs are delivered from a biblical perspective. Both staff and parents should receive a copy of the statement of faith. It is wise to include it in both the staff and parent handbooks along with the applications for both students and staff. Asking staff members to sign their adherence to the program's statement of faith can assure the director that they fully support and identify with the important truths it contains.

Purpose Statements

Purpose statements answer questions about why your organization exists (your mission), what you want to accomplish (your vision), and how the results will be measured (expected student outcomes). Purpose statements encapsulate your organization's priorities. The director, the sponsoring body, and the governing board work collaboratively in developing the purpose statements. An early education program's purpose statement might begin as follows:

> XYZ Early Education Center is a part of the overall ministry of XYZ Church. XYZ Early Education Center exists as an outreach to the community by assisting parents with their overall role as the primary educators of their child. Our main responsibilities are to help young children grow in the social, emotional, creative, spiritual, cognitive, and physical areas of development. We have a strong commitment to God's Word, and we fully integrate godly principles into every aspect of our curriculum. We seek to create a nurturing environment as an extension of the home while assisting children to feel competent. We recognize the window of opportunity for growth during the early years and seek to provide an optimum environment for children's development.

■ Mission statement

It is common for organizations, specifically schools, to create a mission statement. In a broad sense a mission statement is a brief description, usually in one or two sentences, of why your organization exists. It identifies the organization and the values it represents. An early education program that is attached to a K–12 program may have a mission statement that guides the entire organization. Each program needs to evaluate whether the mission statement of the sponsoring organization or of the K–12 program adequately represents the early education target group.

Programs seeking accreditation and pursuing other quality-improvement efforts often begin by developing or refining their mission statement. (See form 2.5 Mission Statement Worksheet.) The process of developing a mission statement involves a collaboration of the program's leaders and should include input from the staff. It can take a few meetings to articulate the previously unstated values and vision. Here is an example of a mission statement unique to early education: "To partner with the family in providing a foundation for early Christian education while developing the whole child in a secure and nurturing environment."

■ Vision statement

Establishing and articulating a vision for your early education program is distinct from creating your mission statement. A mission statement identifies the target group and tells how the program will fulfill the mission, while a vision statement defines what the people in the target group will be like if they are served effectively. (See form 2.6 Vision Statement Worksheet.) In *A Fish Out of Water*, George Barna describes vision as providing "a clear and compelling mental portrait of a preferable future that is conveyed by God to His chosen servants. It is a portrait of a better future that we may participate in developing."[2] The staff members play a key role in influencing how that "better future" will be attained. They each place their own fingerprint on the statement through their individual contributions to the total program. To refine and develop the vision statement, the staff should take time to discuss what is unique about the program and what contributions each member can make. It is important to ask, What fingerprint will this program leave on the lives of the students as we strive to serve them effectively? The answer can be highlighted in various formats that communicate to parents the value and distinctives of the early education program. Purpose statements can also be enfolded into a vision statement.

■ Statement of expected outcomes

Once the philosophy statement is in place, time and attention can be given to articulating a set of expected student outcomes—the measurable change or transformation that will take place in the students that the program serves. ACSI has developed a list of outcomes to serve as a guideline for early education programs. Careful thought needs to be given to outcomes, as the parents and the community will want to know what result to expect from having their children in your program. Identifying student outcomes helps to crystallize what the program's priorities will be and what kinds of learning will be emphasized. Developing goals that are specific to each age group and addressing every facet of a child's development also helps focus teachers on specific areas that should have priority and are appropriate for each child's developmental level. (See form 2.7 Expected Outcomes: Sample Statement.)

■ Guidelines for expected outcomes

The National Institute for Early Education Research defines standards or outcomes as "shared expectations and notions about what matters for children,… standards represent the values of the people who set them."[3] In setting these standards, they also make six policy recommendations:

- Because standards reflect the values of the people who set them, collaboration with families and communities is a key to the successful design and implementation of preschool standards.

- Standards documents should distinguish clearly between program standards and child outcome standards.

- Outcome standards need to be written in ways that take into account the unique ways that young children develop and learn, considering all aspects of school readiness identified by the National Education Goal Panel.

- Standards that address physical health, social–emotional development, and approaches to learning need to have as much emphasis and specificity as those that address cognitive and language development.

- Early education program standards should allow continuity with kindergarten standards, but not at the expense of attention to physical and social-emotional development.

- Standards should be written in ways that allow for appropriate, effective assessment. Assessment policies and practices should go beyond maintaining accountability to fostering program improvement.

Biblical Education Philosophy

It is essential to invest time in developing a biblical education philosophy that articulates the center's beliefs as they relate specifically to the early education program. A cohesive educational-philosophy statement expresses foundational principles that encompass both the spiritual needs of children and the school's approach to the educational process. Thus the school's philosophy encompasses the following areas:

- The nature and needs of young children
  ° The developmental process
    ‣ Individual variation
    ‣ Developmental domains: social, emotional, physical, spiritual, creative, cognitive

° How young children grow and learn (the learning process)

  ▸ Meaningful experience

  ▸ Exploration

  ▸ Interaction with the environment and materials

• How children develop an awareness of and a relationship with God

  ° Priority of teaching biblical truth

  ° Significance of the teacher's role in modeling and meeting children's needs

■ Developing a philosophy statement

Christian early education programs need to be a light in the community, reflecting the love and care for young children that flow from a relationship with Jesus Christ. Because Christian programs are responding to a higher calling and are educating children for eternal purposes, there should be significant differences between Christian and secular programs in their motivation for, and execution of, early education services. Christian programs should be distinct in their staffing and curriculum, their commitment to truth and integrity, and the manner in which young children are cared for and taught. These distinctives relate to and are the outcome of the overall philosophy of the program. The word *philosophy* derives from Greek words meaning "love of wisdom." A philosophy is what holds things together. What is it about your program that holds things together? It should be obvious in a Christian program that the glue is Jesus Christ.

As centers develop philosophy statements, the process becomes a valuable tool in bringing leaders together to search the Scriptures for direction and purpose. A statement supported with Scripture references provides a solid foundation for Christian education.

■ Writing the philosophy statement

In preparing to articulate a philosophy statement, key leaders of the center should gather for an initial discussion as to who will be involved and have significant input. The director, along with the administrator and board, will drive the project. Here are some steps in the process of writing a philosophy statement:

1. *Begin with prayer.* Prayer is essential in directing the thoughts of those writing the statement to identify biblical principles and to rely on the guidance of the Holy Spirit.

2. *Gather sample philosophy statements from other programs.* These, along with information on the topics listed above, will encourage informed participation. (Four examples, forms 2.1–2.4, are provided at the end of this chapter.)

3. *Rely on Scripture references and your statement of faith* to provide the foundation of your philosophy statement. Refer to relevant Scripture passages in the philosophy statement.

4. *As a staff, discuss some of the areas listed above,* particularly those recognized as essential to articulate. Afterward, have the staff return to the classroom and implement some of these concepts with their students. This procedure will reinforce ideas and will allow the staff to see the priorities clearly.

5. *Examine your current philosophy statement,* talk about gaps, and prioritize what is missing.

6. *Reduce the concepts to concise written statements,* item by item, until the final statement contains all that needs to be said.

The final approval and adoption of your center's philosophy statement should come from the program's board or governing body.

■ *Communicating your center's philosophy*

The next step is to communicate your philosophy statement effectively to the staff, the parents, and when appropriate, the students. Philosophy statements should appear in both staff and parent handbooks. The staff should clearly articulate each aspect to the parents, describing how the philosophy will be implemented in the classroom. The staff will need ongoing training in the philosophy, including specific examples of how the center's philosophy impacts the daily classroom activities. These matters need to be addressed frequently so that the philosophy will permeate the entire program. It is the director's responsibility to ensure that the stated philosophy is indeed being implemented in each classroom.

FORM 2.1

Philosophy Statement: Worthington Christian Schools

Statement of Purpose

Worthington Christian Schools (WCS) is a ministry of the Grace Brethren Church (GBC) of Columbus, Ohio. WCS is committed to the education of the children of this church through a curriculum and activities that are based on and are faithful to the Bible. The children of non-GBC Christian families are invited to participate in our K–12 program as space is available. The children of both non-GBC Christian families and non-Christian families are invited to be a part of our center as space is available.

Philosophy of Early Education

We believe that each child is a unique creation of God made in His image (Luke 18:16). We believe one of the ways children learn about God and His purpose and plan for their lives is from the Bible.

We believe that each child learns by actively participating, exploring, and discovering (Proverbs 20:11). Children develop new knowledge and skills based on what they already know and can do, through play, the examination and manipulation of concrete materials, and the use of all their senses. Learning activities should be built around the child's current interests. Children must be encouraged to ask questions, experiment, make choices, and propose solutions. In so doing, they will learn to assume responsibility for their own actions and feelings, and they will gain confidence in acting on their knowledge of the Bible and of their physical and social worlds.

We believe that each child grows developmentally (Luke 2:52). To teach in ways that are developmentally appropriate requires knowing how children develop and learn, and matching to that knowledge the content and strategies planned for them. The WCS PS/K program focuses on concepts and processes, using small group instruction, interactive learning, and active manipulation of relevant, concrete materials to build a solid foundation for academics within a context of meaningful activity.

We believe that each child learns by example (Deuteronomy 6:7). Teachers of young children should hold a biblical worldview and live a Christian lifestyle in their home,

 purposeful design

Early Education DIRECTOR'S MANUAL

FORM 2.1

Philosophy Statement: Worthington Christian Schools (Continued)

school, and community. Play experiences are structured to allow an optimal mix of individual, one-to-one, small-group, and large-group experiences. Planned group activities promote more skillful levels of communication, of social interaction, and of perceptual and motor development.

Mission

Worthington Christian Schools exist to be used by God to disciple students to learn in harmony with God's Word so they may know, love, and serve Jesus Christ.

Vision: Preschool/Kindergarten

The vision of Worthington Christian Preschool/Kindergarten is

- to be a vital outreach ministry of Grace Brethren Church, honoring God, children, and families
- to assimilate many families into the church
- to continually improve our ability to teach young children through professional development, and through mentoring younger teachers
- to be one of the best Christian preschools of choice in central Ohio
- to be, in the future, one of the best Christian birth-through-K childcare programs of choice in central Ohio
- to be, in the future, one of the best Christian adult-daycare programs of choice in central Ohio

Policies

The Worthington Christian Schools Advisory Board has adopted policies for our schools. A copy of the policy book is available in the office. All staff members are encouraged to become familiar with all the policies. Those specific to early education have been included in the handbook.

Nondiscrimination Policy

Grace Brethren Church and Worthington Christian Schools maintain a firm policy prohibiting discrimination against any race, color, or national and ethnic origin, admitting

 purposeful design

Early Education DIRECTOR'S MANUAL

FORM 2.1

Philosophy Statement: Worthington Christian Schools (Continued)

all students to the rights, privileges, programs, and activities generally available to students at the schools. In addition, the schools do not discriminate on the basis of race, color, or national and ethnic origin in the administration of educational policies, admissions policies, scholarship and loan programs, and athletic and other school programs. Nor do the schools discriminate on the basis of race, color, or national and ethnic origin in hiring of either certified or noncertified personnel. All forms of harassment by students, school personnel, or parents that create an intimidating, hostile, or offensive environment will not be tolerated under any circumstances. The administrator, upon receipt of a report or complaint alleging discrimination, harassment, or violence, shall immediately undertake or authorize an investigation.

 purposeful design

Early Education DIRECTOR'S MANUAL

FORM 2.2

Philosophy Statement: Northside Christian Early Childhood Development Center

The educational philosophy of the Northside Christian Early Childhood Development Center is God-centered and is based on the belief that God's laws, principles, ethics, and standards are absolute truth, that the Bible is the inspired Word of God, and that Jesus Christ is the Son of God and the Creator and Sustainer of all things.

Each child is viewed as a separate and unique creation of God. Therefore, every child is accepted and loved. Every child is an individual with his or her own rate of physical, social, emotional, cognitive, and spiritual maturation; therefore, the school environment will influence each child differently. All children will grow in all areas of development through play and interaction with the people and objects in their environment. Young children do not need to be forced to learn. They are motivated by their own desire to understand the world, and thus they learn experientially.

The aim of the Northside Christian Early Childhood Development Center is to provide a loving and nurturing Christian perspective that will foster a positive self-esteem and a child's acceptance of his or her role in life at home, at school, at play, and at church.

This philosophy will be the guiding vehicle for applying biblical principles to teaching practices. All philosophies of subjects, policies of the school and of the school board, curriculum materials, and teaching methods at the Northside Christian Early Childhood Development Center shall conform to this philosophy of Christian education.

Certain objectives have been established in order to implement this philosophy:

1. To teach that the Bible is the inspired Word of God, thus developing attitudes of love and respect toward it (2 Timothy 3:15–17; 2 Peter 1:20–21)
2. To teach biblical character qualities and provide opportunities for the students to demonstrate these qualities (1 Samuel 16:7; Galatians 5:22–23)
3. To teach the students respect for and submission to authority from God's perspective (Romans 13:1–5; Hebrews 13:17; Ephesians 6:1–3)

 purposeful design

Early Education DIRECTOR'S MANUAL

FORM 2.2

Philosophy Statement: Northside Christian Early Childhood Development Center
(Continued)

4. To help students develop a Christian worldview by integrating life, and all studies with the Bible (2 Peter 1:3)
5. To help students develop their identity as unique individuals created in the image of God and to attain their fullest potential (Psalm 139:13–16)
6. To teach students to treat everyone with love and respect as unique individuals created in God's image (Philippians 2:1–4; Ephesians 5:21)
7. To encourage parents to realize and shoulder their responsibility for the spiritual, moral, and social education of their children (Deuteronomy 6:4–7; Proverbs 22:6)

 purposeful design

Early Education DIRECTOR'S MANUAL

FORM 2.3

Philosophy Statement: Baymonte Christian Preschool

The educational philosophy of Baymonte Christian Preschool is based on a God-centered view that God's laws, principles, ethics, and standards are absolute truth, that the Bible is the inspired Word of God, and that Jesus Christ is the Son of God and the Creator and Sustainer of all things.

Each child is viewed as a separate and unique creation of God. Therefore, every child is an individual with his/her own rate of physical, social, emotional, cognitive, and spiritual maturation; therefore, the school environment will influence each child differently. Children will grow in all areas of development through play and interaction with the people and objects in their environment. Young children do not need to be forced to learn. They are motivated by their own desires to understand the world, and thus they learn experientially.

The aim of Baymonte Christian Preschool is to provide a loving and nurturing Christian perspective, which will foster a positive self-esteem and a child's acceptance of his/her role in life at home, at school, at play, and in the child's world.

This philosophy shall be the guiding vehicle to apply biblical principles to teaching practices. All philosophies of subjects, policies of the school board, school policies, curriculum materials, and teaching methods at Baymonte Christian Preschool shall conform to this philosophy of Christian education.

Certain objectives are established in order to implement this philosophy:

1. To teach that the Bible is the inspired Word of God, thus developing attitudes of love and respect toward it (2 Timothy 3:15–17; 2 Peter 1:20–21)
2. To teach biblical character qualities and provide opportunities for the students to demonstrate these qualities (1 Samuel 16:7, Galatians 5:22–23)
3. To teach students respect for and submission to authority from God's perspective (Romans 13:1–5; Hebrews 13:17; Ephesians 6:1–3)

 purposeful design

Early Education DIRECTOR'S MANUAL

FORM 2.3

Philosophy Statement: Baymonte Christian Preschool (Continued)

4. To help students develop a Christian worldview by integrating life, and all studies, with the Bible (2 Peter 1:3)
5. To help students develop their identity as unique individuals created in the image of God and to attain their fullest potential (Psalm 139:13–16)
6. To encourage parents to realize and shoulder their responsibility for the spiritual, moral, and social education of their children (Deuteronomy 6:4–7; Proverbs 22:6)

 purposeful design

Early Education DIRECTOR'S MANUAL

FORM 2.4

Philosophy Statement: Trinity Tots

Because we believe that early childhood is a critical time in the development of children's foundational perceptions of themselves, of others, and of our Lord, we have established a program designed to meet the needs of young children and to promote their development both spiritually and educationally.

Basing our beliefs on Scripture, particularly on the directive of the Lord Jesus to "Let the little children to come to me, and do not hinder them" (Luke 18:16), we believe that young children have the ability and desire to begin a relationship with their God. Spiritual development occurs through the children's relationships with teachers whose words and actions demonstrate God's love and who integrate the truths of God's character throughout the daily activities (Deuteronomy 6:7). Additionally, children discover the nature of God's love and power through biblical accounts of His acts throughout history, presented as accurate recordings of actual events (2 Timothy 3:16). Children are given opportunities to respond to what they learn in daily times of worship through singing and prayer.

The program at Trinity Tots is based on a belief that God created each child a unique individual with his or her own developmental timetable. Thus we accept each child as an individual, allowing for differences in skills and interests while encouraging well-rounded development in every facet of the child's life. The primary source of learning for young children is play, in which they have opportunities to explore the world around them and to develop new levels of competence. Their play experiences enable children to organize and understand themselves and their world. Because learning is an interactive process, teachers prepare an environment in which children may learn through active exploration and interaction with adults, with other children, and with materials. Since children learn most effectively through concrete materials and activities, the curriculum is designed to provide firsthand experiences in a variety of subject areas.

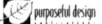 purposeful design

Early Education DIRECTOR'S MANUAL

FORM 2.5

Mission Statement Worksheet

Mission defined:
According to ACSI's Internal Strategic Plan, the *mission* is defined as "what we will offer our target group to fulfill our vision."

Sample mission statement:
"To establish a partnership with the family while at the same time providing a foundation of early Christian education with the focus on developing the whole child."

Steps in developing a mission statement:
Get together with your leadership or staff, and formulate a mission statement. You will need to

- Discuss the important distinctives of your program
- Include the people who are your target for service
- Prioritize the important components
- Ask, How will this statement help us fulfill our vision?

Draft:

FORM 2.6

Vision Statement Worksheet

Vision defined:
According to ACSI's Internal Strategic Plan, the *vision* is defined as "what the people in the target group will be like if we effectively serve them."

Effectively serving the people in your group requires that you give consideration to the unique personal calling on your life and the specific gifts and abilities you will use to accomplish your vision.

Example:
"To lead in the area of early education, providing specific training that will facilitate professional and spiritual growth in others."

Individual activity:
Take some time to consider an individual vision statement. You will need to

- Prayerfully consider what God has put on your heart
- Think of what you feel passionate about
- Ask, How can God use my gifts to effectively serve others?
- Ask, How will fulfilling my vision impact the target group?

Draft:

FORM 2.7

Expected Outcomes: Sample Statement

The aim of XYZ Early Education Center is to prepare children and their families spiritually, socially/emotionally, physically, and cognitively for the coming years of formal schooling. Children will do the following:

SPIRITUAL
Understand that God is a loving God[1]
- Understand that Jesus is God's Son
- Know that Jesus wants to initiate a personal relationship with each person

Understand that the Bible is a special book[2]
- Understand that the Bible is God's Word
- Know that the Bible is truth (with stories that are fact, not fantasy)
- Comprehend that Bible truths contain character lessons

Use prayer to express their thoughts and needs to God
- Understand that prayer is talking to God
- Know they can request God's help to take care of them
- Know they can ask for God's help in being kind and thoughtful to others

Freely share about God, Jesus, and the Bible with others
- Talk about spiritual things as "real"
- Speak spontaneously about spiritual things

Have a desire to attend church
- Have a cultivated interest in learning about God, which causes the desire
- Perceive the church environment as welcoming and safe

Know that God created the world
- Have enjoyed direct experiences with nature[3]
- Know that God wants each person to care for the world

FORM 2.7

Expected Outcomes: Sample Statement (Continued)

Enjoy the process of moving from curiosity to satisfaction in a project because God delights in their work[4]
- Take pride in their own work
- Have positive attitudes about involvement in projects

SOCIAL/EMOTIONAL
Value familial relationships and understand the importance of obeying parents and teachers
- Enjoy and initiate friendships with a variety of individuals[5]
- Develop friendships with those who may not be the same gender, race, or age, or may not have the same ability
- Benefit from the inclusiveness of the emotional culture of the classroom, which celebrates the gifts and talents of all members

Begin to learn the art of sharing
- Share their own ideas with friends and family
- Share toys or other items with friends and family

Begin showing empathy and kindness[6]
- Show empathy to family members
- Express empathy to friends

Use language to express self, developing positive kinds of conflict resolution
- Express both positive and negative emotions
- Observe teachers who model and scaffold to this end

Develop self-confidence in self-initiated activities[7]
- Gain competence through age-appropriate activities
- Have opportunities to share their new skills with others
- Master new skills through encouragement and direction from the teacher

FORM 2.7

Expected Outcomes: Sample Statement (Continued)

Begin to exhibit self-control
- Begin to understand and control their emotions
- Begin to act appropriately, whether or not they are directly interacting with an adult

Be comfortable participating in group discussions[8]
- Enjoy and participate in child-to-child and child-to-adult interactions
- Communicate effectively using their own words
- Be able to attend to others' comments

PHYSICAL
Acquire and refine the fundamental skills of balance, movement, touch, and coordination[9]
- Enjoy rhythm and movement
- Explore fundamental movements through the time, the activities, and the equipment available to them
- Actively pursue gross motor activity

Acquire and develop fine motor skills[10]
- Become acquainted with and have time to use the appropriate equipment and materials that aid in this development

Recognize that their body is created by God and take special responsibility to care for it
- Be introduced to health and nutrition
- Make good food and activity choices

Cognitive
General
- Be able to engage with others in learning activities, including the ability to explore, create, experiment, observe, plan, analyze, reason, investigate, and question[11]

- Initiate investigation as a result of carefully observing their surroundings

 purposeful design

Early Education DIRECTOR'S MANUAL

FORM 2.7

Expected Outcomes: Sample Statement (Continued)

ENJOY CREATIVE EXPRESSION
- Be encouraged to express creativity within their own multiple intelligences as they are provided the materials for this expression
- Be free to work with media that uniquely express the creative element for process art
- Write songs and stories
- Use imagination in dramatic center play
- Find creative solutions to problems that arise during center play

NUMERACY
Understand math vocabulary, concepts, and directed activities
- Have appropriate counting, sorting, and comparing skills
- Work well with manipulatives to achieve an appropriate transition into formal schooling[12]

LANGUAGE AND LITERACY
Understand the importance and use of language in the environment
- Be able to participate in receptive language activities using literature as the foundational tool
- Have a desire to look at books with text and illustrations
- Engage in expressive language experiences that foster growth in language proficiency[13]

Have cultivated prewriting skills in the context of emergent literacy[14]
- Be able to write their own name and some alphabet letters
- Spontaneously choose to use writing implements
- Understand that print carries meaning

Be aware of different sound-letter relationships[15]
- possibly begin to hear rhyming sounds in prominent words
- become phonemically aware through classroom activities designed for that purpose

 purposeful design

Early Education DIRECTOR'S MANUAL

FORM 2.7

Expected Outcomes: Sample Statement (Continued)

EXPECTED OUTCOMES FOR FAMILIES
The aim of *XYZ Early Education Center* is to prepare children and their families spiritually, socially/emotionally, physically, and cognitively for the coming years of formal schooling.
Parents will
- Understand the importance of being the primary educator of their child and of participating in the educational process[16]
- Partner with the school in providing an enriched educational experience for their child
- Understand the significance of continuing Christian education through the elementary, secondary, and college years

Endnotes
1. John Trent, Rick Osborne, and Kurt Bruner. 2003. *Parents' guide to the spiritual growth of children.* Wheaton, IL: Tyndale House.
2. Pam Boucher. 1999. *Teaching in Christian weekday early education.* Nashville, TN: LifeWay.
3. Anita Rui Olds. n.d. *Children come first* (video presentation). Chester, NY: Plough Publishing/Community Playthings.
4. Geraldine Addison Carey and Kay Vandevier Henry. 1988. *Teaching in church weekday education.* Nashville, TN: Convention Press.
5. Rheta DeVries and Lawrence Kohlberg. 1989. *Constructivist early education: Overview and comparison with other programs.* Washington, DC: National Association for the Education of Young Children.
6. William Damon, The moral development of children. *Scientific American* (August 1999), 72–78.
7. Karyn Henley. 2002. *Child-sensitive teaching: Helping children grow a living faith in a loving God,* rev. ed. Nashville, TN: Child Sensitive Communication, LLC, 44.
8. Ibid., 47.
9. Barbara T. Bowman, Suzanne Donovan, M. Susan Burns, eds. National Research Council. 2000. *Eager to learn: Educating our preschoolers.* Washington, DC: National Academies Press, 279–91.
10. Ibid.
11. Ibid.
12. Ibid.
13. Ibid.
14. Ibid.
15. M. Susan Burns, Peg Griffin, and Catherine E. Snow, eds. National Research Council. 1999. *Starting out right: A guide to promoting children's reading success.* Washington, DC: National Academies Press.
16. Glen Schultz. 2003. *Kingdom education: God's plan for educating future generations.* Colorado Springs, CO: Purposeful Design Publications.

 purposeful design

Early Education DIRECTOR'S MANUAL

GOD'S DESIGN FOR GROWTH

Chapter 3

And Jesus grew in wisdom and stature, and in favor with God and men. (Luke 2:52)

Growing Just the Way God Planned

■ *Respecting God's timetable*

In Psalm 139 we are able to get a small glimpse into God's workmanship as He created each one of the children who attend our early education programs. In verses 13 and 14, the psalmist says,

> For you created my inmost being;
>   you knit me together in my mother's womb.
> I praise you because I am fearfully and wonderfully made;
>   your works are wonderful, I know that full well.

It is an incredible thing to realize that God personally formed each person to His liking with a specific plan in mind. We see a glimpse of God's individual design reflected in the life of each child. As Christian early educators we need to be regularly reminded of this truth. God has a plan for every one of the children we teach, and He causes each one's growth in His time. Part of the challenge for those who work with young children is monitoring and supporting their individual timetables. Each child is unique, and each child's development will progress within the limits God has established. Exposing a child to new experiences certainly affects the expression of his or her skills and gifts, but the basic timetable that guides the unfolding of a child's abilities follows God's design and remains unaltered. Because each child's time-table reflects God's design, we need to respect the individuality of each child.

The process, not the product

There is currently a great emphasis on preparing young children for school success. On occasion, school readiness is narrowly defined as a small set of skills and knowledge, mainly academic. Because of societal pressure to attain this kind of readiness, early educators may be tempted to overlook the array of concepts and abilities the young child is actually developing.

It is generally accepted that many aspects of a child's personality, attitudes, and dispositions toward learning are established by age five. With this fact in mind, the Christian early education program can play a significant role by helping to develop a child's character and ability to function well in life. Much of what happens in an early education setting focuses on the socialization of the child. This focus corresponds well with the observation that success in life depends greatly on how well a person gets along with others and adapts to change. Wise early educators encourage well-rounded development in all aspects of a child's life.

Fostering but not forcing development

Living in a society that stresses immediate results may tempt parents and teachers to be impatient with a child's rate of growth. Some parents want their children to walk and talk at an early age because they see these achievements as a personal reflection on them. There is a fine line between exposing children to new experiences that help them take the next step in their development and pushing them beyond their ability in order to speed up their development. There is great joy in watching children walk or run when they are ready and in celebrating all the steps that lead to that particular skill. On the other hand, there can be nothing more frustrating for children

than struggling with a skill when a parent or teacher is pushing them to perform beyond their limits. Young children should be allowed to participate in new experiences and learning opportunities without feeling pressured to perform. Part of the delight of childhood is the child's ability to freely explore new ideas and interests in a supportive environment without the pressure of having to meet grown-up expectations. In *Miseducation*, David Elkind says,

> It is all too easy for us as adults to forget just how inexperienced infants and young children really are and how much they have to learn about the world of objects, sights, sounds, colors, shapes, relationships of up and down, of behind and on top of, plants, animals, trees, and much, much more…. Infants and young children are not just sitting twiddling their thumbs, waiting for parents to teach them to read and do math. They are expending a vast amount of time and effort in exploring and understanding their immediate world. Healthy education supports and encourages this spontaneous learning. Early instruction miseducates not because it attempts to teach but because it attempts to teach the wrong things at the wrong time. When we ignore what the child has to learn and instead impose what we want to teach, we put infants and young children at risk for no purpose.[1]

Respecting the Individuality of Each Child

Normative and individual growth patterns

As mentioned above, children grow at their own rate and pass through developmental stages that may frequently be measured through observation. Some years ago, researchers established age-group norms for specific developmental milestones. These norms can assist those working with young children to recognize stages and milestones in a child's developmental progress. A director or teacher can use this information to assess children according to a developmental timeline. Such assessments aid teachers in creating lesson plans that will help guide the children through this developmental sequence. Parents can also benefit from descriptions of their child's progress. Such information should always be used for the purpose of helping children move forward in their development.

However, the established norms should be used with caution. The National Education Goals panel has held that formal assessment of preschool-age children is not sufficiently reliable to be used in drawing significant conclusions about individual children.[2] Because of the wide variation that is normal in the development of young children and in light of the rapid pace of their developmental growth, assessments should not be used for making comparisons between children or for demonstrating a given child's success or superiority.

Children who demonstrate a slower developmental timetable by moving through the stages of growth at a much slower pace should be respected and valued for their individual milestones as much as those who develop faster and sooner. Teachers who understand child development recognize that children grow at different rates and that their growth within the different domains will vary. Although aware of measurable timelines, teachers know that individual children can demonstrate their progress in a variety of ways within their own time frame. Understanding these concepts helps staff and parents to be aware of upcoming stages, allowing the child the flexibility to be his own person who is respected for his individuality.

■ Redefining normal

Many times we describe behavior as normal or abnormal. Although the distinction may be accurate in general, we need to be careful to separate our view of the child from descriptions of her behavior. We may observe abnormal behavior in a child, but such behavior does not define the child as abnormal. Placing such labels on children is demoralizing, and it creates a climate that is emotionally harmful to both the children and their parents. Broadly, normality is a function of being created in the image of God. Scripture reveals that in this sense we all meet the criteria for normality. With this general understanding, we accept and celebrate children in all their individual differences while working toward common goals for overall development and character growth. We encourage activities and environments that facilitate a child's growth, and we address areas that need attention, recognizing that she will ultimately benefit as the growth process continues.

■ Early intervention

As young children grow, red flags may appear in their rate of progress—delays in certain areas of development. Teachers and directors who see such red flags need to pay attention and address the delays with the parents. Doing so in a timely way can make the difference in whether a child will begin to progress at a more normal rate. Issues that are ignored can become problematic and can cause delays in other areas of development. Staff members need to be trained in recognizing possible warning signs and in communicating with parents about them. Waiting until a child begins kindergarten before addressing such issues is not in the child's best interest. Rather, any noticeable delay should be addressed regardless of the child's age and should continue to be monitored as he develops.

Special Needs
■ Respecting the diversity of children's needs

Each child comes to an early education program with a variety of needs in a variety of areas, including emotional, physical, functional, and cognitive. The needs vary among children. Each child is so complex an individual that the needs often become evident only over time, and the circumstances of life can create additional needs. Some children's needs are obvious even in the early stages of getting to know them. These children are vulnerable to being labeled as "special needs" children. In essence, all children have special or individual needs, so we should use caution in applying labels to them. Educators need to avoid stereotyping children by assigning them prematurely to a category that can unnecessarily limit their later participation in a regular school environment. It is wise to be aware of the significant diversity among children and of the need for adults to accept their differences and to provide for their needs.

■ Being an inclusive school

The more we understand the diversity of children, the more clearly we see our responsibility for creating inclusive environments. In recognizing that children come to us with diverse needs, we have a healthy and accurate view of children in general. This understanding safeguards us from jumping to conclusions about whether individual children will be able to reach their potential as God intends. When we keep children's diversity in mind, we are less likely to set up barriers to their being successful in a regular classroom environment. We need to follow Jesus' example of welcoming children into His arms by accepting children into our programs. Those who believe in Christian education should be leading the way in making our programs accessible to children with varying needs.

As many of us are aware, special accommodations may need to be made to meet the unique needs of certain children. Directors need to participate in ongoing training about various special needs, and they need to pass their knowledge on to their staff. In addition, school districts and communities may provide support services or consultants who will make a helpful contribution. Directors should be proactive in developing a referral list of available resources and in regularly assessing how well their learning environments accommodate each student.

Conscientious directors will want to ensure that their staff and facility can accommodate each child's special needs. The process begins with a parent's first inquiry into the program, when school staff gather information about the child's abilities and needs. It is helpful to ask about the child's history, including special supports and accommodations he has received. Ask the parent whether those who have provided support services for the child have made recommendations regarding his ability to be successful in this environment. The next step is to meet the child and invite the parent to observe in the classrooms. It is helpful if the parent can bring any evaluative information on the child. After observing the classroom, ask the parents what they think about the way their child interacts in this environment and what kinds of barriers would need to be removed. Talk with the parents about your staff and any training they've had for meeting the child's particular needs. Ask whether any ongoing support services will be available to the staff as they work with the child. As you continue to gather information, invite the child to participate in the class for a day while a parent stays in the classroom. After the visit, the teachers can share their observations and questions about any needed modifications. The director should confer with the teacher and parent to discuss how the day went, and they should come to consensus about strategies that will help the child succeed. Such discussions will go a long way toward providing the support the child needs and determining the best environment for him.

■ The ADA and the Christian early education center

The Americans with Disabilities Act (ADA) is a federal civil-rights law that was passed in 1990. This law has important implications for both the employees of an early education center and the children they serve. Among other things, the ADA prohibits discrimination in employment decisions by childcare centers and family childcare providers with fifteen or more employees. The law protects applicants for employment and current employees in these situations:

- They have a physical or mental impairment that substantially limits one or more of their major life activities, like walking, hearing, seeing, speaking, learning.
- They have a history of one or more of these impairments.
- They are perceived to have a disability.

Childcare programs operated by religious organizations are not required to comply with the Title III section of the ADA, which deals with building accessibility, but they may need to comply with state accessibility laws, which may provide greater protection for people with disabilities than the federal ADA guarantees. Directors need to check state requirements to identify their schools' responsibility. For instance, under state law or regulations, a school may be required to do any or all of the following:

- Eliminate restrictive admissions policies that single out children with disabilities and treat them differently.
- Assess on an individual basis whether a child with a disability can be cared for in the program with reasonable accommodations.
- Make reasonable accommodations so that children with disabilities can be included in its childcare program.

Unique Characteristics of Early Learners

■ *Developmental needs*

Those who design early education programs need to keep in mind certain unique characteristics of the early learner. First, we know that young children learn primarily through their senses. Thus we offer them activities that focus on the senses, such as music, cooking, sensory play, and hands-on manipulative and art media that use small- and large-muscle

coordination. Classrooms that rely primarily on pencil-and-paper tasks fail to capitalize on young children's natural drive to learn through their senses. Second, we know that children learn through play experiences. Play experiences allow them to represent their ideas with symbols, a process that builds the foundation they will need later to learn abstract concepts such as sound-letter relationships, a key element in literacy.[3] Another benefit of play is the opportunity it gives young children to make choices among options, such as deciding how to use materials and, in socio-dramatic play, learning to take another child's perspective. David Elkind defines character as "the disposition to make socially responsible choices." According to Elkind, "When children have the opportunity to engage in true play, they are learning to consider options and make choices." He says further, "Children who are given these opportunities internalize the sense that they are competent to act independently and responsibly. It becomes part of their self-concept."[4] Early education environments need to be rich in materials that foster play, and children must be given sufficient time to engage in these activities.

Young children's capacity to understand the world differs from older children's. Piaget describes a preschoolers' stage of development as "pre-operational thought," a term that refers to the fact that they are concrete learners with limited ability to understand abstractions. Because young children perceive the world concretely, the classroom environment needs to be rich in hands-on materials that spark cognitive learning. Early educators who recognize these differences will create an environment that is child friendly and age appropriate. Gross-motor activities also play a primary role in development, providing the experiences children need to develop the basic systems of the body such as the vestibular (sense of balance), bilateral (two sides of the body working), proprioceptive (skilled movements) systems, and spatial awareness.

■ Emotional needs

The younger the child, the greater her need for the emotional security provided by the consistent adults in her world. Because children are vulnerable to circumstances that are beyond their control, we educators must be aware of their great sense of dependence. Children need to feel loved and accepted as well as to have an overall sense of their own competence. Teachers help meet these needs when they offer loving guidance that accepts children's unique timetables and when they create an age-appropriate environment that facilitates learning experiences geared to the children's level. Children need to be respected and heard. They need adults in their lives who will meet their physical and emotional needs in a timely way, thus helping them develop a sense of trust. It is through the modeling and support of sensitive adults that children develop the essential ability to cope with and adapt to the circumstances of life.

The Role of Teachers in Meeting Individual Needs

As noted earlier, it is essential for the preschool director and staff to understand that each child is created as an individual, with a unique developmental timetable. Thus early educators need to understand the vital role they play in meeting children's needs.

Adults meet the *physical* needs of children by

- Teaching them how to keep the bodies God gave them strong and healthy
- Assuring an environment free from physical harm or disease
- Providing opportunities for large- and small-muscle and motor development
- Balancing their day with active and quiet times

- Developing in them an awareness of dangerous situations
- Providing snacks and meals that are rich in nutrients

Adults meet the *emotional* needs of children by

- Understanding that they are a special part of God's plan
- Showing unconditional love for them
- Providing a safe and secure environment
- Respecting and listening to each one
- Responding to their needs with warmth and consistency
- Building a sense of security by clearly defining expectations
- Not doing for them what they can do for themselves

Adults meet the *social* needs of children by

- Teaching them to respect themselves, their family, and others
- Providing appropriate and frequent interactions with adults
- Honoring their need for both time alone and time with other children
- Creating places to play in the classroom that encourage conversation and collaboration
- Balancing their day with structured activities and opportunities for choice
- Providing them skills and strategies for problem-solving with other children without using aggression

Adults meet the *cognitive/intellectual* needs of children by

- Developing in them an awareness that God has given parents, teachers, and others for them to learn from
- Allowing them to explore and to ask questions
- Encouraging them to learn about the world through all their senses

- Providing opportunities for them to create and think of new ideas
- Exposing them to real-life materials and tools that can be used in constructive and imaginative ways
- Introducing them to academic skills through a variety of meaningful hands-on activities and age-appropriate instruction
- Providing a wide range of successively challenging activities that are appropriate for the wide range of development displayed by young children

Adults meet the *spiritual* needs of children by

- Making spiritual truths come alive through modeling them in daily classroom activities
- Teaching spiritual concepts that are geared to a young child's cognitive level
- Using simple language to describe spiritual concepts
- Demonstrating consistency between what they tell children about God and His love and how they treat children
- Taking advantage of teachable moments in helping children see the beauty of God's world
- Spontaneously praying with a child or helping a child pray in response to a situation

In Luke 2:52, we see how Jesus developed in a balanced way—in wisdom (cognitive development), in stature (physical development), in favor with God (spiritual development), and in favor with other people (social and emotional development). Balanced development takes place only when parents and educators accept children as individuals and make allowances for their different skills and interests. While members of the preschool staff have different roles, every staff person influences the children. All staff members must recognize the needs of each child, whether or not that child is their direct responsibility.

As this book has demonstrated, scriptural principles underlie any genuinely Christian early childhood education program. We have just examined the vital role of adults in children's growth and development, a role that is mandated by Scripture. You may wish to turn to form 3.1 at the end of this chapter: Scripture Passages That Reveal God's Design for Our Children.

FORM 3.1

Scripture Passages That Reveal God's Design for Our Children	
Jesus values children.	*Matthew 18:1–6* *Matthew 19:13–15* *Mark 10:13–16* *Luke 18: 15–17*
God is intimately involved in children's lives from the very beginning.	*Psalm 139:13–16* *Jeremiah 1:4–5*
Childhood is a stage of life distinct from adulthood.	*1 Corinthians 13:11*
Children's thought processes are distinct from those of adults.	*1 Corinthians 14:20*
Children are capable of having a relationship with the Lord and can grow spiritually.	*2 Timothy 3:15*
Children are heirs to God's promise of salvation.	*Acts 2:39*
Children must be taught spiritual truths, and adults must be able to answer their questions.	*Deuteronomy 6:20–21* *Psalm 78: 4–8* *Proverbs 22:6* *Romans 10:14*
Children are to be taught God's Word through all the day's activities.	*Deuteronomy 6:6–7*
Children are able to praise and worship God.	*Psalm 8:1–2* *Matthew 21:15–16* *1 Samuel 1:27–28*
A child participated in one of Jesus' miracles.	*John 6:9*
Children are a blessing.	*Psalm 127:3*
Children are to obey their parents.	*Ephesians 6:1–4*
Child guidance should be motivated by love.	*Proverbs 3:12*

purposeful design

Early Education DIRECTOR'S MANUAL

SPONSORSHIP AND GOVERNANCE

Chapter 4

Slaves, obey your earthly masters with respect and fear, and with sincerity of heart, just as you would obey Christ. (Ephesians 6:5)

Sponsored and Stand-Alone Programs

Many early education programs are created out of the genuine desire of a local church or other sponsoring organization to express Christ's love to the community. Maintaining a good relationship with that community is key as the program grows and prospers. Such a relationship requires the diligent effort of both the sponsoring organization and the early education program.

In addition to programs with a church or other sponsor, there are independent stand-alone programs that are not associated with a sponsoring organization. Their owner or corporation must make an extra effort to develop a board or advisory committee to help them self-regulate. For legal and ethical reasons, accountability to parents, staff, and students should never rest on one person. A board or committee should be formed of select individuals who reflect the stated philosophy of the program and who have the time, talent, and interest to contribute significantly to its overall success.

■ Church-school partnerships

Churches have a well-known history of reaching out to their communities with the gospel by forming ministries that meet genuine community needs. Many early education programs are formed to meet the very real need of providing care and education for young children in the local church family. Many others share that same mission, though they are not directly connected with a church.

It is the local church that is most likely to initiate a new early education program. In establishing a partnership between the church and the program, leaders of both must share an understanding of the sponsoring church's overall mission. A church begins a new program for any of several reasons, but the overall goal should be to extend the church's ministry to the community, reaching children and families for Christ. Each entity, the church and the early education program, needs to see the other's work as complementary, contributing to common outcomes. Each needs to respect the other's role in the kingdom of God.

Early in the process, it is helpful to have members of the church board who are also on the early education program's board. This practice helps to ensure consistency and a focus on the overall mission. At times, the leaders of churches and early education programs find themselves at odds because they lack awareness of a shared mission. It can be difficult for a program and its sponsoring church to establish an effective relationship if the program's leaders are not involved in the church. Without a sense of mutual investment in the success of the two ministries, their relationship is more like that of landlord and tenant than of partners in an integrated effort. Both ministries should seek a healthy interdependence while each one maintains its distinctive role.

It is common for early education programs to struggle with the balance of ministry and fiscal responsibility. These programs are distinct from church ministries in several ways:

1. Early education programs provide an educational service to the community.

2. Early education programs by nature carry a large responsibility for the care of young children.

3. Parents are paying for a service to their child that requires moral and fiscal accountability.

4. Many early education programs are required to have a license to operate and are accountable to the state for the care, health, and safety of the children.

Churches need to approach the operation of an early childhood program with an awareness of the differences between the daily ministry of an early education program and the weekly ministry of Sunday school. Because children typically spend many hours in a center, it needs to include enriching materials and equipment beyond what might be acceptable for a Sunday morning program.

Trust develops between the church's leadership and the early education director and staff when each respects the value and uniqueness of the other's ministry. In most cases, church programs and child-care programs share facilities and classroom space. Regular and open communication about the care of their common environment is essential for a successful partnership. Leaders can maintain unity and harmony by meeting together as needed to work through the challenges that result from sharing space. It is also helpful if both departments share success stories in order to maintain a focus on the mission and vision of the church and its early childhood programs.

■ *Guidelines for a shared-space agreement*
Whenever an early education center shares space with other ministries, there is always the potential for conflict. Ministry leaders can more successfully resolve shared-space issues if they have discussed and agreed to the guidelines *before* a dispute arises.

The Iowa State University publication *Child Care: Financial Basics* [1] provides the following helpful suggested topics to include in a shared-space agreement:

1. *Days and times of operation of each program,* including accommodations needed for special

programs or events, school holidays, and summer months

2. *Primary use areas*, including classrooms, office space, bathrooms, storage, and playground

3. *Specialized secondary space*, which may include gym, computer room, alternative outdoor space, cafeteria, meeting rooms

4. *Responsibility* for cleaning, security, building maintenance, playground upkeep and repair, regulation of the heating and air conditioning systems

5. *Job description* for shared staff (custodial, maintenance, secretarial)

6. *Budget projections* for expected payments of shared costs

7. *Procedures for communicating* concerns and resolving problems

8. *Timeline* for reviewing policies (e.g., annually, biannually)

Many church-related early education programs have found it valuable for the center staff to meet with the members of the Sunday school staff who share the same classrooms. A time of fellowship around a meal or coffee creates opportunities for building relationships. When these meetings include time to pray for one another, early education staff members are encouraged to see the ministry volunteers as co-laborers. A relationship is strengthened, for example, when an early education teacher leaves a quick note of affirmation for a Sunday school worker. Although the early education staff may have to take the lead in initiating and maintaining such relationships, the ongoing benefits are worth the effort. Some areas of discussion might include the following:

- Praying for one another
- Sharing God's blessings between the preschool-childcare program and the Sunday school program

- Discussing communication strategies and guidelines for room use
- Discussing expectations for room set-up
- Agreeing on what materials will be left out and which ones will be put away
- Formulating classroom rules for the children
- Replacing consumable materials
- Clarifying the source of funding for new materials and equipment

Establishing and Training a Governing Board

A new early education program will need to set up a governing board to oversee policy development and to maintain the accountability of the program. The board plays a significant role in the ongoing development of the program. It provides leadership by setting policy, hiring the director, establishing the philosophy and direction of the program, overseeing finances, developing program goals, and reporting back to the church board when appropriate. In *Serving God on the Christian School Board*[2], Roy Lowrie outlines several responsibilities of a governing board:

- Exercise spiritual leadership and prayer
- Establish broad policies
- Hire a competent administrator
- Maintain fiscal stability
- Provide adequate facilities and equipment
- Plan and work for the future
- Establish public relations
- Maintain open communication
- Keep right relationships with the state, accreditation associations, and government agencies
- Provide faculty and staff salaries and benefits
- Exercise financial authority

Members of the early education board are typically selected in the same way as church board members, by a nominating committee. For programs not associated with a church, board members are initially selected from the community to serve in the start-up process.

A church selects its board members on the basis of how their professional expertise will contribute to the overall development of its program. An early education program should follow a similar plan. Thus it is important that the early education board include members who have, or have had, children in the program. Such members enrich the board by bringing a fresh perspective on relevant parental issues. It is important to select persons who can provide professional expertise in education, medical issues, legal issues, finance, social work, and family, and it is essential that those selected be able work well as a team. (See form 4.1 Governing Board Application.)

The program leaders need to establish bylaws defining how future board members are selected and how long they will serve. Many boards consist of five to ten members, the number depending on the size of the program. Continuity of service is important. In order to provide consistency for the director and the program, no more than two or three board members should rotate off each year. Also, members should be discouraged from serving for an extended period (beyond six years).

New board members should participate in an orientation process that covers meeting protocol, bylaws, roles and responsibilities, and accountability issues. Each new member should receive a notebook containing the bylaws, a list of board members, staff and parent handbooks, and other documents.

New members need instruction on the differences between the roles of board members and staff members. Individual board members should be aware that they cannot make a decision or require action independently, without the approval of the board as a whole.

An ongoing training program is recommended for both new and experienced board members. The board chairperson serves as a role model, providing ongoing training by setting standards and offering opportunities for growth. Because so many aspects of an early education program are unique to that program, board members need to be trained initially and then periodically brought up to speed on important issues. ACSI offers a number of training materials and opportunities.

■ Establishing bylaws

During the initial phase of an early education center, the board is responsible for drawing up the bylaws for its operation. Establishing bylaws is the primary way in which an organization defines its role and function. Bylaws are rules for the center's governing board to follow. (See form 4.3 Early Education Center Bylaws for a sample bylaws document.) Subsequently, the board makes policy decisions and provisions for the operation of the center. Dorothy Sciarra and Anne Dorsey[3] suggest several areas to include:

- Name and purpose of the organization
- Selection of board members, or how they are elected or appointed
- Officers to be elected, their duties, and their terms of office
- Replacement of board members
- Frequency of meetings
- Standing committees, their function, and their reporting requirements
- Relationship of the staff to the board
- Rules governing the conduct of meetings
- Procedure for amending the bylaws

ACSI has identified on its website (www.acsi.org) specific organizational requirements for Christian schools. You can consult the website for updated information on relevant issues for school boards to address.

■ Policy of nondiscrimination

It is important for those preparing documents for the governing board to review the applicable legal requirements carefully. ACSI publishes the *Legal/Legislative Update,* an excellent resource for the administration and the board. In the sidebar is an excerpt from an *LLU* article entitled "Your School Must Meet Several IRS Nondiscrimination Requirements to Keep Its Tax Exemption."

■ Developing a philosophy statement

Developing a detailed philosophy statement is a vital step in defining the program. (See chapter 2, "Philosophy and Mission of Christian Early Education.") The philosophy statement will be a guiding force in developing the focus of the program and in setting program goals. Staff members will be selected and oriented on the basis of the philosophy statement and the program goals.

■ Establishing policies and procedures

The board will establish appropriate policies and procedures. The board will set the course of action, and the director will develop procedures to ensure the implementation of policy. The center's written policies, which will dictate how decisions are made, should include the topics listed below. (See form 4.4 School Board Policies for a more complete list of areas for which policies should be written.)

- Personnel
- Program
- Parent involvement
- Curriculum
- Student care and discipline
- Standards, including child-staff ratios and group size
- Admissions
- Tuition and payment
- Budget issues
- Health and safety
- Food service
- Volunteers
- Facilities

Organizational Requirements. Your school must include a statement in its charter, bylaws, or other governing instrument, or in a resolution of its governing body, that it has a racially nondiscriminatory policy (RNP) as to students, and therefore does not discriminate against applicants and students on the basis of race, color, and national or ethnic origin.

Statement of Policy. Your school must include a statement of its RNP as to students in all its brochures and catalogs dealing with student admissions, programs, and scholarships. The following statement is acceptable to the IRS:
The _____ School admits students of any race, color, and national or ethnic origin.[4]

The board must also make provisions for the operation of the center. Some of their major considerations will be

- Selecting a director
- Providing for staff training
- Maintaining facilities and equipment
- Preparing and approving the budget
- Setting tuition rates
- Establishing a salary schedule
- Complying with state and federal law
- Evaluating the director
- Auditing financial records
- Arbitrating problems with the director and parents

Typically, board work is done in committees. The bylaws spell out all the standing committees, which include personnel, finance, facilities, program, and nominating committees. Standing committees may meet on a regular basis to carry out work that is designated by the board. Once a committee has done a particular project, it reports its findings back to the board for discussion.

■ Hiring the director

One of the first and most significant tasks of the governing board is overseeing the hiring of the early education director. (See chapter 6, "The Role of the Director.") Since the director is responsible for hiring and supervising the staff, he or she is the board's sole employee. Much prayer and careful consideration should go into hiring the director. A job description should be written that includes any state licensing requirements and qualifications that a candidate must comply with, along with additional requirements and qualifications of the school itself. It is recommended that the job description and contract be examined by a professional who is experienced in labor and human resource laws.

The governing board must ensure that the director is adequately compensated in salary and benefits, which should reflect the responsibilities and standards established for the position. Compensation should be comparable to that of other administrative positions that require the same level of education and experience. Your ACSI regional office may be able to give you specific wage and benefit information about ACSI early education centers in your part of the country.

■ Reporting and communicating

The director is hired to oversee the day-to-day operation of the early education program. While the board is not responsible for the program's daily operation, there should be regular communication between the board and the director. (See form 4.2

Organization Chart for a sample reporting structure.) The relationship should be a direct one, with the director actually attending board meetings. Communication should flow easily between the chairman of the board and the director in planning board meetings and identifying issues that need to be addressed. Confidence and trust are imperative for a good working relationship. The governing board and the director should support each other publicly and privately.

In some cases the director may report to an administrator, who then reports to the board. In this situation, the director would submit a written report to the board, and systems need to be put in place to ensure thorough and open communication between the administrator and the director. In order to effectively represent the needs of the early education program, the administrator must be kept abreast of current issues that need to be addressed. It is suggested that the board chairman have open communication with the director as well so that information can flow freely and any remaining gaps can be filled.

Accountability

Matters of accountability are important to establish up front, and they need to be addressed with both the board and the administration. In any healthy organization, checks and balances will be established along the way. The board plays a significant role in establishing accountability practices, ensuring that the program and its leaders are achieving the stated student outcomes and are maintaining accountability in other areas.

■ Evaluating the program

The early education program can be evaluated on a regular basis in a variety of ways. Typically, the center's leadership looks at student assessments and teacher evaluations separately, but in evaluating the program's overall effectiveness, these pieces play an essential role. In an evaluation of the overall program, it is important for evaluators to look at all areas. These would typically include the following:

- Children's progress in relation to defined outcomes
- Level of needs met with the families served
- Professional growth of the staff
- Financial stability
- Director's ability to lead and to fulfill the mission
- Effectiveness of board oversight

The board, the administration, the staff, and the parents should all be involved in collecting feedback and putting together the information needed for an evaluation, and they can access that information through surveys and through summaries of student and teacher assessments. Once collected, the data can be condensed and put into a report format. Some information may be confidential and should be made available only to the director and the board. Other information can be summarized or condensed and made available to the staff and the parents. By walking through this process, the school communicates to the parents and the community that excellence is its priority. Other agencies are indirectly involved in establishing benchmarks for health-and-safety compliance as well as quality control. Some agencies and organizations focus on minimal compliance, while others focus on establishing quality levels. Their standards, requirements, and guidelines include the following:

- State licensing requirements
- Fire department compliance
- Health department guidelines
- City requirements
- OSHA requirements
- State employment requirements
- ACSI accreditation standards (See form 4.5 Accreditation Standards.)

- Environmental rating scales
- National health and safety standards

Collecting data from these agencies and organizations will result in a final evaluation report that represents a broad range of feedback. It would be natural and appropriate to move on and establish short- and long-range goals based on the findings in the report.

■ Evaluating the director

The roles and responsibilities of a director are so great that at times the task may seem overwhelming. It is difficult for directors to step back and assess what they are doing and how effectively they are leading. If they are to be evaluated, others need to give the feedback necessary to help directors improve their skills. There are several useful ways for a board to organize such feedback. The task typically involves some kind of an evaluation procedure, which can take several different forms. Informal evaluation can be done through oral or written interviews, anonymous surveys of the staff, or specific questions asked by parents and the director. These questions should focus on areas of strength and of possible improvement, and they can be open ended as well as guided. Rating scales can also be useful in measuring overall effectiveness.

A formal evaluation process focuses on standardized questions that may be similar to those on staff evaluations. Other questions may be drawn from specific items in the job description. Evaluation forms collected from other programs may prove helpful to those formulating an evaluation tool. Forms that give room for self-evaluation and for establishing short-range goals may be helpful in addressing specific areas. It is always good to know how the director sees her job performance in relation to her own and others' expectations. According to *Child Care Administration*[5], some broad categories that may be considered in developing such evaluation tools are these:

- Management responsibilities, including planning
- Leadership abilities
- Interpersonal skills
- Communication skills
- Conflict resolution
- Decision making
- Time management
- Curriculum development
- Networking with the community
- Professionalism as an educator

Other areas include:

- Spiritual leadership
- Submission to authority
- Fulfillment of the program's evangelical mission
- Integrity of leadership

In some cases the board is directly involved in evaluating the director, and in other cases evaluation is delegated to an overseeing administrator or pastor. Board members, administrators, and pastors who do not interact with the director on a consistent basis will have a hard time measuring her in the above areas. An effective measure of the director's job performance requires input from people who work closely with her on a daily basis.

FORM 4.1

Governing Board Application

<church/school name> Early Education Center	

Title: Governing Board Member
Qualifications: Shows evidence of Christian maturity and a strong grasp of the essence of Christian and early childhood education.
Oversight Early Education Center Director:

Job goal: The governing board shall oversee the affairs of the early education center and shall develop policies to assure that the center exceeds state licensing standards.

Name:	Date:
Address:	
Home phone:	Work phone:

Give an account of your personal relationship with Jesus Christ:

Church membership:

Present church/ministry responsibilities:

Educational background:

What personal and professional strengths would you contribute as a member of the early education center's governing board?

Briefly discuss any other areas of service and/or leadership experience as well as your desires for *<church/school name>* Early Education Center—things you would like to change or accomplish:

How are you now assisting and supporting *<church/school name>* Early Education Center?

How have you assisted and supported the center in the past?

 purposeful design *Early Education* DIRECTOR'S MANUAL

FORM 4.2

Organization Chart

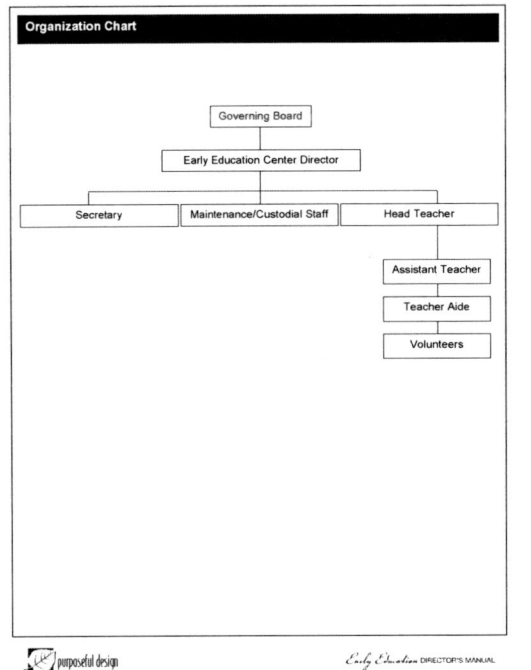

 purposeful design *Early Education* DIRECTOR'S MANUAL

FORM 4.3

Early Education Center Bylaws

Preamble: Whereas the *<governing body>* has duly authorized the organization and operation of an early education center under the general supervision of the *<governing body>*, the following bylaws are hereby adopted to govern the operation of said center.

Name: The early education center shall be known as the *<church/school name>* Early Education Center.

ARTICLE I—Purpose
Section 1
It shall be the purpose of *<church/school name>* Early Education Center to provide an opportunity and a program of growth for young children between the ages of *<age>* and *<age>* years inclusive. This program shall include guidance for growth physically, emotionally, socially, mentally, and spiritually. The center shall be operated in compliance with the minimum rules and regulations for early education centers in the State of *<name of state>* as required by the State of *<name of state>* Department of *<name of department>*.

ARTICLE II—Governing Body
Section 1
The affairs of the early education center shall be governed by a governing board consisting of at least five members. Members of the center's governing board shall not be eligible for employment on the staff of the center.

Section 2
The normal appointment to the early education center's governing board shall be for a term of *<number>* years, with no member serving more than three consecutive terms.

Section 3
The center's governing board shall elect its own officers, including a chairman, cochairman, secretary, and treasurer. Each will serve for one term. The director of the center shall be considered an advisory member of the governing board.

Section 4
The center's governing board shall meet at least once each quarter on its own appointment as to date, hour, and place of meeting. A majority of the board shall constitute a quorum. Special meetings may be held at any time upon a call by the board chairman or the center's director.

Section 5
The minutes of all meetings shall be kept by the secretary and shall be available to the governing board upon request.

ARTICLE III—Personnel
Section 1
All personnel of the early education center shall be qualified as required by the State of *<name of state>*, Department of *<licensing agency>*.

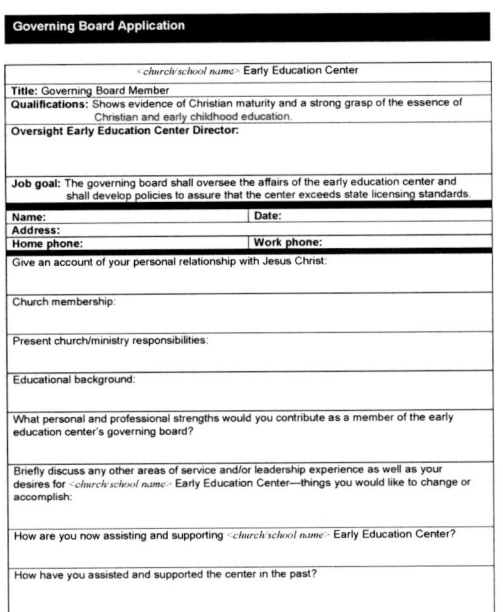 purposeful design *Early Education* DIRECTOR'S MANUAL

FORM 4.3

Early Education Center Bylaws (Continued)

Section 2
The staff shall consist of a director, an assistant director, teaching personnel, and office personnel as set forth in the current standards for early education centers of the State of *<name of state>*, Department of *<licensing agency>*.

Section 3
The director of the center shall be appointed (hired) by the center's governing board.

Section 4
The teaching staff shall be appointed (hired) by the center's governing board upon the recommendation of the director of the center.

Section 5
The center's governing board shall be responsible for setting personnel policies: sick leave, vacations, benefits, and other such policies.

ARTICLE IV—Administration and Financing
Section 1
It shall be the responsibility of the center's governing board to supervise the financial transactions concerning the operation of the center.

Section 2
The center shall be financed by a tuition charge to be determined by the center's governing board. The tuition shall be paid in advance by the month.

Section 3
The director of the center shall prepare an annual operating budget. This budget shall be confirmed by the center's governing board.

Section 4
The center's director shall receive funds and shall establish and maintain a bookkeeping system in sufficient detail to record all receipts and disbursements. Moneys received will be deposited by the director of the center. The director will pay salaries and expenses, and will maintain a cash fund.

Section 5
The director shall be responsible for preparing a quarterly financial status report, which shall follow the budget outline. This report shall be submitted to the center's governing board.

Section 6
A yearly report on the progress, equipment, and finances of the center shall be given to the governing board in written form by the director of the center, for presentation at the January board meeting.

purposeful design *Early Education* DIRECTOR'S MANUAL

FORM 4.3

Early Education Center Bylaws (Continued)

Section 7
Terms of employment for the director and staff of the center shall be established and approved by the center's governing board.

ARTICLE V—Amendments
Amendments to these bylaws may be initiated by the center's governing board. Each amendment must be passed by a majority vote of the governing board.

FORM 4.4

School Board Policies

ACSI membership	**Financial Policies**
Accreditation	Acceptance of gifts or donations
Availability of board policies	Audits
Bylaws:	Budget
Preamble	Checking and other accounts
Name	Delinquent accounts
Statement of faith	Emergency tuition aid/grants
Philosophy of education	Extended session fees
Board of directors	Facility use policy
New board members	Field trip fees
Duties of the board	Financial relationship to church
Officers of the board	Fundraising
Meetings	Investments
School administrator	Long-term debt
Indemnification	Multiple-child tuition discounts
Faculty and staff	Payroll
Dispute resolution	Petty cash
Students	Receipts and disbursements
Amendments of the bylaws	Recording of financial transactions
Educational philosophy	Refund policy
Educational philosophy: *review and revision*	Registration fee
Establishment of policy	Returned checks
Line of authority	Salaries
Name of school	Staff tuition discounts
Nondiscriminatory policy	Tuition
Relationship to church	Tuition payment schedules
Statement of faith	
Statement of faith: *use of*	
Statement of purpose	
Statement of purpose: *review and revision*	

FORM 4.4

School Board Policies (Continued)

Personnel Policies

Absences	Keys
Accidents, injuries, and safety	Lesson plans
Assignment and placement	Lifestyle statement
Biblical worldview integration	Loyalty requirements
Breaks	Medical benefits
CPR training/first aid certification	Nondiscriminatory policy
Child abuse reporting	Organizational chart
Christian conciliation	Pay periods
Classroom supplies	Performance evaluations
Conditions of employment	Personal phone calls
Conduct outside the classroom	Reduction in staff
Contracts of employment	Remuneration for those resigning or dismissed
Corrective/termination procedures	Release of children
Disciplinary policy statement	Resignation process
Dress code	Salaries
Educational philosophy	Selection of staff
Establishing personnel salaries	Statement of faith
Exit interviews	Substitutes
Field trips	Supervisory responsibilities of staff
Fire drills	Tuition discount
Grievance procedures	Written or verbal communication with children,
Grounds for dismissal	parents, and staff
Harassment policy	Vacations
Health requirements	Workers' compensation
Holidays	
In-service education	

FORM 4.5

Accreditation Standards

For ACSI accreditation, the following *specific* policies and/or procedures are requested:

Admission policies: *section 1.0 data attached #2*
Statement of faith: *section 1.0 data attached #3*
Written statement of the center's philosophy and its application to training children:
    section 1.0 data attached #4, accreditation standards 1.1.5, 2.3
Policy on student discipline: *section 2.0 data attached #3*
Food service policies and procedures: *section 5.0 data to be supplied #1*
Procedures for preventive maintenance: *section 6.0 data attached #3*
Policies and procedures for emergency drills and evacuation: *section 7.0 data attached #1*
Health service policies: *section 7.0 data attached #3*
Attendance policies related to illness: *section 7.0 data attached #4*
Policies and procedures related to communicable diseases and blood-borne pathogens:
    section 7.0 data attached #5
Policy on hiring of personnel relating to health and safety: *section 7.0 data attached #11*
Policy relating to the reporting of child abuse: *section 7.0 data attached #12*
Policy on administering and storing medications: *section 7.0 data attached #16*
Policy on supervision of children: *section 7.0 data attached #18*
Policy for sharing information in student records with parents or others: *section 8.0 data attached #8*

Although not explicitly referenced, a number of policies and/or procedures need to be developed in response to specific accreditation standards. *The following list is not exhaustive:*

Section 1: Philosophy and Policy-Making Body
Policies and/or procedures for
• Annual evaluation of the director: *standards 1.2, 1.2.2*
• Annual evaluation of the center: *standards 1.2.1, 1.2.3*
• Staff compensation and retention: *standard 1.4.4*

FORM 4.5

Accreditation Standards (Continued)

Section 2: Administration
Policies and/or procedures for
- Staff members' spiritual and professional qualifications: *standard 2.4*
- Staff evaluation: *standards 2.5.2, 2.5.3*
- Public relations: *standard 2.7*
- Staff planning time: *standard 2.10.2*
- Staff meetings: *standard 2.10.2*
- Staff schedules, breaks: *standard 2.10.4*
- Leadership in director's absence: *standard 2.10.5*
- Children's transitions: *standard 2.10.6*
- Student records: *standard 2.11*

Section 3: Personnel
Policies and/or procedures for
- Staff ratios: *standards 3.3, 3.3.1*
- Sensitivity to culture, language, and special needs of children: *standard 3.4*
- Staff training in Christian philosophy of the program: *standard 3.8*
- Staff training in employee policies: *standard 3.10*
- Staff handbook (with policies for paid holidays, sick leave, and personal or vacation days; guidelines for increased compensation based on experience, job performance, and professional development; insurance or other benefits; resignation and termination procedures; and grievance procedures): *standard 3.10.2*
- Staff in-service training: *standards 3.11, 3.11.1, 3.11.2*
- Job descriptions: *data attached #3*

Section 4: Curriculum
Policies and/or procedures for
- Evaluating and revising the curriculum: *standard 4.1.1*
- Facility/program modifications for children with special needs: *standard 4.1.2*

 purposeful design

Early Education DIRECTOR'S MANUAL

FORM 4.5

Accreditation Standards (Continued)

- Daily schedule (length of group times; balance between large-group, small-group, and individual choice): *standards 4.3, 4.3.1, 4.3.2, 4.3.3, 4.3.4*
- Use of passive media: *standards 4.3.9, 4.6.3*
- Child observation and assessment: *standards 4.5, 4.5.1*
- Curriculum plans for each age group: *standard 4.5.2*
- Curriculum guidelines for intellectual, physical, social, emotional, and spiritual development: *standards 4.6, 4.7, 4.8, 4.9, 4.10*

Section 5: Nutrition and Food Service
Policies and/or procedures for
- Food preparation: *standard 5.1*
- Menu composition: *standards 5.1.1, 5.2.1*
- Nutrition education: *standard 5.1.3*
- Parent-provided food: *standards 5.3, 5.3.2*
- Mealtime procedures: *standards 5.4, 5.4.4, 5.4.5*

Section 6: Physical Environment
Policies and/or procedures for
- Arrangement of space (learning centers): *standard 6.3.2*
- Cleaning (restrooms, diapering areas): *standards 6.4, 6.6*
- Bedding, laundering schedule: *standard 6.5*
- Inspection of playground equipment: *standard 6.13*
- Playground surfacing: *standard 6.13.2*
- Storage, rotation of equipment/toys: *standard 6.15*

Section 7: Health and Safety
Policies and/or procedures for
- Staff health records: *standard 7.1.3*
- Alerting staff to children's health conditions: *standard 7.6*
- Staff members' CPR/first aid certification: *standard 7.9*

 purposeful design

Early Education DIRECTOR'S MANUAL

FORM 4.5

Accreditation Standards (Continued)

- Monitoring fire extinguishers and smoke detectors: *standard 7.10.4*
- Emergency closing plan for contacting parents: *standard 7.10.7*
- Storage of potentially hazardous materials: *standard 7.11*
- Arrival and departure procedures: *standard 7.14*
- Student transportation: *standard 7.15*

Section 8: Family and Community Relations
Policies and/or procedures for
- Parent communication (handbook, newsletters): *standards 8.1, 8.2*
- Parent conferences: *standard 8.3.1*
- Observation methods: *standards 8.3.2, 8.4.1*
- Parent orientation: *standard 8.4.2*
- Documenting and communicating significant changes in individual children: *standard 8.4.3*
- Parent education programs: *standard 8.5*
- Parent involvement: *standard 8.5.2*

 purposeful design

Early Education DIRECTOR'S MANUAL

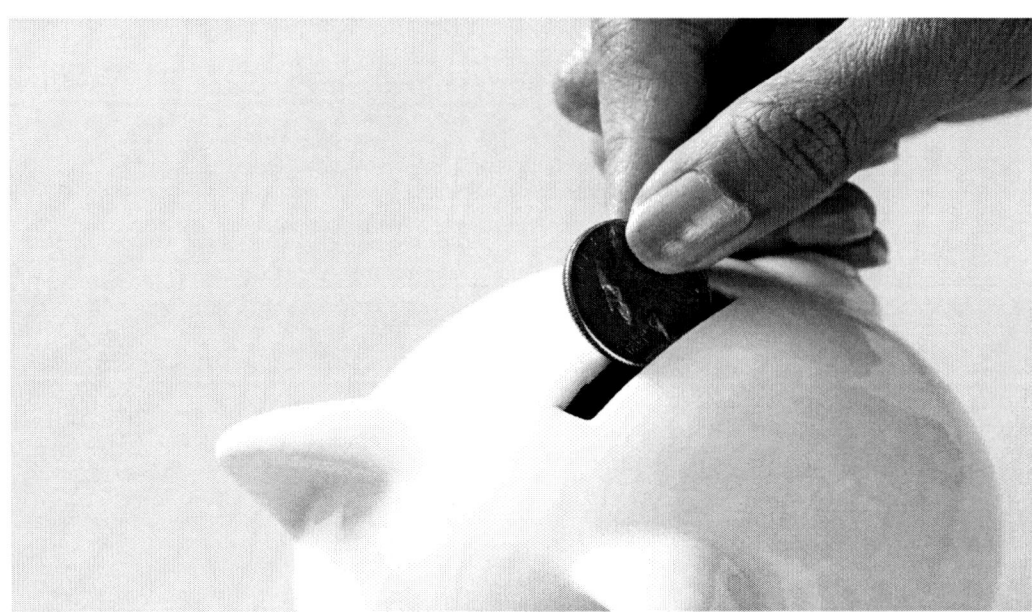

Chapter 5

Now it is required that those who have been given a trust must prove faithful. (1 Corinthians 4:2)

Wise Stewardship

In accepting the responsibility of caring for young children, early education programs not only commit to providing safe and enriching environments; they also assure parents that they will continue to offer those environments until the children outgrow the program. When a lack of sufficient funds forces a program to close prematurely, children face the difficult task of forging relationships with new teachers and playmates. One of the ways we honor children is through wise stewardship of program finances, ensuring the continuity of care that children and families need.

■ Church financial partnerships

Starting and funding an early education program can be an exciting adventure. Because of the necessary financial investment, church programs need to give significant time and thought to the matter. In a passage that suggests the value of planning ahead, Jesus referred specifically to the cost of discipleship. Speaking to a large crowd, He said,

> Suppose one of you wants to build a tower. Will he not first sit down and estimate the cost to see if he has enough money to complete it? For if he lays the foundation and is not able to finish it, everyone who sees it will ridicule him, saying, "This fellow began to build and was not able to finish." (Luke 14:28–29)

There are a few important principles that we can glean from this passage in relation to the operation of a church-based early education program:

1. Churches need to consider seriously the actual costs involved in starting an early education program and be realistic about the financial resources available to fund it.

2. Counting the cost involves more than simply crunching numbers. It may also involve a study committee that surveys the community to learn the need for such a program and its benefits for the children.

3. Building a quality early education program involves creating a stable environment that will support the growth of young children. At times, this task includes maintaining financial reserves to enable the program to continue through unstable times.

4. Laying a solid foundation, a step that is crucial to the success of the program, includes attracting and retaining quality staff members and providing appropriate facilities that have the space needed for learning.

5. Early education programs should not be entered into with the goal of using them to fund other programs within the sponsoring church, K–12 school, or other ministry. Rather, the goal is to offer families a quality program for young children while providing appropriately for staff needs and facility maintenance.

Financial independence

Early education programs need to achieve financial independence. Once a program has begun, its goal should be to become self-sufficient. It is important to track the new program through established budgets to verify its financial health. A program begun in partnership with a sponsoring church or other organization still needs to have a separate budget in order to track its own income and expenses. Programs that combine their budgets or share income pools with other entities will have difficulty determining the degree of their financial success. Itemizing income and expenses by department will provide the director with tools for ensuring accountability and good stewardship.

Another sensitive issue is excess revenue. If an early education program is fortunate enough to have excess income, its administration and board members have an ethical responsibility to ensure that the excess revenue is reinvested in the program. The extra funds may be used to establish a reserve for emergencies, to increase staff salaries, to replace supplies, or to make improvements in the facility. Rarely does a program generate so much revenue that its leaders are at a loss to know how to use it all. In fact, because of the low child-adult ratios required of programs for young children, the early education field is particularly labor intensive. Investing any excess revenue in staff compensation, training, and benefits will have an ongoing impact on the children.

Training for the director

The early education director may view the budget as a daunting responsibility. It is recommended that the governing board assist the director in accessing appropriate training until confidence has been established. A knowledgeable board member or church member may be able to act as a consultant by walking the director through the budgeting process. At a minimum, the director should be oriented to the terms and information included in the monthly financial reports.

In a church-sponsored early education program, a church administrator may also be responsible for the program's budget. However, the director's expertise in early childhood issues, her familiarity with the daily operations of the program, and her understanding of its long-term goals make her input essential in developing and maintaining the early education center's budget.

■ Ethical considerations and accountability

As noted above, it is important to maintain good stewardship and to monitor financial practices in order to operate in a way that is consistent with biblical principles. To deviate from this practice is to risk the credibility of the program and the testimony of the school. Parents expect that ethical standards will be upheld and that the tuition they pay will be used wisely and will be channeled into the program. To help protect the program from potential problems, the school should establish basic guidelines, including the following:

- Assure that all tuition collected is deposited in a timely way.
- Hire qualified bookkeeping staff with strong ethical values.
- Have two staff people involved in collecting and recording tuition.
- Have an additional staff person, other than the director, be in charge of purchasing and petty cash to ensure accountability.
- Have reserve funds for emergency situations and replacement costs.
- Have the program audited or reviewed annually.
- Establish a school board to oversee the program's financial operation.
- Consult an accountant for guidance in financial best practices.

Budgeting Principles

In order to manage and guide a program properly, the early education director needs to be familiar with the basic principles of budgeting. At its simplest level, a budget is a tool for planning and control.

Through the process of budget development, the board and the director strategically plan how the financial resources of the center will be used to achieve its goals. (See form 5.1 Annual Budget.) Once a center has been operating for a number of years, it is common to base future budget projections on previous ones. While this method is valuable for predicting enrollment trends, it can make it easy for the center to simply reproduce its spending patterns

Additional Support

Private organizations or individuals can be another financial resource, providing tax-deductible donations. Such a donation can be a welcome bonus, enabling a center to develop a new program or establish a scholarship fund. Many early education programs organize fund-raising projects to provide extra funds. While the revenue collected from fund-raising is not enough to keep a program in operation, the extra funds may enable the center to replace outdoor play equipment or to meet other facility needs. Another kind of subsidized funding is in-kind support. This support comes in the form of items or services that the center receives from another source without having to pay for them. An example is the use of a facility at little or no cost. Church-sponsored programs are often able to benefit from this in-kind support that allows the program to have lower overhead costs.

from year to year while giving little thought to its mission. A wise director connects proposed expenditures to the center's expected student outcomes by funding equipment, materials, and programs that directly support the school's overall goals for children. When financial decisions are guided by their impact on the children's developmental outcomes, resources are aligned with staff efforts in fulfilling the program's mission.

■ Planning and goals

Many schools guide the development of their program by establishing both short-term and long-term goals. Short-term goals focus on immediate needs that the center will face in the coming year, such as developing curriculum, purchasing supplies and materials, and creating parent and staff handbooks. These goals can be established and reviewed by the board and the staff throughout the school year. Targeting them will increase the effectiveness of the overall program and will strengthen the quality of the care and education that are provided.

Long-term goals involve issues that are essential for the continued success of the school and can be addressed over a period of years. They may include decisions about enrollment, accreditation, finances, facilities, staffing, and staff training. A program often needs to regroup every few years in order to refocus and ensure that it is meeting the current needs of the students. A good practice is to review the center's philosophy and vision statements and to readdress the essential elements of the program. Goals should be specific enough to be measurable, and they should be incorporated into yearly evaluations of the program by both the parents and the staff.

■ Ongoing replacement costs

Over time, a center's equipment, furnishings, and facilities will need to be replaced. Therefore, it is imperative to accumulate a cash reserve designated for these expenses. A good rule of thumb is to amortize these costs over a period of time to allow for depreciation. Saving a portion of the annual tuition revenue will help the center address such needs. A center that sets aside five to ten percent of its yearly income will have sufficient resources to meet its future needs. As these set-aside funds increase, it is tempting for administrators, church personnel, and board members to cast an eye on the accumulated reserve. The director and school board members need to be aware of this tendency. They must be proactive in regularly reminding the school and church leaders what these reserve funds are for and how replacing materials and equipment will benefit the overall facility.

A successful center will maintain a balance between setting aside excess revenue for replacement costs and reinvesting that revenue into the program. It is a good practice to maintain three months of revenue in reserve for emergency situations, a policy that represents good stewardship and enables the program to be independent from other programs.

■ Types of income

Tuition. The primary source of income for most Christian early childhood education programs is monthly or weekly tuition. Before you set tuition rates, you need to consider several matters, including the actual cost of providing your services, the prevailing market rates, and any discounts you may consider offering. Additionally, when viewing tuition as a budget item, you must take into account utilization rates, or the degree to which the center operates at capacity throughout the year.

Fees. Revenue from tuition can be supplemented by various one-time or annual fees, including the following:

Enrollment/reenrollment or registration fees are paid when a child is enrolled or reenrolled for the following year. They are collected in advance of the opening of school and should be set aside as a part of that school year's income. Many schools allocate a small portion of their enrollment or registration fees for their annual ACSI membership dues.

Supply fees, which are collected before the first day of school, are used to purchase such items as curriculum materials and art supplies. Instead of collecting another fee from parents, some centers incorporate the cost of supply items into the tuition. Some centers have the parents purchase supplies to bring to the classroom, and thus the children establish a bond with the center before the first day.

Contributions and fund-raisers. There are likely to be opportunities for the center to receive income through individual contributors and fund-raising efforts. However, such income may not be available until the center is well established and has been in operation for several years.

■ Establishing tuition rates

Surveying local market prices. It is helpful to take a yearly survey of tuition rates charged by programs in your vicinity and even outside it. (See form 5.2 Survey of School Rates.) You can connect with these programs through telephone directories and licensing websites. Knowing about the programs and the children they serve will help you understand the distinctives of your own program. Comparing market prices in your area will keep you on top of what rates are reasonable. Programs that fall in the low range may be perceived as substandard in both facilities and staffing, while programs in the high range are hard to afford and may be accessible only to high-income families. When you know your community and how much parents can afford to pay, you are in a position to establish appropriate tuition rates that will not force you to jeopardize the quality of service you provide.

A thorough tuition survey will include programs that are similar to yours in size and structure, both within

and outside your local area. Keeping in touch with local programs will help you recognize the trends in your community. Additionally, you will want to collect information on salaries and benefits offered by other local early education employers. It is wise to survey both privately and publicly funded programs so that you will be aware of the range of wages available to the staff you will be recruiting.

Other considerations. Because tuition may be the chief source of income for your center, the tuition rates must reflect the actual costs of providing early care and education. Rates will vary according to the ages of the children being served and the scope of the program, including the number of days and hours of attendance. For example, the cost of caring for infants and toddlers is significantly higher than the cost of serving older, preschool-age children because of the high adult-to-child ratio necessary to meet the younger children's needs. Often, fees from the older children's classrooms subsidize the tuition rates of the younger children.

The director must be aware of how the various tuition rates contribute to the actual cost within each department. Additionally, daily schedules affect overall tuition income. Half-day tuition rates often reflect a higher fee per hour than full-day rates. The combined fees of the children enrolled for two days a week and those enrolled for three days a week may amount to more than the fees of children enrolled for five days a week. A director who is informed about how these variations affect the annual tuition income is better prepared to anticipate and respond to changing enrollment patterns.

Tuition reductions. Some early education programs offer a range of tuition reductions, including discounts for siblings, discounts for children of school employees and church staff, and waived fees for absent children. The director must be aware of the cumulative financial impact of such policies and must confront the annual cost to the program of each specific tuition discount. Centers offering discounts when a child is absent because of illness or a family vacation, or when the center is closed for a holiday or in-service day, must take into account the fact that expenses remain constant in most of these instances. Offering discounts to staff members whose children are enrolled in the program can be a successful method of recruiting and retaining teachers, but the costs to the program are significant when staff-to-child ratios are high. When developing policies on employee tuition discounts, the director may want to seek legal advice to ensure that the policies comply with federal laws. For example, a recent IRS ruling stated that church employees not working for the school do not qualify for tax-free tuition discounts.[1]

■ Financial stability

Determining the actual cost of providing high-quality childcare and early education requires a detailed review of the expenditures involved in delivering such a program. The expenses are generally classified as either variable or fixed. Variable expenses—payroll, food, consumable supplies—fluctuate with changes in enrollment. Fixed expenses remain fairly constant regardless of other variables such as the number of children enrolled in the program.[2] For example, each month's use of the facility may cost a predetermined amount.

Expenditures must be closely monitored to ensure financial stability. Keeping an accurate count of the number of children in attendance during childcare hours allows directors to maintain appropriate staffing ratios. Additionally, directors can practice good stewardship by purchasing supplies in bulk, by taking advantage of discounts available to ACSI member schools, and by evaluating equipment and curriculum materials in light of their value for children.

When reduced enrollment results in reduced income, an early education center must scrutinize expenditures closely and introduce cost-cutting measures. At times, haphazard management results in financial loss. When staff members aren't adequately trained, the center is not getting appropriate value for the money it spends on their salaries. Poor employee performance is costly, both to the children and to the program's reputation.

Similarly, conscientious management brings financial benefits. A center must not underestimate the value of intangibles. Staff members are more likely to stay in a center where morale is good, reducing the cost of recruitment and orientation. Greeting parents warmly by name, listening to their concerns, and responding to them promptly costs nothing but builds strong relationships and results in free word-of-mouth advertising.

Budgeting Practices

■ From start-up to established center

The first step in budget preparation is defining the categories for various types of income and expenses. You will need enough categories to help you track your center's income and expenditures, but not so many that the amount of detail becomes overwhelming. (See form 5.3 Annual Budget Worksheet.)

If you are opening a new early education program, you will need to develop a budget for the start-up period, prior to opening, when a director is hired and initial investments in equipment are made. (See form 5.8 Classroom Equipment and Supplies.) After children are enrolled and the school begins generating income, a first-year budget will help guide the operation. This budget will need to reflect the time it often takes to build enrollment to capacity. Once the center has become established, an ongoing budget can be developed that reflects the needs of an existing center.

■ *Projecting income*

To make a ball-park estimate of the center's income, the director can estimate the number of students to be enrolled in each class and multiply the total for all classes by the amount of the tuition. (See form 5.4 Planning Income.) If the center is a new one, the enrollment may not be at capacity. In budgeting for ongoing programs, planning should be realistic, with past income history serving as a guide. Tuition rates for the following school year should be established in November or December. While it is important for the school's tuition rates to be comparable to those of other centers in the area, the total amount of tuition must meet the center's financial needs adequately. No director should fall into the trap of starting with low tuition rates in the hope of raising them later, when enrollment has increased or the center is more successful. Also, the center's income is affected by any tuition assistance programs or tuition discounts for children of the staff.

■ *Projecting expenses*

In evaluating existing budgets, directors are often interested in the typical distribution of expenses. (See form 5.5 Planning Expenditures.) The following averages are suggested in "Child Care: Financial Basics"[3]:

- Personnel   55–70 percent
- Occupancy   15–20 percent
- Meals/snacks   2–5 percent
- Supplies   3–5 percent
- Equipment   2–3 percent
- Insurance   2–3 percent
- Other services   3–4 percent
  (accounting, legal, training, transportation)
- Profit/surplus   5–7 percent

Many factors will affect these percentages. An early education center operating in an established church with a debt-free facility may pay only the utility expenses

and no rental fees. In such a situation, additional finances may be invested in the staff and program. In determining the percentage to be allocated to each category, a number of areas need to be considered:

Personnel

- Factors that affect personnel costs
  ° Adult-to-child ratio
  ° Expectations for staff members in terms of education and experience
  ° Percentage of the staff at various education levels: head teachers, teachers, and teacher assistants
  ° Hours of operation
  ° Children's attendance patterns
- Salaries
- Benefits
- Substitutes
- Professional development
- Payroll taxes

Occupancy

- Rent or mortgage
- Facility: property taxes, maintenance, renovation/repairs
- Utilities: water, gas, electric, telephone, Internet/email access

Meals/snacks

- How many meals and/or snacks will be served each day?
- Will the center participate in a federally subsidized food program?
- Will snacks be supplied by parents?
- Will meal and snack supplies be delivered by vendors?
- If food items are purchased locally, what are the reimbursement expenses for employee wages and transportation?

Supplies

- Consumable materials, including art and learning materials (See forms 5.7 Purchase Request Form and 5.9 Supply Requisition.)
- Donated materials that can be accessed

Equipment

- Nonconsumable items such as furniture, audio/visual equipment, and office equipment
- Items that might be built with donated labor rather than purchased

Insurance

- General liability
- Vehicle
- Errors and omissions
- Officers' and directors' liability insurance (for board of directors)
- Medical or accident insurance
- Property insurance

Other Services

- Legal: legal defense reimbursement program
- Marketing:
  - Telephone directory
  - Signs, etc.
- Transportation:
  - Ongoing
  - Occasional (e.g., field trips)
- Professional:
  - Membership in professional organizations (ACSI, etc.)
  - Accreditation
  - Conferences and training
  - Subscriptions and professional resource books

Profit/Surplus

- Ongoing replacement costs:
  - Furniture
  - Indoor equipment
  - Playground equipment
  - Carpeting
  - Facility upgrades

■ *Following a schedule*

With timely preparation, the director is able to project the school's year-end cash position accurately. In other words, in May/June of the current year, the approximate cash position for May/June of the next year can be projected, giving the director time to make any necessary adjustments. The following schedule will help the director and governing board develop a budget in a timely manner:

- November/December—Determine the tuition and wage/benefits packages for the next school year, and present these to the governing board for approval.
- February/April—Determine all other budget costs.
- May—Present a semifinal budget to the governing board for approval.
- September—Revise the budget and the projections to reflect actual enrollment.

After a budget summary and a detailed budget have been prepared, the final step is to make month-by-month projections. This step begins with dividing the income and expense figures into twelve monthly amounts. Many new or small centers do not take this step, but it is important. Completing month-by-month charts can make the difference between a well-prepared budget plan and a haphazard one. (See form 5.6 Yearly Financial Spreadsheet.)

Church-related centers may choose to follow the church's fiscal year, which typically runs from July 1 through June 30. Income and expenses cannot be divided equally by twelve. It isn't that simple because some months will have high expenses, while others, such as July and August, will not. Therefore, the amount of expected income and expenses for each month, for every item, should be determined. Month-by-month projections can be made by using data based on experience and by looking for trends in income and spending. A monthly percentage of total receipts and expenditures for each account can be assigned. By multiplying this percentage by the budgeted amount, the director can forecast next year's monthly receipts and disbursements quickly and quite accurately. A computer can save time by facilitating the procedure. The director should be careful, however, to evaluate each account according to whether it is more appropriate to budget by the percentage method or by actual cash projections.

Cash surpluses and needs can be projected for each month by accumulating totals on a month-to-month basis. This information is extremely important for a school that is operating on a tight budget.

If the majority of staff members are hourly employees who are paid twice a month, monthly payroll expenses will vary with the number of days in the month. Similarly, when employees are paid every two weeks, the total biweekly payroll may be quite consistent during months of steady enrollment. This principle also applies to tuition collection. Some centers charge parents a set amount for each month, others do the same for each week. Particularly when working primarily with hourly staff, directors need to look closely at the relationship between the number of payroll hours in each month and the amount of tuition being billed.

Additional payroll expenses accrue when teachers go on vacation and substitutes must be hired to replace them. If the majority of teachers take paid vacations during the summer, an increase in expenses for salaries may result. Some directors encourage staff members to take their vacation hours during periods when many children are typically absent, such as Christmas holidays. In periods of low enrollment,

replacement staff may be unnecessary, reducing the impact of vacation hours on payroll.

■ Accounting systems

Accounting systems are put in place to ensure good financial practices. The systems can vary according to location, but a few general principles should be considered. Accounting systems involve a systematic approach to managing finances.

It is a best practice to have personnel with some expertise in accounting manage the center's finances. Although a center can get by with personnel who have limited financial skills, it is best to have professionals. Financial mistakes can be costly and can create roadblocks that hamper a center's continued growth. Tracking income and expenditures is an ongoing process that requires regular attention. Computer programs and ledger cards are two ways of tracking income, while detailed documentation with computer technology is the main way of tracking expenses. Regular reports need to be generated at least once a month, comparing the center's expenditures with the amounts budgeted. This practice will help give an overall view of the program's financial health.

Collecting and recording funds. Funds should be collected on a consistent basis. Policies regarding payment schedules and consequences for delinquent accounts should be detailed in the parent handbook and should appear periodically in the monthly newsletter. Some programs require parents to sign a financial agreement detailing such policies as frequency of payment, penalties for late payment and returned checks, and termination notices. Collecting tuition and handling delinquent accounts can be a difficult area for the director to manage considering her numerous other responsibilities and the positive tone she wants to set with the parents. If the necessary resources are available, it is a good practice to involve selected support staff in the collection process.

A set procedure should be established for making tuition payments. Periodic reminders, such as a small sign near the sign-in sheets announcing the first of the month, are a help to busy parents. Ongoing follow-up of delinquent payments is essential. Failure to make timely payments can quickly get out of hand if tuition income is not tracked on a regular basis. Parents should be notified right away if their payment is late to verify their intent and to work out a plan acceptable to both the director and the family. Allowing delinquent payments to build up over time creates a financial hardship for both the family and the center.

Incoming funds should be recorded promptly, and receipts supplied for cash payments. These practices allow for early tracking of outstanding accounts and good follow-up with families. When tuition checks are not recorded or deposited in a timely manner, there is a loss of potential interest income as well as the risk of missing funds. It is desirable when possible to assign to separate persons the responsibilities of recording payments and of making deposits. Strict procedures for handling funds help to maintain the integrity of the center.

Maintaining cash flow and reserves. Wise business practices can help assure constituents that the center will continue to be fiscally sound and will use responsibly the resources God has provided. A cash reserve of five percent of the expense budget is considered conservative in the business community. Such a reserve will help to cushion the center against hardship resulting from emergency expenses or miscalculations in the budget. Some centers are unable to set aside as large an amount as five percent, so they budget a small amount each month and accumulate the recommended percentage over a period of three to five years.

Financial Oversight
▪ Regular statements
A monthly financial summary provides an overview of the program's finances. Budget reports comparing actual income and expenses with projections allow the director to apply controls such as spending limits and payroll adjustments. The summary should list each category of the budget along with a budgeted amount and the actual income and expenditures.

This overall picture is useful in helping the director see whether too little is coming in or too much is being spent. If the summary shows a failure to balance income and expenses, adjustments can be made the following month. Expenses usually follow a particular cycle, so enough cash should be kept in reserve to cover those months in which income is especially low. The monthly financial summary is a useful tool that can guide the director in making important financial decisions. It will enable her to monitor the spending cycle in each category and to determine whether any adjustments need to be made.

▪ Financial audits
An audit is a detailed review of the program's income and expenditures.[4] Audits are generally conducted by certified public accountants (CPAs). The auditor will check various financial activities to assure that all legal requirements are being met. Finding a qualified auditor who is familiar with the particular type of program will be important. In preparing for an audit, the director needs to make sure that all accounting systems are up-to-date and easily accessible to the individual or team. Christian early education centers that are associated with church organizations will participate in the audit of the entire organization. To maintain a 501(c)3 status, the center must abide by government requirements. Auditors typically review the records, affirm good accounting practices, and make recommendations for improvement. Follow-up documentation may be needed

in addition to subsequent visits. Auditors who sign off on the report have placed their professional integrity on the line as they verify the accuracy of the documents.

A requirement for ACSI accreditation of an early education program is an audit or financial review summary by someone in the accounting field. A financial review is a less stringent and less expensive process than an official audit. Still, a review serves to verify the accuracy of the accounting processes and helps assure the center of its financial well-being. Alternatively, in order to fulfill this requirement for accreditation, the program may submit a financial procedures checklist.

FORM 5.1

Annual Budget

INCOME				
Tuition				
Infants (8 x $6,750)	$54,000	After-school care (50 x $3,500)	$175,000	
Toddlers (21 x $5,750)	$120,750	Lost revenue	<$950>	
Preschoolers (40 x $4,750)	$190,000	**Total gross tuition**	**$538,800**	
Other Income				
Enrollment fees	$5,000			
Grants and awards	$20,000	Fund raisers	$10,000	
USDA food program	$25,000	**Total other income**	**$60,000**	
TOTAL INCOME	**$ 598,800**			
EXPENSES				
Personnel				
Administration		*Support Staff*		
Director (1 x $31,000)	$31,000	Custodian (1 x $15,500)	$15,500	
Assistant director (1 x $26,000)	$26,000	Cook (1 x $15,500)	$15,500	
Administrative assistant (1 x $20,000)	$20,000	FICA, workers' compensation, unemployment	$84,050	
Teaching Staff				
Teachers (11 x $18,250)	$200,750			
Assistant teachers (6 x $15,500)	$93,000			
Aides (2 x $7,000)	$14,000			
Substitutes ($5,000)	$5,000	**Total Personnel**	**$504,800**	
Operating Expenses				
Rent	$24,000	Kitchen and janitorial supplies	$1,000	
Utilities and phone	$15,000	Insurance	$3,000	
Advertising	$1,000	Licenses	$500	
Food	$35,000	Staff development/training	$3,000	
Office supplies	$1,500	Petty cash	$500	
Classroom equipment and supplies	$10,000			
Total Operating Expense	**$94,500**			
TOTAL EXPENSES	**$599,300**			

FORM 5.2

Survey of School Rates

School	Date	Sessions	Rates	Registration Fee
Name: Location:		M–F Full: M–F Half: MWF Full: MWF Half: TTH Full: TTH Half: Lunch:		Annual: One Time:
Name: Location:		M–F Full: M–F Half: MWF Full: MWF Half: TTH Full: TTH Half: Lunch:		Annual: One Time:
Name: Location:		M–F Full: M–F Half: MWF Full: MWF Half: TTH Full: TTH Half: Lunch:		Annual: One Time:
Name: Location:		M–F Full: M–F Half: MWF Full: MWF Half: TTH Full: TTH Half: Lunch:		Annual: One Time:

FORM 5.3

Annual Budget Worksheet

Income Category	Yearly Income	Last Year Ending
Totals		

Expense Category	Yearly Income	Last Year Ending
Totals		

FORM 5.4

Planning Income

Income Category	Projected Income
Category: Items:	
Category: Items:	
Category: Items:	
Category: Items:	
Category: Items:	
Category: Items:	
Category: Items:	
Category: Items:	
Category: Items:	
Category: Items:	
Totals	

FORM 5.5

Planning Expenditures

Expense Category	Projected Expenses
Category: Items:	
Category: Items:	
Category: Items:	
Category: Items:	
Category: Items:	
Category: Items:	
Category: Items:	
Category: Items:	
Category: Items:	
Category: Items:	
Totals	

purposeful design   *Early Education* DIRECTOR'S MANUAL

FORM 5.6

Yearly Financial Spreadsheet

	Sep	Oct	Nov	Dec	Jan	Feb	Mar	Apr	May	Jun	Jul	Aug	Totals
Income													
													Total Income
Expenses													
													Total Expenses

purposeful design   *Early Education* DIRECTOR'S MANUAL

FORM 5.7

Purchase Request Form

Teacher:

Date:

I see these as priority items that need to be purchased for my classroom for the upcoming year:

Item	Timeline	Purpose	Quantity

I would like to have these items available in my classroom for the upcoming year:

Item	Timeline	Purpose	Quantity

I suggest we purchase these items for the entire program for the upcoming year:

Item	Timeline	Purpose	Quantity

purposeful design   *Early Education* DIRECTOR'S MANUAL

FORM 5.8

Classroom Equipment and Supplies

Space-saving art storage	Single traditional puzzle holder
Kinder Smocks (12)	First Puzzle Set, Animals
Conical-tip markers (2 packs)	Early Learning Puzzle Set
Big brush bucket (30 ct.)	Easy Grip Pegged Puzzles (3)
1 gallon school glue	Dress-up tree
Tempera paints, assorted colors (12)	Pretend play cooking set
Crayon assortments, large size (200 ct.)	Healthy Play food set
Student scissors (12)	Multiethnic School Dolls (4)
Do-a-Dot markers (6)	Doll cradle
Assorted foam brushes (12)	Child's 2-way mirror
Watercolor paint trays (12)	Dexter's Dressups set
Art display paper (3 rolls)	3-unit kitchen set
Art display paper rack	Deluxe maple tables and chairs set
Extra-white sulphite drawing paper (3 reams)	Bean bag chairs (2)
White newsprint (2 reams)	Small carpet
Sponges (10 pack)	Childcraft Complete Kitchen set
No-spill paint cups (set of 10)	Learn to Read / *See* book set
Classroom Clay Creations Kit	Learn to Read *About Me* book set
Dip & Print sponge class sets	*Beginner's Bible* (2)
1 gallon white school paste	Teacher planning book
All-purpose double easel	Scheduling pocket chart
Portable CD player	Super spots stickers
Wood rhythm stick kit	Heavy-Duty Kindermat (12)
Rhythm band instrument set (25 player)	Virco V90 Chairs (12)
Children's music CDs (4)	Virco Activity Table (trapezoid)
Assorted CDs (4)	Virco Activity Table (rectangle)
Softworks Hand Puppets	Mattkleen Disinfectant (2)
Lego Duplo Basic Medium Set	Triple section folding storage
Lego Explore Being Me World People Set	Adult rocker
Interlocking Stars	Standard cork bulletin boards (3)
Beads and laces	Library book display (single sided)
Links	Sharpie twin pack (pack)
Stickle Bricks	Bic Round Stic Pens (12 pack)
Fit-A-Space	Fiskar teacher scissors
Giant nuts and bolts	Classic economy stapler
Deluxe road system kit	Clock
Stowaway storage boxes (10)	Classroom American flag
Mathematical Discoveries Kit	Classroom Christian flag
Circle time class kit (flannel boards)	Unisource paper towels (case lot)
Small Wonders Kit	Unisource toilet paper (case lot, 6 rolls)
Exploring Magnets Kit	Trash can liners (100 pack)
Insect kit	Unisource soap (case lot, 4 boxes)
Superior Listening Center	Trash can (with lid)
Big-screen microscope (2)	Broom
Unit block set (119 pieces)	
Wonderfoam counting mat	

purposeful design   *Early Education* DIRECTOR'S MANUAL

FORM 5.9

Supply Requisition

Name:			
Position:			
Date requested:		Date needed:	

Item:	Quantity:	Cost:	To be purchased from:

Comments:

purposeful design

Early Education DIRECTOR'S MANUAL

THE ROLE OF THE DIRECTOR

Chapter 6

Whatever you do, work at it with all your heart, as working for the Lord, not for men. (Colossians 3:23)

Spiritual and Educational Qualifications

■ A godly leader

As Christian administrators, we are called to follow God's example of leadership. As God extends His grace and mercy to us as His leaders, shouldn't we also extend grace and mercy to those we lead? The keys to becoming a godly leader are expectations, communication, and appreciation. Setting realistic expectations for the staff, children, and parents lays a foundation for godly leadership. It is essential that we communicate those expectations, but just as important is how we communicate them. Finally, showing appreciation as we communicate our expectations will help to keep our relationship with the staff an open one.

In order to follow God's example of leadership, we need to spend time in His Word. If we rely only on our strength to do our best, we will fail. A godly leader not only has a personal relationship with God through His Son Jesus Christ but also leads a life of prayer. The Holy Spirit plays a significant role in guiding the director each step of the way. God's Word gives us a promise in the book of Joshua: "Constantly remind the people about these laws, and you yourself must think about them every day and every night so that you will be sure to obey all of them. For only then will you succeed. Yes, be bold and strong! Banish fear and doubt! For remember, the Lord your God is with you wherever you go" (Joshua 1:8–9, TLB). Our success depends largely on our reliance on the Holy Spirit.

As we pursue excellence in our spiritual lives, our professional lives will follow suit. In order to have professional insight, we need expertise and experience in early education. Our responsibility for leading the staff—including teachers, assistants, and office personnel—demands that we have the necessary professional expertise. Those of us who are currently directors, or are seeking to be, need to consider earning a degree in child development or a related field. Doing so will give us the credibility we need to provide leadership that encourages our staff to move forward in their own professional careers. Education in the field of early childhood education will introduce us to new concepts and will give us the knowledge we need to direct our staff effectively. In order to be strong leaders, our skill level needs to surpass that of our staff, who will respect us more if we keep at least one step ahead of them. Many professionals rely heavily on experience. Of course experience is valuable, but experience alone will not allow us to keep up with current trends and provide the leadership our staff needs. In *A Fish Out Of Water*[1], George Barna defines leadership by what it is not:

- Leadership is not influence.
- Leadership is not getting things done efficiently.
- Leadership is not controlling the decision-making process through power and position.
- Leadership is not being the most popular among peers.

In contrast, Barna describes leadership as "the process of motivating, mobilizing, resourcing, and directing people to passionately and strategically pursue a vision from God that a group jointly embraces."[2] Barna says the following about the role and purpose of a leader[3]:

- Leaders get people excited about God's vision.
- Leaders enable people to be genuinely inspired.
- Leaders mobilize people around a common cause.

- Leaders bring together people of like minds and hearts and blend their abilities toward bringing a vision to reality.
- Leaders do the *right* things for the *right* reasons, at the *right* time.

Having a realistic concept of leadership will help the director understand what her priorities should be in moving the center forward. Many times directors feel that they need to be gifted in all areas and that they must manage the complete operation of their center single-handedly. This false assumption can lead quickly to burnout. Effective leaders will delegate tasks, giving themselves time to pursue opportunities for moving the program forward in the vision God has for it and surrounding themselves with people who are gifted in a variety of areas.

■ Understanding child development

In order to be an effective leader of a preschool/childcare center, a director needs a strong working knowledge of early education, a requirement that goes hand in hand with the education requirement already addressed. Directors are called on regularly to make decisions that will be in the children's best interest. They have a significant impact in developing the curriculum and guiding how it is taught. Thus directors need to be knowledgeable about the ages and stages of young children. It is important for a director to have classroom experience in teaching and caring for young children. Without both education and experience, directors may find themselves in a situation in which certain staff members with a higher level of expertise will choose not to accept or rely on their director's counsel and leadership. Education and experience help a director develop her basic skills, but it is also important that she expose herself to various types of programs by visiting schools, serving on accreditation teams, and taking courses that enable her to be on the cutting edge. It is easy for a director to compare her own program with those that are deficient in certain areas, but exposing herself to the best of the best will make her more realistic about where her own program needs to grow.

■ Leadership styles and abilities

God has uniquely designed each of us, giving us gifts and talents that prepare us to fulfill a specific role. If He has called you to the ministry of working with young children, He will equip you with the necessary abilities to do your work. With this calling comes the responsibility to use in a productive way the gifts God has given. Early education leaders need to relate well with the center's staff, parents, and students. Those not gifted in working with people should reevaluate their calling to determine whether a career in early education is a good fit.

Each director has a unique style, but all styles should include showing respect for others, valuing and never humiliating them. Also, the same director will demonstrate different leadership styles in different situations, and a good leader will know which style is appropriate at a given moment. Situations that call for immediate action may indicate a *directive approach*. For example, sometimes a director needs to make an immediate decision about a matter that affects the health and safety of the children. There may be little time to discuss with others what ought to be done. Staff members may need to be reminded about matters of policy or job performance. A director's ability to give clear, consistent direction to the staff and the children will provide the needed security and stability. But directors should be careful not to use a directive approach in making every decision, as the result would be a staff that feels cut off from the decision-making process.

Often an administrator will have the time and opportunity to consult with the staff regarding an issue. Such consultation allows for a *participatory approach* to decision making. The participation of the staff is likely to result in a better outcome,

including their buy-in to the decisions that are made. Even when a director exercises her right to make the final decision, staff members have been heard and various perspectives discussed.

Still another style is the *collaborative approach*, in which the director and the staff members have equal say and input in the decision-making process. The director can delegate responsibilities, giving staff members the role of making a decision or a change based on a consensus. This approach allows the staff to feel they have contributed to the overall success of the program. The rule of thumb is to involve the staff in decision making as much as possible while providing clear and consistent direction.

The director can assess her own management style by

1. Understanding her personal style of leadership
2. Researching various approaches to management
3. Developing a plan for improvement

A Director's Responsibilities

The day of a visit by prospective parents, a state licensing official, or a representative from the health department will be the day when the toilets are clogged, three teachers are out sick, the pet rabbit is on the loose, little Johnny throws up, and the director is training a new staff member. A director will wear many hats in the course of a day. A look at the job description is enough to frighten Superman. However, a director who has reasonable expectations, good organizational skills, and above all flexibility will meet each day's challenges confidently and will enjoy each day's blessings.

■ Job description

Identifying the scope of the director's responsibilities requires a clear understanding of the overall early education program. Each program makes unique demands, and those demands depend on the type of program, its size, its hours of operation, the available financial support, and the reporting requirements. Job descriptions for the director need to take into account all aspects of the program. General categories include the following:

- Determining ongoing community needs
- Planning the budget and monitoring finances
- Communicating regularly with the governing board
- Purchasing and maintaining equipment and supplies
- Hiring, training, evaluating, and firing staff
- Marketing the program
- Providing professional development opportunities
- Staying current in early childhood education and early childhood legislative issues
- Maintaining relationships with families
- Maintaining positive involvement with children
- Monitoring health and safety standards
- Actively evaluating the program and implementing quality improvements
- Achieving and maintaining accreditation
- Developing and maintaining the instructional program
- Developing the facility and physical environment
- Maintaining relationships with regulating agencies

A clearly defined job description will help the prospective director understand the scope of her responsibilities and identify performance expectations. Evaluation tools need to be based on the stated objectives. Job descriptions should be in place before a director is hired, allowing applicants to look over the job requirements and the board to state its expectations clearly. (See form 6.1 Job Description: Early Education Center Director.)

▪ Scope of responsibility

As can be imagined, the scope of the director's responsibility is huge. A person in the position can experience feelings of stress and isolation. One of the responsibilities is to work at helping staff and board members understand their respective roles in meeting the responsibilities God has given them. Thus, the governing board bears the responsibility of fulfilling the requirements established by governing agencies to care for the education, health, and safety of young children. Directors need to communicate the board's role clearly and ensure that they are active in making policy decisions that relate to that responsibility. Staff members need to be aware of their role in the instruction and supervision of the children.

▪ Disciplinary action

At one time or another, a director will have to deal with a difficult staff situation, one that will require much prayer and discernment to address. The director should keep in mind that the people involved are the main focus of the problem, and she should make every effort to handle them with care and respect. It is easy to overreact in the heat of such a situation. Sometimes distance and time alone will enable the parties involved to make the right decision. We are called by God to handle our employees in the spirit of fairness and love. With this fact in mind, here are a few principles we can follow when addressing a conflict situation:

- Always listen first and gather the information from all parties.
- Spend time in prayer both privately and with each staff member involved.
- Ask yourself, What is the most loving thing I can do in this situation? Sometimes the answer involves following established policies and letting reality happen for a staff member.
- Always offer a balance of grace and truth.
- Be consistent in your decisions.

It is important to document staff situations and to track them as they continue and are finally resolved. *Child Care Administration* discusses four levels of warning that can guide a director in taking disciplinary action when necessary[4]:

- Level 1: a simple verbal warning that alerts the employee to unsatisfactory behavior
- Level 2: a written warning given to the employee that documents unsatisfactory conduct
- Level 3: a return of the employee to probationary status for a certain amount of time
- Level 4: the termination of employment

It is important that all levels of action be supported by documentation.

Professional and Personal Growth and Support

Professional growth is an ongoing process throughout a person's career. Those who choose a career in education recognize that they will be lifelong learners. Formal education and practical experience are the best combination for those who hope to provide a stimulating environment for staff and children. Directors are constantly in the refining process and are growing both personally and professionally. As adults we need to grow and develop in all areas. The process takes work, and growth does not come easily, but the payoff is worth the effort. Over time, as God reveals our gifts and talents, He is also revealing the areas of weakness we face every day. Coming to terms with our weaknesses and working on them helps move us forward and refines us into His image. We cannot become good leaders unless we are willing to commit to a refining process.

Just as the preschool/childcare director supports the staff, she needs to be supported too. Such support can come from the governing board, the staff, the parents, and the children. Other sources of encouragement include professional organizations such as a local preschool directors' group, professional seminars, and publications.

Keeping current in early childhood education can be a challenge for the busy director. Publications in the fields of early education and children's ministry can help keep the director abreast of innovative educational ideas. Seminars and workshops offer excellent training opportunities. For the early education director, professional growth must have a high priority, since her insight into early childhood issues will impact every child the preschool/childcare center serves.

Another source of support for directors can be other directors. Director networking groups have value because they enable interaction among directors, who can support each other spiritually, educationally, and professionally. The group can be designed to meet the needs and time constraints of the directors who make it up. If a group becomes formally organized, its members should create statements of philosophy, purpose, and goals/objectives. These statements will give direction to the organization and will help ensure its success. Directors can take turns hosting the meeting at their centers, or they can find other locations. They can also take turns serving as chairperson. Each meeting should include time for informative presentations, prayer, and much fellowship. Guest speakers can present information on center administration and early childhood education. Some topics for meetings include the following:

- Prayer support (most important)
- Curriculum
- Teaching methods
- Snack suggestions
- Policy information
- Handbook ideas and information
- State and local regulatory information

- Philosophy
- Review of children's books and videos
- Personnel issues
- Special-day event ideas
- Professional growth ideas and opportunities
- Fund-raising ideas
- Promotion and recruitment ideas
- Student enrollment
- Parent information issues and involvement
- Field-trip ideas and information
- Community resources

Some networking groups have sponsored Christian seminars for administrators and teachers. Others have pooled their resources to create a lending library of books and videos for staff training and development. Some ACSI regions have strong director support groups already in place, and other regions are in the process of developing such groups. Check with the ACSI early education representative in your region for more information.

Short- and Long-Range Planning

Planning, both short- and long-range, is essential to the health of an early education ministry. The planning process, which should involve the board and the entire staff, includes identifying specific steps that will assist the director in fulfilling her dreams for the preschool/childcare center.

Long-range planning is a systematic process of moving the organization toward clearly stated objectives. Remember, long-range planning is not the same as forecasting, which is predicting how the program will look if things continue as they are.

Seven ingredients are necessary for a successful long-range plan:

- The plan must be enthusiastically supported by the director, who communicates it to the staff members who will implement it.

- The plan will reflect the management style of the director, who is responsible for providing leadership.
- All staff members should be involved in carrying out the plan. A sense of ownership in the plan is essential to its success.
- The plan must be both efficient and timely, and it must not involve busywork.
- The process must be more important to the staff than the product. The process provides the format for dealing with the future of the ministry.
- The director and board must make a commitment to the plan and the process.
- The long-range planning process requires considerable time and effort on the part of all participants. The following broad questions must be addressed:

  ○ What are we?
  ○ Where are we?
  ○ Where do we want to go?
  ○ How can we get there?
  ○ How will we measure our progress?

God has plans for our early education ministry: "For the Lord Almighty has purposed, and who can thwart him? His hand is stretched out, and who can turn it back?" (Isaiah 14:27). God desires that Christians aim for noble plans: "But the noble man makes noble plans, and by noble deeds he stands" (Isaiah 32:8). God also desires that Christians be diligent in carrying out those plans: "The plans of the diligent lead to profit as surely as haste leads to poverty" (Proverbs 21:5). Finally, God asks His people to trust Him through the entire process: "Commit to the Lord whatever you do, and your plans will succeed" (Proverbs 16:3).

There is great benefit in both short- and long-range planning. Short-range planning, which can be done as a board or a staff, establishes the priorities for the coming year. Planning should be done at all levels to ensure that no one succumbs to "the tyranny of the urgent." A plan is different from a goal. Goals focus on what you would like to achieve, while a plan explains how you will reach those goals. In a quality Christian early education program, planning will include the activities, the curriculum, the calendar, and the organizational details. Without proper planning, the quality of the program will suffer significantly. Careful planning requires time spent in prayer. A good starting point is asking the Lord to reveal His priorities.

■ Developing a calendar: Event planning

Running an early education program requires careful planning of the activities and events that happen weekly, monthly, and annually. The nature of a school environment requires that planning be a continuous process. When one event ends, the next one is beginning. Without a master calendar, it is easy to lose sight of upcoming activities. Here are a few suggestions to keep the process moving:

1. Plan in advance for the upcoming year, usually in early summer.

2. Print out a blank calendar for the upcoming year and select tentative dates for the activities.

3. Meet with the staff and go over the events, ensuring they are spread out over the year and flow well from one to another.

4. Check with your facility or church to reserve room dates.

5. Make any final changes or edits.

6. Publish your calendar for the upcoming year.

Keep in mind that the focus should always be on what is best for the children. Events at their preschool/childcare center can be exciting for young children. They should be as stress free as possible, an enjoyable experience for everyone.

■ Time management

Time is a valued and sometimes elusive commodity for the preschool/childcare director. God wants us to be wise stewards of our time and His business. Proper time management saves physical energy and contributes to a sense of order and professionalism. The successful director knows how to budget time to ensure that the needs of the center are being met.

A personal calendar is an essential tool for time management. At the beginning of each month, the director can develop a monthly calendar that includes all the month's activities for the center as well as any specific director activities. Other activities can be added on a daily and weekly basis. The program's secretary and/or assistant director should have a calendar that corresponds to the director's calendar. Also, everyone on the faculty and staff needs to have a calendar of the center's activities and other important staff information. Monthly activity calendars are also helpful to parents.

Flexibility is vital in any service job. The director must realize that, while a daily plan is essential, situations will arise that take priority over any event already scheduled. There will be days when the director will feel that none of the planned activities have been accomplished. At such times it is important to remember that, although the plans were not fully carried out, that hour spent with an insecure staff person, a hurting parent, or a child who needed to be held might have been as important as any scheduled activity, if not more important. Maintaining a schedule flexible enough to allow for interruptions must be a priority.

■ Delegation

Another important ingredient in time management is delegation. Myron Rush defines *delegation* as "transferring authority, responsibility, and accountability from one person or group to another."[5] The many tasks included in a director's daily responsibilities can be overwhelming and can quickly lead to burn-out. Although the director is responsible for seeing that all these tasks are completed, it is unrealistic to expect a director to complete them all herself. A director should delegate any task that can be done as well or better by another staff member—a program supervisor, the assistant director, a classroom teacher.

The Bible tells us that Moses, following the advice of his father-in-law Jethro, delegated some of his leadership responsibilities (Exodus 18:13–26). Not only will the director benefit from delegating, but other staff members will be developing leadership skills.

The following are some tasks that may be delegated:

- Program management
  ° Coordinating events
  ° Implementing fund-raisers
  ° Record-keeping and reporting to governing agencies
  ° Coordination and purchase of supplies
  ° Performing safety inspections and implementing safety routines
- Parent interaction
  ° Writing newsletter articles
  ° Planning parent education events
  ° Maintaining a parent bulletin board
- Staff supervision
  ° Scheduling substitutes
  ° Performing classroom observations
  ° Orienting new staff members
  ° Providing feedback on lesson plans
  ° Coaching and mentoring staff members
- Other areas of responsibility as appropriate

When planning a schedule, the director must make and take time for rest and relaxation. Attending a special seminar, or just taking a personal day off, can do much to rejuvenate and refresh. Occasionally, it may be necessary to work late or even on a weekend. However, the director must be disciplined enough

not to let late hours and weekend work become a habit. Directors should also be willing to leave the facility from time to time. There is more to life than being a director. Developing a strong support system will prevent the director from falling into the trap of believing she is irreplaceable.

Getting Together

■ Staff meetings

Directors should set aside regular times for staff meetings. Staff meetings can be valuable opportunities for the director to build relationships with staff members and foster teamwork among them. The number and purpose of the meetings may vary, depending on the type of program, but they should be scheduled consistently. Many programs find it valuable to meet weekly. Programs in which teachers get together each morning for prayer may not need to hold staff meetings as often because there is already a daily flow of communication.

Successful staff meetings have a defined purpose and follow a plan. (See form 6.3 Staff Meeting Planning Chart.) For example, the meeting could begin with prayer and a short devotional. Then it could cover such areas as reminders of upcoming events and presentations on curriculum ideas. Staff members know that their needs and ideas are valued when they have the opportunity to contribute agenda items for upcoming meetings. A staff meeting can include some training, but its primary purpose is to inform the staff of ongoing expectations and to communicate about important issues. Although professional growth may result from staff-meeting activities, these meetings should not be mistaken for in-service training.

■ In-service training

In-service training offers guided instruction on an issue related to early education or the care of young children. Separate time should be set aside for this purpose. Often, directors utilize the orientation time at the beginning of the school year to provide such professional guidance. They also schedule in-service days throughout the year. As directors observe the activities in their classrooms, they can quickly see those areas that need to be reinforced and developed in their teachers. Bringing in guest speakers can be an effective way to provide the needed training. In-service training provides enriched instruction that helps move the staff forward professionally.

Here are some general guidelines for planning for in-service training:

- Begin with an annual orientation, including a review of the center's philosophy and its employee policies.
- Adjust training to the experience level of the staff.
- Focus on long-term growth.
- Brainstorm needs and possible topics with your staff.
- Provide a suitable time and place away from distractions.
- Bring in other professionals.
- Provide on-site workshops for convenience.
- Facilitate group discussions with your staff.
- Involve teachers in presenting curriculum ideas.
- Set an example of ongoing training to encourage professionalism.

Meeting Expenses

■ Budget development

Developing a budget for the early education program is an important step in moving toward good fiscal stewardship. A plan needs to be in place to ensure that the required funds are available to operate the program—that the income is adequate to cover the expenses. To determine how much income will be adequate, the director needs to estimate the anticipated expenses. For programs just getting off the ground, this process can be a nail-biter, as there

is no way of knowing what the first enrollment will be. Established schools will be able to estimate their income more accurately and can propose a budget that will need only small adjustments. Sometimes a sponsoring church or K–12 school will use funds from other programs to establish an early education program. However the program is funded, it is important to track the start-up expenses. As enrollment grows, the program will become more financially independent. Eventually, such programs can reimburse the sponsoring organization for some of the start-up costs and then reinvest the surplus back into the program. (See also chapter 5, "Managing Finances.")

■ Purchasing equipment and supplies

Start-up costs for a center include whatever equipment and supplies are needed to begin operating. As the enrollment grows, ongoing purchases are made to enhance the program. Directors can make the purchases themselves, or they can delegate the job to a staff person. If she delegates the job, the director must take care to ensure that good decisions are made about product durability and cost. Many directors purchase equipment and supplies through catalogs, making it easy to compare prices for similar items. Catalog purchasing can be convenient, since the items are delivered directly to the school.

In deciding whether to purchase an item locally or through a catalog, the director or other buyer needs to review the price, shipping costs, delivery schedule, methods of payment, and provision for returning items purchased. Also, centers maximize their purchasing dollars by paying invoices promptly.

In summary, the director or other buyer needs to do the following:

- Check shipping costs
- Note delivery schedules
- Benefit from the experience of other professionals

- Make price comparisons
- Purchase high-quality equipment and supplies
- Pay bills on time

▪ Tracking inventory

It is important to take an annual inventory of consumable and nonconsumable materials, supplies, and equipment. An inventory of nonconsumables, such as classroom furniture and office equipment, is important for insurance purposes. An annual inventory of consumable supplies allows the director to track their use and purchase appropriate quantities in the future. During the school year, staff members should report their need for specific items they run out of, such as construction paper or colors of paint. Some centers place large annual orders for art supplies and other consumables in order to qualify for discounts. Some educational supply companies offer discounts to ACSI centers.

Regulations and Standards

▪ Regulatory agencies

Nearly all states have regulatory agencies that license preschool/childcare centers that meet specific standards. In some states, all centers with a certain number of students enrolled must be licensed. In other states, licensing is optional. Even where licensing is not required, a knowledge of the regulations set forth by the licensing agencies can help a center maintain minimal standards that ensure an environment appropriate for young children.

Besides licensing agencies, other state and local regulatory agencies may have standards that your center must meet. The Christian director is responsible to be educated in these requirements and to provide a high-quality program that not only meets but exceeds them. (See form 6.4 Areas of Possible Federal and State Regulation.)

▪ Licensing requirements

It is the director's responsibility to be familiar with current regulations that govern early education programs. Many states require specific training in this area. Directors need to have a current copy of the regulations, and they should review them often with their staff. Some directors find it burdensome to inform staff of these regulations periodically. However, keeping your staff well informed helps them understand what it means to provide a safe and healthy place for young children. In addition, it familiarizes them with the specific supervision requirements and adult-child ratios that need to be enforced at all times. Licensing agencies focus on a few specific goals. Their mission is to promote the health, safety, and quality of life of each facility through the administration of an effective collaborative regulatory enforcement system. They seek to fulfill this mission by

- Promoting strategies to increase voluntary compliance
- Consulting with care providers, and providing them with technical assistance
- Working collaboratively with clients, their families, advocates, care providers, regulatory agencies, and others involved in community care
- Training staff in all aspects of the licensing process
- Educating the public about licensing
- Promoting continuous improvement and efficiency throughout licensing[6]

Licensing departments now have websites that explain the regulations and offer help for centers desiring to be in compliance. Updates are posted on a regular basis along with other important information.

A positive relationship with the licensing agency is key. We need to view licensing agencies in the same way we view other helpful community agencies, since they exist to protect young children. As believers, we try to be supportive of our communities and of their governing agencies. This position sends a positive message and gives us a testimony that honors the Lord.

Local licensing or other regulatory agencies mandate specific requirements for the operation of early education programs. The director's first responsibility is to be informed about the requirements and proactive about staying up-to-date. Her second responsibility is to comply with the requirements. Nonprofit faith-based programs are not exempt from licensure unless their exemption is indicated, as it is for certain church ministries that are exempt from selected federal and state requirements. Such exemptions can create a perception among church staff that, if the school program belongs to the same corporation, the same provision for exemption may apply, but this perception may not be true. A school can generally be defined as a "public accommodation," meaning that the school offers a service to the community. Each state is distinct in its regulatory requirements.

Leaders of churches and K–12 programs should become knowledgeable about the specific requirements for preschool/childcare centers when they consider starting one. Ignorance is never an excuse for failure to comply with federal and state requirements. Scripture is clear on the issue of being subject to the government. Regulations exist to protect the welfare of young children and to establish minimum requirements that ensure an appropriate level of care. If mandated adult-to-child ratios exist, they should be followed. Directors need to ensure that their center meets these standards, since programs that are not in compliance can face serious legal consequences. Adequate records must be maintained, including the appropriate paperwork. Several pieces of information need to be kept current if the center is to act as guardian over the children while they are present. (See form 6.2 Attendance Chart.)

■ Accreditation

The director's commitment to complying with state licensing regulations is essential, as it ensures children's basic health and safety while in out-of-home care. However, young children also need and deserve early education centers that enrich their lives and actively foster healthy growth. Accreditation has been designed to complement licensing, exemplifying higher standards of care and education and enabling the early education program to have a more significant impact on the child's life.

There are a number of evaluation tools for measuring individual components of early education programs. However, accreditation is recommended as a comprehensive evaluation tool that considers every aspect of the program. The accreditation team makes an in-depth review of the program, the staff, the curriculum, the environment, and the written materials that guide the entire operation. While local licensing and other regulatory agencies provide external pressure to conform to standards, the emphasis in accreditation is on self-monitoring and ongoing improvement.

There are several accreditation instruments from which to choose. However, faith-based programs are best served by an accreditation tool that reflects their Christian distinctives. Although the ACSI accreditation program shares some common elements of content and purpose with other accrediting associations, the philosophy that underlies ACSI accreditation carries important distinctions. Those serving in Christian early education programs recognize that they are accountable for the manner in which they deliver the program, and that accountability is not only to children and parents but to God Himself. Buoying them up under this weighty responsibility is the awareness that along with this higher accountability there exists a higher purpose—impacting children spiritually for eternity. Although ministry to young children has value in meeting children's present needs, there is also an eternal side to the daily care and nurture of children.

Finally, Christian early educators believe in the value of children and in the significant role of parents, beliefs that are based on Scripture. The motivation for the high level of care we provide comes from an authority outside ourselves, for we understand that children are created in God's image, and valuing and serving them is not done through mere sentimentality. We respect the biblical role of the family because that role is ordained by God. These are some of the motivating beliefs that set Christian early education programs apart.

When parents are looking for a quality early education center, accreditation is an indicator that the program values young children enough to pursue excellence in every aspect of its operation. ACSI accreditation, for example, requires centers to perform a self-study evaluating every aspect of their program against standards that represent best practices in the field. In general, the programs must document how they are promoting children's growth in the cognitive, social, emotional, physical, and spiritual areas. A significant feature of ACSI accreditation is the emphasis on children's spiritual development, viewed as an integral component of their overall development. To this end, accreditation requires the center's leadership and staff to examine the impact of the teacher/child interactions, the environment, and the program upon children's spiritual development. In this sense, accreditation measures the program's spiritual vitality along with the effectiveness and strength of the program and curriculum.

Parents who choose an ACSI-accredited preschool/childcare center can be assured that the program is meeting high standards in a number of areas:

- Philosophy and policy-making
- Administration
- Personnel
- Curriculum
- Nutrition and food services
- Physical environment
- Health and safety
- Family and community services

The ACSI accreditation process includes the following components:

- Review of the accreditation standards, which reflect best practices in all aspects of program implementation.

- Completion of a self-study that involves the active participation of and feedback from all staff members. The self-study is a systematic assessment of the extent to which the program meets and exceeds the accreditation standards, as well as the program's stated goals. A survey of parents is conducted to ensure that their perspective is considered. As a result of this process, program improvements are implemented. The program's completed self-study document includes the findings made in the assessment along with supporting documentation.

- On-site verification of the self-study by a team made up of trained peer evaluators with expertise in early childhood education. The visiting team will spend two to three days observing classrooms, interviewing staff, and writing a report that documents the extent of the program's compliance with the accreditation standards.

- An accreditation decision made by the National Early Education Accreditation Commission after reviewing the program's self-study, visiting team report, and supporting documentation.

• Submission of an annual report detailing the center's response to the recommendations of the visiting team.

• Renewal of accreditation after a limited term.

The ongoing evaluation that takes place because of the annual reporting and periodic accreditation renewal ensures that the center is in a continual improvement process that results in better and more effective programs for children. An added benefit of accreditation is the staff members' growth that results from their participation in the process. In 1 Thessalonians 5:21, we are exhorted, "Test everything. Hold on to the good." As administrators and staff recognize and celebrate the strengths of their program, their commitment is strengthened, and further refinement and development is often the natural next step.

■ *Reporting child abuse*
Any member of the preschool/childcare center staff who has reasonable cause to suspect that a child is being abused or neglected must immediately report that suspicion to the appropriate social service agency or local law enforcement agency. In addition, the person must report the suspected abuse or neglect to the director. Note that reporting to the director does not absolve the teacher of the legal responsibility to report to the appropriate public agencies. Every state has a child-abuse reporting law that is designed to ensure that the case will be reported and that guarantees confidentiality to the person reporting the suspicion. In most states, it is a misdemeanor to knowingly fail to report situations where a child's physical health, mental health, or welfare has been, or may be, adversely affected by abuse or neglect.

■ *Monitoring applicable legal requirements*
In addition to the direct program oversight exercised by licensing agencies, the early education center is subject to a myriad of federal, state, and local requirements. On a local level, the center may be affected by zoning determinations, county health department requirements, and fire safety inspection and supervision. Federal laws exist that restrict discrimination in hiring, require all employees to complete I-9 forms, and mandate the filing of specific information about each person hired. Federal laws also charge the center with developing written policies prohibiting sexual harassment and documenting an exposure control plan related to blood-borne pathogens, including mandatory interactive training on universal precautions. There are federal laws mandating minimum wage requirements, providing guidelines for the administration of benefits, and requiring the posting of specific employment laws. Additionally, federal law regulates leave policies for persons in uniformed service and employees serving on jury duty. Federal requirements also apply to the maintenance of employee records.

Although the majority of the laws relate to employment issues, there are also federal mandates for testing the water supply and maintaining records of chemicals used at the facility. In many instances, the federal requirements listed above are also addressed by state law. The director must know both the federal laws and the state requirements that may elaborate on them and that may be more restrictive.

The preschool/childcare center must comply with all requirements, even the most stringent. Because the requirements can be extremely complex and are constantly being updated, it is impractical to include a complete description of applicable laws in this publication. One of the most valuable aspects of ACSI membership is access to excellent publications that highlight these issues of compliance. ACSI regularly updates a Legal Compliance Checklist that highlights federal laws affecting private schools. ACSI posts the checklist on its website (www.acsi.org). The director is responsible to become familiar with these areas of compliance and to monitor changes in state and federal requirements as they occur. To fulfill this responsibility, the director must actively pursue this knowledge through reading such ACSI publications as the *Legal/Legislative Update* and through attending appropriate conferences and training programs. In some instances, the early education center is a component of a large church or school that maintains human resource or business administration staff who regularly monitor compliance with applicable laws. Even when the director is not ultimately responsible for maintaining compliance with federal rulings, it is imperative that she be aware of which individuals in the organization are fulfilling these responsibilities. In summary, competent directors understand and comply with the applicable federal and state regulations.

Influencing Public Policy

Beyond staying informed of existing laws, directors should monitor proposed legislation that may have impact on early childhood education programs. Advocacy begins with information. Professional newsletters and publications often highlight upcoming legislation. On the ACSI website, directors can go to *Legal/Legislative Issues* and then to *Legislative Tracking* to access a searchable database detailing proposed legislation in each state. The site displays summaries of legislative bills along with an indicator of each bill's status and an indication of ACSI's position, if applicable. After learning about proposed legislation and the issues involved, the director can assess its potential impact and formulate a position to communicate to public officials. Along with expressing her views directly to decision-makers, an advocate can alert others to areas of legislative concern, mobilizing colleagues, teachers, and parents. By spreading the word, the director maximizes her influence. She gives community officials a sense of how many schools and families will be affected and what they think about the matter. This kind of involvement is an important barometer of a director's professionalism and a critical means of advancing the influence of the Christian early education center.

FORM 6.1

Job Description: Early Education Center Director

Under the supervision of the school principal, the director of the early education center is responsible for the general supervision and management of the early education program.

Responsibilities:
1. Oversee curriculum and program development.
2. Oversee compliance with the requirements for state licensing and the state department of social services.
3. Implement a staff development program. Recruit qualified staff members. Provide ongoing training. Disseminate information on current educational research and practices. Provide professional growth opportunities for staff members. Conduct employee performance appraisals.
4. Provide spiritual leadership to staff, children, and parents, both through example and through actively promoting spiritual growth through staff devotions and in personal parent contacts.
5. Ensure that children's actual experiences are consistent with those we say they will receive. (Perform ongoing assessment of program quality.)
6. Respond to parents' and staff members' concerns, solve problems, and resolve differences.
7. Implement public relations plan. Develop community awareness of the early education program. Recruit new families to meet ongoing enrollment needs.
8. Inform parents of school events and policies through monthly newsletters, the parent handbook, and other written communication as necessary.
9. Submit to the board monthly reports detailing early education center enrollment and other significant issues.
10. Provide oversight to the maintenance of the physical grounds, buildings, and equipment, ensuring safety. Develop the physical environment to effectively promote children's development.
11. Perform administrative tasks necessary to the operation of the school:
    Provide adequate staffing for the number of children enrolled.
    Set employees' regular work schedules.
    Arrange for substitutes as needed.
    Submit employees' hours worked to accounting department.
    Oversee the ordering and purchasing of supplies.
    Conduct staff meetings.
    Provide care for ill and injured children.
12. Oversee annual school events (back-to-school night, open house, children's musical programs, field trips, etc.).
13. Report children's special needs, difficulties responding to discipline, etc., to parents. Work together with parents and teachers to promote children's successful integration into a classroom setting.

Early Education DIRECTOR'S MANUAL

FORM 6.2

Attendance Chart

Remember to sign the chart where indicated.

Child's Name	Time In	Signature of Person Responsible	Time Out	Signature of Person Responsible

Early Education DIRECTOR'S MANUAL

FORM 6.3

Staff Meeting Planning Chart

Month/Date	Upcoming Events	Reminders	Discussions	Training
September				
October				
November				
December				
January				
February				
March				
April				
May				
June				

Early Education DIRECTOR'S MANUAL

FORM 6.4

Areas of Possible Federal and State Regulation

(Note that the following outline lists pertinent issues but is not exhaustive.)

Personnel
* Labor law
  – Wages
  – Overtime
  – Rest and mealtimes
  – Termination procedures
* Record-keeping
  – Employment applications
  – Employee health records
  – Professional qualifications
  – Criminal record clearance
  – Physicals
  – Record of hours worked
* Benefit policies
* Anti-harassment policies
* Leave policies
  – Jury duty
  – Uniformed services
  – Family and medical leave
* Required postings of employment laws
* Bloodborne pathogens
  – Exposure control plan
  – Training in universal precautions
* ADA

Children
* Immunizations
* Required enrollment forms
* Health records
* Suspected child abuse

Insurance
* Liability
* Workers' compensation

Facility
* Zoning laws
* Building codes
* Fire regulations

Environmental issues
* Lead contamination
* Asbestos hazards
* Material Safety Data Sheets (MSDS)

Volunteers

Racial nondiscriminatory policy
* Reflected in brochures, etc.
* Published annually
* Record-keeping and reporting requirements, if applicable

Copyright laws/licensing

Early Education DIRECTOR'S MANUAL

SELECTING AND WORKING WITH STAFF

Chapter 7

And David shepherded them with integrity of heart; with skillful hands he led them. (Psalm 78:72)

Setting Standards

The most important responsibilities of the preschool/childcare center director are recruiting, hiring, and supervising the staff. As important as the curriculum and the facility may be, they are secondary to the employees. The center's success can be measured by the degree to which it reaches its goals, and achieving those goals depends mainly on the staff. Parents measure the center by the staff. Selecting employees begins with prayerful consideration of each applicant. The goal is to determine whether prospective employees

- Share the philosophy and goals of the center
- Meet the center's established job qualifications
- Have the skills and disposition to fulfill the responsibilities of the position

The director of a preschool/childcare program, along with the governing board, should prayerfully set the standards for those who will serve on the staff. First, staff members must be committed Christians who exhibit a life controlled by the Holy Spirit. Evidence of Christian commitment is seen in an active pursuit of spiritual growth, involvement in a local church, and a lifestyle consistent with biblical principles. Furthermore, the faith of the staff members must shape their view of the profession and must influence every aspect of their job performance. They must be qualified educationally, having completed formal course work in child development and early childhood education, and having acquired sufficient knowledge and experience to assume the responsibilities of the position. They should demonstrate personal attributes that will contribute to healthy relationships with children, parents, and other staff members. These attributes include dedication, warmth, sensitivity, emotional stability, good health, maturity, patience, and the ability to develop trusting relationships. Staff members must display an attitude of professionalism, having respect for and commitment to the field of early childhood education. Staff members who have a strong sense of professionalism will demonstrate integrity, maintain confidentiality, reflect on their work, and strive to refine their expertise.

By their nature, early education programs make great demands on the physical and emotional energy of employees who work directly with children for long hours. Staff members must constantly be alert to prevent children in their care from suffering physical or emotional harm. They must be prepared to offer parents encouragement and assistance as needed. They must be team players, able to work harmoniously with fellow employees.

The Hiring Process

■ *Determining staffing needs*

Determining the preschool/childcare center's staffing needs is the first step in the hiring process. (See form 7.1 Position Assessment Worksheet.) Establishing a teacher-to-child ratio is necessary. State and local regulatory agencies have regulations regarding the teacher-to-child ratio, and in some cases their guidelines are adequate. However, the foremost responsibility of the program is to honor the Lord by providing the highest quality of care in a safe and loving environment. In order to provide care of exceptional quality, the center may establish standards that exceed the minimal ratio guidelines.

Adult-to-child ratios. The following chart shows a recommendation for minimal adult-to-child ratios. It is just one recommendation. The director should check with her state and/or local regulatory agency for the minimum requirements in her own region.

RECOMMENDED MINIMAL ADULT-TO-CHILD RATIOS[1]

Infants–12 months	1 staff to 3 infants
13–30 months	1 staff to 4 children
31–35 months	1 staff to 5 children
3-year-olds	1 staff to 7 children
4-year-olds	1 staff to 8 children
5-year-olds	1 staff to 8 children

Group size for each class should not exceed twice the adult-to-child ratio. (For example, the maximum group size for infants is six; for 3-year-olds, the maximum group size is fourteen.) When the children are in mixed-age groups, the adult-to-child ratio and group size should be suitable for the majority of children in the group.

There may be a temptation to set higher ratios than those recommended above. However, lower ratios may be needed to successfully meet children's needs and provide a high-quality program. Strong programs generate a favorable community reputation and full enrollment. Ultimately, the quality of the program will determine its long-term success.

Staff positions. In establishing the adult-to-child ratios, the director must also take into account the qualifications and job titles of those who will staff the classroom. Most states have specified qualifications for various positions—teacher, assistant teacher, aide—and guidelines for the proportion of staff members needed for each job classification. Restrictions concerning conditions under which aides can supervise children without a teacher being in the classroom should also be in place. After researching the minimum requirements for staff qualifications in these areas, the director and governing board will need to set their own standards.

■ *Preparing job descriptions*

Once the director has established what the staff needs are, it is time to prepare an appropriate job description for each position. Job descriptions should be reviewed and updated regularly. (See forms 7.8, 7.9, and 7.10 for sample job descriptions.)

General guidelines. Prospective employees need the opportunity to review the job description before they apply. The job description will help the director and the prospective employee determine whether the applicant's skills and abilities match the center's needs. The job description should be concise, and it should include the following:

- Job title
- Qualifications: educational, spiritual, experiential
- Reporting relationships
- Duties and responsibilities
- Essential functions

The job description is not merely a valuable tool for selecting employees; it also guides the director in supervising and evaluating the staff member, since it defines the desired performance of one in the position. Gathering samples of job descriptions from other centers can be a helpful first step in the process. However, each center's job descriptions must be "forged from the perspectives and convictions of the schools using them."[2] In the process of formulating performance expectations for each position, the director gains valuable insights that assist in training staff members to fulfill the expectations and in evaluating the degree to which they have attained the performance objectives.

Essential functions. A statement identifying the essential functions of the job is a key element of the job description. "An essential function is one that, if removed, would fundamentally change the job."[3] Essential functions "identify the result

to be achieved, not solely the manner in which a job is performed. This requires a close analysis of the physical and mental requirements of each job and what functions are essential to perform that job."[4] The essential functions should be described in enough detail for a potential applicant to determine whether she would require "reasonable accommodations" because of a health problem or disability. The phrase "reasonable accommodations" is defined by the EEOC as "a modification or adjustment to a job, the work environment, or the way things usually are done that enables a qualified individual with a disability to enjoy an equal employment opportunity."[5] Directors need a thorough understanding of the provisions of the ADA. An excellent resource in this area is ACSI's *Christian School Personnel Forms*, which can be ordered from the Customer Service Department at 800-367-0798. (See form 7.12 Employment Applications and the ADA.)

■ *Recruiting staff*

Finding eligible applicants for the center's staff can be the most frustrating job for any director. Most directors do not have the luxury of a file drawer full of applications. Nor do they have the advantage of unlimited time for seeking new employees. Thus, to find the best applicants, the director must do some recruiting.

Preparing to recruit. Before beginning outside recruitment, the director should do the following:

- Pray that the Lord will bring the right applicant to the center.
- Look within the center's staff for possible promotions.
- Keep an "Application on Hold" file; accept applications even when there are no positions open, informing each applicant that the application will be kept on file for a year. (See form 7.3 Letter to Update Application Files.)

- Network with other Christian preschool/ childcare center directors.
- Advertise at local churches, Christian schools, and other Christian ministries.
- Advertise through Christian job networks.
- Advertise in the local Christian newspaper or newsletters.
- Advertise through the preschool/childcare center newsletter.
- Advertise on the local Christian radio stations.
- Get acquainted with the early childhood education department head of your local community college, who may know of a student who wants to teach in a Christian preschool/childcare center.
- Contact the job placement offices of local Christian colleges.
- Review lists of people available for employment through the ACSI teacher listings.
- Encourage young people in your local church, or those who attend a Christian high school, to develop an interest in early childhood education.
- Be alert to parents who volunteer in the classroom and display skills and potential in working with young children; encourage them to obtain training and to consider a ministry in early education when they return to the workforce.
- As a last resort, advertise in your local newspaper; always remember that applicants from secular sources need a more careful screening.

Discrimination issues. It is essential for directors to be familiar with guidelines protecting individuals from discrimination in employment. Title VII of the Civil Rights Act of 1964 prohibits employers from discriminating against applicants on the basis of race, sex, religion, and national origin. Additionally, the Age Discrimination in Employment Act (ADEA) prohibits employment discrimination against applicants over age forty, and the Americans with Disabilities Act (ADA) prohibits discrimination against those with physical and mental disabilities.

Under federal law, there are six protected classifications in the employment setting: race, sex, religion, national origin, age, and disability. These federal protections apply specifically to organizations that employ fifteen or more. However, states also have their own civil rights statutes, which may apply to employers of fewer than fifteen.

Fortunately, there are provisions in Title VII that permit nonprofit religious organizations to discriminate in hiring on the basis of religious criteria, an exemption that has been upheld by the Supreme Court. In order for this exemption to apply, the organization must consistently apply the religious criteria to its hiring and employment practices. Additionally, the religious aspect of the early education center must not be historic or incidental but must play a significant role in the operation of the program. For more information, consult "Your School May Discriminate on a Religious Basis in Personnel Decisions: Understanding the Religious Exemption Clause of Title VII," which is available in the ACSI publication *Christian School Personnel Forms*.

Compliance with antidiscrimination laws is a serious responsibility for anyone involved in hiring. Directors should pursue further training and receive ongoing information in these areas to protect their early education programs from possible litigation and claims of bias.

■ Working with applicants

The employment application. The employment application or packet is likely to be the first contact a potential employee has with your early education center. The information in the application packet should tell the prospective employee something about your center's philosophy. Reviewing the applicant's completed application will be an important step in the screening process. Information in the application packet should include the following:

- General information about the center
  - ° The center's statement of faith (See form 7.13 Statement of Faith.)
  - ° A statement that the center does not discriminate in employment on the basis of age, race, color, national or ethnic origin, sex, or disability
  - ° A statement about child abuse investigation
  - ° An appropriate job description
  - ° Requirements of the position
  - ° An application form, which should request
    - ▶ Applicant's name
    - ▶ Permanent address
    - ▶ Telephone number
    - ▶ Date of availability
    - ▶ Educational background
    - ▶ Work experience
    - ▶ Personal references
    - ▶ Three professional references
    - ▶ Personal statement of Christian beliefs
    - ▶ Personal statement about any criminal conviction
    - ▶ Education and experience documentation, if required
    - ▶ Position applied for
    - ▶ Salary range
    - ▶ Questions regarding the position

Reviewing the application. Once the employee application packet has been completed and returned to the director, the screening process continues. The director should look for neatness, correct grammar and spelling, employment dates for previous jobs and reasons for leaving them, and thoroughness displayed in answering questions. After the director has reviewed the applications, they can be categorized into *potential employees* and *not potential employees*. Remember, all information on every

application is confidential and should be treated as such. Applicants who are not suitable should be informed promptly and graciously. (See form 7.5 Letter to Applicant Not Hired.) If the applicant seems promising, the following steps can be taken:

- Interview former employer by telephone.
- Request college transcripts.
- Ask for written personal and professional references. (See form 7.2 Reference Letter.)
- Study the applicant's job résumé.

If the information is favorable and the director is satisfied that the preschool/childcare center and the applicant are compatible, an employment interview is scheduled.

■ The employment interview

The employment interview is a significant step in hiring staff. The interview should be formal yet comfortable for the director and the applicant. It can be brief and focused if the director asks predetermined questions. The director should design questions that will elicit a clear profile of the applicant's character and competence in working with children and adults. (See form 7.11 Important Skills for Early Education Teachers.) Questions may focus on the applicant's educational philosophy, past experiences in similar settings, and future goals. Describing a common classroom scenario, such as a conflict between children, and asking the applicant to detail how she would respond in such a situation can yield a revealing answer. Asking her to describe her strengths and weaknesses as well as her interest in working in the early education ministry can bring enlightening results. The same questions should be asked of all who apply for a given position. Interview questions should be reviewed to make sure they do not pertain to any of the areas in which discrimination is prohibited. (See form 7.14 Interview Questions for Early Education Applicant.)

The director prepares for the interview by thoroughly reviewing the application, noting any "red flags" or special concerns and getting a sense of the applicant's background. The director sets a positive tone by beginning the interview on time, greeting the applicant warmly, and starting with prayer. The director can set the applicant at ease by beginning with a brief explanation of what to expect in the interview process. Because the interview often gives the employee her first impression of the center, it is an opportunity to convey professionalism and other positive characteristics of the program. During the interview, the applicant should have an opportunity to ask questions. At the end of the interview, it may be appropriate to discuss wages and benefits in general terms. However, the specifics should be included in a written offer of a contract or work agreement. (See form 7.15 Teacher Contract.)

Sometimes the director may wish to get a second opinion before hiring an applicant. A member of the governing board or an appropriate staff member can help the director conduct a team interview, lending additional insight. In some cases a second interview is needed to further narrow the field. The applicant may also be asked to return at a later time and lead an activity with the children, allowing the director and supervising teacher to observe her skills firsthand.

As the initial interview is concluded, the applicant should be told by what date she will be contacted. The director must see that the applicant is notified by that date, one way or another. (See form 7.6 Interview Evaluation Worksheet.) Finally, the director should encourage the applicant to spend time in prayer and should also pray, along with the governing board, that the right decision will be made.

■ Preemployment orientation

When the director decides to make a job offer, one step remains in the evaluation process. Preemployment orientation (PEO) is the final way to confirm the decision. The PEO gives the applicant the opportunity to come to the center during a regular school day to study, observe, and work. (See forms 7.16 Preemployment Orientation/Observation Worksheet and 7.17 Preemployment Orientation Worksheet.) The PEO lasts from four to six hours and includes time for the applicant to study the following:

- The appropriate job description
- The preschool/childcare center employee handbook
- The center's philosophy
- The center's parent handbook
- The center's curriculum
- The center's application packet, including tuition information
- State and local regulatory organizations' rules and regulations
- Safety procedures
- Fingerprint/security check information
- Employee medical information
- Time sheet/time card procedures

Afterward, the director should give the applicant time to ask questions concerning the above materials.

Another important part of the PEO is a guided tour of the center. Before the tour, the applicant receives a checklist of people to meet, items to find, and discoveries to make. Next, she has an opportunity to interact with the children, the staff, and the parents. This is not the time for the applicant to assume teaching responsibilities but simply to have personal contact with the children and parents under the supervision of the director and/or a head teacher. (See form 7.7 Observation and Evaluation of Prospective Employee.)

The remaining PEO time is reserved for a conversation between the applicant and the director. If the director is confident that the applicant is well qualified, she can offer a contract/work agreement. Whatever decision is made about hiring the applicant, she should be compensated financially for her PEO time. A few dollars spent before the employment decision is made can help prevent employment problems in the future.

The following recommendations are for anyone making a hiring decision:

- When in doubt, don't! If, after earnest prayer and counsel, the director is hesitant about a particular applicant (though some of the qualifications may look good), she should usually turn the application down. Panic can set in when the coming school year looms, and the temptation is to act in haste to fill a spot. Hasty decisions often bring adverse results.
- Cover all the bases. Screen and evaluate carefully!
- Above all, do not compromise in the area of the applicant's Christian testimony.
- Spend time in prayer over each step in the employment process.

■ Working with new employees

New-employee orientation. After the applicant has accepted the position, the director must equip her to be successful in her new position. (See forms 7.19 New-Employee Checklist and 7.20 Staff Personnel Form.) The specifics of new-employee orientation will vary with the position being filled. A teacher's assistant and a head teacher will need to master different kinds of information. Regardless of the job title, the new staff member should receive a copy of the evaluation form that corresponds with her job description, and the director should review the process of evaluation with her. Allowing the new staff member several days to shadow someone currently serving in the position will give her an opportunity to see in action the procedures found in the staff handbook. A new employee is given much information, and it takes time to process it all. Assigning the new person to an existing staff mentor provides a vital avenue for ongoing dialogue. The length of the training or orientation period may range from six weeks to six months, depending on the organization, but it should be consistent within the organization.

New-employee evaluation. After the school's designated training period, the new staff member should receive a formal evaluation. This evaluation gives the director and the staff member an opportunity to confirm that the job placement is successful. Classroom observation and feedback from coworkers and/or immediate supervisors will inform the evaluation. A separate evaluation form for new staff is valuable, as it can highlight the essential areas that are the initial evidence of a good match between the school and the early educator. The new-employee evaluation form should be based on the job description for the position, but it should focus on key competencies that can reasonably be achieved within the training period. Of course, the new staff member needs to receive ongoing verbal feedback throughout the training period. However, meeting with the new person to review the formal evaluation at the end of the training period brings closure to the orientation process and provides valuable accountability for both the staff member and the director.

Possible areas to include on a new-employee evaluation form are the following:

- Evidence of Christian character
- Interaction with children (is warm, attentive, aware of individual characteristics, etc.)

- Rapport with parents (recognizes and knows names)
- Implementation of safety procedures (universal precautions, releasing children, etc.)
- Familiarity with the program's philosophy (can put in own words)
- Relationship with staff
- Punctuality
- Attendance record
- Implementation of the job description

■ Working with substitutes

A plan for recruiting, training, and retaining substitutes is essential to the smooth operation of the early education center. Licensing regulations may specify eligibility qualifications for substitute staff members. Places to find substitute teachers are similar to those that centers access when they are seeking permanent staff. Additionally, directors may want to inquire of former staff members (including retired staff), college students who are home on school breaks, church Sunday school teachers, and current and former parents in the preschool/childcare program.

Although substitute staff are often accompanied in the classroom by permanent staff who give on-site guidance, the substitute still needs formal orientation. At a minimum, she needs the following:

- A tour of the center
- An introduction to all other staff members
- Review of essential health, safety, and security procedures
- Information on recording hours, and when and how to pick up paycheck
- Written instructions regarding the daily schedule and plans for the group of children she will be working with
- An overview of the program's philosophy and curriculum

Retaining substitutes is not easy, as they are often the director's best job candidate when a regular position becomes available. Maintaining good relationships with substitutes requires communication, consideration, and respect. These can be expressed as follows:

- Find out how early in the morning and how late in the evening you may call with an assignment.
- Express appreciation regularly and through multiple avenues (oral and written, small gifts, prayer card, etc.).
- Include substitutes in staff social events when appropriate.
- Train permanent staff members in ways they can contribute to a substitute's success.
- Remind substitutes of the important role they play in meeting young children's need for emotional security.

Staff Compensation

The largest and most important item in the early education center's budget is staff wages and benefits. Whether or not the director and the governing board are aware of it, the quality of the early education program is determined at the time when the staff wages and benefits are set. Unfortunately, preschool/childcare centers have earned the reputation of paying their staff substandard wages and offering few if any benefits. An effort to make the program affordable to parents or a desire to subsidize a larger school system has often resulted in the sacrifice of reasonable employee wages and benefits. As a result, early education staff members have one of the highest turnover rates of any profession in the country.

■ Salary scales

The director needs to work with the governing board in developing effective compensation and retention strategies that provide incentives for staff to improve their skills and advance professionally.

(See form 7.25 Financial Worksheet.) These goals can be accomplished by creating a salary matrix that includes equitable starting wages and incremental increases for additional education. A thoughtful approach to the salary scale or schedule and the staff members' career ladders will raise the level of staff professionalism.

In designing the salary scale, the board and the director can consider several questions about how to divide up the "pie" of compensation dollars:

- How much education will an employee need to advance to the next step? (By creating a midpoint increment between a Child Development Associate and an Associate of Arts degree, the staff may view the advance as more attainable.)
- How can increased job responsibilities be rewarded?
  - How many staff levels are acknowledged? (For example, supervisor, assistant supervisor, head teacher, teacher, assistant teacher, aide)
  - Can stipends be given for specific projects or time-limited additional responsibilities?
- Will wages automatically increase with each year of experience completed?
- Will a cost-of-living adjustment be applied to the entire scale?
- Will new staff members be allowed to transfer experience from other early education centers? At what rate of conversion?
- Will salary *steps* reflect the following?
  - A percentage increase from the base (creates greater variance between high and low salaries)
  - A fixed amount (e.g., $0.50 per hour)
- When do salary increases become effective?
  - Anniversary date
  - Beginning of new school year

Additionally, when the board and director are reviewing retention strategies, the following areas should be considered:

- Benefit packages
  - What do staff members need or desire?
  - What benefits are offered by other schools?
    - Reimbursement for professional growth expenses (tuition)
    - Medical
    - Vacation
    - Sick leave
    - Retirement
- Nonmonetary rewards
  - What do staff members value/want?
    - Diverse job responsibilities
    - Professional growth opportunities
    - Opportunities for advancement
    - Physical environment (staff lounge, classroom improvements)
  - What systems does the center have in place to support high morale?
    - Open communication
    - Input into decision-making
    - Autonomy in fulfilling job responsibilities

■ Staff schedules

Setting staff work schedules can be a challenge as the director attempts to meet the needs of the program and the staff members. Maintaining appropriate staffing levels is critical for financial survival.

Staffing needs. The director needs to review enrollment and attendance patterns to determine how many staff members are needed during each hour of the day. Often, staff scheduling involves balancing both full- and part-time work schedules. The work schedule may change during the course of the year in response to staff turnover, changes in enrollment, and staff absences. (See form 7.21 Time-Off Request.) Updated staff schedules should be posted for reference and distributed to all staff as far in advance of the change as possible. Some issues to resolve when working on staff schedules include the following:

- Opening and closing personnel
  - ° Special qualifications of staff
  - ° Specific guidelines for staff
- Staff rest and lunch breaks
  - ° How to minimize the impact of transitions on children
- Lesson-plan preparation time
  - ° Time allowed (may range from 2 to 5 hours a week)
  - ° Best time of day and week
  - ° Personnel involved

Rest and meal periods. Because working with young children is physically and emotionally demanding, staff are typically given a ten- to fifteen-minute break for each four-hour period of work. These breaks are commonly considered working time and are mandated in some states. Meal periods (lunch breaks), which are typically thirty minutes or more, do not need to be compensated as work time as long as the employee is completely relieved from duty during the entire meal period. Even inactive duties, such as supervising napping children, constitute working time and cannot be performed during an unpaid lunch break. State laws may include additional requirements for rest and meal periods and should be reviewed.

▪ Payroll

All staff members must be paid at least the federal minimum wage, and the state may set a minimum wage that is higher than the federal minimum. Procedures need to be in place for accurately recording employees' hours worked each day. Policies for the length of the pay period, pay dates, and payment at termination need to be established and communicated with the staff. State laws should be consulted in developing these policies.

▪ Overtime

Any hours worked in excess of forty hours each week shall be compensated at one and one-half times each employee's regular rate of pay. Employees may not waive their rights to overtime compensation. Early education staff may be exempt from overtime requirements only if they meet the tests for professional exemption as a "bona fide teacher":

> However, the professional employee exemption as applied to teachers contemplates an employee with a high level of education and specialized training as distinguished from a general academic education. Work that can be performed by employees with education and training below the college level generally would not be considered work of a bona fide professional level under the regulations defining the exemption for bona fide professional teachers. Similarly, though preschools may engage in some educational activities, preschool employees whose primary duty is to care for the physical needs of the facility's children would ordinarily not meet all of the requirements for exemption as teachers under the applicable Regulations, 29 CFR 541.3.[6]

Educational background and the nature of the teacher's primary duties are key factors. States may have additional standards for qualifying as exempt, including salary provisions. Careful research and legal consultation is strongly advised in determining the status of the various early education staff positions.

▪ Out-of-class responsibilities

Though the majority of their time is spent working directly with children, early education staff often have additional responsibilities, including these:

- Parent conferences
- Staff meetings
- Lesson-plan preparation
- Evening parent events

Directors need to determine a reasonable number of hours the teachers are allotted to perform these additional responsibilities, and they need to develop a way for teachers to record the time they spend in them so that they are appropriately compensated. If work spent on nonclassroom responsibilities causes the employee to exceed forty hours in one week (or over eight hours in one day in some states), the overtime rate of compensation applies. Scheduling substitute teachers to release teachers from their responsibilities with children is one way to give teachers time to fulfill nonclassroom responsibilities without exceeding forty hours in one workweek. Compensation policies for nonclassroom responsibilities need to be clearly communicated to the staff. It is the director's responsibility to ensure that staff members are complying with the policy.

■ *In-service training*

Many states require an annual number of hours of ongoing training for those who work with young children. Often this training is completed outside the employees' regular work hours. The preschool/childcare center is required to pay staff for the time spent on in-service training, unless the following criteria are met: (1) the training takes place outside normal scheduled hours of work, (2) the training is voluntary, (3) the training is not job-related, and (4) no other work is performed during the training period.[7] However, rulings on this issue have varied from state to state, particularly in determining whether the training is voluntary and/or not job-related. Distinctions in interpretation reflect the differences in state requirements for staff training. In some states, the preschool/childcare center is charged with ensuring that all staff members complete a specified number of in-service hours. In others, the burden for completing the hours is placed upon the teacher, as a means of maintaining her certification. In general, when the individual staff members are deemed responsible for completing the in-service training, the early education center does not have to

pay them. When the center is required to monitor and certify that the annual hours have been completed, the center must pay for the training hours.[8] Because the issue is complex and open to interpretation, directors should contact their state's office for the Employment Standards Administration (E.S.A.) Wage and Hour Division for a determination.

Staff Handbook

The most important document the director will ever write is the staff handbook. The early education center's staff handbook is a powerful tool in hiring, training, and supervising staff. It is the employees' resource for policy and procedure information. Every applicant going through the preemployment orientation must have an opportunity to read through the staff handbook. Upon becoming an employee of the preschool/childcare center, the applicant should receive a personal copy.

Preparing a staff handbook is tedious and time consuming. Operational policies and procedures are established as the preschool/childcare center grows and develops. It may take several years of reviewing and rewriting before the director is satisfied with the finished product. Even then, the staff handbook should be updated regularly. All information necessary for the smooth operation of the center should be clearly explained in the staff handbook. (See form 7.18 Topics to Include in Staff Handbook.)

All personnel policies detailed in the staff handbook will need to be thoroughly researched to ensure they comply with applicable state and federal laws. Therefore, it is worth the expense to have the handbook audited by an attorney with expertise in these areas.

■ *Annual review of staff handbook*

Reviewing the staff handbook is a central part of new-staff orientation. However, current staff members also need to be reminded of the center's policies and procedures. Therefore many early education centers incorporate an annual review of the staff handbook into the orientation in-service at the beginning of each school year.

Making this review meaningful to the staff can be a challenge. In planning a time of reviewing policies and procedures, the director begins by deciding what the staff will need to know and be able to do as a result of the training, prioritizing the content to be covered. On the basis of those goals, the director plans appropriate activities. Activities that actively involve the staff will be the most effective and memorable. Some ideas for accomplishing this purpose include these:

- Jigsaw approach:
  ° Divide the handbook into sections.
  ° Assign a section to each pair or small group of staff.
  ° Have each group read and summarize for the entire staff.
- Game show:
  ° Create a set of questions that can be answered in the staff handbook. (Emphasize newly added content or areas of which the staff particularly needs reminding.)
  ° Divide the staff members into teams. Give them bells or buzzers.
  ° Read questions. The first team to find the answer in the handbook rings in.
  ° A team member announces the page number where the answer is found and reads the answer.
  ° All staff members must turn to the page in their handbook and look at the answer.
  ° Keep score. Award silly prizes.

■ *Annual review of Christian philosophy*
The new school year all-staff orientation is also an ideal time to review the center's Christian philosophy. Much thought and prayer is invested in developing the documents that include the philosophy. These documents will have limited impact unless staff members translate them into daily classroom practice. The goal of the annual review is to ensure that teachers have a thorough understanding of the school's philosophy and that they can apply it in the classroom. Use activities during this review that require teachers to

- Think about the philosophy.
- Talk about it with others.
- Generate practical application ideas.

Some activities to consider include the following:

- Have staff look up the Scriptures that support the philosophy statement.
- Role-play explaining the philosophy to a parent or to a new teacher.
- Ask staff to develop lists of classroom examples that are *not* consistent with the center's philosophy. Have them explain why the activity is inappropriate and what they would do to change it.
- Divide staff members into small groups and assign each group to a different area of the classroom or a different time of the center's day. Ask them to list every opportunity to demonstrate the center's philosophy in that area or during that time.

Safety Practices for Employees

Employers have a moral and legal responsibility to provide a safe work environment, protecting their employees from illness and injury. In establishing procedures to promote workplace safety, directors need to consider the unique characteristics of the preschool/childcare center environment and the specific risks presented by young children that create occupational health hazards for staff. Early educators are regularly exposed to infectious disease. Classroom activities and equipment, together with small, active bodies, often create tripping hazards. Depending on the age of the children being served, the work may involve lifting. Working with young children in a group setting can often be stressful, particularly when the caregiver is isolated or doesn't receive enough support.

■ Preventive measures

Inspection. The first step in protecting staff health is identifying hazards. Directors need to inspect all areas of the facility, including classrooms, playgrounds, hallways, restrooms, break room, and offices. Conducting the inspection with a board member and/or church or preschool/childcare center staff member multiplies the director's ability to perceive potential dangers.

The purpose of the inspection is twofold. First, it is to identify hazards: for example, uneven pavement that might cause a teacher to trip. Some of these hazards will be correctable and should be taken care of immediately. Others, such as energetic children darting across the playground, can't be eliminated, but they must be identified and managed. By heightening staff members' awareness and sharing ways to respond to these risks, the director is demonstrating concern for the staff's safety. The second purpose of the inspection is to identify ways to improve the work environment by minimizing the physical strain connected with the teachers' daily responsibilities.

Walk through the classrooms, observing teachers at work and asking yourself these questions:

- Is adult-sized furniture available so that staff members are not always sitting in awkward positions?
- Can storage and furnishings be arranged to minimize repetitive lifting?
- Are there supports such as steps for toddlers to climb up to the changing table and step stools for staff to use when accessing items from tall shelves?

Focus on repetitive actions performed by teachers and the physical requirements imposed by daily routines. Keep in mind the range of activities that span the day's schedule as you complete the staff safety walk-through.

Training. After assessing the work environment, you will have a concrete idea of the challenges of your particular facility and playground. Next you will want to train staff members in how their actions can minimize hazards and protect their health. (See forms 7.26 On Health and Safety and 7.27 Beginnings Workshop.)

■ Federal requirements

Exposure to bloodborne pathogens. The Occupational Safety and Health Administration (OSHA) requires all employers to adopt a written "Bloodborne Pathogen Exposure Control Plan" that includes the following at a minimum:

1. The exposure determination for each job classification in your program
2. The procedures for evaluating the circumstances surrounding an exposure incident
3. The schedule and methods for implementing sections of the standard covering
- Methods of compliance
- First-aid reporting procedures
- Hepatitis B vaccination
  ° Vaccination follow-up
  ° Post-exposure follow-up
- Communication of hazards to employees through in-service training
- Record keeping[9]

Employee classifications reflect the extent of occupational exposure to blood and blood products encountered by persons in each job position. There are three classifications or groups. It is likely that all those who work in an early education center will render first aid as part of their primary job responsibilities, which places them in the first group.

Those who are in the first group need to receive in-service training and be offered pre-exposure hepatitis B vaccine series, at school expense. Schools also need to supply any protective equipment needed, such as latex or vinyl gloves. Directors need to ensure that all staff are thoroughly trained in universal precautions. They also need to monitor staff to make sure they consistently practice universal precautions. An extensive resource on this topic, which includes sample forms, is "Responding to OSHA's Final Rule for Occupational Exposure to Bloodborne Pathogens," which is included on ACSI's website and in the ACSI publication *Christian School Legal and Administrative Issues*.

Hazardous chemicals. The Worker and Community Right to Know Law requires employers to develop a written comprehensive hazard-communication program. A list of potentially hazardous chemicals (such as cleaning products, pesticides, and certain office products) must be compiled, and Material Data Safety Sheets (MDSS) must be obtained. The hazard-communication program needs to include provisions for container labeling, the collection and availability of MDSS, and an employee training program.[10]

▣ Strategies promoting staff health
Establishing a safe workplace is not accomplished once and for all, but requires ongoing attention and maintenance. Some of the ways in which schools encourage a healthy staff are indirect. For example, making comfortable space available for staff members' breaks helps minimize stress in teachers and helps meet their physical need for rest. Consistently enforcing the policy of excluding ill children from attending school protects both the staff and the other children. Making sure that all classrooms are well ventilated benefits everyone. Personnel policies that provide employees with health care and sick leave are critical.

Relationships with Children
Recent advances in brain research have confirmed what we have known through Scripture, that relationships are central to children's development. Early educators nurture children when they respond to them warmly and demonstrate sensitivity by giving focused attention to each child. Relationships give young children what they need to develop into healthy individuals.

▣ Staff-child interaction
Providing a variety of activities and materials is only a small part of the teacher's responsibility. The quality of the program is only as good as the quality of the interaction between the teacher and the children. Respectful and supportive teachers will

- Look at children when they are talking and listen to what they have to say
- Sit low or kneel to be at eye level when talking to a child
- Give children choices whenever possible
- Observe children at play and work, and plan activities to enhance their skills and talents
- Speak with children in a soft, loving, courteous manner
- Guide children who have a hard time making choices
- Smile and laugh easily and often
- Show an interest in children's indoor and outdoor activities

One of the profound responsibilities and significant ministries of early educators is their influence on children's self-image and their social, emotional, and spiritual development. Because the children's social and emotional development occurs in the context of individual relationships with family members and other caregivers, the time children spend at the early education center can have a lasting impact. Teachers play a significant role in initiating and shaping their relationship with each individual in their class, influencing the child's ability to trust, relate to others, take pleasure in relationships, and feel effective both now and in the future.

When teachers invest in children's healthy social and emotional development, they are laying a foundation for children's spiritual development. Helping children learn to trust and have positive expectations of the people in their world is the first building block in learning to trust God and have positive expectations of Him. We want children to know that God is good and loving, consistent and not capricious. Children learn these truths as they experience their teacher as good (invested in the child's well-being), loving (warm and responsive), and consistent. Directors can encourage their staff to think about how they have personally experienced God's character and what they can learn through Jesus' example. The staff members can reflect on how they have experienced God's unconditional love and how Jesus has modeled for them an example that they can emulate in their own relationships with the children. We are commanded, "Be imitators of God, therefore, as dearly loved children and live a life of love, just as Christ loved us and gave himself up for us as a fragrant offering and sacrifice to God" (Ephesians 5:1–2).

Teachers' relationships with children must be guided by biblical principles. At times, those who work with young children need to have their minds renewed in this respect, through prayer and meditation on God's Word. Having a staff discussion of scriptural principles on this subject can be an effective method for transforming staff-child interaction. The following are some Scriptures for teachers to consider in this area:

- *God initiates relationship.*
  But God demonstrates his own love for us in this: While we were still sinners, Christ died for us. (Romans 5:8). God, who has called you into fellowship with his Son Jesus Christ our Lord, is faithful. (1 Corinthians 1:9)

- *God's kindness draws people.*
  Or do you show contempt for the riches of his kindness, tolerance and patience, not realizing that God's kindness leads you toward repentance? (Romans 2:4)

- *God is consistent in His goodness.*
  Every good and perfect gift is from above, coming down from the Father of the heavenly lights, who does not change like shifting shadows. (James 1:17)

- *God encourages us to be others-directed, to adapt our responses to the needs of others.*
  We who are strong ought to bear with the failings of the weak and not to please ourselves. Each of us should please his neighbor for his good, to build him up…. Accept one another, then, just as Christ accepted you, in order to bring praise to God. (Romans 15:1, 2, 7)

- *We are encouraged to adapt our communication to our hearers (to speak their language).*
  Though I am free and belong to no man, I make myself a slave to everyone, to win as many as possible. To the Jews I became like a Jew, to win the Jews. To those under the law I became like one under the law (though I myself am not under the law), so as to win those under the law. To those not having the law I became like one not having the law (though I am not free from God's law but am under Christ's law), so as to win those not having the law. (1 Corinthians 9:19–21)

■ Supervision of children

Directors must instill in their staff the significant responsibility of keeping children safe, which can be accomplished only through diligent supervision. The director must provide specific guidelines, regularly remind the staff of them, and monitor their application. The supervision guidelines need to be tailored to the unique challenges of the facility. For some facilities, such as one that has an extremely large playground, a diagram designating the stations where staff members need to be in place will be necessary.

Following are some basic principles of supervision:

• Teachers need to be alert to children's movements. Distractions must be minimized (for example, conversations with other staff).

• Teachers need to be aware of the movements of the entire group. Although conversation with individual children is encouraged, teachers need to look up often, scanning the entire area.

• Adults need to be physically near the children. (For example, if the majority of the children are playing in the sandbox, staff members should be stationed in the area that is closest to them but that still allows the best view of the entire playground.)

• Teachers must never put themselves in a position where they are unable to supervise children by sight.

• Staff members need to count the number of children in their group on a regular basis, particularly when transitioning from one area of the facility to another.

■ Managing behavior

The importance of child guidance. Guiding children in their behavior will be one of the greatest challenges a classroom teacher will face on a daily basis. The important thing for an early education professional to recognize is that children by nature need to be guided in how they act and relate to others. Appropriate behavior does not come naturally. Early educators know it doesn't and are prepared to offer children their guidance. Working with the parents is also essential to making a difference in the lives of the children. Early educators often encounter parents who are themselves struggling in the area of child guidance, and teachers can offer expertise that will give them important tools to use. The term "child guidance" should be interpreted literally, since the process is one of guiding children, not controlling them or forcing their behavior. The distinction is important, as some emphasize the use of discipline, including punishment, to manage and control behavior. The difference involves using an approach that demonstrates respect for the child.

Establishing boundaries. The key to managing behavior is to establish and communicate appropriate boundaries. Drs. John Townsend and Henry Cloud have described a boundary as a "property line."[11] Young children need boundaries. In an early education classroom, boundaries give children structure and define expectations, allowing them to be who they are within certain limits. Boundaries also help to keep the bad out and to define and keep the good in. Those that live within healthy boundaries are able to foster and grow in respect and love for each other. Teaching young children what love and respect look like will help them develop in a healthy way. Children feel more secure when limits are set for them than when everything is allowed.

Communicating expectations. One way for teachers to set boundaries is by communicating their expectations. Depending on the age of the child, teachers can communicate their expectations and rules for behavior directly in a school environment. Children will pick these up very quickly. Younger children can learn them through behavior modification and reinforcement. At the beginning of the school year, the teacher should establish classroom rules and should reinforce them every day to ensure that the children understand them clearly. Asking questions is a way to check children's understanding, as their answers tell the teacher how well they comprehend expectations.

Teachers need to discuss consequences with both the children and their parents. A classroom management system is helpful in reinforcing positive behavior. As children grow and develop, the rewards for appropriate behavior should move gradually from external to internal. As early educators, we find that children can give a variety of reasons why they behave in particular ways. Our challenge is to uncover the clues that will help us understand their behavior better. Reminding ourselves that they are beginning to develop self-control will help us be patient as they are working through these issues.

Setting limits on destructive behavior. Much of the children's daily classroom behavior can be managed quite easily with reminders and redirection. When unacceptable behavior escalates to such a point that children become destructive to themselves or others, teachers should take quick action to protect all the children's well-being. Throughout each day, teachers and caregivers must closely monitor children whose impulses are likely to lead them to behave in destructive ways. Behavior is usually consistent inside and outside the home. If a child displays destructive behaviors, teachers or caregivers need to develop an action plan, cooperating with the parents to get a handle on how the child responds to their correction and guidance. Appropriate guidance is key, as children will have particular developmental limitations. All children need to know that if they hurt others or themselves they will be corrected immediately. Staff members should focus on the behavior they seek, and they need to set strong limits on harmful behavior.

Creating a positive tone in the classroom. Much of behavior management in the classroom is reminding children of what they know and making them aware of how their behavior is affecting others. Remembering that this process takes time, we can relax and reinforce behaviors that demonstrate small steps in the right direction. The children will not be perfect all the time, but we will see progress. We accept young children in their immaturity, and we help guide them toward maturity. Above all, children need to know they are loved and accepted for who they are. Early educators can convey their love and acceptance through the power of the Holy Spirit as they remember the model that Jesus sets in His unconditional love for us.

Their teachers' words can have a powerful effect on the children. Encouraging words are an excellent way to extend grace to young children. Scripture admonishes, "Do not let any unwholesome talk come out of your mouths, but only what is helpful for building others up according to their needs, that it may benefit those who listen" (Ephesians 4:29). One of the most exciting aspects of early education ministry is an awareness of how our words and actions can give evidence of the grace of God.

Directors need to be a strong support to the teachers in the classroom, clearly communicating that they are on the teachers' side. At the same time, directors can observe the situation and provide insight in how best to serve the children and support them in their growth process. Over time, a director can change the classroom tone from negative to positive through role modeling and communicating expectations. Teachers need to know that, when a child's behavior is out of control, the director will listen and take appropriate action, and will follow through with the child's parents.

Balancing grace and truth. Grace can be defined as "unmerited favor," while truth is the real world in which we live.[12] Healthy relationships are founded on knowing when to show grace and when to allow reality to come into a person's life. Each of us needs friends to tell us the truth but also to cut us some slack at times. The most effective teachers are those who have experienced a healthy balance of grace and truth. Teachers who have been given too much grace or too much truth may tend to handle guidance issues in the same way. Either pattern can be destructive to a child, especially one who needs what the teacher cannot give. By being aware of these issues, teachers can bring into focus the words or actions that will benefit the child. An experienced teacher will have a good feel for whether the child needs to experience consequences or to be cut some slack. The following are some situations in which teachers and caregivers would tend to be more gracious with a child:

- A child is facing a traumatic experience.
- A child has lost an important relationship.
- A child is overtired.
- A child feels threatened.
- A child faces a new situation.
- A child has experienced a physical injury.
- A child manifests developmental delays.
- A child is ill.

Circumstances that would warrant immediate intervention and an element of truth would include the following:

- A child is causing harm to another child.
- A child is causing harm to himself or herself.
- A child places himself or herself in danger.
- A child is defiant.
- A child has been reminded and redirected.
- A child exhibits impulsive negative behavior.

The best equation for growth is a balance of grace and truth, along with the element of time. The role of time in allowing growth to happen is crucial. It is easy to get frustrated with particular children. But as we wait and watch for signs of growth over a period of time, we continue to encourage growth in each child.

Behavior management techniques. Both teachers and parents are always looking for helpful techniques to use with young children. What works for one child may not work for another. Having a variety of tools will give the teacher options for handling situations as they arise. In *Positive Discipline for Preschoolers*, Jane Nelson outlines seven positive discipline teaching tools:

- Positive time out
- Selective attention: ignoring the behavior, not the child
- Acceptance: holding without being hooked
- Consequences and solutions
- Follow-through
- Kindness and firmness
- Humor and laughter[13]

Working with parents. One of the best helps in guiding a child's behavior is a strong relationship with the parents. Parents play a key role in teaching their child to practice self-control and to respect others. Some parents will even look to you for guidance in these areas. Parents who ask for help are likely to follow through on your suggestions and be able to work through the process. The three areas that need to be reinforced with teachers and parents are communication, consistency, and follow-through. Communication of expected behavior is essential, and it can take a variety of forms. Repetition is important to reinforce learning. Consistency in expectations and consequences is the cornerstone for understanding. Follow-through is an essential part of developing self-control in a child. What you say should be what you do. Children who understand consequences are better equipped to face life's challenges.

Management of Staff

■ *Relationships on the staff team*

Just as positive relationships between the director and staff are essential to an effective early education program, healthy relationships *among* the staff members have a considerable influence on staff members' effectiveness. The director sets the stage for good relationships by setting standards for staff interaction, communicating those standards, and modeling the kinds of communication and relationships she expects to see. Setting an example by believing the best about each staff member helps create a positive culture. Directors lay the foundation for a strong team by being proactive about building relationships through planning social activities, creating memories through establishing meaningful traditions, and, most important, prioritizing time for staff to pray together. Creating a sense of community so that each staff member experiences care and support yields long-term benefits. Setting clear expectations of all staff members and detailing specific job responsibilities minimizes confusion and misunderstanding. Reminding staff of the destructive consequences of gossip and communicating a firm stand against it is the first step in combating a common struggle. Addressing inequities in workload and schedules derails resentment.

In truth, staff members need to be equipped to resolve the conflicts that are the inevitable outcome of working closely in an early education setting. Fortunately, God's Word has provided a wonderful resource in the principles found in Matthew 18:15–17. The director can review the passage with staff members, laying the foundation for presenting the procedures she expects them to follow in resolving conflicts:

- Keep the matter confidential.
- Keep the circle small. Go directly to the person who offended you, or whom you believe you offended, and share your perspective.
- Be straightforward. Address the issue honestly and directly.
- Be forgiving. Once the issue is resolved, reestablish the relationship.
- If the matter can't be resolved between the two of you, take it to the next level of authority.[14]

■ *Maintaining staff morale*

The mission of the Christian early education center can be accomplished only by people—many people—working together toward shared goals. In leading an early education staff to attain their goals, the director needs to attend to staff morale. Lumsden defines *morale* as "the professional interest and enthusiasm that a person displays toward the achievement of individual and group goals in a given job situation."[15] A teacher's enthusiasm not only influences her own accomplishment; it also sparks (or dampens) the spirits of the rest of the staff.

At the other end of the spectrum from a teacher with high morale is the one who is experiencing burnout. Burnout is reflected in "a loss of concern for and detachment from the people with whom one works, decreased quality of teaching, depression, overuse of sick leave, efforts to leave the profession, and a cynical and dehumanized perception of students."[16] Imagine the impact that a teacher who is experiencing burnout has on the children and on the rest of the staff. Burnout may be a common and natural consequence of the demanding job of working with young children, but can a director afford to allow it to take hold in her staff?

Work environment. One way a director actively combats burnout is by taking a thoughtful and intentional approach to developing a healthy work environment. The first step is assessing the current climate of the center, getting a sense of staff-member perceptions. This step involves asking questions and listening to the staff. Formal surveys can be helpful, as some of the director's assumptions may be wrong. In fact, Bloom found that early education administrators consistently rated the organizational climate more favorably than teachers did.[17] Because of her position, the director may have limited vision—another reason for regular dialogue with the staff. Additionally, when the director inquires about her staff members' thoughts, feelings, and opinions so that the staff feel heard by the administration, she communicates that she respects and values them as individuals.

Shared principles. One of the substantial benefits of being guided by a biblical worldview is the cohesion it provides, allowing all areas of life to be organized around Christian principles. When the same scriptural principles that underlie our philosophy in working with children are guiding our philosophy of staff management, there is a consistency that strengthens both aspects of the program. Thus the provisions we make for the beauty and comfort of the staff lounge mirror the care and planning we invest in preparing the classroom environment. When we recognize that individual staff members have unique tastes and desires, and make room for the differences, we are as responsive to our staff as we expect our staff to be to the children. Environment communicates expectations. For example, we set children up for success when they can find materials and put them away, as this practice encourages their independence. Similarly, when staff members are trusted with responsibilities, we communicate our high expectation and our confidence in their competence. Just as children grow when they are given choices, teachers who exercise autonomy in carrying out their work and have input into decisions that affect them will grow in job satisfaction and the ability to do exemplary work. The chart below contrasts some qualities of healthy and unhealthy work environments:

CHARACTERISTICS OF WORK ENVIRONMENTS

Healthy	Unhealthy
Open communication Direct communication Dialogue	Hidden agendas Rumors Gossip Too little communication
Fairness	Favoritism
Predictability	Inconsistency
Trust	Suspicion
Laughter	Shrill voices
Peace	Tension
Clear expectations	Confusion
Security	Fear
Structure/order	Chaos
Shared Vision	Purposelessness or cross-purposes
Fun	In a rut Same old same old

■ *Regular communication with staff*

The director must take time to communicate regularly with individual staff members. Checking to make sure a teacher has the necessities for a successful day, giving this one a hug or a pat on the back, saying a quick prayer with that one—all send the message that the director really cares. Daily communication also helps the director stay in touch with the children and the classroom activities. Lunch and breaks spent with the staff can be times of relaxed and informal communication.

A "Monday Memo," or weekly staff newsletter, is an important source of encouragement and information for the staff. The memo can include Scripture verses and inspirational thoughts, notices about upcoming events, creative classroom ideas, teacher commendations, prayer requests, and other important information.

Regular staff meetings are important in developing and maintaining teamwork as well as communicating information about the center's program. The meetings should be held on a regular schedule. Everyone's time is valuable. Most directors and teachers have few spare hours, even for a staff meeting. If the director plans carefully, the staff meeting will be worthwhile for all attendees. A written agenda is helpful for making sure all information is covered and ending at a preset time. (The agenda also serves as good notepaper for the teachers.) Most staff meetings are informational; however, the director may also want to call planning or training meetings. The agenda for these can allow for discussion and teacher input. The director will be the main facilitator in the staff meetings. However, teachers or other appropriate staff persons should be included, perhaps in leading a devotional or prayer time, sharing a classroom experience or teaching idea, explaining lesson plans, or voicing general concerns. The staff meeting is not the place to discuss personal staff supervision issues. The director is responsible for piloting the meeting in a professional way that is honoring to the Lord and to the staff.

■ Staff supervision

The success of the entire early education program depends on the success of each staff member, and the director contributes to that success through staff supervision. Often the director dreads the evaluation process at least as much as the staff members do. Because the process can make both parties uncomfortable, the director needs to renew her mind about the purposes of staff evaluation and pass this positive perspective on to the staff.

Staff supervision goes far beyond an occasional classroom observation or an annual evaluation. It actually begins before hiring, since the recruitment, application, interview, and preemployment orientation are all part of staff supervision. In fact, these early opportunities can lay the groundwork for successful communication between the director and

the teacher. It is the director's responsibility to do everything possible to enable new employees to be successful in their positions. Components of the staff supervision process include informal observation, formal observation, self-evaluation, and an annual employee evaluation.

Annual employee evaluation. Everyone wants to know it: "How am I doing?" The annual formal evaluation is a summary of the staff member's performance for the year, both in the classroom and in all other areas of performance (punctuality and parent relations, for example). (See form 7.22 Teacher Evaluation.) The annual evaluation is comprehensive and includes the staff member's self-evaluation, the director's written evaluation, and an evaluation conference. Before the evaluation the director reviews the evaluation form with the staff members, explaining any terms as necessary. The staff members are oriented to the elements of the evaluation process and are given a schedule for completing the self-evaluation component.

Staff self-evaluation. Self-evaluation gives staff members the opportunity to reflect on their own job performance. (See form 7.23 Self-Evaluation of Teacher.) They rate their own performance, using the same form the director uses in the formal evaluation. This activity should help staff members set goals and prepare to benefit from the evaluation conference, which should include time for them to discuss the self-evaluation with the director.

Evaluation conference. Using the same form the teacher (or other staff member) used for self-evaluation, the director records her ratings of the teacher's performance, basing them on information she has gathered throughout the year in formal and informal observations. (See form 7.24 Employee Progress Report.) After preparing a written evaluation, the director schedules and conducts a conference with the teacher. Before the conference, the teacher should have time to read through a copy of the director's written evaluation and to share her self-evaluation.

The director should arrange to hold the conference in a private area where there will be little possibility of interruption. The purpose of the conference is to reconcile the teacher's self-evaluation with the director's evaluation. The meeting should always begin with prayer, and then the director and teacher should review the evaluation process together and the areas in which the teacher was evaluated. The teacher receives written and verbal affirmation for her accomplishments along with guidance for her future performance, including any corrective action she needs to take. She is given an opportunity to respond in writing to the evaluation, noting any concerns or areas where she and the director did not reach agreement. After their talk, the director and the teacher sign both the original and the copy. The teacher keeps the copy, and the director puts the original into the teacher's file.

If the teacher's job performance has been unsatisfactory, the director should *not* wait until the annual evaluation to call attention to the situation but should deal with it immediately, working with the employee and following the procedures necessary to correct the problem. The staff evaluation should be a time of encouragement, not a time to surprise the teacher with a poor performance evaluation.

Informal observation. As stated above, the director should communicate regularly with each staff member. She should also spend time in the classrooms on a regular basis, perhaps choosing a different time for each visit in order to observe a variety of activities. Afterward, a short note lets the teacher and/or assistant teacher know that the director cares about what is happening in that class. Although in the course of the day, directors are regularly present in the classrooms, time for informal observation needs to

be prioritized and placed on the director's schedule. Otherwise, urgent demands may divert her attention from these valuable drop-in visits to the classroom. The purposes of informal observation are to keep the director informed and to provide opportunities for her to affirm, guide, and correct the staff on an ongoing basis.

Formal classroom observation. While the focus of the annual staff evaluation is broad, the emphasis of formal classroom observation is often more narrow, focusing on the teacher's interaction with the children and guidance of their learning and on her skill in setting up the classroom environment. According to Caruso and Fawcett, "Two basic things help teachers to grow: One is relevant professional information and the other is continuing feedback."[18] Formal classroom observation sets the stage for the director to provide feedback to her staff. Feedback helps a teacher to be more aware of what she does and how she does it, information that empowers the teacher to change and adapt. If feedback is to be professionally beneficial, it must focus on the teacher's behavior and not her traits, which are relatively fixed. Feedback needs to be specific and accurate, reflecting observations and not inferences.

Formal classroom observations should be scheduled in advance. However, teachers may prefer not to know the schedule so they won't be anxious beforehand. The actual observation should last for an entire activity period, giving the director an overview of the transitions between the activities. The observation form should be provided to the staff member ahead of time.

Prior to observation, areas of focus must be determined. Several types of observation form can be considered. A *closed* form, such as a checklist of predetermined skills or a rating scale, reflects a method of observing that is scientific and helpful for documenting the frequency of specific teacher behaviors, such as praising a child and responding in a child's words. An *open* observation form emphasizes narrative, describing a teacher's words and actions, much like an anecdotal record. A *combined* observation form includes elements of both types: categories of specific teacher behaviors along with space for comments and descriptive information. The observation form should include specific practices and activities that are consistent with the philosophy of the center and that support children in their progress toward the expected student outcomes. Directors may want to select items from a published observation form or create their own form, basing the items on the focus of the observation. (See forms 7.28 Observation Form and 7.29 Peer Observation Form.) When teachers are included in the process of developing the observation criteria, they have a deeper understanding of what the director is looking for and are more fully committed to implementing the desired practices.

Post-observation conference. After the observation, the director meets with the staff member to discuss what she observed. The teacher and director discuss What happened? What did it mean? and What next? The post-observation dialogue is a natural opportunity for the director to guide the teacher in reflecting on her caregiving and teaching behaviors, resulting in greater awareness. The teacher's background, level of maturity, and professional attitudes will affect the director's role in this conference. For new and young staff unaccustomed to self-evaluation, the director will need to take the lead and guide the conversation. In conferences with teachers who are highly committed to the field and able to do abstract thinking, the director will function more as a supportive peer in providing an outside perspective. Additionally, the director will need to take into account the backgrounds of the individual teachers (education, life stage, culture) and be aware of how those factors influence communication.

Benefits of staff evaluation. When teachers receive feedback that strengthens their skills, they improve—a result that affects the children by affecting the overall quality of the program. Staff evaluation also creates indirect benefits, influencing the entire culture of the center. A formalized system of staff observation and evaluation sends a powerful message to the staff, communicating that they are capable of growth and expected to grow. It encourages them by reinforcing the idea that their work with children is valuable and requires expertise. Ultimately, involvement in a well-executed staff-evaluation program raises staff members' self-confidence and helps them view themselves as lifelong learners who are engaged in complex professional activities.

Systematic staff evaluation is not only essential to program improvement, it also protects the program, ensuring that staff members implement the program consistently in accordance with established guidelines. In addressing areas of minimal compliance and marginal performance, staff evaluation processes ensure that the director is aware of staff performance issues and is actively addressing them, creating accountability for both the director and the marginal performer. The consequences of negligent staff behavior for children's physical and emotional safety are extremely serious. Ongoing supervision and evaluation procedures must be planned and implemented to protect the reputation of the program and, most importantly, the children who are served.

■ Confrontation of staff

Discipline situations. One of the most difficult parts of the director's job is dealing with staff discipline situations. These are usually rare. Sooner or later, however, every director will be involved in confronting one or more staff members. A director who needs to address a staff member about job performance, attitude, or another issue must prepare for the conference by doing some homework.

Prayer is essential! The director who looks to the Lord in prayer and is guided by the Holy Spirit will be sensitive to the issues involved in the situation. Prayer can prevent any seeds of bitterness from taking root in the heart of the director or the staff member, so that the director can confront the employee in love and can preserve the dignity of both.

The director must not put off a confrontation. The situation will not go away; in fact, it will usually get worse! Before the interview, the director should make sure she has all the information possible about the situation and then should remember to document, document, document!

When confronting the staff member, the director should stick to the issues, ask pertinent questions, and let the person know she is listening and wants to work through the situation. Using a documentation tool such as form 7.32 Growth Improvement Plan will help make the director's expectations and suggestions clear. If a time is set by which improvements should be made, it must be a specific date. A description of the situation, the director's suggestions or recommendations, and the time expectations should be put in writing for the employee to sign. The director should give the employee a copy. After the meeting is over, the director should again remember to document what happened. No one knows when a confrontational situation will rear its head again. A follow-up interview should be scheduled to encourage the staff member and to evaluate her progress.

In this as in other situations, a code of confidentiality must be followed! The situation is between the administration and the employee, and the director should not share it with anyone who is not involved.

Termination of employment. There are situations that cannot be resolved by making suggestions or setting improvement goals. In these situations it is important for the director and the governing board to work together. *Accurate documentation is essential in any termination process.* (See form 7.4 Employee Separation/Evaluation Report.) The staff handbook should have a section about the center's policies on termination and the process involved. The director and the governing board should be aware of the legal aspects of terminating an employee. ACSI offers a variety of resources that are helpful to administrators dealing with these issues.

Director Evaluation

Input on the job performance of the center's director is as important as the observation and evaluation of the teacher. The governing board or the appropriate supervisor should give the director an annual written evaluation. The director may also choose to ask the staff to provide input through a written evaluation. This staff evaluation may be optional and anonymous. The teachers should understand that the purpose of the director evaluation is to help the director improve in her job performance. The director will need to develop the ability to accept both compliments and constructive criticism from the staff in a way that honors Christ.

Staff Professional Growth

Many states require of staff members a certain number of professional growth hours per year. (See forms 7.30 Professional Growth Plan and 7.31 Professional Growth Track.) Whether or not professional growth is state mandated, staff members of early education centers need to sharpen their skills in early childhood education. In addition to sending the staff to early childhood seminars, workshops, and conferences, the director should provide on-site, in-service activities. When planning in-service training, the director should use a combination of facilitators from within the early education center and from outside sources. Having a diverse pool of presenters broadens staff members' knowledge and perspective.

Another way to enrich staff members is to arrange for them to visit and observe other early education programs. It is beneficial to prepare teachers by defining the purpose of the observations and making time afterward for debriefing and reflection.

The center that encourages professional growth clearly puts a high priority on developing and maintaining quality in its early childhood education. Therefore, conference registration fees for the staff should be included in the annual budget. Dates for annual events, such as ACSI early education conferences and teacher conventions, can be obtained from the ACSI regional office so that school closures for in-service days can be included in the school calendar and announced before families complete the registration process.

Additional funds can be set aside for staff to attend incidental seminars or training sessions that may be offered during the year. When the director comes across a seminar that is scheduled on a weekday, she can schedule substitutes, releasing one or two teachers to attend. These staff members can present the information to the rest of the staff at an in-service meeting. Thus the benefits of the seminar are maximized, as the teacher making the presentation learns even more as she shares the new information.

Subscribing to early childhood education journals and periodicals is a cost-effective way for a center to update the staff and inform them about their profession. Investing in a variety of early education curriculum resource books is essential for generating new ideas. Periodicals and books should be housed in a central location, cataloged topically, and made readily available to all staff members.

Unfortunately, many early childhood periodicals, seminars, and other professional growth opportunities do not reflect a Christ-centered worldview. The director and staff should assess the available professional growth opportunities and materials and prioritize those that reflect a Christian approach to early education. Secular presentations and materials may also be valuable resources for the staff and can help them stay abreast of trends in the field. Teachers' professional growth is encouraged when the director engages staff in discussion following a secular training event, analyzing the materials and the content of the presentation in light of the early education center's Christian philosophy. By highlighting the valuable information and sifting unbiblical content and viewpoints from it, the director models critical thinking and guides the staff in becoming critical consumers of research.

Early Education Certification

ACSI early education certification options have been designed to enable Christian early education programs to uphold their commitment to a biblical philosophy while encouraging the professional development of their faculty and staff. Those whom God has called to work with young children have accepted a high calling; it is therefore vital that their lives be characterized by both spiritual and academic integrity.

The director can play an important role in raising staff members' awareness of ACSI early education certification and credentialing opportunities and in supporting staff members through the process by distributing brochures and answering questions. Professional growth is encouraged when the center's salary schedule provides a "step" increase for ACSI certification. When the staff members achieve certification, the director can highlight this information in the parent newsletter, providing public recognition for the teacher and enhancing the center's credibility.

FORM 7.1

Position Assessment Worksheet

<church/school name> Early Education Center

Position title:	Date:
Classroom/age group:	Hours of employment:

Education needed:

Experience desired:

Wage/benefits available:	Target hire date:

Coworkers:

Key responsibilities:

purposeful design   *Early Education* DIRECTOR'S MANUAL

FORM 7.2

Reference Letter

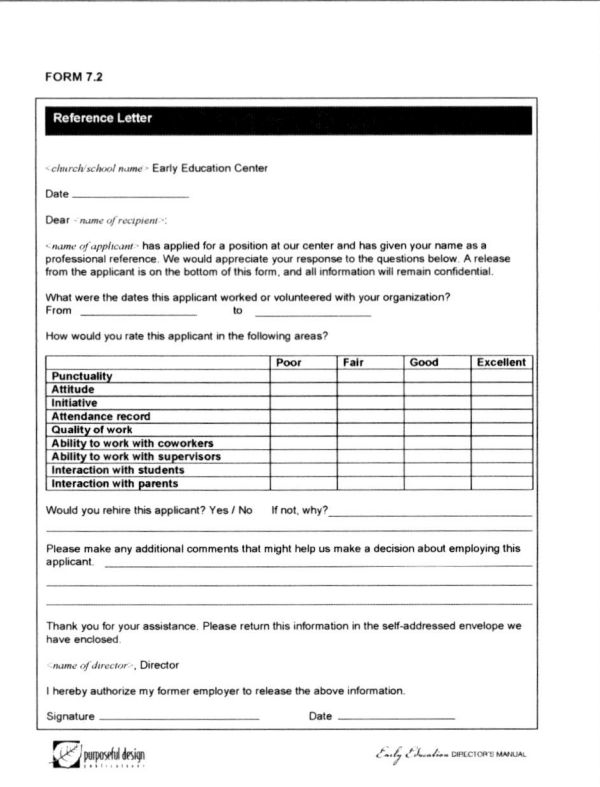

<church/school name> Early Education Center

Date _____

Dear *<name of recipient>*:

<name of applicant> has applied for a position at our center and has given your name as a professional reference. We would appreciate your response to the questions below. A release from the applicant is on the bottom of this form, and all information will remain confidential.

What were the dates this applicant worked or volunteered with your organization?
From _____ to _____

How would you rate this applicant in the following areas?

	Poor	Fair	Good	Excellent
Punctuality				
Attitude				
Initiative				
Attendance record				
Quality of work				
Ability to work with coworkers				
Ability to work with supervisors				
Interaction with students				
Interaction with parents				

Would you rehire this applicant? Yes / No   If not, why?_____

Please make any additional comments that might help us make a decision about employing this applicant. _____

Thank you for your assistance. Please return this information in the self-addressed envelope we have enclosed.

<name of director>, Director

I hereby authorize my former employer to release the above information.

Signature _____   Date _____

purposeful design   *Early Education* DIRECTOR'S MANUAL

FORM 7.3

Letter to Update Application Files

<church/school name> Early Education Center

Date _____

Dear *<name of applicant>*:

We are in the process of updating our teacher application records. Your application has been on file with us for some time. We appreciate your interest in our school.

It will be helpful to us if you would let us know your preference regarding your application. Please indicate your preference(s) below:

☐ Keep my teaching application on file for current and/or future consideration.

☐ I am interested in substitute teaching. My current phone number is _____.

☐ My name/application may be released to other Christian schools for their teacher or substitute search upon their request.

☐ Please discard my application.

☐ Other.

Please return this form in the enclosed reply envelope. We will assume that no reply after 30 days means that we should discard your application.

May the Lord bless you as you seek His will and direction in your life.

Sincerely,

<name of director>, Director

Sample from ACSI's *Personnel Forms Resource Packet*

purposeful design   *Early Education* DIRECTOR'S MANUAL

FORM 7.4

Employee Separation/Evaluation Report

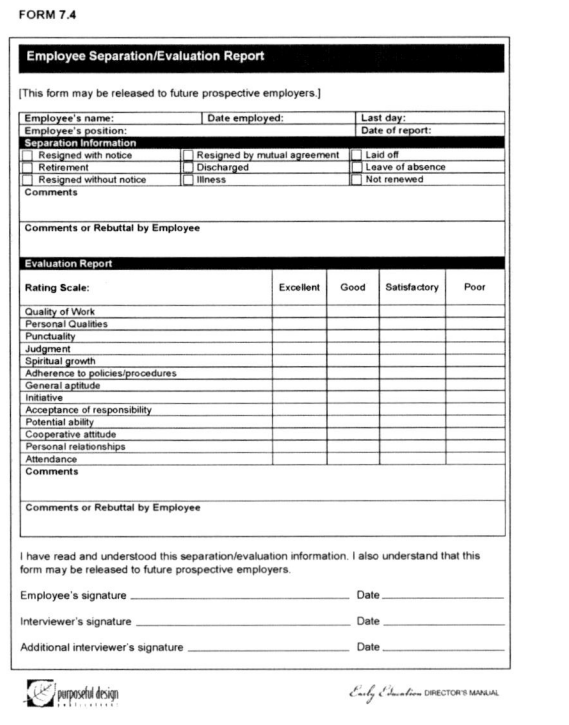

[This form may be released to future prospective employers.]

Employee's name:	Date employed:	Last day:
Employee's position:		Date of report:

Separation Information

☐ Resigned with notice	☐ Resigned by mutual agreement	☐ Laid off
☐ Retirement	☐ Discharged	☐ Leave of absence
☐ Resigned without notice	☐ Illness	☐ Not renewed

Comments

Comments or Rebuttal by Employee

Evaluation Report

Rating Scale:	Excellent	Good	Satisfactory	Poor
Quality of Work				
Personal Qualities				
Punctuality				
Judgment				
Spiritual growth				
Adherence to policies/procedures				
General aptitude				
Initiative				
Acceptance of responsibility				
Potential ability				
Cooperative attitude				
Personal relationships				
Attendance				

Comments

Comments or Rebuttal by Employee

I have read and understood this separation/evaluation information. I also understand that this form may be released to future prospective employers.

Employee's signature _____ Date _____

Interviewer's signature _____ Date _____

Additional interviewer's signature _____ Date _____

purposeful design   *Early Education* DIRECTOR'S MANUAL

FORM 7.5

Letter to Applicant Not Hired

<church/school name> Early Education Center

Date

Dear *<name of applicant>*:

Thank you for your interest in employment opportunities at *<church/school name>* Early Education Center. We have filled the position for which you applied. We thank you for taking the time and effort to contact us. We certainly wish you every success in your career search activities.

Sincerely,

<name of director>, Director

FORM 7.6

Interview Evaluation Worksheet

Applicant's name _____   Date _____

Rate each area: (3) Above Average (2) Average (1) Below Average	
Education	
Experience with children	
Verbal communication	
Attitude	
Ability to work with coworkers	
Flexibility	
Appearance	

Perceived areas of strength

Perceived areas of weakness

Overall impression

Name of interviewer _____

FORM 7.7

Observation and Evaluation of Prospective Employee

Applicant's name:	Date:

Staff observer:

Classroom/age group:

Rate each area: (3) Above Average (2) Average (1) Below Average
Give examples whenever possible

Arrives on time	
Interacts well with children	
Is aware of children's abilities	
Is alert to health and safety concerns	
Is able to handle transitions	
Encourages children to help themselves	
Has good attitude toward children	
Communicates well with adults	
Manages classroom well	

General observations

Has experience with children	
Is able to put book knowledge into practice	
Needs additional training	
I would/would not be comfortable working with this person	
I need to observe more to evaluate appropriately	

Comments

FORM 7.8

Job Description for Teacher

Title: Teacher

Spiritual Qualifications
Each employee at *<church/school name>* Early Education Center must have received Jesus Christ as his/her personal Savior and must believe that the Bible is God's Word and is the standard for faith and daily living. The employee shall be a Christian role model in attitude, speech, and actions toward others. This requirement includes being committed to God's biblical standards for sexual conduct (1 Corinthians 6:18–20). He/she shall be a member in good standing at a local evangelical church that has a statement of faith. He/she shall be willing to show by example the importance of Scripture study and memorization, prayer, witnessing, and unity in the Body of Christ. He/she shall be in wholehearted agreement with the center's statement of faith and its Christian philosophy of education. He/she shall have the spiritual maturity, academic ability, and personal leadership qualities necessary to "train up a child in the way he should go."

Physical Qualifications
Employees of *<church/school name>* Early Education Center must be able to observe, hear, and respond to the needs of children and to emergencies or conflicts that might arise in a classroom, on the playground, or in common areas. Employees must have the ability to lift children of up to fifty pounds from the floor to waist high ten to fifteen times a day; to crouch to a child's height and maintain eye contact at a child's level; to sit on the floor; to stand tall enough to reach children who are on play equipment; and to determine and communicate cognitive, social, and physical needs of children orally and in writing in the English language. Employees must feel confident that they can care for up to *<number of children>* children alone and can handle the stress, tension, and exasperation of daily contact with staff members, parents, and children. (One exception is that employees between ages 16 and 18 will not have sole charge of a group of children.)

Other qualifications
1. Meets the state of *<name of state>* requirements and qualifications for head teacher.
2. Has a minimum of two years' experience working with young children in a classroom setting, preferably with at least one year as head teacher.
3. Possesses an ability to interact effectively with parents, peers, and administrative staff.
4. Has at least nine semester hours of college-level credits in child growth and development or early childhood education.
5. Will complete the ACSI philosophy of Christian education class (offered during orientation week) within the first year of employment.
6. Such alternatives to the above qualifications as the director may find appropriate.

Reports to: Early Education Center Director

General Description of Duties
The early education teacher is responsible for planning and implementing an appropriate educational program for the children assigned to his/her class, following the guidelines in the center's approved curriculum. The teacher is also responsible to fulfill assigned duties and

FORM 7.8

Job Description for Teacher (Continued)

tasks, attend ten hours of in-service per school calendar year, attend designated school events, and abide by the terms and policies of the school as presented in the early education center staff handbook and policy handbook.

Performance Responsibilities
Spiritual
Demonstrates Christian maturity in attitude, actions, and speech, showing a consistent walk with Jesus Christ. In all work is sensitive to the spiritual needs of people.

Classroom Management
1. Will plan, supervise, and implement the program for the class in accordance with the policies and the Christian philosophy of <church/school name> Early Education Center.

2. Will plan, implement, and supervise a daily classroom program in early education that will address the spiritual, physical, emotional, social, and mental needs of the individual child in a group environment. Will plan and use an age-appropriate curriculum that permits the child to exercise his/her initiative and will help the teacher to respond within a relatively controlled and clearly defined structure.

   It is the teacher's responsibility to write lesson plans using materials from numerous resources. These lesson plans are to be turned in to the center's director twice a month.

3. Will treat all children with dignity and respect. Will follow the basic school discipline formula, taking the initiative to clearly communicate discipline concerns to the director and to the parents. Will abide by a code of confidentiality in all discipline cases.

4. Is responsible for the ordered arrangement, appearance, decor, and learning environment of the classroom.

5. Is responsible for an equal share of joint housekeeping responsibilities of the staff.

6. Will attend all staff meetings and training sessions. Staff meetings are held on a weekly basis for teachers in the early education center.

7. Will implement methods for effectively utilizing the teacher, including clear communication and supervision. Will give input to the director on assistant teacher evaluations.

8. Will plan and implement methods of establishing a positive liaison with parents. This duty includes making daily contact with parents as well as attending specific events and meetings: e.g., Meet-Your-Teacher Day, Back-to-School Night, open house, conferences. Will initiate extra conferences as needed throughout the school year with the input of the director.

Early Education DIRECTOR'S MANUAL

FORM 7.8

Job Description for Teacher (Continued)

9. Will evaluate on an ongoing basis the spiritual, social, emotional, and intellectual level of each child. Will give a formal evaluation two times in each school year.

10. Will assist in designated public-relations events sponsored by the school.

11. Will maintain current infant/child CPR and first-aid certification.

12. Additional duties:
    • Ordering classroom supplies
    • Reporting maintenance needs in the classroom
    • Performing additional duties as assigned by the director
    • Publishing a monthly parent newsletter

13. Is supervised during the school year by the director and any other designated administrators. Is observed throughout the year by the director, and is given both informal and formal evaluations.

Early Education DIRECTOR'S MANUAL

FORM 7.9

Job Description for Assistant Teacher

Title: Assistant teacher

Qualifications
1. Shows evidence of Christian maturity and a strong grasp of the essence of Christian education.
2. Meets the state requirements and qualifications for assistant teachers.
3. Such alternatives to the above qualifications as the director may find appropriate.

Reports to Early education director
Early education teacher

Performance Responsibilities
Spiritual:
Demonstrates spiritual maturity in attitude, actions, and speech, showing a consistent walk with Jesus Christ; in all work is sensitive to the spiritual needs of people.

Classroom Management
1. Assists in implementing the daily program under the direction of the teacher and the director.
2. Assists in preparing the learning environment, setting up interest centers, and preparing needed materials and supplies.
3. Assists in supervising the classroom and playground; is responsible for discipline in the classroom/playground in accordance with the early education discipline formula under the direction of the teacher and/or director; treats all children with dignity and respect.
4. Assists with general housekeeping tasks.
5. Maintains a professional attitude in communicating with the teacher, director, children, and parents.
6. Attends staff meetings and training programs as deemed necessary by the teacher and/or the director.
7. Is willing to fulfill responsibilities and procedures as presented in the early education staff handbook.
8. Performs additional appropriate duties as assigned by the teacher and/or director.

Early Education DIRECTOR'S MANUAL

FORM 7.10

Job Description for Teacher Aide

Title: Teacher Aide

Qualifications
1. Shows evidence of Christian maturity and a strong grasp of the essence of Christian education.
2. Meets the state requirements and qualifications for a teacher aide. Must be at least 16 years old.

Reports to Early education teacher

Performance Responsibilities
Spiritual
Demonstrates spiritual maturity in attitude, actions, and speech, showing a consistent walk with Jesus Christ. In all work is sensitive to the spiritual needs of people.

Classroom Management
1. Assists in the implementing of the daily program under the direction of the head teacher, assistant teacher, and director.
2. Assists in preparing the learning environment by setting up and preparing needed materials and supplies.
3. Assists in supervising the classroom/playground. (Aides age 18 and under will not be supervising the classroom/playground alone.)
4. Is responsible for general housekeeping tasks as assigned by the teacher, the assistant teacher, and/or the director.
5. Maintains a professional attitude.
6. Treats all children with dignity and respect.
7. Attends staff meeting and training programs as deemed necessary by the director.
8. Exhibits a warm and friendly personality to children, staff, and parents.
9. Accepts additional appropriate duties as assigned by the teacher, assistant teacher, and/or the director.

Early Education DIRECTOR'S MANUAL

FORM 7.11

Important Skills for Early Education Teachers

Communication
- Ability to build open relationships based on mutual respect with parents, children, and other staff members

Staff and parents
- Ability to work through conflicts (to problem-solve and to negotiate solutions)
- Ability to perceive self as part of a team
- Willingness to share space and materials with others

Children
- Ability to relate to each child according to his/her individual needs, interests, and abilities
- Ability to use classroom management techniques that build children's ability to make choices and be self-directed
- Ability to share information effectively with parents in a nonjudgmental, nonthreatening manner

Child development
- Ability to understand and apply principles consistent with the school's philosophy of education
- Ability to evaluate activities and materials in light of their developmental value for the child
- Ability to promote the children's self-help skills and independence
- Ability to support the children in their efforts and discern when to offer assistance and when to allow them to work through a situation on their own
- Ability to promote children's exploration of situations and materials by asking questions and by providing appropriate materials and guidance
- Ability to observe children actively and frequently and to use the information gained in planning subsequent activities

Organizational concerns
- Ability to maintain and use observational records of children
- Ability to plan and implement a wide variety of activities that are balanced in their scope and are relevant to the lives of young children
- Ability to develop and maintain a classroom environment that is safe, orderly, and aesthetically pleasing

Professional concerns
- Ability to represent the early childhood profession positively in the community, through effectively communicating the center's mission and its value for children
- Interest in learning more about child development and the ability to apply new information
- Ability to self-evaluate and to generate goals, and the ability to receive feedback from others

Early Education DIRECTOR'S MANUAL

FORM 7.12

Employment Applications and the ADA

Q & A Topic: Complying with the ADA on Employment Applications

Q. Our school has a policy against discrimination in employment on the basis of a disability. In implementing this policy, what can we include or not include on an application for employment?

A. The Americans with Disabilities Act prohibits Christian schools with 15 or more employees (whether part-time or full-time) from discriminating in employment on the basis of a disability. One of the purposes of the ADA is to eliminate medical questions or prevent an employer from obtaining information that would disclose whether or not an individual is disabled. Asking medical-related questions could cause an employer to decide not to hire a prospective employee. Thus the Act places certain prohibitions on questions.

For example, the United States Court of Appeals of the Tenth Circuit recently considered several questions on an employer's application. In *Griffin v. Steeltek, Inc.* (No. 97-5103), an employer had asked whether or not a prospective employee had received workers' compensation or disability income payments. These types of questions are prohibited. The Court also ruled that a question asking, *Have you physical defects that preclude you from performing certain jobs?* was impermissible. This was true even if the applicant was not disabled.

Questions (even if in an oral interview) that require a prospective employee to describe or identify medical conditions or any prior health problems are inappropriate. Asking employees how many days they have missed in the past due to sickness or health is inappropriate. Asking a prospective employee how many days of family medical leave he/she has taken is also inappropriate. The application should not contain any questions about a person's physical or mental impairments.

The ADA gives specific guidelines on what an employer may ask. The employer should have a job description that includes a list of the "essential functions of the job."* The employer should provide this job description to the prospective employee, including the essential functions. The employer may ask an applicant if he/she can perform each of the essential functions. If an applicant cannot perform an essential function, the employer may then inquire into what is needed to reasonably accommodate the applicant so he/she might be able to perform the essential functions.

Because the ADA is a very fact-specific statute, and reasonable accommodations may depend on the particular circumstances of the school and of the prospective employee, schools should seek legal advice if there is any question about whether or not to provide a requested reasonable accommodation.

*ACSI sells the *Personnel Forms Resource Packet*, which contains a model teacher's job description that lists the "essential functions" of the job. It also shows how to include the physical requirements of a job in a job description. Call 800-367-0798 for information or to order.

Author: Attorney John L. Cooley

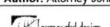

Early Education DIRECTOR'S MANUAL

FORM 7.13

Statement of Faith

<church/school name> Early Education Center

We believe there is one God, eternally existent in three persons—Father, Son, and Holy Spirit (Genesis 1:1, Matthew 28:19, John 10:30).

We believe the Bible to be the inspired, the only infallible, authoritative, inerrant Word of God (2 Timothy 3:16, 2 Peter 1:21).

We believe in the deity of Christ (John 10:33); His virgin birth (Isaiah 7:14, Matthew 1:23, Luke 1:35); His sinless life (Hebrews 4:15, Hebrews 7:26); His miracles (John 2:11); His vicarious and atoning death (1 Corinthians 15:3, Ephesians 1:7, Hebrews 2:9); His resurrection (John 11:25, 1 Corinthians 15:4); His ascension to the right hand of the Father (Mark 16:19); His personal return in power and glory (Acts 1:11, Revelation 19:11).

We believe in the absolute necessity of regeneration by the Holy Spirit for salvation because of the exceeding sinfulness of human nature; and that we are justified on the single ground of faith in the shed blood of Christ and that only by God's grace alone are we saved (John 3:16–19, John 5:24, Romans 3:23, Romans 5:8–9, Ephesians 2:8–10, Titus 3:5).

We believe in the resurrection of both the saved and the lost; of them that are saved to the resurrection of life, and of them that are lost to the resurrection of damnation (John 5:28–29).

We believe in the spiritual unity of believers in our Lord Jesus Christ (Romans 8:9, 1 Corinthians 12:12–13, Galatians 3:26–28).

We believe in the present ministry of the Holy Spirit by whose indwelling the Christian is enabled to live a godly life (Romans 8:13–14, 1 Corinthians 3:16 and 6:19–20, Ephesians 4:30 and 5:18).

Please read this Statement of Faith carefully and indicate below your degree of support:

☐ I fully support the Statement as written without mental reservations.

Signature _____

☐ I support the Statement except for the area(s) listed and explained on a separate paper. The exceptions represent either disagreement or items for which I have not yet formed an opinion or conviction.

Signature _____

Modified sample from ACSI's Personnel Forms Resource Packet

Early Education DIRECTOR'S MANUAL

FORM 7.14

Interview Questions for Early Education Teacher Applicant

- When and how did you receive Jesus Christ as your personal Savior, and how has He changed your life?
- What are you doing to grow in your relationship with Jesus Christ?
- What church do you attend, and how are you involved in its ministry?
- Why have you chosen to work with young children?
- What do you enjoy the most about this type of work?
- What do you find the most difficult about this type of work?
- How would you lead a young child to Christ?
- Describe your educational philosophy.
- Describe your philosophy for classroom management and for guiding children's behavior.
- If you were going to start an early education center, what would it be like? (curriculum, environment, staff, etc.)
- What do you think are the most important aspects of effective working relationships between fellow teachers?
- What do children need from their teacher?
- How do you talk and listen to a child?
- What do parents need from their child's teacher?
- What is the best way of communicating with parents?
- What does the director need from her staff?
- What skills do you have that prepare you for this job?
- What strengths would you bring to this position?
- Do you feel daily lesson plans are important? Why?
- Do you feel parental involvement is important in the early education classroom? Why? How will you involve children's parents?
- Explain confidentiality and how it relates to any problem in an early education center.
- What weaknesses will you need to address as they relate to this position?
- How would you assess children's development?
- How would you incorporate assessment into the curriculum?
- Describe how you would communicate children's progress to their parents.

What would you do if ...
- Two children are fighting over the same toy.
- A parent complains that her child doesn't want to come to school because no one plays with her.
- A parent wants to know why the three-year-olds aren't learning to write letters and numbers.
- A parent complains that a teacher in another class was yelling at the children.
- A 10-year-old has been withdrawn and moody lately. She is not playing with her best friend and seems very distant.

Early Education DIRECTOR'S MANUAL

FORM 7.15

Teacher Contract

<church/school name> Early Education Center

Believing that God has led in this decision, the school board of *<church/school name>* Early Education Center has appointed *<name of teacher>* as *<name of position>* for the *<year>* school year. This contract begins *<date>* and ends *<date>*, depending on satisfactory performance of assigned duties. In so doing, we recognize and affirm the ministry of teaching for *<name of teacher>* as a God-ordained vocation. We rejoice that God has brought *<name of teacher>* to us as a "fellow laborer" in this ministry. This contract provides a framework of mutual obligation and responsibility to assure the orderly operation of an exemplary program at *<church/school name>* Early Education Center.

By accepting this appointment, said teacher specifically acknowledges that this contract is for a limited duration and that all rights and privileges herein shall terminate upon the expiration date of this contract, unless voided earlier pursuant to the provisions of paragraph 21 below. The parties agree that no rights of tenure or presumption of continued employment are conferred or implied by this contract or by a number of consecutive contracts. The parties further agree that no right to notice of renewal or nonrenewal of the contract is conferred or implied.

Gross salary or hourly wage for this period of employment will be $*<amount>* payable in *<number>* installments of $*<amount>* on the 5th and 20th of each month, beginning on the 20th of the first month of contract. Fringe benefits are listed on the attached Financial Worksheet.

Conditions of Employment

1. The teacher affirms that, as part of the qualifications for this position, he/she is a born-again Christian who knows the Lord Jesus Christ as Savior (John 3:3, 1 Peter 1:23).

2. The teacher gives testimony that he/she has a sense of God's will, that teaching is his/her calling, and that teaching in *<church/school name>* Early Education Center is God's direction at this time.

3. The teacher will manifest by precept and example the highest Christian virtue and personal decorum, serving as a Christian role model (1 Timothy 4:12) to pupils both in and out of school (Luke 6:40), and as an example to parents and fellow faculty members in judgment, dignity, respect, and Christian living. This includes, but is not limited to, refraining from such activities as the use of alcohol, tobacco, and illicit drugs as well as the use of vulgar and profane language (Colossians 3:17, Titus 2:7–8, 1 Thessalonians 2:10, 5:18, 5:22–23; James 3:17–18).

4. The teacher will faithfully attend and financially support a local church whose fundamental beliefs are in agreement with the statement of faith of this school (Hebrews 10:25).

5. The teacher accepts without verbal or mental reservations both the statement of faith and the educational philosophy and objectives of this school and is committed to upholding them.

purposeful design publications — Early Education DIRECTOR'S MANUAL

FORM 7.15

Teacher Contract (Continued)

6. The teacher has read the teacher job description and agrees to abide by the requirements listed. The teacher has also read and agrees to abide by the regulations set forth in the faculty and student handbooks, as well as any additions made by the school board during this contract year. He/she agrees to cooperate in every way with the school authorities and adhere to the policies adopted by the school board.

7. The teacher will provide the administrator with a copy of a valid teaching certificate or an official transcript of all college and graduate studies prior to the first day of school or will make other acceptable arrangements with the administration, or this contract is voided.

8. The teacher agrees to work toward and apply for ACSI teacher certification. A teacher new to this school must complete the requirements for ACSI certification within three (3) years of commencing to teach at this school before being eligible to be considered for a new contract in the fourth year.

9. All state medical requirements for a teaching position with proof of such must be filed with the school before the start of school. Upon request, the teacher agrees to submit to a physical examination by a licensed physician at school expense and furnish the school with a copy of a physician's report.

10. Assignment to a room is to be made at the discretion of the director after consultation with the teacher. He/she agrees to accept his/her proportionate amount of supervision outside the regular classroom assignment. The extent of such supervision and assignment is to be determined by the director, who will seek as far as possible to achieve equity in all staff assignments.

11. The teacher will strive at all times to understand, appreciate, love, and serve the pupils entrusted to him/her for instruction and will to the best of his/her ability provide for their fullest spiritual, intellectual, physical, and emotional development.

12. The teacher will maintain a classroom atmosphere that is conducive to learning. This includes maintaining a professional appearance.

13. The teacher agrees to be present on time for faculty devotions and staff meetings.

14. The teacher will avoid as much as possible highly debatable topics that tend to divide evangelical believers. A student is to be referred to his/her local church if a debatable topic of a theological nature arises.

15. The teacher agrees to attempt to resolve differences with others (parents, fellow workers, administration) by following the biblical pattern of Matthew 18:15–17. Should he or she have unresolved issues with the employer after utilizing the Matthew 18 principle, the parties agree to be bound by the following mediation and binding arbitration agreement in an attempt to resolve issues and bring reconciliation:

purposeful design publications — Early Education DIRECTOR'S MANUAL

FORM 7.15

Teacher Contract (Continued)

16. The parties to this agreement are Christians and believe that the Bible commands them to make every effort to live at peace and to resolve disputes with each other in private or within the Christian community in conformity with the biblical injunctions of 1 Corinthians 6:1–8, Matthew 5:23–24, and Matthew 18:15–20. Therefore, the parties agree that any claim or dispute arising out of, or related to, this agreement or any aspect of the employment relationship, including claims under federal, state, and local statutory or common law, the law of contract, and law of tort, shall be settled by biblically based mediation.

    If resolution of the dispute and reconciliation do not result from mediation, the matter shall then be submitted to an independent and objective arbitrator for binding arbitration. The parties agree that the mediation and arbitration process will be conducted in accordance with the "Rules of Procedure for Christian Conciliation" ("Rules") contained in the Peacemaker Ministries booklet *Guidelines for Christian Conciliation*. Consistent with these "Rules," each party to the agreement shall agree to the selection of the arbitrator. The parties agree that if there is an impasse in the selection of the arbitrator, the Institute for Christian Conciliation division of Peacemaker Ministries in Billings, Montana (406-256-1583), shall be asked to provide the name of a qualified person who will serve in that capacity. Consistent with the "Rules," the arbitrator shall issue a written opinion within a reasonable time.

    The parties to this contract agree that these methods shall be the *sole remedy* for any controversy or claim arising out of the employment relationship or this agreement, and they *expressly waive* their right to file a lawsuit against one another in any civil court for such disputes, except to enforce a legally binding arbitration decision. The parties to this agreement have had an opportunity to consult legal counsel before signing this agreement.

17. The teacher agrees that the Bible dictates the standards for sexual behavior. Any promiscuity, or homosexual or other deviant sexual behavior, is forbidden and as such violates the bona fide occupational requirement of being a Christian role model. The unique roles of the male and female are clearly defined in Scripture. Romans 1:24–32 states that God recognizes homosexual and other deviant behavior as perverted. Deviation from scriptural standards in sexual behavior is grounds for termination. (Romans 13:12–14; 1 Corinthians 6:9–20; 1 Timothy 4:12; 2 Timothy 2:19–22; 1 Peter 1:15–16, 2:15–17)

18. The teacher acknowledges that he/she is fully aware of his/her obligations under state law regarding child abuse reporting requirements and that he/she will fulfill those obligations.

19. Any previous agreements, whether written or oral, are fully merged into this agreement, and no agreement, statement, or promise other than those contained in this contract shall be valid or binding on either party. This contract shall be interpreted under the laws of the State of *<name of state>*.

purposeful design publications — Early Education DIRECTOR'S MANUAL

FORM 7.15

Teacher Contract (Continued)

20. **Fringe benefits**
    It is understood that the school is not liable to reimburse any teacher for any unused benefit in the fringe benefit package. Teachers may not choose to receive cash in lieu of any benefit.

    Sick days
    Teachers shall be permitted *<number>* sick days per year. Should additional one-year contracts be offered in the ensuing years, unused sick leave may be allowed to accumulate to thirty days, to be used for extended illness only. A prorated payroll deduction will be made for each day absent over the allotted days for both full- and part-time teachers.

    Personal and professional days
    Two personal days may be taken by full-time teachers with advance coordination and approval of the principal. One professional day may also be taken to attend a conference or visit another school for professional growth and development. These days do not accumulate from year to year.

    Vacation days
    The teacher will receive all standard school holidays including Christmas and spring vacations.

    Medical insurance
    The school shall pay *<percentage figure>* percent of the medical insurance premiums for full-time teachers working 30 or more hours per week. This insurance will become effective 30 days after initial employment begins and shall continue in effect for the contract period. It shall also continue to be in effect between contract periods for returning faculty members. Otherwise, the policies will be terminated on the last day of employment. Teachers electing coverage who work less than thirty hours per week shall pay the proportionate difference of the premium between their part-time hours and the 30 or more hour-a-week position. For example, the school would pay two-thirds of the premium of a person working 20 hours per week.

    If the teacher's spouse has duplicate family coverage, and the teacher signs a waiver, he/she will be given a taxable gift of $*<amount>* proportional to the number of hours worked as consideration for the waiver.

    Free tuition
    A full-time teacher shall receive free tuition during the school year for his/her children. A part-time teacher will receive a proration of the benefit based on the number of hours per week contracted.

    Life and disability insurance
    The school will pay the fees for all full-time teachers to be covered by a $*<amount>* group term life insurance policy and a group disability insurance policy. These policies shall become effective 30 days after initial employment begins and shall continue in effect for the

purposeful design publications — Early Education DIRECTOR'S MANUAL

FORM 7.15

Teacher Contract (Continued)

contract period. They shall also continue to be in effect between contract periods for returning faculty members. Otherwise, the policies will be terminated on the last day of employment. Part-time teachers may elect to have the insurance fees deducted from their wages and participate in these group policies providing they work enough hours to meet the requirements of the policies.

Graduate study assistance for full-time faculty
The maximum possible annual allowance awarded for graduate study will be one-half the cost of textbooks and one-half the tuition costs for up to eight hours of graduate study as budgeted funds permit. See *Faculty Handbook*.

21. The teacher must give the board one month's prior written notice of intended resignation unless a different termination date is mutually agreed upon. If the teacher resigns or is terminated during the period of service covered by this contract, payment shall be made of the same proportion of the annual salary as the number of days of actual duty bears to the number of days covered by the contract. All fringe benefits will end on the last day of employment. All the employer's property that is in the teacher's custody must be returned before he/she is entitled to final payment of any amount due upon separation.

Where cause exists, the board may terminate this contract, provided the teacher has been informed in writing of the cause or causes for discharge and has been given an opportunity to respond to them prior to final termination. Failure to request a hearing with the board within seven days of delivery of the termination notice shall waive the teacher's right to such a hearing, and the termination is final. Dismissal may be immediate or with longer notice, depending on the reason for dismissal.

Cause as used herein includes but is not limited to any conduct tending to reflect discredit on the school or on the teacher, or tending to seriously impair his/her continued usefulness as a Christian role model for the students. The *Faculty Handbook* and the *Policy and Procedures Manual* give full details regarding termination of contract.

This contract will be valid only if it is signed and returned by *‹date›*.

I have read and understand the duties, responsibilities, salary, and benefits and will abide by the terms and conditions of this contract.

Teacher_____ **Date** _____

We at *‹church/school name›* Early Education Center extend our warmest welcome to you. We pledge our prayer support and help as you minister to the needs of our students.

Board Chairman
Director _____ Sample from ACSI's *Personnel Forms Resource Packet*

purposeful design | *Early Education* DIRECTOR'S MANUAL

FORM 7.16

Preemployment Orientation/Observation Worksheet

‹church/school name› Early Education Center

Thank you for applying to work at our early education center. We appreciate the time you are taking today to come in for the preemployment orientation and observation. You will be assigned a staff trainer, who will be available to answer any questions you have during your time of orientation and observation. Our purpose today is for you to read through important information regarding our program and your employment here at *‹church/school name›* Early Education Center. You will also be taken by one of the staff trainers on an in-depth tour of our facilities. And finally, you will visit a selected classroom to observe the staff, the children, and the parents in our facility. Feel free to ask questions of the staff; however, try not to interrupt the flow of the daily class schedule. Since we do ask input from the staff regarding your time in their class, we would like you to interact with the children under the supervision of the head teacher in the class.

As you go through the day, please check off the following tasks as you complete them:

☐ **Sign in on the timesheet.**

☐ **Meet with a staff trainer for reading orientation.**

☐ **Complete reading materials.**

☐ **Take a tour of the early education center.**

☐ **Observe a classroom.**

☐ **Observation classroom** *‹classroom number›*

☐ **Head teacher** *‹name of head teacher›*

☐ **Meet with director.**

☐ **Complete remaining payroll information.**

☐ **Sign out on the timesheet.**

purposeful design | *Early Education* DIRECTOR'S MANUAL

FORM 7.17

Preemployment Orientation Worksheet

‹church/school name› Early Education Center

Applicant's name _____ Date _____

Background information		Center Information	
History of the center		Safe place for personal property	
Purpose, goals, philosophy		Staff cubbies	
Funding sources		Teachers' lounge	
Organizational structure		Teachers' restrooms	
Population served		Snacks and beverages	
Staff Handbook		Teachers' breaks	
Work schedule		Coffee	
Clocking in and out		Lunch	
Payroll period		Phone calls and messages	
Benefits and how to apply		Guests/visitors to center	
Vacation		Teachers' books	
Sick leave		Children's books	
Leave without pay		Supplies and equipment	
Health insurance		Ordering procedures	
Pregnancy/paternity leave		Working with coworkers	
Bereavement leave/pay		Administration structure	
Calling in sick/other		**Classroom Orientation and Notebook**	
Reimbursement of expenses		Daily schedule	
Training and conferences		Greeting children and parents	
Procedures for resignation and termination		Taking attendance	
Center Requirements		Procedures for sick or injured children	
Staff and department meetings		Mealtimes	
Conferences and seminars		Nap routines	
First aid/CPR training		Health checks	
Parent events		Medication	
Meet-the-Teacher Night		Ouch reports	
Christmas program		Accident forms	
Open house		Dealing with toileting accidents	
Spring program		Reporting suspected child abuse	
Conferences		Children's files	
Confidentiality		Communications to parents	
Licensing standards		Weekly notes	
Emergency Procedures		Personal notes	
Fire drills list		Opening and closing procedures	
First aid supplies		Center discipline policy	
School closures		Playground rules	
		Handling birthdays and holidays	
		Referring parents	

purposeful design | *Early Education* DIRECTOR'S MANUAL

FORM 7.17

Preemployment Orientation Worksheet (Continued)

Applicant's signature _____ Date _____

Director's signature _____ Date _____

purposeful design | *Early Education* DIRECTOR'S MANUAL

FORM 7.18

Topics to Include in Staff Handbook

- Staff welcome
- Short history of the center
- ACSI accreditation
- State licensure
- Organizational structure of the center (organization chart)
- Center's bylaws
- Statement of faith
- Application packet
- Job descriptions for all positions
- Supervision and evaluation procedures/plan
- Termination procedures
- Sexual harassment policy
- Overtime/compensatory time
- Paydays
- Holidays
- Sick leave
- Personal days
- Vacation days
- Employee tuition discount
- Insurance
- Medical leave of absence
- Injury benefits
- Bereavement leave
- Jury leave
- Leave without pay
- Unauthorized leave
- Dress code
- Center's program procedures
- Philosophy

- Classroom discipline
- Classroom environment
- Staff meetings
- Lesson plans
- Staff development
- Substitute procedures
- Program components and curriculum
- Supply and equipment information
- Health, accident, and illness procedures
- Universal precautions
- Child abuse policy and procedures
- Disaster procedures
- Preschool child procedures
- Daily health checks
- Attendance of children
- Release of children
- Late pickup of children
- Classroom/playground rules
- Field trip procedures
- Van/car rules
- Communication on behavior to children/parents/staff
- Discipline procedures
- Verbal communication with children
- Verbal/written communication with parents
- Confidentiality
- Teamwork with other staff

FORM 7.19

New-Employee Checklist

‹church/school name› Early Education Center

Name _____ Application received _____

Interviewed by _____ Interview date _____ Time _____

- ☐ Statement of faith signed
- ☐ Staff handbook read and agreed upon
- ☐ Observations complete for:
  - ☐ 3-year-old class
  - ☐ 4-year-old class
  - ☐ Prekindergarten class
  - ☐ Other
- ☐ Observation evaluations completed
- ☐ Reference check completed
- ☐ Employment agreement signed/ nonemployment letter sent
- ☐ Tour of facilities completed
- ☐ Phone number and birth dates given
- ☐ Personnel file
- ☐ Copies of driver's license and social security card
- ☐ Emergency information
- ☐ W-2 form completed
- ☐ I-9 form completed
- ☐ Payroll information

- ☐ Health exam results
- ☐ TB test results
- ☐ CPR/first aid course verification
- ☐ Fingerprint card
- ☐ Payroll deductions (if applicable)
- ☐ Minor's permit (if applicable)
- ☐ Vacation/sick days forms
- ☐ Completed reference forms
- ☐ Telephone reference documentation
- ☐ Employment packet completed
- ☐ Orientation questionnaire completed
- ☐ Insurance information given/completed
- ☐ Mid-probation meeting
- ☐ Probation completed

Additional comments _____
_____
_____
_____
_____

FORM 7.20

Staff Personnel Form

‹church/school name› Early Education Center

Name _____ Phone _____
Address _____
Date of birth _____
Social Security Number _____ Orientation/Hire Date _____
Allergies _____
Emergency Contact Number _____

- ☐ First Aid/CPR
- ☐ W-4 Information
- ☐ Background Check
- ☐ Employment Verification
- ☐ Universal Precautions
- ☐ Payroll Information
- ☐ Medical Insurance
- ☐ TB Test

Job Description

Hourly Wage/Benefits

Other Information

FORM 7.21

Time-Off Request

‹church/school name› Early Education Center	
Name	Today's date
Date(s) requested off	to
☐ Medical	
☐ Personal	
☐ Vacation	
Time requested off	
Time off approved by	
Substitute request	
For Office Use Only	
Substitute phone number	
Substitute contacted	
Substitute confirmed	
This Time-Off Request form must be submitted two weeks prior to date requested	

FORM 7.22

Teacher Evaluation

Self-Evaluation
I believe that this year I excelled in these areas:

These areas were a struggle for me this year:

Next year I plan to work on these areas:

Director's Teacher Evaluation
I was impressed with your ability to do the following:

These areas seemed to flow very well in your classroom:

Perhaps you could use more support in these areas:

Next year we will assist you as follows:

FORM 7.23

Self-Evaluation of Teacher

<church/school name> Early Education Center

General Evaluation		
Do I like and respect myself?	Yes	No
What are some of my strengths and weaknesses?		
With my peer staff		
With the children		
Am I accepting of the individual differences of the children in my care?	Yes	No
Am I striving to give each child every opportunity to develop his/her capacities to the limit?	Yes	No
Am I flexible? Am I using my resourcefulness and imagination to try new things to help the children grow and learn through doing?	Yes	No
Do I consciously build on the learning and the experiences that the children received from their previous teacher?	Yes	No
Do I effectively help each child think for himself/herself? Do I help build judgment and controlled behavior in each child?	Yes	No
Am I continuing to grow professionally to help children become contributing, effective members of society?	Yes	No
Evaluation of the Job		
Do I like my work? If not, why not?	Yes	No
Is my work fulfilling?	Yes	No
Am I satisfied with my salary or hourly wage?	Yes	No
Am I in agreement with the philosophy and objectives of the school?	Yes	No
Have I the physical health needed to meet the demands of the job?	Yes	No
Teacher-Parent Relationship		
Do I inspire confidence in the parent by showing an interest in the child and a friendly, cooperative desire to understand him/her?	Yes	No
Do I work cooperatively with the parent in order that the parent and I may understand the child's progress and his/her developmental problems?	Yes	No
Do I work cooperatively with my fellow staff members in the interest of the growth of each child and his/her parents?	Yes	No
Do I keep information about the school, the staff, and the children confidential (not sharing it with anyone)?	Yes	No
Teacher-Staff Relationships		
Do I like and respect my fellow staff members?	Yes	No
Am I accepted by the school staff?	Yes	No
Do I contribute to a strong staff morale?	Yes	No
Do I show professional attitudes toward all the school staff?	Yes	No

---

FORM 7.23

Self-Evaluation of Teacher (Continued)

Am I supportive of my fellow workers outside of the school?	Yes	No
Professional Attitudes		
Do I conduct myself within the recognized ethics of the profession?	Yes	No
Do I avail myself of every opportunity to grow within the profession through in-service training as well as courses taken outside?	Yes	No
Am I willing to seek and try new ideas?	Yes	No
Am I able to accept and apply constructive suggestions?	Yes	No
Do I plan personal out-of-school activities in such a manner that professional obligations in the school can be met?	Yes	No
What are my greatest interests outside of my teaching? Am I finding them fulfilling?	Yes	No
Additional comments		

FORM 7.24

Employee Progress Report

<church/school name> Early Education Center

Name of teacher	Date		
1. Does the teacher arrive on time?		Yes	No
2. Does he/she plan and carry out programs consistent with the philosophy of the early education center?		Yes	No
3. Does he/she follow the schedule?		Yes	No
4. Does the teacher come prepared for			
a. Bible?		Yes	No
b. music?		Yes	No
c. science?		Yes	No
d. language arts?		Yes	No
e. literature?		Yes	No
f. creative activities?		Yes	No
g. free play?		Yes	No
5. Does he/she work happily with this group of children and still have control?		Yes	No
6. Is he/she conscious of the need to give attention to health and safety factors (with both environment and children)?		Yes	No
7. Does the teacher understand the needs of different age groups, and is he/she able to plan the work to fit the interests of the group?		Yes	No
8. Do you think the teacher is best fitted for this age group?		Yes	No
9. Is the teacher aware that a child's response is determined largely by the teacher's attitude?		Yes	No
10. Is the teacher willing to assume duties in any area of operation?		Yes	No
11. Is the teacher's relationship with other staff members pleasant and professional?		Yes	No
12. Does he/she keep the children's records in order and up-to-date?		Yes	No
13. Is the teacher available to parents for conferences when indicated?		Yes	No

FORM 7.25

Financial Worksheet

Employee's name	
Teaching assignment	School year
Years step	
Education column	
Base salary $	

Additional duties	Compensation
	$
	$

Total Salary $	
Fringe benefits $	
Health insurance $	
Group life insurance $	
Group disability insurance $	
F.I.C.A contribution $	
Tuition discount $	
ACSI convention registration $	
Total benefits $	

Total remuneration for this contract position $	
Employee's name	
Employee's legal name	
Present address	
Home Phone	Social security number
Date of first hire	
Birthplace	Date of birth

Name, address and phone number of person(s) to be notified in case of emergency

Doctor's name	Phone

Health Insurance Waiver

I, *name of employee*, choose to waive my right to employer-paid health insurance.

Signature of employee	Date

 *Early Education* DIRECTOR'S MANUAL

FORM 7.26

On Health and Safety

- Identifying potential hazards
  - Provide information on common causes of workplace injury, including identifying trip hazards.
  - Include specific hazards common to early education settings.
- Safe procedures for lifting
  - Hold child or object close to body and bend from knees. Avoid twisting body when lifting
  - Avoid lifting children. Encourage children's independence whenever possible
  - When a child has a playground fall, crouch next to the child and provide comfort. Allow the child to walk to the area where first aid will be administered. If the child is not able, leave the child where he is and stay with him until he's ready or call for additional medical assistance
- Safe procedures for carrying loads
  - Divide large loads into two smaller loads and make two trips
  - Use a cart.
  - Have another staff member help you.
- Interacting with children on the floor
  - Avoid sitting for too long on the floor without back support
  - Lean against a wall or sturdy furniture, using a pillow for back support.
  - Do stretching exercises [1]
- Guidelines for handwashing
  - Effective method/procedures
  - Frequency
    - Upon arrival
    - Before and after eating, handling food, feeding a child, giving medication
    - After diapering, using the toilet or helping a child use a toilet, handling bodily fluid, handling uncooked food, handling pets, cleaning or handling garbage [2]
- Recognizing signs of communicable illness
  - Characteristics of common childhood illnesses
  - Methods of illness transmission
  - Guidelines for excluding children showing signs of illness
- Communicable illnesses that present particular risk to staff who may become pregnant
  - CMV, Chicken pox, Fifth disease, Rubella, Hepatitis B [3]
  - Encourage staff in child-bearing years to alert their primary health-care providers to their field of employment. It is advisable to get screened to determine immunity to specific communicable diseases prior to becoming pregnant
- Promoting wellness
  - Rest, diet, and exercise
  - Routine health examinations
  - Stress management
- General safety practices
  - Wear shoes that protect and support feet and make it easy to negotiate classroom and playground obstacles.
- Environmental hazards
  - Special handling instructions of any chemicals the employee is exposed to; for example, the need to mix bleach water solutions in a well-ventilated area
- Training in bloodborne pathogens exposure control plan
  - Tailored to job classification
  - Universal precautions
  - Procedures for using and disposing of gloves
  - Staff training in this area must include federally-mandated content, and needs to be interactive. This following excerpt from *Responding to OSHA's Final Rule for 'Occupational Exposure to Bloodborne Pathogens'* [4] details required training content:
    - How to obtain a copy of the regulatory text and an explanation of its contents
    - Information on the epidemiology and symptoms of bloodborne diseases
    - Ways in which bloodborne pathogens are transmitted
    - Explanation of the exposure control plan and how to obtain a copy
    - Information on how to recognize tasks that might result in occupational exposure

 Early Education DIRECTOR'S MANUAL

FORM 7.26

On Health and Safety (Continued)

- Information on the basis of selection, types, proper use, location, removal, handling, decontamination, and disposal of personal protective equipment
- Information on hepatitis B vaccination such as safety, benefits, efficacy, methods of administration, and availability
- Information on whom to contact and what to do in an emergency, including HIV/HBV exposure
- Information on how to report an exposure incident and on the post-exposure evaluation and follow-up
- Information on warning labels and signs, where applicable, and color-coding
- Question-and-answer session on any aspect of the training by a health care professional

Federal requirements
Exposure to Bloodborne Pathogens. The Occupational Safety and Health Administration (OSHA) requires all employers to adopt a written "Bloodborne Pathogen Exposure Control Plan" to include the following at a minimum:
1. The exposure determination for each job classification within your program
2. The procedures for evaluating the circumstances surrounding an exposure incident
3. The schedule and method for implementing sections of the standard covering
   - Methods of compliance
   - First-aid reporting procedures
   - Hepatitis B vaccination
     - Vaccination follow-up
     - Post-exposure follow-up
   - Communication of hazards to employees through in-service training
   - Record keeping

Endnotes
1. Cal/OSHA Consultation. *Ergonomics for very small business.* Child Care Providers (poster) http://www.dir.ca.gov/dosh/dosh_publications/Erg_ChildCare.pdf.
2. American Academy of Pediatrics and American Public Health Association. 2002. *Child care providers' health and well-being: Applicable standards from caring for our children.*
3. ACSI, Responding to OSHA's final rule for "Occupational Exposure to Bloodborne Pathogens," *Christian School Legal and Administrative Issues* (also available on the ACSI website).
4. Susan S. Aronson. 2001. *Taking care of caregivers: Wellness for every body.* Child Care Information Exchange (July), 40–44.

 *Early Education* DIRECTOR'S MANUAL

FORM 7.27

Beginnings Workshop

Wise Moves	
Challenge	**Wise Moves**
Lifting children, toys, supplies	Avoid lifting by having children climb steps with help. Pull child or object to be lifted as close as possible directly in front of you; squat and wrap your arms around whatever you are lifting. Then tighten stomach muscles and use thigh muscles to raise yourself and your load. To lower objects and children, slide them down your body to the level where you can squat or kneel to put them in their destination.
Inadequate work heights	Reorganize your supplies so that frequently used objects are stored in places where you can reach them easily. Store heavy objects at waist height so that you don't have to lift them. Adjust diapering and similar work surfaces to waist height. Use adult-sized chairs whenever you can. If you can't sit next to the children as you help them, squat or kneel on a kneepad. Use step stools to reach high places.
Lifting infants in and out of cribs	Do not use cribs with floor-level mattresses or those that do not have a side that you can drop when putting children in or out. Get yourself and the child as close to the crib side as possible before you lift.
Frequent sitting on the floor without back support	When possible, sit against a wall or a piece of furniture that supports your back. Sit with a little pillow in the small of your back when you can. Stretch when you get up.
Carrying heavy objects or children	Use carts and strollers. Let children climb up with a step stool. If possible, divide heavy loads into several smaller loads, use carts that can be slid under each load, and then tilt the load onto a cart.
Awkward posture to open windows or adjust objects	Move objects away from the window to get as close as possible to it. Put one foot on a step stool for better leverage. Lubricate the window mechanism to make the window easier to open. When the job is hard, ask a coworker to help you.
Sweeping/picking up crumbs and small toys from the floor	Use a long-handled dustpan and broom. Keep separate clean ones for toys and for things going into the trash.
Caring for children with special needs	Get specific training from the child's physical therapist about how to move and carry the child.
Caring for children during active play when sudden moves may be needed	Avoid twisting. Practice turning and bending to intercept a running or falling child so that the moves become natural. Bend your knees when pushing children in swings. Use good body mechanics when you help children on and off equipment.

King, Gratz, Scheuer, and Claffey. The ergonomics of child care: Conducting worksite analyses. Work 6 25–32. Child Care Information Exchange 7/01—52 Permission to reprint granted

 *Early Education* DIRECTOR'S MANUAL

FORM 7.28

Observation Form

Teacher:	Date:
Classroom:	Time:
Ages of children:	
Observer:	

Overall theme and curriculum for the month:

Activities the children are engaged in:

General observations:

Learning needs that are being met:

Suggestions for increased learning and effectiveness:

Planned activities during observation:

Student response to activities:

Needs of the children:

Suggestions for next time:

purposeful design   *Early Education* DIRECTOR'S MANUAL

FORM 7.29

Peer Observation Form

Peer Observer:
Teacher:
Date:
Time:
Activity:

What activities were the children engaged in?

Did they seem to respond well to the direction by the teacher?

Were the activities presented in such a way as to develop competence in the children?

Observations of the children:

Areas of strength of the teacher:

Suggestions for improvement:

Other comments:

purposeful design   *Early Education* DIRECTOR'S MANUAL

FORM 7.30

Professional Growth Plan

Teacher:	Date:

My long-range professional goals are as follows:

I plan on working on the following area this year to achieve my long-term goals:

I hope to have this finished by (month and year):

This year I plan on developing myself professionally in these two areas:

Area	Timeline	Specifics
1.		
2.		

I make an agreement to receive _____ hours of professional growth training by doing as follows:

Attending conventions, conferences, workshops _____ hours

Attending a class _____ hours

Reading books and articles _____ hours

Observing in other classrooms _____ hours

Signatures:

Teacher: _____ Date: _____

Director: _____ Date: _____

purposeful design   *Early Education* DIRECTOR'S MANUAL

FORM 7.31

Professional Growth Track

Teacher:				School Year:		
Months	Date	Class	Seminars	Observations	Articles/Books	Total
September						
October						
November						
December						
January						
February						
March						
April						
May						
June						
July						
August						
Comments						

Grand total:

purposeful design   *Early Education* DIRECTOR'S MANUAL

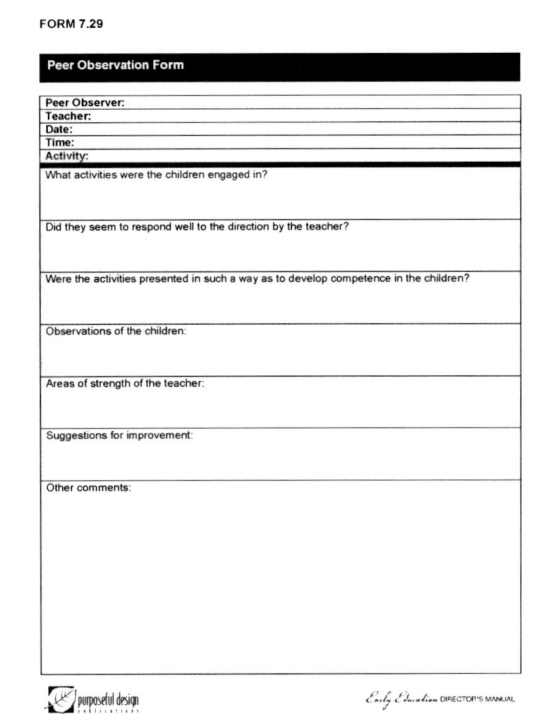

FORM 7.32

Growth Improvement Plan

The purpose of this Growth Improvement Plan is to help you, under the leadership of the director, to increase your skills as an early educator. The decisions you make in your job performance affect the entire early education team as well as the children and their parents.

Employee	Date
Situation	

What were my actions/decisions?

Why does the situation need to be changed?

How might I handle such situations in the future?

How do my actions/decisions affect	
children?	
parents?	
fellow staff members?	

When do we meet again?	Date

We, <staff member's name> and <church/school early education director's name> agree on this Growth Improvement Plan and understand that the plan will be reevaluated. If progress has not been made, the following actions will be taken to correct the situation:

purposeful design

Early Education DIRECTOR'S MANUAL

CURRICULUM DESIGN AND IMPLEMENTATION

Chapter 8

"For I know the plans I have for you," declares the Lord, "plans to prosper you and not to harm you, plans to give you hope and a future." Jeremiah 29:11

What Is Curriculum?

Curriculum has been described as the "design of experiences and activities developed by the teachers to help children increase their competence; this should be thought of as including everything that happens to children during their time at the preschool."[1] This broad definition encompasses all the teacher says and does. It includes the classroom environment, the materials made available to children, and the daily class routines. Effective curriculum is not haphazard but reflects a comprehensive plan that guides all that happens in the class. Curriculum in Christian early education programs addresses the spiritual implications of children's development within every domain, recognizing the interplay of physical, social, emotional, cognitive, and spiritual development and the need for full maturity in each area in order to fulfill God's purposes.

Biblical Integration

As Christian early educators, one of the most important things we can do is to focus on the spiritual development of our young children. How children view God and what role He plays in their lives will determine their future. Unless spiritual development is nurtured, children will miss out on the very meaning of life and the joy that comes with a life well lived. With our desire for children to become healthy, whole persons comes the responsibility for building strong spiritual foundations to help prepare them for life. Ultimately, much of what life is about is a spiritual or moral issue. According to George Barna, most adult Christians had placed their trust in Christ by age thirteen.[2] By then a child's spiritual identity has been put in place. This fact places a tremendous responsibility on parents, schools, and churches—to make the most of every opportunity.

Christian early education programs are committed to helping children develop a biblical worldview, which is a coherent, God-centered view of all of life. Because of this commitment, the Bible permeates every aspect of the curriculum and is the central guide for all that is taught. Those who plan curriculum must exercise caution so that the spiritual component does not become a separate subject area, set apart from all others. Christian programs are distinct in this regard. "Biblical integration brings to light the truth (or error) of any subject by interpreting it through Scripture. Biblical integration is concerned with wholeness."[3] Biblical integration is not complete unless it includes God's purposes as a whole. Young children must learn about their Creator, His redemptive plan, and what He wants to accomplish through them, or efforts at biblical integration are reduced to bits and pieces of content that can be meaningless to children. Simply quoting Scripture is not practicing integration. The principle exemplified in each Scripture must be communicated, along with ways in which that principle applies to the life of the child. Spontaneous teachable moments of drawing attention to God's creation are a part of bringing the curriculum alive and cultivating children's spiritual development. In these and other ways, teachers play an essential role in helping children connect biblical truth to their daily lives.

A Biblically Integrated Early Education Program

Christian early education programs integrate Christian principles and biblical concepts throughout the day and across the curriculum. Additionally, staff members recognize their significant role in introducing children to Christ through both modeling and direct instruction. If a program is to be biblically integrated, its leaders must make its spiritual mission their priority. Here are some considerations for evaluating the degree of biblical integration in your program:

■ *Guiding statements*

- Scripture is interwoven in written documents and in classroom and program activities.
- The program's mission encompasses a spiritual purpose and has a spiritual impact on the child, the child's family, and the community.
- The philosophy of the program reflects biblical principles.
- The program has developed biblically based student outcomes for all areas of development.

■ *Intentionality*

- Children's spiritual development receives focused attention, is planned for, and is assessed.
- Prayer is an integral part of program planning and implementation.
- Staff members take advantage of every classroom opportunity (routines, environment, transitions) to communicate God's love to the children and to incorporate prayer and worship into the program.

■ *Staff*

- In recruiting and selecting staff, administrators seek those who have a vital relationship with Christ and a passion for Christian education.
- Staff members dedicate themselves to the work of the Holy Spirit and to the renewing of their minds in the likeness of Christ so that they can be living examples in daily classroom life.
- Staff members are instructed in principles and techniques for integrating faith and learning so that they are able to teach biblically integrated lessons.

- Staff members receive ongoing training in topics related to young children's spiritual development.

▪ Instruction

- The Bible is taught as the source of truth. Bible stories are presented as actual happenings and are taught in ways appropriate to the children's developmental level.
- The biblical principles that are taught are meaningful and relevant to the experiences of young children and take into account their cognitive limitations.
- Within every domain, lessons reflect a Christian worldview. Teachers consider how the content they present relates to the whole of God's truth, and they shape children's understanding accordingly.
- Teachers guide children to think critically, preparing them to test information in the light of God's truth.
- Instruction within every domain is designed to help children understand God's world and their redemptive role as God's image bearers within His world.

▪ Interaction

- Staff members are alert to opportunities to connect biblical truth to children's daily experiences, guiding children to recognize God's sovereignty.
- Staff members model and join children in spontaneous prayers responding to God's creation with gratitude and requesting His help in faith.
- Staff members guide children in applying biblical principles in resolving conflict.
- In conversations with children, teachers clarify, filter, and correct misinterpretations, leading children into truth.

Best Practices in the Early Education Curriculum

The variety and innovation found in early education programs is truly something to celebrate. Avenues for promoting children's growth encompass a range of strategies. However, excellent early education has a few foundational principles at its core.

▪ Understanding child development

As discussed in chapter 3, in planning their early education programs, directors must take into account the characteristics specific to the young learner. Just as a high-school geometry teacher needs an in-depth understanding of advanced mathematics, an effective early educator needs specialized knowledge of child development. Early educators should be grounded in the principles that characterize growth and learning, as well as specific characteristics common to each age group. (See form 8.1 Developmental Profile and 8.2 Suggestions for Recording Children's Development.) This foundational awareness of how young children learn is essential for successful teaching. Directors should not assume that each staff member has a thorough understanding of child development. An applicant's knowledge of child development should be assessed and determined before he or she is hired. Or such knowledge may be developed over time through coursework, conferences, and in-service training. Children benefit from adults who have a clear understanding of what they need. It is the director's responsibility to ensure that the curriculum reflects this understanding.

▪ Active learning

There are significant cognitive differences between young children and adults. Preschool children have difficulty with abstractions; they learn best through concrete experiences. Therefore, early educators must facilitate and guide children's learning rather than simply dispense knowledge. Guided experiences with the world around them encourage children in their intellectual development. Young children are full of energy. They are constantly moving, touching, and interacting with materials, leading to hands-on learning, or "learning by doing." As they interact with their environment, children gather information, make assumptions about it, and test their assumptions. Thus their experiences form the basis for their knowledge and enable them to find meaning and order in their world. In early education, children need to touch, handle, and discover for themselves rather than just listening to lectures or filling out worksheets.

Early education programs allow children to choose from a variety of activities in self-selected learning centers. These centers offer the materials, the time, and the independence children need to make choices and thus discover on their own. (See form 8.3 Centers Checklist.) Children who are often moved from one activity to another as a large group have little time for social interaction and exploration. Children who are required to sit for long periods of time can become frustrated, and their frustration limits their learning. More importantly, time that could be spent in rich, active learning experiences is lost.

Play has purpose

Play is a natural avenue for growth and learning. Thus there is wisdom in cooperating with God's design by making the most of children's play opportunities. Teachers maximize children's play through the selective provision of materials and the sensitive use of questions and comments. Play promotes children's development simultaneously in every domain. Play allows children to experiment and explore, to try out ideas, to move their bodies, to use their imagination, and to be in control. Repeated experiences with play and with learning materials lead to a feeling of competence, one of the most significant feelings of early childhood. Allowing children to be independent and to do things for themselves fosters

confidence. Children who challenge themselves to try new experiences develop competence. Play provides a safe and effective arena in which children can develop foundational skills and the essential perception of themselves as effective, capable persons.

> God has made all of us different. So what we want to provide in our classrooms is variety and flexibility. We provide some activities to see, some to hear, and some to touch and do. We use music, and puzzles, and role play. We try to be sensitive to children who like to work in groups and sensitive to children who enjoy working alone. Children are usually willing and able to do activities that don't match a learning preference of theirs, if they know that sooner or later they will get to do something that appeals to them.[4]
>
> —Karyn Henley

Responsive curriculum

In a class of twenty four-year-olds, it's normal to see a wide range of abilities. Variations in development are also normal in early childhood, and the early education curriculum needs to account for that reality. An effective early education curriculum is responsive to individual needs. The curriculum needs to be implemented in a flexible way, with teachers modifying the activities according to each child's ability to participate. Open-ended materials and activities that provide a range of challenges are some of the best ways of accommodating individual needs.

Integrated learning

Early educators recognize that children's learning cannot always be neatly compartmentalized into subject areas or development domains. Many typical early childhood activities nurture learning in a variety of disciplines. (See form 8.9 Planning Thematic Units.) For example, a child involved in a classroom cooking project is learning math and science concepts, participating in literacy experiences, and engaging in language development. The overlap among subject areas and developmental levels requires teachers to be vigilant in selecting the most enriching activities, including experiences that allow for in-depth investigation. In considering the content to be taught, early educators should choose topics that are meaningful to young children. Unfamiliar concepts are made relevant to children as teachers connect new information to prior experiences.

> Integrated curriculum is an effective approach with preschool-age children because it makes use of their strengths as learners. It offers them interesting and meaningful projects they can explore fully with their hands, bodies, minds, and senses. [5]

■ Balanced programs

The concept of balance in an early education program refers to an awareness of the needs of the whole child and of how the child's needs determine the schedule and the structure of the day's activities. As noted above, the curriculum is not focused solely on the cognitive development of children but also on their physical, social, emotional, and spiritual needs. There should be a balance between time spent in child-initiated activities and time spent in teacher-directed experiences. In child-initiated activities, the child is active in making choices, creating plans, and acting on those plans through play. However, the teacher leads the learning and development of the children by determining the content they are exposed to and the experiences that are provided for them. Teachers need to pay attention to the length

of group times for various age groups, recognizing that children's ability to attend to and benefit from large-group instruction will vary among the age groups. Some fear that providing a program that allows for the active involvement of the children will lead to chaos, lack of structure, and low expectations for their learning. This fear results from a misperception— the assumption that an open-ended program like this is not intentional, purposeful, and well thought out. This assumption can lead to an aversion to messy or noisy activities. However, in a balanced program, the teacher is not passive. Instead, the teacher plays an active role, observing and interacting with children, scaffolding their learning. The teacher is intentional in selecting activities for which the benefit to the child is the supreme value.

Developing a Curriculum Framework

Curriculum is sometimes misunderstood as merely purchased materials, such as textbooks or workbooks. Confusing these curricular resources with the curriculum framework is a misperception that can narrow a program's focus and impact. Programs that rely on purchased materials to dictate their activities and priorities run the risk of failing to meet their stated objectives or to fulfill their overall mission. It is tempting to assume that purchased materials will assure a high-quality program. True, such materials can be valuable resources in supporting the school's own curriculum framework. However, because each school is unique in its philosophy, mission, and community, the curriculum must be purposefully designed to align successfully with the school's distinctive culture. There is an overwhelming body of knowledge to choose from when one is determining what should be taught. When individual teachers make decisions in isolation, the instructional program is weakened because there is no clear vision of the educational process from beginning to end. Curriculum development requires careful planning and schoolwide participation before classroom instruction so that each experience can build toward a larger goal. This process empowers the teacher to be an effective educator and allows the child to receive a more complete education. A well-designed curriculum framework brings coherence and unity to the school's instructional program. It also provides a basis for assessing the program to identify its strengths and weaknesses before reviewing and adjusting it accordingly.[7]

A curriculum framework is an intentional plan that outlines the foundational components of the curriculum. The framework includes the essential elements of the content to be taught and guides the context in which learning takes place. This content is developed from the expected student outcomes and the context from the center's overall philosophy. Establishing a curriculum framework ensures a focus on *where we're going* as educators and protects us from misdirected activity and wasted effort. Having outcomes in mind from the beginning of the educational process provides us with a scaffold on which to construct activities that will support children in reaching these outcomes. Children benefit because they will learn in an environment designed to facilitate their reaching their full potential, a setting in which their well-rounded development is not left to chance. When we clearly articulate our program's goals, parents benefit by being able to understand the expected outcomes and to support their children's development toward them. Parents are also assured of the wise use of their tuition dollars toward education that is focused and purposeful. Teachers benefit from having a picture of what they're working toward, and that picture assists them in planning a total program and specific activities that facilitate the children's development.

■ *Components of the curriculum framework*

- Guiding statements: Mission, vision, and core values
- Philosophy of teaching and learning

Balanced Programs Use a Variety of Strategies

How should teaching be done in early education programs? Research indicates that many teaching strategies can work. Good teachers acknowledge and encourage children's efforts, model and demonstrate, create challenges and support children in extending their capabilities, and provide specific directions or instruction. All of these teaching strategies can be used in the context of play and structured activities. Effective teachers also organize the classroom environment and plan ways to pursue educational goals for each child as opportunities arise in child-initiated activities and in activities planned and initiated by the teacher. This panoply of strategies provides a tool kit from which the teacher can select the right tool for the right task at the right time. Children need opportunities to initiate activities and follow their interests, but teachers are not passive during these initiated and directed activities. Similarly children should be actively engaged and responsive during teacher-initiated and directed activities. Good teachers help support the child's learning in both types of activities. They also recognize that children learn from each other and from interactions with the physical environment. Since pre-school programs serve so many ends simultaneously, multiple pedagogical approaches should be expected.[6]

Key Principles for Effective Curriculum Development

- The curriculum framework flows from the early education program's philosophy of teaching and learning.
- Curriculum is designed to accomplish the overall outcomes for the children in the program.
- Staff input is incorporated into the curriculum planning process.
- Curriculum is tailored to the characteristics and needs of each age group.
- Curriculum is adjusted to meet the unique needs of the children enrolled in the program.
- Resource materials are accessed to support the curriculum. These resources are not referred to as the curriculum.
- Teachers are held accountable for implementing the curriculum framework.
- The curriculum framework is shared with parents in order to facilitate a partnership with the home.

- Expected student outcomes (ends)
- Goals and objectives for each age group
- Suboutcomes, or benchmarks
- Sequence
- Learning context
- Assessment

Guiding statements. Written documents articulating the philosophy, the mission, the vision, and the core values of the center define the purpose of its early education program. These documents are the foundation of the curriculum framework.

Philosophy of teaching and learning. A written philosophy of teaching and learning is essential to a unified, effective program. This document expresses the program's beliefs about the nature of growth and learning in the young child and the instructional practices that flow from those beliefs. Additionally, Christian early education programs articulate their perspectives on the process of spiritual growth and formation in young children. The program's views on spiritual development will impact the delivery of the curriculum, the role of the teacher, and the context of the classroom.

Expected student outcomes (ends). Outcomes are the competencies and characteristics that children will have attained when they complete the early education program. The outcomes broadly identify the program expectations for each student in the spiritual, physical, cognitive, social, and emotional domains. ACSI has a set of model outcomes to use as a guide, which is included in chapter 2.

Goals for each age group. Outcomes define what the end product will look like, but goals for each age group will help in determining how those outcomes will be achieved. (See form 8.8 Objectives.) Goals should be progressive, building on competencies gained each year. If outcomes are established in each developmental area, then goals for each age group can be written in relation to each of these outcomes. This process creates a base for achieving the outcomes. Developmental goals can be segmented into three components: skills, knowledge, and dispositions, which have been defined as follows:

- Skills: small units of action (counting, drawing a circle)
- Knowledge or content: vocabulary, facts, concepts (knowing the name of the circle, understanding the concept that numerals represent quantity)

- Dispositions: tendencies to respond to a situation in a certain way (kindness, curiosity)[8]

By ascertaining the skills, knowledge, and dispositions that we want the children to gain, we can more effectively plan instructional activities and educational strategies that will help them reach those goals. At the end of the process, the program will have a list of developmental goals for each age group, within each domain, based on the expected outcomes. These age-group-specific goals can be provided to parents and referenced by staff members for use in lesson planning.

Suboutcomes, or benchmarks. Because goals can be very broad, it is valuable to break them down into more specific descriptions that can be demonstrated and measured.[9] These descriptions, or *benchmarks*, clarify the goals and help teachers recognize the many small components a child displays on the way to achieving the goal. For example, the goal "Develops a sense of responsibility" might have several benchmarks, including "Pushes chair into the table after lunch." When teachers work together on establishing benchmarks for the goals, they know when they observe behaviors that verify a child's progress.

Sequence. Once the skills to be developed, the content to be delivered, and the dispositions to be nurtured have been identified for each age group, these benchmarks can be sequenced, so that teachers know when concepts will be introduced. This process serves several purposes. Skills and knowledge that must be learned sequentially can be introduced at the appropriate time and to the appropriate age group and can move from simple to complex. Having a planned sequence reduces overlap or duplication of material covered by the different age groups. Finally, charting the sequence of the benchmarks ensures that key components are not omitted or overlooked.

Age-level expectations must be held with an awareness of the wide variation in abilities that is considered normal in young children. Because of these normal variations, children in the four-year-old class may be functioning with three-year-old skill in some areas and with four- or five-year-old skill in others.

Learning context. The learning context encompasses the classroom environment, the materials available to the children, the learning strategies teachers use with individuals and groups, and the daily schedule. Because a significant amount of what young children learn happens as they interact with classroom materials, the learning environment also delivers the curriculum and must be planned. The role of the environment and the materials in the curriculum will be addressed comprehensively in chapter 9. As children play, they are learning in many domains simultaneously. Thus, when planning curriculum, teachers need to take play into account as an avenue for learning. Teachers need to be sensitive to teachable moments as well. Instruction happens as teachers interact with children on the playground and in centers, asking questions that lead children to discovery and supporting children in their play to lead them to new concepts.

This component of the curriculum framework documents the strategies teachers will use in leading children's learning as well as the techniques teachers will use to support children's development during times of routine care (toileting, mealtimes, naptimes). Since *everything that happens during the child's day can be considered curriculum*, children miss out when early educators overlook opportunities to make daily routines meaningful. Closely related to these routines are the strategies teachers use to help children make smooth transitions between activities.

The daily schedule also helps to shape the learning context. Elements such as the length of group times, the amount of time devoted to child-initiated learning, and the balance of time spent indoors and outdoors are components of the daily schedule that should be thoughtfully planned and recognized as valuable resources for achieving the program's goals. The director sets standards for each element of the learning context, communicates the standards to the staff, and monitors the effectiveness of each element.

Assessment. The framework for curriculum is not complete unless it includes a written plan for assessing the children's progress toward the goals. The program must identify performance standards that define how children can demonstrate that they have achieved the expected outcomes. Strategies for collecting information through observation and for using that information to inform the curriculum need to be articulated and communicated to the staff. Teachers must clearly understand the expectations for observation—frequency, focus, and guidelines. They will also need to be given guidelines, training, and tools for making evaluative judgments based on the observations they have collected and for communicating to the parents an overall assessment of each child's progress. At the end of the year, the preschool director will collect and review these assessments as a means of evaluating the program.

■ Steps in developing the curriculum framework

Program administrators initiate the process of curriculum development. The planning process involves the following:

The director begins the process:

1. Develops a philosophy of teaching and learning. Staff members will provide input, but the director guides the process. If a philosophy statement exists but is ambiguous or difficult to explain, the director should edit it for clarity. If the philosophy statement is incomplete,

the director should identify the overlooked areas and address them.

2. Creates a list of expected student outcomes that describe what she wants children to "look like" when they leave the early education program.

3. Predetermines guidelines for how to encourage the staff to be involved in the process.

4. Schedules a planning session with the staff, beginning the process with prayer.

The planning session with the staff includes the following:

1. reviewing the program's mission, philosophy, and expected student outcomes.

2. reviewing and defining the curricular approach used in the center, such as theme-based, skill-based, or literature-based.[10]

3. brainstorming monthly emphases, to be used programwide, that will support the curricular approach used in the center.

4. aligning the learning objectives that will guide each month's curricular delivery.

5. ensuring that the activities will be tied to learning objectives for children, all directed toward achieving the expected student outcomes.

6. reviewing age-appropriate strategies that will be utilized to introduce concepts.

7. planning each month's Bible themes, verses, character traits, and Bible truths.

8. creating a chart presenting a yearlong overview of the program's curriculum framework.

9. creating a one-page monthly overview identifying the areas to be covered. The monthly overview can include
   • Bible truths
   • character traits

- language
- literacy
- numeracy
- science
- music
- art
- motor skills
- social/emotional development (life skills)

A number of programs use a thematic approach to curriculum based on monthly themes or topics of interest to young children, with weekly units to support each theme or topic. (See form 8.9 Planning Thematic Units.)

Translating monthly overviews into weekly plans. Lesson plans play an important role for both the teacher and the director. Thoughtful teaching relies on understanding how each planned activity supports the overall expected student outcomes. The process of preparing lesson plans allows the teacher to think through these issues. Plans should indicate how the activities are intended to impact the children in each developmental area, as well as what spiritual emphasis they will have. Lesson-plan forms should reflect the content areas outlined in the curriculum framework to ensure that the planned activities will encourage learning and development in each area. Lesson planning begins with the *end*, or where we want children to be at the end of the year. Daily, weekly, and monthly activities should be planned strategically to get children to that place.

Webbing. Webbing, which is the brainstorming part of lesson planning, involves selecting a unit theme or topic and brainstorming ideas for teaching specific areas.[11] Using the monthly overviews, teachers can develop individual web units to break the monthly plan down into specific activities. They can create web units by creating a chart with the theme in the middle of the page and the content areas surrounding the theme, as follows:

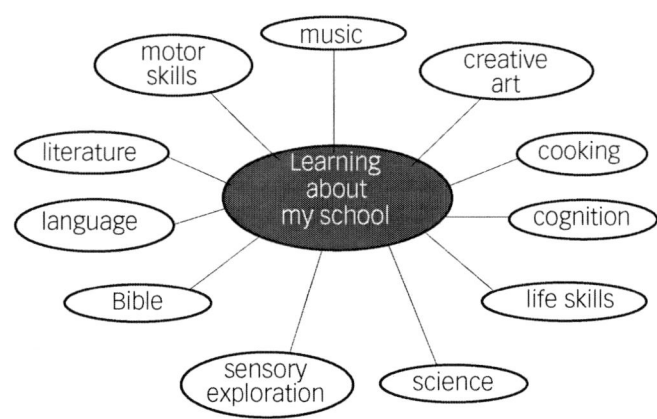

Under each content area, teachers should leave room for a list of activities. The process works best when a group of teachers brainstorm the activities. It can be helpful to divide the teachers into groups according to the ages of the children they teach. The next step is deciding which of the ideas generated have the most merit. To decide, teachers examine which of the proposed activities line up with the goals and benchmarks in the curriculum framework and then use the selected activities to develop their lesson plans. In order to ensure a balanced approach to learning, the lesson plans should contain the appropriate learning categories, which include these:

Bible	literacy	numeracy	language
creative art	music	life skills	cognition
science	motor skills	social/ emotional	sensory exploration

Head teachers should turn in weekly lesson plans to the director (or other appropriate staff person) for a review of content. Such a review helps the director stay abreast of classroom activities and accomplishments, and ensures that these are consistent with the program's philosophy. Lesson plans should be returned promptly to staff members with comments, both commendations and recommendations. Teachers should make their lesson plans as specific as possible so that parents and other staff members will be familiar with the activities for the week. After teachers have finalized their plans, they can select supplies and materials to have ready for each day. Monthly themes and weekly unit topics can be listed on the lesson plans, which can indicate the activities for each day of the week and possibly the order in which they will be done. As teachers implement their lesson plans, they should note how effective the activities were, including how well the children learned and how much interest they showed. Later, they should modify the lesson plans accordingly to better meet the children's needs.

Selecting resources. It is not an easy task to create a curriculum framework, let alone to develop learning components for each area of a child's development. The resources you'll need range from teacher activity books to complete course units that cover a year or a specific topic. Whether it is separate activities that you find to use in a certain lesson plan or complete guides for language arts or Bible, these resources can be valuable tools for implementing your program's curriculum framework and supporting your lesson plans.

The first step in selecting resources for a curriculum framework is to evaluate the needs. If the teacher is currently using a published curriculum, she will want to evaluate how well it aligns with each component of the program's curriculum framework. Is it compatible with the philosophy of teaching and learning? Do the activities provided correspond with the expected student outcomes? Are there certain skills or content areas that are not covered? Identifying and documenting the gaps between the resources available and the resources needed is the beginning of the search for resources. After assessing how well the current resources align with the curriculum framework, the teacher prioritizes the gaps, deciding

which ones are the most significant and should be addressed first. Next she generates a list of possible resource materials and selects the most promising for review. If any program in the community is using an interesting resource, it can be beneficial for the teacher to make an appointment to observe its use firsthand. The process of review should be guided by developing a rubric that identifies the children's needs and allows the teacher to weigh the pros and cons of each resource against those needs. (See form 8.11 Evaluation of Early Education Center's Curriculum.) A teacher will follow a similar process if her program relies primarily on teacher-developed resources. Whether curricular resources are purchased or developed, the evaluation and selection process needs to be comprehensive.

Monitoring curriculum implementation. In order for the program to be as effective as possible, the staff must be fully committed to implementing its philosophy and its stated objectives. This implementation involves ongoing professional learning and a strong desire to succeed in accomplishing specific goals. Directors need to identify the expected standards for implementing the curriculum framework. They need to inform teachers clearly of what is expected in teaching methods, types of activities, and the balance they need to provide in implementing their daily plan. Knowing these expectations will help teachers know whether they are on target. The director needs to conduct regular observations to ensure that the program is being implemented as planned.

Teachers should be aware of the overall program goals in order to work toward meeting them in the classroom. The director needs to check classroom environments on a regular basis, evaluating the available materials for appropriateness. She also needs to observe the types of activities that are offered. Giving staff clear expectations in these areas will minimize environments that are not suited for specific age ranges. New materials should be incorporated into each classroom on a regular basis, both by sharing and rotating existing materials among the classrooms and by having a regular plan for purchasing new items. Directors will need to give teachers direction about when lesson planning should be done and when the lesson plans need to be submitted.

Development and Learning by Domain

Seeking to meet the needs of the whole child, early education directors carefully monitor the program's curriculum to ensure that appropriate attention is given to each aspect of the child's development. This desire to provide a balanced program requires directors to segment the curriculum into categories based on developmental domains or learning content areas. Certainly, children's growth and learning will occur *across* domains and content areas, and skilled teachers take advantage of that reality. Despite the inherent limitations of an imposed structure, curriculum planning would be impractical in its absence. Directors need to consider the influence of a particular structure on the types and variety of learning experiences provided for children.

■ Spiritual development

The most significant aim of an early education program is helping young children develop a relationship with Christ. Expected student outcomes for children's spiritual development and the program's philosophy of teaching and learning set the stage for the early educator's work in this area. In the spiritual endeavor, early educators rely on the Holy Spirit, praying for the children in their class daily and seeking to be the Christlike model children need. In planning for children's spiritual development, early educators keep children's cognitive limitations in mind. They use language children can understand, select content that is meaningful to children, and clarify concepts they may find confusing. Curriculum in this area encompasses what children need to know about God, opportunities to respond to this knowledge, and ways children can apply biblical truth in daily life.

The importance of the Word of God. Early educators should integrate Christian principles into all program activities, but in addition the daily schedule should include a separate worship and Bible time. From the time children are very young, it is important for them to be exposed to Scripture. Placing God's Word in front of them each day through lessons, music, prayers, and verses helps children integrate biblical truth into their daily lives. Children need to see their teachers read the Word of God on a regular basis and refer to it often. The director should encourage the teachers to make their worship and Bible time alive and exciting for the children. An unprepared teacher reading a Bible story in a monotone will send the message that the Bible and worship are boring.

The words we use as educators can be powerful in shaping children's understanding of spiritual truths. We need to be mindful of how young children perceive the things we teach. We know that children learn concretely and therefore take almost everything literally. As a result we want to be careful not to mislead children into thinking that the stories they hear from the Bible are fiction. One way to avoid this misunderstanding is by reinforcing the idea that the events recounted in the Bible really happened and referring to them as Bible truths rather than stories.

Teaching children memory verses is one method of hiding God's Word in their hearts. Memory verses should be simple and brief, yet they should convey a message about how we are to live and conduct ourselves. In order for these powerful words to have a lasting impact, they need to be taught in a way that is developmentally appropriate. Here are a few guidelines for teaching memory verses:

- Have the Bible open as you teach a verse so children will understand that it is a part of God's book.
- Tell children where the verse is found in the Bible, and show them the place.
- Use a verse, or portion of a verse, that is no longer than one sentence.
- Talk about what the verse means and how it applies to the children's lives.
- Say the verse a few times before having children repeat it.
- Have the children repeat the verse together from time to time throughout the day.
- Avoid putting children on the spot by asking them to recite the verse if they do not volunteer.

The Bible tells us how to teach biblical truths to children: "These commandments that I give you today are to be upon your hearts. Impress them on your children. Talk about them when you sit at home and when you walk along the road, when you lie down and when you get up. Tie them as symbols on your hands and bind them on your foreheads. Write them on the doorframes of your houses and on your gates" (Deuteronomy 6:6–9). As these verses suggest, biblical truths are not taught just at scheduled "Bible times." Teachable moments present themselves throughout the day. As each school day begins, teachers should lead the children in prayer and praise for the day God made and throughout the day should lead them in giving thanks for what they see, hear, touch, smell, and taste.

The priority of prayer. Children need to be taught that communication with the Father is essential and that prayer is a conversation with God. Teaching children the discipline of folding their hands and closing their eyes can be effective in helping them stay focused on praying. The classroom environment should be one in which children are encouraged to pray during group time, snack time, lunch time,

and throughout the day. Spontaneous prayers of thanksgiving should be common in Christian early education centers. Children who often see adults modeling prayer are more likely to feel comfortable with praying aloud and with practicing this discipline in their own lives.

Chapel times. Chapel times take many different forms. Some schools come together for chapel daily, twice a week, or once a week. Sometimes each class has its own chapel time. The most successful chapel times are interactive ones held in a location where children are comfortable and free of distraction. Chapel times that mimic church services by having the children sit in pews are often not the best, since small children may not be able to see or to sit comfortably. Thinking through why the center has chapel time and what the children are intended to get out of it will help the program leaders clarify their priorities. They also need to decide who will plan the chapel time, including someone to lead in singing and someone to present a Bible lesson or truth. Some programs utilize their director, while others create a rotating schedule for staff members. On occasion, programs may involve church leaders. Those who plan chapel should know enough about young children to make the chapel time appropriately short and to use appropriate methods. Both classroom time and chapel time have a stronger impact when leaders have a plan specifying what Bible truths they will teach and in what sequence.

Moral development. Instruction in biblical truth involves teaching children how to tell right from wrong. Including stories that focus on right choices helps children to develop their moral compass. The Bible should be the central focus in teaching these truths. This teaching may lead into discussions about sin or the bad choices we sometimes make. Teachers can help children relate to these truths by keeping the concepts simple and talking at their level without shaming them. Unless they understand right and wrong, children will find it difficult to understand the concept of a Savior. Some schools may avoid these truths out of fear that some parents might be put off. The reality is that these truths may be the reason the parents chose a Christian program for their children.

Accountability. The staff should be trained in planning for children's spiritual development, and directors can hold teachers accountable by reviewing lesson plans, observing in the classroom, and holding discussions at staff meetings. Measuring the children's spiritual development is difficult but not impossible. Some methods include observing their behavior and noticing their interest in spiritual things. It is important to give feedback to the parents so that they can stay informed and can be united with the school in reinforcing their children's spiritual training at home.

Leading a child to Christ. The most rewarding experience a parent or teacher can have is to lead a child to a knowledge of God through a personal relationship with Jesus. The preschool age is not the time for mass evangelism, but it is a time when parents and other adults are making a lasting impression on the child. Those with whom children associate daily can lead them to Christ. The preschool staff will be effective in leading children to Christ if they are prepared, as follows:

- Each staff person must know Christ personally as Savior and Lord. The life of each staff member should portray Christ so that children see evidence that He is at work in people they know.
- The teacher must know every child personally and show genuine love and affection for each one.
- The teacher should pray for each child on a regular basis.
- All staff members should be sensitive to the

spiritual, emotional, social, physical, and intellectual needs of the children and should model Christ as they strive to meet those needs.

- Each staff member needs to know how to explain the plan of salvation in simple terms, using language that young children can understand.
- The staff should communicate with the parents when a child is expressing an interest in knowing Jesus as Savior. If the parents are Christians, they will want to be actively involved in leading their child to Christ.

Talking about spiritual things with one's children can be a rewarding experience. Children should be encouraged in their faith development. They should know that if they are interested in receiving Jesus as their Savior, their teacher is very willing to walk them through that experience.

When a child makes a commitment to Christ, the Christian teacher can continue to train and encourage the child in his or her faith. As children grow physically by eating nourishing food, so they grow in Jesus by receiving daily spiritual nourishment. Nevertheless, teachers of young children should avoid saying too much at any one time. Instead, they should build slowly, precept upon precept. The process takes time and dedication, but it is well worth the cost. It is what Christian early education is all about.

■ Social and emotional development

Early educators are keenly interested in social and emotional development. They know that the early years are crucial in children's developing self-concept, social competence, and ability to trust, all of which profoundly impact their spiritual development. Foundational beliefs about their own worth are established through the children's early experiences. Dispositions to care for others and to participate in community are formed when children are young. The Christian early education curriculum cultivates children's healthy development in these areas both indirectly through daily classroom routines and directly through planned instructional activities.

Children are taught that they are made in God's image, and this truth is reinforced by how they are treated and how they are taught to treat others. They are instructed in biblical principles that relate to social relationships, and the classroom structure gives them opportunities to put these principles into practice in various ways:

- Developing friendships
- Resolving conflicts and negotiating solutions
- Sharing, taking turns, and cooperating
- Helping and contributing to the classroom community
- Accepting others and developing positive attitudes toward differences
- Taking responsibility for their own actions
- Developing self-control
- Respecting themselves and others
- Expressing their thoughts, feelings, and needs in words
- Expressing their emotions in biblically acceptable ways
- Acquiring self-help skills and experiencing personal competence
- Collaborating with other children in investigation and learning
- Demonstrating empathy and care for others and responding to needs with helpfulness
- Treating others as they would like to be treated

Early educators show attitudes and practice behaviors that foster healthy social and emotional development. Thus they

- are responsive to individual children's needs

- are emotionally engaged, listening to the children, showing interest in their work, celebrating their accomplishments
- ensure that the classroom is an emotionally safe place for children, dealing firmly with bullying and teasing
- show an interest in the child's family
- provide secure, predictable classroom routines with consistent expectations

Children also benefit from exploring content knowledge related to the social sciences. Some of the concepts they encounter include these:

- appreciation and respect for God's plan for the family
- geographic features of the local community
- the role of some community workers
- awareness of holidays and historic events
- basic facts about the nation they live in

■ Physical development

From a neurological and physiological standpoint, perceptual and motor development is fundamental to learning. Physical development encompasses general health and nutrition, gross-motor coordination, and fine-motor skills. The curriculum addresses physical development through both individual choice and teacher-led activities. Teachers guide children to explore different ways of moving their bodies, leading them in purposeful activities designed to promote perceptual motor development. These movement activities can often be combined with music. At the same time, equipment specifically designed to encourage preschool children's physical development is available to children both on the playground and in the classroom. Suggestions for movement experiences and equipment that should be provided are included in chapter 9.

Teacher-led learning to promote large- and small-muscle development includes activities designed for the following:

- strengthening large and small muscles leading to controlled, purposeful movements
- developing body awareness
- exploring rhythm and various forms of creative movement
- exploring balance, position in space, and coordination of body movements

Teacher-led learning related to general health and physical well-being includes topics such as these:

- nutrition and healthy food choices
- physical activity as a key to good health
- appreciation and respect for the human body
- maintaining personal safety

■ Cognitive development

Learning across multiple domains. Mental growth and stimulation happen through a child's dynamic interaction with the environment, with other children, and with the teacher. Foundational thinking skills and general cognitive dispositions of curiosity and inquiry are cultivated in activities the child experiences in each of the content areas. Play is a significant vehicle for learning, and early educators have an active role in designing play experiences, providing stimulating materials, and engaging children's thinking through conversation. Suggestions for materials for child-initiated experiences in the following areas of cognitive development are included in the next chapter (on environment). Therefore, this section will focus on the teacher's role in guiding learning in these areas and the basic components that should be addressed. Neither teacher-guided activities nor child-initiated experiences provide a complete education on their own. Both are essential components of effective learning experiences.

Thinking skills. Early educators lead children to engage in inquiry that develops their ability to observe the environment and reflect on what they encounter. As a result, children grow in their ability to do the following:

- solve problems
- make predictions based on prior knowledge or experience
- understand cause-and-effect relationships

Children's growth in this area is guided by the teacher's questioning. Practices that promote children's thinking skills include these:

- asking children open-ended questions
- giving children "wait time" before asking them to respond
- asking children to think of ways of solving problems and to propose alternative possibilities
- encouraging children to formulate their own questions

Creative exploration and expression. Historically, one of the hallmarks of early education programs has been an emphasis on having children experience the creative arts. Children's engagement in creative activities supports cognitive development and integrates physical, emotional, and social development. Artistic expression can also be a way for children to express their thoughts and feelings to God. Teachers facilitate children's art experiences by providing a wide variety of materials and demonstrating techniques for various art media as appropriate to children's physical development.

Sensory activities. In an infant/toddler program, art projects focus on sensory experiences with paint, pudding, and other nontoxic materials. Safety and appropriateness should be kept in mind along with transitions for setup and cleanup. Toddlers love to scribble on anything. This activity leads to fine-motor control and eventually to writing. Having sufficient time and materials for these skills to develop is important. As children enter the preschool years, their interests, attention span, and skill level change dramatically. Art experiences should support this development. The process of making choices as they create art is more important than the actual products that children make. Activities will vary, but some common ones include tearing, cutting, gluing, painting, collage making, modeling with clay, and drawing with chalk, crayons, or markers. Children love to see their artwork displayed, and teachers can display their creative work on boards placed at a child's level, creating special frames and captions, and taking photographs of their artwork.

Dramatic play. Dramatic play encourages growth in all areas. Teachers promote language development by making available a variety of props to stimulate children to create fictional, real-life, and biblical scenarios that they can act out. Dramatizing situations builds children's language and social skills. Teachers need to allow children adequate time to get deeply involved in these play experiences. Dramatic play can take place both indoors and outdoors. Dramatizing a familiar story helps children understand a sequence of events, and acting out a Bible story gives the teacher a glimpse into the children's level of comprehension.

Sensory learning. Sensory learning takes place through integrating activities in which children use their senses—touching, tasting, smelling, seeing, and hearing. Sensory tables can be encouraged for the sense of touch, cooking for taste and smell, visual patterning for developing visual discrimination, and language and music for auditory discrimination. Water, sand, and mud activities allow children to develop their tactile system and touch receptors. These activities can be done both outdoors and indoors through the use of a sensory table. Teachers should support and make provision for these activities in spite of the inconvenience of cleaning up afterward.

Music, poetry, and chants. Music and singing in the classroom provide a wide variety of enriching experiences and support language and literacy development in particular. Fingerplays, chants, poetry, and nursery rhymes are forms of language play that prepare children for reading. Music can be used alone or in combination with instruments designed for children to use in the classroom. Through music, children are exposed to the concepts of volume, pitch, tempo, and rhythm. Their musical tastes and knowledge are broadened as they hear recorded music representing various cultures and musical styles.

Science. Although young children are not ready for the sophisticated and abstract concepts typically associated with the sciences, they are naturally curious about their world and interested in living organisms and in the physical environment. Teachers can cultivate children's inborn curiosity and guide their desire to discover. As children explore and observe their world, they are acquiring some of the basic competencies used in scientific investigation. Teachers support children's acquisition of these skills by providing activities that allow children to do the following:

- use their senses to gather information about the physical world
- describe their observations
- conduct simple experiments
- use tools such as a magnifying glass

Content areas related to children's understanding of science concepts include these:

- earth science: properties of rocks, soil, water, and air
- changing seasons

- features of weather
- life cycles of living organisms
- plant life

Language and literacy development. Children's language skills begin to develop in infancy. The preschool years are a time of rapid language growth in which parents and teachers lay the groundwork that enables children to become successful readers when they reach school age. Thus language and literacy development is a major focus of an early education curriculum.

Language. Children need multiple experiences with listening, speaking, and reading to develop a broad vocabulary, the ability to express their thoughts, and the ability to comprehend the words and sentences they hear. Language development is supported by interactive conversations between children and their teachers. The fuel for these conversations is rich sensory experiences provided in the curriculum. Early educators regularly foster language development by

- engaging children in conversation that builds on the children's interests
- encouraging children to ask questions and describe experiences
- encouraging children to express themselves in complete sentences
- giving children words to describe their experiences, thus expanding their vocabulary

Literacy. Just as language development includes both receptive and expressive components, children's literacy development culminates in their being able to take meaning from print and express thoughts with written words. As children develop, they begin to link language to the written page and to understand the concept of letters as symbols, eventually learning the sounds the letters represent. The ability to put words on paper progresses through various stages, beginning with scribbles that children may

say are "words." As children develop small-muscle control, they become increasingly able to form individual letters, and they learn to write their own name.

An appreciation for the written word needs to be developed at an early age. Teachers can promote such an appreciation by making available books that have meaning to the child, are enjoyable, foster imagination, reinforce known concepts, and introduce new ones. Early educators read aloud to children daily, recognizing that this activity is one of the most powerful ways of promoting literacy. Through interactive read-aloud experiences, children are introduced to the conventions of written language and the way stories are structured. When teachers enthusiastically share stories, children develop a love for words that propels their interest in learning to read.

Literacy concepts that teachers introduce to children include

- phonological awareness: understanding that language has structure and that words are made up of sounds and syllables
- print awareness: recognizing that print and written symbols convey meaning and awareness of the many purposes for writing
- alphabet knowledge: familiarity with the forms and functions of alphabet letters
- print conventions: understanding that books are read from front to back, pages are read from top to bottom, and sentences are read from left to right

Teachers support literacy development by providing activities that encourage children to

- predict story outcomes on the basis of the illustrations or of prior knowledge
- use rhyming words
- pay attention to the sounds that make up words and note their differences

- dictate stories and label drawings
- recognize common words in their environment
- recognize and write their own name
- know the names of the letters that make up their names
- understand the difference between letters, numbers, and words
- pretend to read (looking at pictures or at a book, and making up a story)
- follow one- and two-step directions
- become aware of the sequence of events in a story and retell familiar stories
- become competent in the use of writing instruments

Understanding Concepts Is Key

Developing expertise requires both a foundation of factual knowledge and skills and a conceptual understanding that allows facts to become "usable" knowledge. In the preschool years, key concepts can be quite basic and therefore easily overlooked. In mathematics, for example, children need to develop more than verbal counting skills and number recognition. They need to grasp "quantity." Similarly, emergent literacy requires not just that children recognize letters, but that they grasp the concept of "representation" involved in written words and illustrations. Because the preschool years are a time when children are rapidly developing skills and acquiring new knowledge, the importance of concepts can be overlooked. Curricula can be judged on the extent to which they promote learning of concepts as well as information and skills.[12]

Math. An informal understanding of mathematical concepts begins early in life, as children's curiosity and desire to explore lead them to notice patterns and discover relationships. Play experiences that allow children to manipulate materials are essential for the successful development of math concepts. Building with unit blocks and other forms of construction play is a vital part of children's math learning. Teachers play an active role in extending children's understanding of math concepts and in introducing math vocabulary through both directed activities and everyday classroom experiences.

Mathematical concepts and knowledge that teachers explore with children include the following:

- quantity (more, less, full, empty)
- measurement (time, length, weight, height)
- one-to-one correspondence
- spatial relationships and position words (over, under, beside)
- names of geometric shapes
- names of numerals
- terms describing position in a sequence (first, middle, last)

Teachers support children's acquisition of mathematical concepts and skills by providing activities that allow children to do the following:

- count
- identify likenesses and differences
- sort and classify objects by color, shape, or another characteristic
- order objects by specific characteristics (such as shortest to longest)
- represent information on a graph
- extend patterns

Assessment

A curriculum is only as successful as the growth and learning it stimulates. For this reason, it is imperative to assess children's learning and development as a means of refining the instructional program. For the classroom teachers, assessment refers to the process of observing children and collecting information about their growth for the purpose of using that information in their teaching. Because children's growth is uneven and episodic, learning must be assessed over time and demonstrated in the context of the child's activities.[13] Teachers rely on informal assessment to show them how to teach effectively.

■ Benefits of assessment

Because implementing assessment effectively requires a significant amount of time, energy, and expertise, it helps to focus on the many benefits of assessment to the child, the family, the teacher, and the whole program.

Assessment benefits the child because it

- validates the child by requiring that he or she be well known to the teacher
- assures that the child's development is attended to carefully and not left to chance

Assessment benefits the family because it

- assures parents that teachers are skilled professionals who are deeply interested in their child
- keeps parents informed and affirms their God-given role in the child's life
- gives parents insight into their child in a new setting
- gives parents an opportunity to share their insights
- connects the school to the home
- helps parents see and understand their child's progress

Assessment benefits teachers because it

- gives them insight into individual children's needs, strengths, and competencies
- leads them to professional development opportunities that increase skills

- increases their understanding of child development and the learning process
- gives them confidence in communicating with parents
- helps them develop the habit of keen awareness of children and their progress
- helps them design interesting and challenging activities

Assessment benefits the school because it

- helps answer the questions, Are we achieving our goals for children? Are we fulfilling our mission?
- gives evidence of how children in the school are growing and changing
- promotes innovation in classrooms and responsiveness to children's needs
- strengthens the school's reputation as an *education* center, as well as a *care* center

■ Types of assessment

In the typical early education center, most staff members will be engaged in assessment for the purpose of understanding children better and supporting their future growth. The term *assessment* also refers to measures used *outside* the classroom for a variety of purposes. Developmental screenings are quick and efficient assessments that help to identify children who may need further diagnostic testing, particularly in the area of health or of general development. Diagnostic testing is used to determine whether a child has a special need or disability as well as to measure the extent of the special need. Readiness assessments are used to decide whether a child will be successful in a kindergarten classroom as demonstrated by the attainment of specific skills and knowledge. A readiness test has value only when the areas evaluated match the skills that are needed to function in the classroom the child will be attending.[14]

When selecting a published assessment tool, directors must take into account the published purpose of the test, recognizing that tests are designed to achieve a specific purpose and will be valid only when used for that purpose. Thus, developmental screenings, readiness tests, and diagnostic tests are not interchangeable. In addition to using tests for their intended purpose, directors should use only tests that have demonstrated their reliability and validity. A reliable test will consistently produce the same results, and a valid test will measure what it is supposed to measure. Because reliability and validity are essential to formal assessment, classroom teachers shouldn't design their own screening tests because such tests will *not* be valid. However, teachers *do* need to be actively involved in designing forms for the ongoing assessment of children. With appropriate training, teachers can learn to be effective in conducting observations and gathering information about children's progress, steps that are critical for the informal assessment that is the classroom teacher's domain.

■ Observation

Observing children's behavior is a process of developing objective and accurate descriptions of children's activities. It is a skill that is refined over time through practice. Teachers who have a good understanding of child development will be most effective in their teaching strategies. Observing a young child involves paying careful attention to details of the child's behavior, recording those details in a structured manner, and assessing the implications of the child's actions. (See form 8.10 Pre-K Teacher's Observations for Kindergarten Placement.) A system of recording must be developed to document and preserve what teachers have seen and heard. Observations need to be

• Planned. Teachers need to plan their observations Their weekly lesson plans should indicate who and

what they will observe that week. Otherwise, the observation is unlikely to happen and will not be systematic if it does.

• Ongoing. To provide an accurate picture of the child, the observations must be captured over a period of time, in different situations, at different times of day.

• Practiced. With practice, teachers will become more skilled. Observing is a complex skill, so the director must provide ongoing training. Good observers note details and set aside any preconceptions so that they can record an accurate description of the child.

• Referenced in planning. The information gained through observing becomes the basis for individualizing the program to meet the children's needs. The teacher will need to adjust the lesson plans to meet the needs that are revealed through the observations.

In addition to validating children's achievements, observation provides teachers with vital information that they can use to meet other classroom needs. Information gained through observing helps teachers

• make changes in the classroom environment if, for example, the arrangement of the centers is not working

• clarify a concern, validating the need to refer a child for developmental screening

• gain insight by revealing patterns in problem situations, such as a particular child's misbehavior, a child's problem in separating from parents, or a problematic time of day (clean-up time or transition into the classroom from the playground)

Recording observations. Teachers may think, "I'm *always* observing children, so why do I need to write anything down?" Part of the reason for doing so is to remember what was observed, to compare current observations with past ones, to draw conclusions that may not be obvious, and to record progress. Observations must be documented to be useful for planning and reporting to parents. There are a variety of tools to use in recording observations, each with distinct purposes, advantages, and disadvantages. Some examples include the following:

Developmental checklists help teachers record the child's achievement of observable developmental milestones. These checklists help teachers focus on children's developmental growth in all areas as distinguished from specific skill accomplishments. (See form 8.7 Assessment Checklist.) Developmental checklists are often published in child development texts or parenting books. Because true developmental checklists are based on research and observation of a large number of children, published sources can be relied on.

Time sampling is especially effective when the teacher wants to know how often a certain behavior is happening and what circumstances surround specific behaviors. It can be a helpful tool when dealing with discipline problems or children showing signs of regression. The teacher creates a chart for an entire day in fifteen-minute increments. When she observes a specific behavior, she records it on the chart, noting what precipitated the event. She uses this information to understand the child's behavior and to see whether specific events trigger certain behaviors. It is also a good method for quantifying the challenging behavior, an important step before discussing the situation with parents.

Anecdotal records are descriptive accounts of specific episodes in the child's day. They provide information about the child's interactions with other children, with the teacher, with materials, and with ideas. Anecdotal records are useful for gathering information about a child in any area of development. The details in an anecdotal record can be particularly valuable in understanding a child's social development and problem-solving abilities.

Interviews and conversation involve asking questions when children are playing, a practice that gives teachers insight into children's thinking and problem-solving skills.

Language samples involve taking note of children's conversations with friends or in small-group and whole-class discussions to assess expressive language development.

Skills checklists are lists of skills appropriate to each age group. These lists allow teachers to record the children's accomplishments so that they can be seen at a glance. In contrast to developmental checklists, skills checklists can be created by teachers and tailored to list specific skills the teacher needs to know about. Sometimes a skills checklist will correspond with a particular classroom activity. For example, a teacher planning to observe in the art center will prepare for the observation by considering which skills children might display as they work. By creating a grid with all the children's names listed vertically and the identified skills listed horizontally, teachers can record information for several children at one time. The information can then be transferred to each child's record. Alternatively, teachers can create a checklist for each child that includes all the skills the early education center is working toward. This checklist might include a space to indicate the date when the child first demonstrates the skill and another date when the child demonstrates proficiency. This type of checklist recognizes that children's skills emerge on a continuum. The child who can accomplish a task with assistance displays a different level of progress than a child who cannot achieve with the same assistance, even though neither child has mastered the skill yet.

Collecting observation and assessment information. Information about a child's accomplishments must be organized so that it is accessible to the teacher for lesson planning and for parent conferences. Portfolios are typically used to store recorded observations and work samples. (See form 8.12 Early

---

Media for Recording Observations: Pros and Cons

Teachers use a variety of materials for recording and storing their observations, each kind having good points and bad:

- **Index cards:** come in various sizes; are easily sorted; fit neatly in a file box
- **Notebooks:** help keep information all in one place; are good for showing the child's growth over time
- **Sticky notes:** have benefits similar to those of index cards but are less durable
- **Gummed labels:** limited writing space may be a positive, as it forces teachers to be concise; limited flexibility, as labels can't be reorganized

---

Education Portfolios.) Teachers using portfolios generally prepare a file for each student at the beginning of the school year. They then save samples of the child's drawings, paintings, and writings and place them in the folder on a regular basis, often weekly. The portfolio items should be chosen purposefully, to demonstrate the child's progress toward a specific outcome or goal. Teachers can also allow children to choose work that they want saved in their portfolio, thus helping them to be active participants in their learning. This systematic accumulation of each child's work provides children, parents, and teachers with a wonderful visual documentation of the children's growth. Portfolios are helpful to teachers not only for documenting children's progress but for identifying those children who seem to be struggling in specific areas.

■*Sharing assessment information with families*
Because God places children into families, the things we learn about children during their time at school should be shared with their parents. (See forms 8.4, 8.5, and 8.6.) Although it is time-consuming, preparing assessment information and sharing it with families is one way to keep parents actively involved in their child's growth and development. Parents learn about the child's behavior in the early education setting, which may be different from the child's behavior at home. Through such sharing of information, teachers can be the parents' window into their child's world at school.

It is easy for a teacher to feel like the "expert" when telling parents about their child's growth. However, every parent is the primary expert on his or her own child. Both parents and teachers have their own kind of expertise to contribute. Teachers can share their experience with a wide variety of children and their understanding of typical child development, while parents offer a breadth and depth of information about their own child. (See form 8.13 Parent Feedback Form.) Thus everyone benefits when the child's assessment conference is a collaborative process.

FORM 8.1

Developmental Profile
(four-year-old)

Child's Name		Birth Date	
Teacher		Session	

SOCIAL DEVELOPMENT

Relationships with other children

☐ Outgoing	☐ Friendly	☐ Shares	☐ Teases
☐ Cautious	☐ Ignores	☐ Participates	☐ Aware of others' feelings
☐ Shy	☐ Takes turns	☐ Cooperates	

Stage of play

☐ Solitary	☐ Parallel	☐ Cooperative

Relationship with adults at school

Attitude toward teacher (trusting, dependent, demanding, over-sensitive, comfortable, listens, ignores, accepts)

Class activities

Attitude toward routines such as cleanup, toileting, circle time (assists, resists, needs help, self-reliant)

Favorite activities and friends

Attention span

Comments

EMOTIONAL DEVELOPMENT

Responsiveness toward classroom environment

Degree of independence

Interest in trying new things

Awareness of change

Ability to express needs and wants

Feelings of success or insecurity

Comments

purposeful design   *Early Education* DIRECTOR'S MANUAL

FORM 8.1

Developmental Profile (Continued)

PHYSICAL DEVELOPMENT

Small-muscle development

Hand dominance (right/left/both)

General mastery of specific skills

☐ Grasping with fingers	☐ Using scissors	☐ Using buttons/zippers	☐ Drawing basic shapes
☐ Writing name	☐ Drawing a person		

Large-Muscle Skills

☐ Jumps	☐ Hops	☐ Rides bicycle	☐ Throws
☐ Stands on one foot	☐ Skips	☐ Rolls	☐ Climbs stairs
☐ Catches	☐ Swings		

Body movements (rigid, relaxed, clumsy)

Participation in outdoor activities

Comments

CREATIVE DEVELOPMENT

Interest in music/dramatic play

Interest in stories, finger plays, circle activities

Inside activities (Check interest areas)

☐ Blocks	☐ Library	☐ Housekeeping/dramatic play	☐ Games
☐ Arts/crafts	☐ Writing center	☐ Trucks/cars	☐ Manipulatives

Comments

COGNITIVE DEVELOPMENT

Speech and language/hearing development

☐ Can express needs and wants	☐ Speaks in sentences	☐ Has well-developed vocabulary	☐ Speaks clearly
☐ Follows three-step commands	☐ Stutters/verbal frustration	☐ Able to recall information	

Responsiveness to directions

purposeful design   *Early Education* DIRECTOR'S MANUAL

FORM 8.1

Developmental Profile (Continued)

Level of comprehension skills

Any noticeable areas

Cognitive Skills

☐ Recognizes full name	☐ Knows basic shapes	☐ Knows body parts	☐ Knows colors
☐ Knows positional concepts	☐ Knows phone number		

Comments

Overall Impression

Teacher Signature		Date	

Written by the staff at Grace Christian Preschool, 1992.
Permission given to use for reference by Sandi Brakebush, director

purposeful design   *Early Education* DIRECTOR'S MANUAL

FORM 8.2

Suggestions for Recording Children's Development

Large-Motor
- Take photographs throughout the year of individual children using their motor skills.
- Talk with the children's parents about the importance of physical development and the progress of their vestibular, bilateral, and special awareness systems.

Fine-Motor
- Keep a checklist to record when a child learns how to button, zip, and tie her shoes.
- Include cutting, painting, and pasting art samples.
- Include examples of the children's writing and drawing.

Social/Emotional
- Include a parent survey on the child's interests at home.
- Write anecdotal notes on how individual children take turns and share.
- Use a weekly checklist that records which centers children choose to spend their time in and who plays with whom.

Cognitive
- Throughout the year take photos of the children's block structures.
- Include the children's artwork and drawings in their portfolios.
- Record children's statements about the results of science discoveries.

Literacy and Oral Language
- Include in the portfolios children's illustrations of stories they read or hear.
- Take an inventory of each child's favorite books a few times during the year.
- Include in each portfolio a list of songs the child sings.
- Make audiotapes of children's conversations or retelling of stories in circle time

Creative Expression
- Photograph a child's play dough project.
- Record songs the child sings.
- Include samples of easel paintings and artwork from school and home.

purposeful design   *Early Education* DIRECTOR'S MANUAL

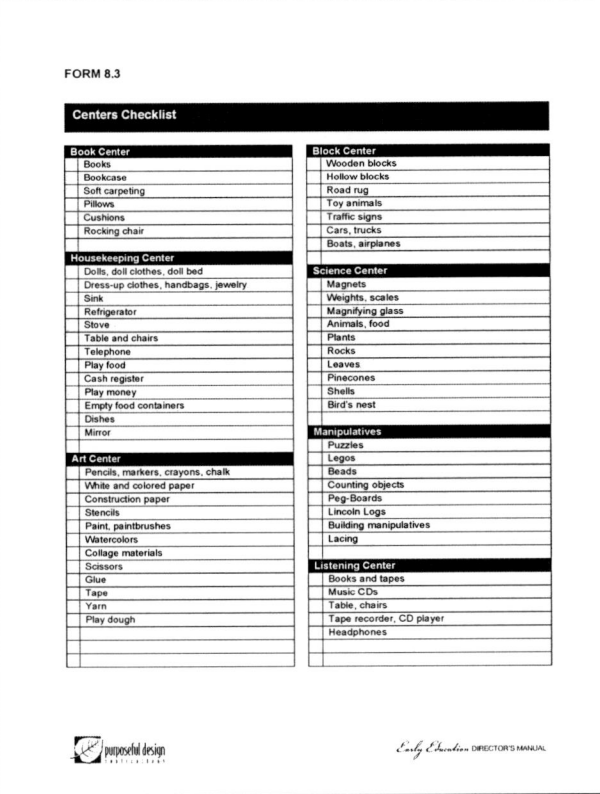

FORM 8.3

Centers Checklist

Book Center
- Books
- Bookcase
- Soft carpeting
- Pillows
- Cushions
- Rocking chair

Housekeeping Center
- Dolls, doll clothes, doll bed
- Dress-up clothes, handbags, jewelry
- Sink
- Refrigerator
- Stove
- Table and chairs
- Telephone
- Play food
- Cash register
- Play money
- Empty food containers
- Dishes
- Mirror

Art Center
- Pencils, markers, crayons, chalk
- White and colored paper
- Construction paper
- Stencils
- Paint, paintbrushes
- Watercolors
- Collage materials
- Scissors
- Glue
- Tape
- Yarn
- Play dough

Block Center
- Wooden blocks
- Hollow blocks
- Road rug
- Toy animals
- Traffic signs
- Cars, trucks
- Boats, airplanes

Science Center
- Magnets
- Weights, scales
- Magnifying glass
- Animals, food
- Plants
- Rocks
- Leaves
- Pinecones
- Shells
- Bird's nest

Manipulatives
- Puzzles
- Legos
- Beads
- Counting objects
- Peg-Boards
- Lincoln Logs
- Building manipulatives
- Lacing

Listening Center
- Books and tapes
- Music CDs
- Table, chairs
- Tape recorder, CD player
- Headphones

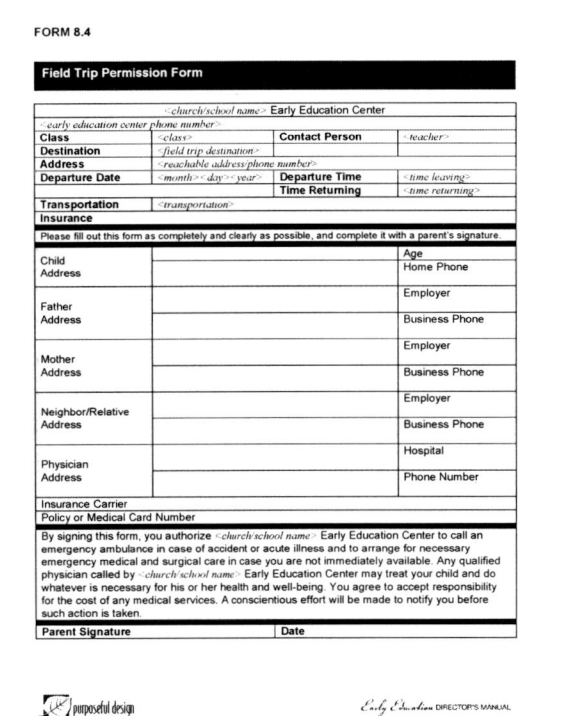

FORM 8.4

Field Trip Permission Form

<church/school name> Early Education Center
<early education center phone number>

Class	*<class>*	Contact Person	*<teacher>*
Destination	*<field trip destination>*		
Address	*<reachable address/phone number>*		
Departure Date	*<month> <day> <year>*	Departure Time	*<time leaving>*
		Time Returning	*<time returning>*
Transportation	*<transportation>*		
Insurance			

Please fill out this form as completely and clearly as possible, and complete it with a parent's signature.

		Age
Child Address		Home Phone
Father Address		Employer
		Business Phone
Mother Address		Employer
		Business Phone
Neighbor/Relative Address		Employer
		Business Phone
Physician Address		Hospital
		Phone Number

Insurance Carrier
Policy or Medical Card Number

By signing this form, you authorize *<church/school name>* Early Education Center to call an emergency ambulance in case of accident or acute illness and to arrange for necessary emergency medical and surgical care in case you are not immediately available. Any qualified physician called by *<church/school name>* Early Education Center may treat your child and do whatever is necessary for his or her health and well-being. You agree to accept responsibility for the cost of any medical services. A conscientious effort will be made to notify you before such action is taken.

Parent Signature	Date

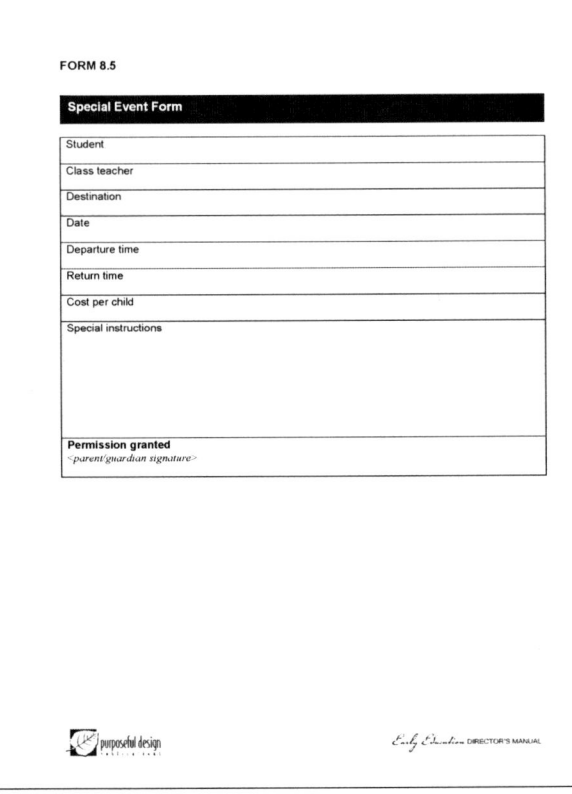

FORM 8.5

Special Event Form

Student	
Class teacher	
Destination	
Date	
Departure time	
Return time	
Cost per child	
Special instructions	

Permission granted
<parent/guardian signature>

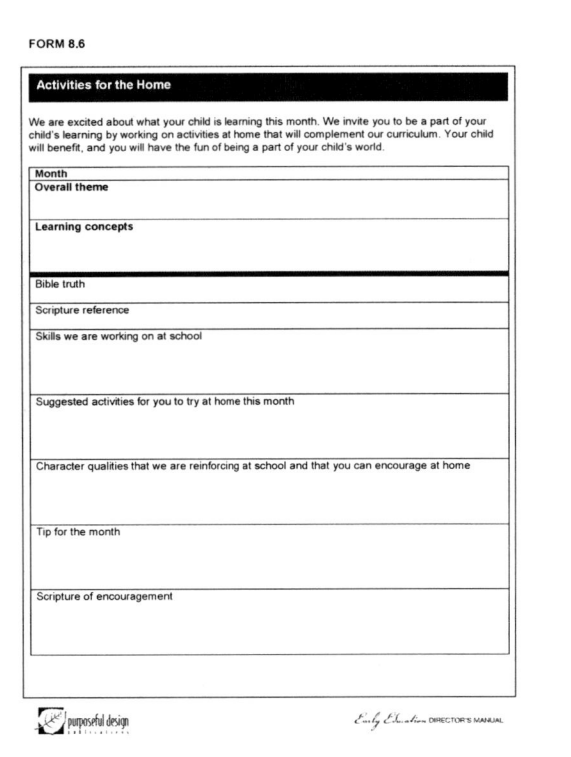

FORM 8.6

Activities for the Home

We are excited about what your child is learning this month. We invite you to be a part of your child's learning by working on activities at home that will complement our curriculum. Your child will benefit, and you will have the fun of being a part of your child's world.

Month

Overall theme

Learning concepts

Bible truth

Scripture reference

Skills we are working on at school

Suggested activities for you to try at home this month

Character qualities that we are reinforcing at school and that you can encourage at home

Tip for the month

Scripture of encouragement

FORM 8.7

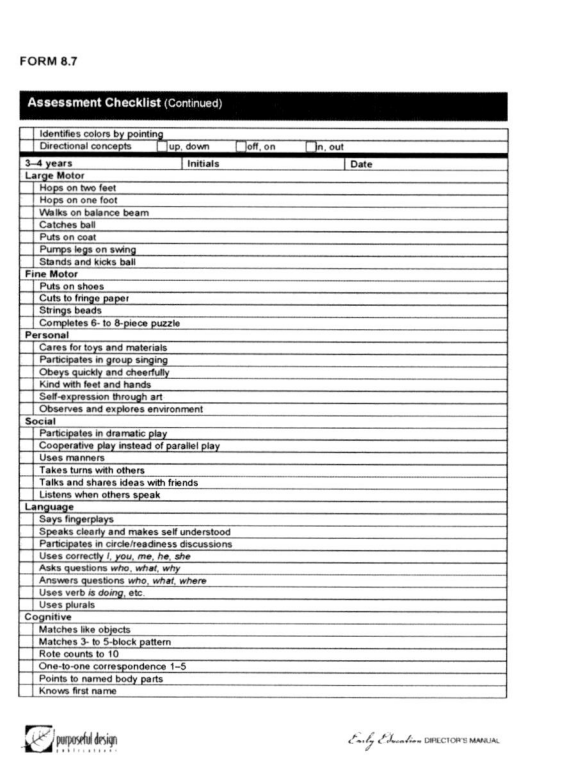

Assessment Checklist

Child's name		Teacher's name
Birthdate		
Home language		
Date of entry		
Age at entry		

2 years	Initials	Date
Large Motor		
Jumps with two feet		
Runs without falling		
Walks on balance beam		
Fine Motor		
Completes 2- to 4-piece puzzle		
Scribbles: circular strokes		
Stacks blocks		
Pours from pitcher with control		
Personal		
Participates in group singing		
Cares for toys and materials		
Listens at circle time		
Expresses self through art		
Observes and explores environment		
Obeys quickly and cheerfully		
Social		
Participates in dramatic play		
Listens when others speak		
Language		
Self-expression with words		
Says fingerplays		
Names familiar objects		
Refers to self by name		
Asks simple questions		
Verbalizes wants		
Explains "N" with 2 words		
Uses *I, me, you*		
Cognitive		
Can name own sex		
Knows first name		
Knows last name		
Can rote count to		
Follows 1-step directions		
Follows 2-step directions		
Matches like objects		
Points to named body parts		
Knows opposites ☐ big, little ☐ fast, slow		

FORM 8.7

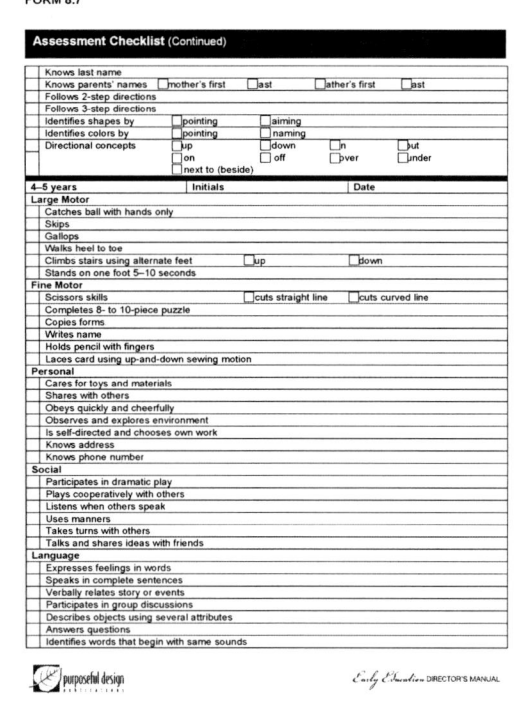

Assessment Checklist (Continued)

Identifies colors by pointing		
Directional concepts ☐ up, down ☐ off, on ☐ in, out		

3–4 years	Initials	Date
Large Motor		
Hops on two feet		
Hops on one foot		
Walks on balance beam		
Catches ball		
Puts on coat		
Pumps legs on swing		
Stands and kicks ball		
Fine Motor		
Puts on shoes		
Cuts to fringe paper		
Strings beads		
Completes 6- to 8-piece puzzle		
Personal		
Cares for toys and materials		
Participates in group singing		
Obeys quickly and cheerfully		
Kind with feet and hands		
Self-expression through art		
Observes and explores environment		
Social		
Participates in dramatic play		
Cooperative play instead of parallel play		
Uses manners		
Takes turns with others		
Talks and shares ideas with friends		
Listens when others speak		
Language		
Says fingerplays		
Speaks clearly and makes self understood		
Participates in circle/readiness discussions		
Uses correctly *I, you, me, he, she*		
Asks questions *who, what, why*		
Answers questions *who, what, where*		
Uses verb *is doing*, etc.		
Uses plurals		
Cognitive		
Matches like objects		
Matches 3- to 5-block pattern		
Rote counts to 10		
One-to-one correspondence 1–5		
Points to named body parts		
Knows first name		

FORM 8.7

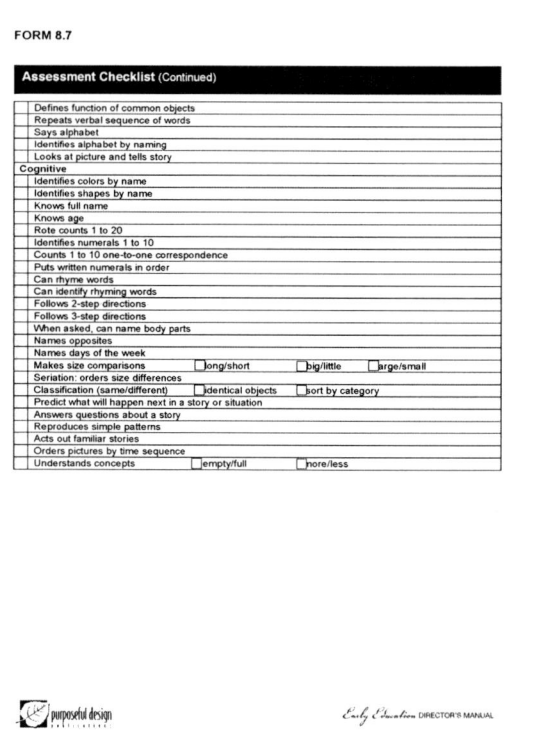

Assessment Checklist (Continued)

Knows last name		
Knows parents' names ☐ mother's first ☐ last ☐ father's first ☐ last		
Follows 2-step directions		
Follows 3-step directions		
Identifies shapes by ☐ pointing ☐ naming		
Identifies colors by ☐ pointing ☐ naming		
Directional concepts ☐ up ☐ down ☐ in ☐ out ☐ on ☐ off ☐ over ☐ under ☐ next to (beside)		

4–5 years	Initials	Date
Large Motor		
Catches ball with hands only		
Skips		
Gallops		
Walks heel to toe		
Climbs stairs using alternate feet ☐ up ☐ down		
Stands on one foot 5–10 seconds		
Fine Motor		
Scissors skills ☐ cuts straight line ☐ cuts curved line		
Completes 8- to 10-piece puzzle		
Copies forms		
Writes name		
Holds pencil with fingers		
Laces card using up-and-down sewing motion		
Personal		
Cares for toys and materials		
Shares with others		
Obeys quickly and cheerfully		
Observes and explores environment		
Is self-directed and chooses own work		
Knows address		
Knows phone number		
Social		
Participates in dramatic play		
Plays cooperatively with others		
Listens when others speak		
Uses manners		
Takes turns with others		
Talks and shares ideas with friends		
Language		
Expresses feelings in words		
Speaks in complete sentences		
Verbally relates story or events		
Participates in group discussions		
Describes objects using several attributes		
Answers questions		
Identifies words that begin with same sounds		

FORM 8.7

Assessment Checklist (Continued)

Defines function of common objects		
Repeats verbal sequence of words		
Says alphabet		
Identifies alphabet by naming		
Looks at picture and tells story		
Cognitive		
Identifies colors by name		
Identifies shapes by name		
Knows full name		
Knows age		
Rote counts 1 to 20		
Identifies numerals 1 to 10		
Counts 1 to 10 one-to-one correspondence		
Puts written numerals in order		
Can rhyme words		
Can identify rhyming words		
Follows 2-step directions		
Follows 3-step directions		
When asked, can name body parts		
Names opposites		
Names days of the week		
Makes size comparisons ☐ long/short ☐ big/little ☐ large/small		
Seriation: orders size differences		
Classification (same/different) ☐ identical objects ☐ sort by category		
Predict what will happen next in a story or situation		
Answers questions about a story		
Reproduces simple patterns		
Acts out familiar stories		
Orders pictures by time sequence		
Understands concepts ☐ empty/full ☐ more/less		

FORM 8.8

Objectives

What is your overall goal?

What do you want to see happen?

At what point in the day will this occur?

How often will this occur?

At what point will the child be successful in this?

Put all of these responses in a one-sentence objective

Educational Objective
During circle time the children will demonstrate they can

by

Select four activities to help accomplish this objective.

1.

2.

3.

4.

FORM 8.9

Planning Thematic Units

Elements of thematic planning include the following:

- Select monthly themes that are rich in learning possibilities. This step involves a careful review of themes traditionally offered. Such a review may result in exchanging favorite themes of less significance for those that are more meaningful. Examining possible monthly themes in light of the expected student outcomes can help you with this sorting process.

- Determine weekly units that relate to the overall monthly theme. The number of units should correspond to the number of weeks in the month. Weekly units are on subthemes of the monthly theme, and they may be progressive. The subthemes are important aspects of the monthly theme that you want the children to learn about. For example,

Monthly theme	Walking through the beginning of school
Weekly unit themes	Week 1: Learning about my school
	Week 2: Making new friends
	Week 3: Learning about my best friend Jesus
	Week 4: Learning about my body and how it works

- Document other components of the curriculum to be covered during the month. These areas may or may not be correlated with the monthly theme.

  – Bible truths
  – Character traits
  – Language
  – Literacy
  – Numeracy
  – Social/emotional development (life skills)
  – Science
  – Music
  – Art
  – Motor skills

FORM 8.10

Pre-K Teacher's Observations for Kindergarten Placement

Child's Name	
Teacher's Name	Date

1. How does the child attend during group instruction?

2. Does the child seek learning experiences without external pressure during free-choice time?

3. Does the child stay on task? Is he or she easily distracted?

4. Does the child have difficulty sitting still? Under what circumstances?

5. Do you feel that the child is immature? If so, how does he or she manifest immaturity?

6. Is small-muscle development a concern?

7. Can you provide any other information relevant to the child's successful kindergarten placement?

FORM 8.11

Evaluation of Early Education Center's Curriculum

Teacher's Curriculum Evaluation

What are your thoughts regarding the center's overall curriculum?

What are the strengths of the curriculum plan?

Where are the gaps that should be covered for next year?

What are some areas that the children really connected with?

What are some additional resources that would enhance the curriculum?

FORM 8.12

Early Education Portfolios

September
Make a file for each child in your classroom.
Design a survey for parents to fill out on their child.
Take a photo of each child doing his favorite activity.
Have each child practice writing his or her name.
Put into each portfolio a sample of the child's cutting ability.
Have the child draw a self-portrait.
Complete at least one observation of each child, including your notes in the portfolio.

October
Complete a skill-level assessment of each child.
Observe and record a conversation with each child.
Take photos and write down the comments children make about their own pictures.
Write an assessment describing the children's strengths and their needs.
Establish goals for the year and write a behavioral objective for the child.

November and December
Gather more samples of the children's work, making sure your samples document their learning and progress, or any delays that are evident.
Literature: Write down their thoughts; record whether or not they comprehend a story; record responses to questions.
Art: Art-project samples, easel painting, storytelling, Lego projects, or building projects.
Critical thinking: Maze activities, sequencing, puzzles and other activities that you can record their responses to. What do you think? How would you...?
Fine-motor skills: Include samples of the child's printing, coloring, drawing, cutting, gluing, etc.

January
Review each child's goals to see whether you are making any progress. Update your goals for the child, and establish new ones if necessary.
Complete an assessment of each student in the social, emotional, creative, physical, spiritual, and cognitive areas.
Schedule a parent-teacher conference to discuss the progress and share the portfolios.

February
Add more photographs.
Include any observation notes for the month.
Add a few more samples of the child's work.

March
Have the child draw another self-portrait, and note any progress over the last one.
Allow the children to review their portfolios. Record their comments and discuss their progress with them.

April
Gather more examples of each child's work and progress.
Add additional photos and anecdotal notes.

May
Review summary sheets and goals, and do a developmental profile again to note any progress on each child.
Schedule a parent-teacher conference and discuss the child's progress. Make a recommendation for the child's placement next year. Show the portfolio and examples of the child's work.
Gather any final examples.

June
Go over the portfolios with the children and praise them for the way they have grown.
Send the portfolios home with end-of-the-year comments.

FORM 8.13

Parent Feedback Form

We are very interested in your feedback regarding our instructional program for this month. As you know, we seek to partner with you in providing an enriched learning experience for your child. Please respond to the following questions in order to help us meet your child's needs.

Our theme for the month is
What have you noticed that your child has been learning this month in relation to this theme?

Next month's theme will be
What would you like your child to learn this coming month in relationship to this theme?

What are some skills you have been working on this last month with your child?

Is there anything we should be aware of regarding your child?

What are your general observations regarding your child during your time here at our program?

Do you have any prayer requests this month for your child or your family?

ESTABLISHING APPROPRIATE ENVIRONMENTS

Chapter 9

"Whoever welcomes one of these little children in my name welcomes me; and whoever welcomes me does not welcome me but the one who sent me." (Mark 9:37)

A Welcoming Climate

Directors of early childhood education centers have the great privilege of developing the facility and classroom space to create a welcoming climate for the children and families that pass through the doors each day. An environment that reflects good stewardship and attention to detail provides a direct blessing to the children and enhances the program's appeal to prospective families touring the center.

Indoor Space

The director, in cooperation with the staff, plans how best to utilize the indoor space. In evaluating the building and the space available, the director should consider the needs of the individual children. After checking with state and local regulatory agencies, the director should make sure there will be enough indoor space for the number of children to be enrolled. The minimum requirement is typically 35 square feet of floor space per child, including space for equipment. This indoor space requirement refers to classroom space and excludes such areas as the kitchen, bathrooms, office, staff lounge, hallways, and stairways. The regulatory agencies have specific requirements for exits and stairways, and they may require accommodations for non-ambulatory children. They may also have specific requirements for toileting facilities and hand-washing sinks. Classrooms must be well lighted and properly ventilated. Storage areas for supplies must be large enough and well organized for easy accessibility. Office space should be separate from the areas used by children.

The state and local regulatory agencies will provide information about appropriate temperatures. A suggested temperature during cool weather is at least 68 degrees. Ceiling fans or air conditioners can be used during warm weather. It is recommended that all children spend time in the fresh air each day, as vigorous outdoor play is associated with staying healthy. When children stay indoors in cool weather, they are actually exposed to more germs because of their limited access to fresh air.

Challenges for Early Education Environments

Early education programs encompass a range of schedules and purposes, from part-time enrichment programs to full-time childcare. Although all children benefit from a thoughtfully planned environment, the need for high-quality environments increases proportionally with the amount of time children spend in the program. Additionally, the very youngest children feel the environment's influence even more keenly than others. Physical comfort, security, and opportunities to explore are particularly significant for their overall development. Children receiving all-day care in a center face inherent challenges. They must adapt to routines and adult expectations that are likely to differ from those at home and may even vary within the center, depending on the degree of consistency among the staff members. Being a part of a group and having to interact with many people can be stressful for a young child. "A program that occupies two or three hours of a child's day faces far fewer issues of institutionalization—regimentation, autonomy, privacy and comfort—than an all-day program. Children, like adults, can and need to conform to group life some of the time, but not all of the time."[1]

Fortunately, the potentially negative effects of institutionalism can be successfully avoided by developing in each classroom environmental elements that affirm the children's worth, provide comfort and space for them to be alone, and all the while support their learning. How can something as abstract as "classroom space" affirm children's worth or have an impact on their comfort and development? In a program that values children's development of initiative and competence, the classroom environment supports independent learning by ensuring that learning materials are attractively displayed so as to invite children's interest and are organized in such a way that children can return them when they are finished. In the same way, an attractive, carefully prepared environment sends a clear sensory message that children are valued and treasured.

Guidelines for Early Education Facility Development

Form 9.1 Facility Components lists spaces, furnishings, and supplies to acquire as you develop your early education center. The list illustrates the variety of spaces that directors need to plan for when they are designing a new facility. It is helpful to evaluate the existing space against this list, recognizing that every facility has limitations. However, by setting their sights on an ideal environment, directors can address the challenges in their own facility. For programs that are in the process of expanding, directors may want to review the *GSA Child Care Center Design Guide*.

Child Development and the Classroom Environment

In planning environments that support young children, we must be guided by our knowledge of their unique characteristics. How should knowledge of child development inform the way we design our classrooms?

■ *Physical development*
We know that young children are in a period of rapid physical growth, developing new skills and

interests that match and prod their developing abilities. Therefore, classroom space needs to be flexible, and teachers must observe when a child is ready for a new challenge and must adapt the environment accordingly. In the course of a day, young children experience both surges of energy and periods of fatigue. The classroom must provide areas for high-energy activities along with quiet areas for rest, accommodating the energy fluctuations that are a normal part of development for the young child. High-energy activities should be alternated with lower-energy activities. Finally, the classroom environment needs to be safe for children to explore, protecting them from their own immaturity and lack of experience.

Programs that provide a perceptual motor-development program may utilize classroom space for the program activities. The space needs to be open and clear of furnishings so that children have enough room to practice and develop their large-motor skills. The outdoor environment also assists in developing children's large-motor skills. Pieces of equipment such as climbers, slides, swings, and bikes allow children to develop the basic systems of the body, including the vestibular (body position and movement), bilateral (right and left), tactile (touch), and proprioceptive systems (producing stimuli within the body).

■ Emotional development

Just as the school environment provides safe, protected spaces to enable children's physical development, the classroom must provide a nurturing setting for their emotional development by meeting their needs for security, comfort, and significance. The adults in the classroom play a central role in creating a climate of warmth, familiarity, and acceptance that makes young children feel secure and gives the early education center a homelike atmosphere. After all, home is a haven not merely because of its physical comforts but also because the child

can relax there. At home the child is surrounded by people he trusts, he is known intimately, and his uniqueness is appreciated and enjoyed.

Although staff members are key in cultivating an environment that nurtures emotional growth, physical aspects of the environment also influence children's school experiences. One of the ways we know we're in a well-designed space is that once there, we don't want to leave. Beautiful and comfortable places encourage us to linger and enjoy. Teachers create comfortable environments by developing the quality of "softness" in the classroom, by adding pillows, area rugs, cozy furnishings, and living things like plants and animals.

Another way teachers can minimize the institutional feel of the early education center is by creating an environment that is rich and varied. Interesting and beautiful places are those that "have been enriched and equipped with materials from home, from nature, and from the children and adults themselves"[2] We know that children, like adults, are comforted and soothed by orderly and beautiful spaces. When we enhance the beauty of a space by displaying child-created art, the child's ideas and work are validated. By personalizing the classroom in this way, we meet the children's need for belonging and significance. We also help to develop their sense of significance when we trust them with responsibilities for caring for classroom materials, allowing them to see themselves as contributing members of the classroom community. Still another way that the classroom environment can affirm children's worth and build their self-image is by having diverse play materials, posters, and books that reflect the physical characteristics of the children in the program. We need to use the children's names and photographs as often as possible in the classroom decor.

Softness Defined

The dimension of softness was so named because it appeared to indicate a responsive quality of the environment to the child, especially on a sensual/tactile level. It was based on the presence or absence of eleven components:

1. malleable materials, such as clay or play dough
2. sand that children can be in, either in a box or play area
3. laps—teachers holding children
4. single sling swings
5. grass that children can be on
6. a large rug or carpeting indoors
7. water as an activity
8. very messy materials, such as finger paint, clay , or mud
9. child/adult cozy furniture, such as rockers, couches or lawn swings
10. dirt to dig in
11. animals that can be held, such as guinea pigs, dogs, and cats

The softest activity settings are also the most perennially appealing.[3]

■ *Social development*

Closely related to the children's developing sense of self is their relationship with others, which grows from the infant's initial awareness of others as people separate from themselves to the sophisticated, collaborative play of four- and five-year-olds. The physical arrangement of space in the classroom shapes the opportunities it offers for social development. "Different kinds of interactions occur in different types of spaces. Small, enclosed areas support fantasy play, growth of friendships, experimentation with light and objects, and children's games."[4] Smaller

spaces are also seen as encouraging richer language, extended conversation, and greater collaboration between children. In light of these findings, Jeanne Vergeront recommends the creation of nooks, such as a crawl-in cube, or even a box. Although varied equipment is important in supporting complex play, other children are actually the greatest resource for enriching play experiences.[5] A carefully planned classroom provides a range of play spaces, from small spaces in which a child can pursue a task independently to spaces for two children and still larger spaces for four to six. This flexibility allows the children some choice in the amount of social contact they experience throughout the day.

■ *Cognitive development*

Classrooms that facilitate collaborative pretend play not only enhance social development, they strengthen cognitive development at the same time. Elaborate pretend play lays the groundwork for perspective taking and abstract thought.[6] Through varied equipment and materials displayed to attract and maintain children's interest, the physical environment provides raw materials for children's learning. A classroom that is well stocked with real materials, such as items from nature in the science area and such props as recycled food packages in the dramatic play center, provides children with rich opportunities for exploration and dramatic play. Children's emerging literacy and numeracy are supported by classroom areas designated for looking at books, using writing tools, and counting and sorting objects as well as by a print-rich environment throughout the classroom.

■ *Spiritual development*

The environment influences children's spiritual development in both direct and subtle ways. The love and care shown by the staff members powerfully communicate the love of God and the truth of the child's significance. These messages are reinforced when children receive them in a carefully prepared classroom setting. The comfort and beauty of the classroom speak to the child in a sensory language, affirming that the child's needs are important. The environment also provides opportunities for the display of visual images, such as posters that support biblical and character-trait themes. The availability of the appropriate props offers children the opportunity to act out the Bible stories and in that way, through time and repetition, to increase their understanding of them. Another way in which the environment can support children's spiritual development requires flexibility in the use of dramatic play space. (For example, children could use the block play area to re-create the scene of Paul and Silas in prison.) Displaying pictures that reflect a multicultural classroom help children learn to appreciate other cultures. Finally, classrooms that are rich in materials from nature provide numerous teachable moments for encouraging children's sense of wonder. As children explore objects from the natural world, teachers have the opportunity to encourage their understanding and appreciation for God as the source of nature's beauty and design.

Environmental Basics: Setting the Stage

There are fixed structural elements of any facility that create the backdrop or canvas for the children's classroom experiences. The size and shape of the classrooms, the floor coverings, the use of color, and the number and location of windows—all these contribute to the overall feel of the classroom. Functionality increases when water is available in the classroom. The presence or absence of toileting facilities, water fountains, or sinks for children and adults has an impact on the daily classroom schedule and the variety of activities available to children.

■ Classroom layout

One of the most significant elements of the classroom environment is the size of the room and the number of children and adults that use the space.

Thirty-five square feet of usable indoor space per child is typically identified as the bare minimum, and forty to fifty square feet per child is recommended.[7] Frequently, early education programs are located in existing facilities that have a variety of classroom shapes and sizes. In planning space for young children, we need to give careful consideration to the ages of those who will use the classrooms and the optimal group size for the age groups served. Large rooms can be divided into smaller, self-contained spaces through the use of partitions and partial walls. As a rule, the space should be adapted to provide for the optimal group size rather than letting the size of the existing space determine the number of children to be enrolled. In some facilities, this practice may result in classrooms providing more than the minimum amount of square feet per child. However, it is better to err by providing additional space than to exceed optimal group sizes, as young children may find large groups overstimulating and relationally taxing. Spaces become stressful when there is too much furniture, too many learning centers, or too many children crowded into one area.

Beyond the physical dimensions of the classrooms, their appearance is significantly enhanced by the basic backdrops of lighting, windows, and floor and wall coverings. Many early education classrooms accommodate a wide range of activities, meeting children's need for both care and learning. Think of the variety of activities that may occur in a single classroom:

- Snacks and meals are served and prepared.
- Quiet settings for rest and napping are provided.
- Individual learning centers that change as children grow are developed.
- Areas for large-group gatherings are adapted for seasonal activities and special events.
- Large- and small-motor skill activities take place.

Classrooms providing varied activities need flexible and varied space. The space needs to be arranged so that children are visible and can be easily supervised. Flooring should include durable and easily cleaned hard surfaces for meals and messy art projects along with carpeted areas that absorb the sound created by noisier activities such as block-building. Freshly painted classroom walls enhance the aesthetics of the room. Neutral colors for both walls and furniture allow teachers to use color as an accent in drawing children's attention to a particular area. In general, color schemes should be calm and soothing. Walls and furnishings that are too bright can be overstimulating. Classroom walls can be made more functional in several ways, such as adding plexiglass coverings for art display areas and partially carpeting walls to provide tactile stimulation and to absorb sound. Maintenance can be reduced by adding paneling to frequently used areas of the classroom where chairs or cots are stacked.

■ Lighting

Windows enhance the classroom by providing natural light along with glimpses into nature and the outside world. Sunlight streaming through a window not only provides interesting sensory experiences and visual stimulation for the child but softens the effect of fluorescent lighting, which can be harsh and overstimulating. Children may be calmed by reduced lighting, so the addition of a dimmer switch provides teachers with a tool for setting the mood. Though they are more expensive, full spectrum or warm white fluorescent tubes are a beneficial replacement for the cool white tubes.

■ Scale: Creating a child-friendly "classroom"

One of the most basic ways for an early education classroom to create a welcoming environment for young children is to provide space that is appropriately scaled. *Scale* is the size of an object relative to its surroundings. Because of their small size, children may feel intimidated by large open spaces.

Jim Greenman observes that "children, who operate most of the time in outsized surroundings, gravitate to the tiny in spaces, objects, and living things."[8] Contrast the experience of a child eating lunch at a table that comes up to his chin with that of a child sitting in a small chair at a small table. In which environment will the child feel more comfortable? Child-scaled equipment and furniture facilitate success and create a sense that the child belongs in, and is a welcome participant in, the environment. Other ways to be sensitive to issues of scale include the following:

- creating small areas within larger spaces
- lowering parts of the ceiling (with a fabric canopy, for example)
- including some items in the classroom that children can move by themselves, such as pillows and crates[9]
- decorating the lower half of the wall—anything higher is for the adults

To get a sense of how the classroom is experienced by a young child, examine the room from the child's eye level. Is it possible to create level changes within the classroom that will allow children to see eye to eye with adults? Can child-sized hardware and accessories be used, such as sinks, toilets, mirrors, and stair rails? Can the height of the floor be varied through the addition of portable, carpeted plywood platforms on casters?[10]

■ Environment issues of church-sponsored programs

Church-sponsored programs face unique challenges in creating high-quality early education environments. These programs are frequently housed in secondhand spaces not originally designed to serve young children. The classrooms may be of unusual shapes and sizes, may lack convenient access to sinks and toileting facilities, or may be situated far from any outdoor play areas. In addition, church-sponsored programs often share space with other ministries, creating challenges such as storing and caring for classroom equipment and keeping children's building and art projects undisturbed.

The environmental challenges can be considered a trade-off, for many benefits come from being sponsored by a local church, such as ministry resources, infrastructure, and community visibility. However, to prepare quality classroom environments, the director must be aware of the challenges unique to the site and must have a plan for addressing those challenges. There are ways to offset the shortcomings of the available facility and maximize the potential of any given space.

Making the Most of Classroom Space

The organization of classroom space will impact the early education program, affecting how the children respond to one another and to the staff. Creating a classroom that provides enriched activity spaces for play and learning and also meets the functional needs in the daily routines of group care is a challenge. However, the benefits for the children and the teacher are many. The best arrangement of classroom space promotes independence and self-direction.

The arrangement of the equipment can enhance or discourage certain behaviors in children. Wide-open indoor space may encourage behaviors that are more appropriate outdoors. Small, confined spaces may discourage children from participating in an activity. When space is poorly organized, the children are more prone to aimless wandering, which can lead to misbehavior. When clear guidance is not provided by the classroom environment, the teacher must invest significant time in directing children, leaving her less time for interacting with them individually, for taking advantage of teachable moments, and for nurturing relationships.

▪ Planning

High-quality environments do not emerge spontaneously. They are a result of careful planning by teachers and administrators, planning that is guided by the program's desired outcomes for the children. Early education staff should structure their environment so that it supports their goals for the children, both in their short-term experiences of care and their long-term development as individuals. Consistency among a program's philosophy and mission, the way the teaching staff provides guidance, and the classroom environment is a powerful force in shaping young lives.

▪ Guiding principles

Options for arranging space are limited by fixed features, such as the location and number of doors and windows, and the size and shape of the classroom space (i.e., large open spaces or smaller separate rooms). Successful classroom environments include defined interest and activity areas that are separated by boundaries and accessed through clear pathways. Some general principles for planning classroom space are the following:

- Place calm, quiet areas away from active, noisy areas, minimizing distractions and potential disruptions to play and learning.

- Arrange compatible activities near each other, particularly when they share resources such as a sink.

- Provide space that is varied and appropriate in size for the specific activity, with some play spaces sized for one or two children, others for as many as four to six.

- Make available a sufficient number of activities so that children have open play spaces to choose from when they have completed an activity. It is recommended that free choice time provide from one-and-a-half to two-and-a-half more activities than the number of children who will be playing, minimizing overcrowding and ensuring enough variety to capture children's interest.[11]

• Personalize the classroom through displays of children's art, photographs of recent class events, and other visual reminders that each child belongs to the classroom community.

Specific Classroom Spaces

■ Center and classroom entryways

Those first moments of arrival are very important in welcoming children and parents to another day at school. Both the school's reception and sign-in areas and the individual classroom entrances can create a sense of assurance that the children are in a place prepared specifically for them and can entice children to join the group and enter into the day's activities.

Children should have individual cubbies, or personal storage spaces where they can keep their "valuables," which may include items brought from home, artwork they created, or a special rock found on the playground. These cubbies can be personalized with the children's photographs. Cubbies provide private spaces for children to hang their jackets and store their nap belongings. (Many health departments require that children's personal cloth belongings be stored in such a way that they do not touch to ensure that lice and germs are not shared.)

Bulletin boards for parents are posted in the line of sight of the sign-in counter. Information about the program should be attractively displayed, inviting the involvement of parents and affirming the significant role they play. The parent board may also include information about community and church activities, photographs and profiles of the staff, and displays of encouraging or inspirational Scriptures. The parent board should be attractive, and should be regularly updated to ensure ongoing interest. Some schools serve refreshments and morning coffee in the reception area, encouraging parents to linger. A few innovative programs even videotape the day's activities and play the tape at the end of the day, providing a glimpse into the child's classroom life.

■ Interest centers

The classroom should be divided into interest centers that accommodate the variety of types of activities that promote children's development. The interest centers do not need to be large spaces, or even permanent ones, as they may be modified from week to week to reflect changing curriculum themes. *An effective interest center is simply an organized, defined space that encourages children to engage in autonomous learning.* Plentiful materials are a must so that the children can interact with them and benefit from the experience. The space must be flexible enough to accommodate all the day's activities. For instance, the carpeted block-building area may also be used for large-group meetings such as circle times.

The following guidelines will help teachers to organize and arrange interest centers:

• Each center is well defined and easily accessible to children.
• Toys, props, and materials used in the center are accessible to the children.
• Toys, props, and materials are neatly organized and stored. (Pictures cut from toy/preschool supply catalogs can be laminated and taped to shelves and storage areas to help children find the matching toys, props, or materials.)
• All centers can be easily supervised by the staff.
• The teacher's role is to plan the centers, observe children as they work and play, be a resource for them in their play, and evaluate how well the centers are working for the children.[12]

Sufficient time should be allowed for child-directed learning in the interest centers so that the child can become deeply engaged in self-chosen activities. In general a longer-lasting, more focused experience in one or two centers has more value for the child than a fleeting visit to all of them. A minimum of 30 minutes is required for sustained play. When the schedule allows 45 minutes to an hour, more in-depth play can take place.[13]

Boundaries. Interest areas are defined by clear boundaries, with physical markers separating them. A boundary may be provided by a bookshelf or storage unit, stabilized by sufficient width at the base so that it cannot be easily tipped over. Small free-standing room dividers can also provide a visual separation between play spaces. At four feet, they are high enough to block the children's view of other areas but low enough to allow adults to see over them. A space can also be defined by something as simple as an area rug, a tape line on the floor, or a change in flooring from linoleum to carpet. Some unique ways to separate space include using an usher's rope, a free-standing lattice structure, bamboo curtains, or fabric panels. Interest areas may also be set apart by using elevated places, such as a loft or a low platform. All these techniques for separating space share the goals of creating a child-scaled classroom, helping children to focus on a specific activity, and reducing the sense of crowding that may accompany being part of a large group.

Pathways. In planning the location of the different interest areas, the early educator must consider the best way to guide the children from one area to another. The space should be arranged with pathways between areas, allowing children to see their choices and to access areas of interest while providing protection for other interest centers. For example, pathways around the block-building center protect children's works-in-progress from children who are walking through to another interest area.

Places to pause. Just as pathways assist children in moving about the room and previewing activity choices, sometimes children need a "place to pause,"[14] a private space to rest and consider what they would like to do next. When there is no physical provision for privacy, children may filter out or ignore unwanted contact, mentally. Essentially, they are "spacing out" and withdrawing from the classroom, inwardly. When classrooms provide specific areas that allow a child to look out a window, look at a book, or engage in a positive activity alone, a child need not expend emotional energy to protect herself. Some teachers take advantage of unique existing features of their classroom to create private space. For example, a fireplace and hearth can be painted, carpeted, and furnished with books and pillows to create a cozy nook for one or two children. A simple tent can be created by draping a blanket over a small overturned table or between two pieces of classroom furniture. With a flashlight, children will have a quiet spot to explore. Even a large cardboard box can serve children's need to be in a small space, separate from the group.

■ *Typical interest centers and supporting materials*

A child learns best through firsthand experiences, and centers can provide abundant opportunities for a wide range of sensory experiences: touching, smelling, hearing, seeing, and tasting. Interest centers allow the child to create, explore, invent, and learn! Each interest center should indicate clearly to the child what type of play or activity can be done there. The following interest centers should be developed in each early education classroom. Although the centers described here focus on a primary area of learning or development, children do not explore math concepts only in the math center, or have literacy experiences only in the literacy areas. Both math and language development also take place in the construction area, the sensory areas, and so on. The more teachers keep in mind the integration of children's learning, the more they can enrich and extend the opportunities in their individual centers.

Of the centers described below, the first three—the library center, the writing center, and the listening center—are referred to together as *literacy centers*.

Library center. The library area should contain a variety of picture books that children can explore on their own or share with a friend, including some that reflect the themes or concepts currently being taught. The book center should be conducive to quiet reading. This center develops children's familiarity with and interest in books, and exploring these can lead to a lifelong love of reading. Large pillows, comfortable chairs, and a plush rug create a comfortable place for children to examine a book on their own or share one with a teacher or a friend.

The bookshelf needs to be easily accessible and filled with plenty of engaging children's books that are regularly rotated. The books need to be attractive and in good repair, with content appropriate to the children's level and with high-quality text and illustrations. Other materials in addition to books can be included to stimulate children's interest and conversation: catalogs, puppets, flannel-board characters from familiar stories, mounted photographs from magazines, and classroom books created through children's dictation.

Writing center. The writing center gives children an opportunity to explore writing implements and communication tools, develop skills in these areas, and learn to appreciate the value of expressing their ideas in written form. Materials need to be well

organized and attractively displayed, inviting children's participation.

Materials for the writing center

- paints, brushes, easel
- colored chalk, small chalkboards with erasers
- felt-tip markers
- pencils
- paper of many sizes and colors, lined and unlined
- sandpaper letters
- word cards with familiar words
- small alphabet chart
- stencils
- envelopes of various sizes
- index cards
- pads, notebooks
- sticky notes
- greeting cards
- carbon paper, tracing paper, stencils
- magic slate
- small whiteboards
- stamp pads, letters
- pan of sand for finger-writing
- sandpaper letters and numbers
- play dough to form into letters and numbers
- flannel board with letters and numbers
- mailbox
- typewriter

Listening center. The listening center provides a place where children can listen to stories independently, following along in the text of what they are hearing. Although this type of experience with books is no substitute for the interactive reading that occurs when a teacher reads a story, it does capture children's interest and also provides an activity that allows the child some time alone, separate from the rest of the group.

Equipment for the listening center

- child-operated cassette or compact disc players
- recordings of high-quality children's literature, with or without the corresponding books
- headphones

Children will need clear instructions in the correct use of the equipment. Players can be labeled with symbols or pictures as well as words to remind children how to use them.

Dramatic-play/home-living center. As children spend time in dramatic play, they develop oral language and a sense of competence. The center should include the basic furnishings that will encourage children to dramatize home and family situations. These furnishings can also be adapted to a variety of themes with the addition of props. The best, and often the most economical, props are real objects that children can find in their own homes.

Equipment for the home-living center

- unbreakable mirror
- dress-up clothes
- jewelry
- variety of pieces of fabric with multicultural colors and designs
- baby bed
- high chair
- small table, chairs
- storage for food items and accessories: cereal boxes, empty vegetable cans with edges filed smooth, spice containers, real-life small pots and pans, child-sized plastic cups and plates, dry sponge, small dustpan and hand-held broom
- sink
- stove
- refrigerator
- cozy rug
- telephone
- ironing board
- shopping cart
- cash register

Literacy props for dramatic play

The items listed here are not just for the writing center. They are intended to encourage children to include writing spontaneously in their pretend play, reinforcing the usefulness of print.

- menus, order pad, play money
- recipes, marked measuring spoons and cups
- memo pads, envelopes, address labels
- cookbooks, telephone books

The space for the home-living center can be converted into specific themed places for dramatic play if another, more appropriate space is not available. With the addition of props and with minor rearrangement of the space, the children can pretend they are people with various jobs and professions, such as nurses, doctors, postal workers, carpenters, firefighters, and hairdressers. A dramatic-play box containing appropriate clothing and props is a necessity. The teacher may want to bring various dramatic-play boxes to the center throughout the year so that children can pretend they are in the following places:

- pet store
- restaurant
- beauty shop
- barber shop
- bakery
- bank
- campground
- airport or airplane
- post office
- grocery store
- office
- church
- school
- shoe store
- gas station (ideal for encouraging dramatic play outdoors)

The dramatic-play themes are most effective when they are implemented after a similarly themed field trip, connecting them with the children's real experience.

Block/construction center. The block/construction center should be established in an area of the classroom where there is little or no through traffic. The area should have plenty of floor space where children can build, create, and play. Wooden unit blocks, in particular, are essential because they are so versatile and can be used in open-ended play. Research suggests that the child's ability to create complex block structures predicts later mathematical ability. When children build with unit blocks, they learn the names of geometric shapes and have opportunities to explore seriation and classification. When children work on a construction project together, they learn to solve problems. They have opportunities to talk, describing their building, making plans with other children, and deciding what to add next. When one is investing in a set of unit blocks, it is wise to purchase well-made ones. They should be modular (i.e., all sets match and have the same dimensions and proportions). The set of blocks should be large enough to allow children to create elaborate constructions. In addition to the wooden unit blocks, other blocks should be available in a variety of shapes and sizes to use for flat and/or three-dimensional building.

Materials for the block/construction center

- unit blocks
- large hollow wooden blocks
- foam blocks
- waffle blocks
- props, such as people, animals, trucks, cars, boats, airplanes, signs, car floor mat

Manipulatives center. The manipulatives center should have materials appropriate to the children's level of development in eye/hand coordination, body dexterity, and problem solving. Materials to put together and take apart give children opportunities to develop their small muscles.

Materials for the manipulatives center

- blocks that balance or connect
- large beads for stringing
- forms and shapes
- Peg-Boards and pegs
- form puzzles
- wooden puzzles
- magnetic shapes
- matching and bingo games
- pipe fittings
- nuts and bolts
- Tinkertoys
- Lego and Duplo blocks
- locks with keys
- nested boxes
- items for sorting: buttons, rocks, shells
- tongs and cotton balls
- eyedroppers
- farm and school sets
- screwing toys
- lacing cards
- pounding toys

Music center. In the music center the children can explore sounds made with objects of different sizes and shapes. They can make and play instruments, and they can listen to various types of music, including music from other cultures and music of different styles—Christian worship music, hymns, folk ballads, classical music, jazz, and so on. The music center should have a variety of musical instruments and materials that will allow the child to create and experiment with sound and rhythm.

Items for the music center

- homemade instruments
- xylophone
- triangles
- bells
- drums
- sand blocks
- tone blocks
- tambourines
- wind chimes
- cassette and tape player/CD player and CDs
- diverse recordings (regularly rotated)
- creative-movement props, such as scarves and streamers.

Art/creative-expression center. The teacher should prepare the art center to give children opportunities to create, experiment, practice skills, release feelings, and express themselves in a nonthreatening way. When children spend time in the art center, they have many opportunities to make decisions and implement their ideas, activities that build confidence. A daily craft or art project does not take the place of an art center. The art center should encourage free expression. The only direction the teacher gives there should be the different media she brings in for the children to use. In other words, the art center should be totally child-directed. Coloring books have far less value to children's development than most other materials and have no place in this center. The preschool director needs to make sure the teachers understand what art for young children is. A variety of books discussing open-ended art for children should be available in the teacher resource library. The teacher might ask the children what materials they would like to see in the art center; it is amazing what they will come up with. The art center will need to be located near the water source in the classroom.

Items the art center should have at all times

- scissors (child-sized, left- and right-handed)
- paper (manila paper, construction paper, coffee filters, newsprint, wax paper, textured papers, cardboard)
- sticky dots
- crayons
- colored chalk
- watercolor paint
- hole punches
- staplers
- tape
- markers of various sizes
- yarn
- glue and glue brushes (can be old watercolor brushes or child-sized glue brushes)
- cloth fabric
- feathers
- clay
- felt pieces
- craft sticks
- pencils
- paints
- easels
- painting smocks

Science center. The science center should stretch the children's minds and imaginations as they discover some of the wonders of God's world. Here, children can learn about the natural environment, experiment and try out their ideas, and develop problem-solving and questioning skills. The items in the science center should change regularly and may reflect the current season. Children should be encouraged to bring in found items, both from the playground and from their experiences away from school.

Materials to introduce science in exciting ways

- thermometer
- flashlight

- prism
- magnifying glass
- magnets
- plants
- animals
- fish
- insects
- shells
- grain
- variety of seeds
- dried leaves, flowers
- bird nests
- rocks
- feathers
- plastic tubing
- funnels
- eyedroppers
- clear plastic jars with lids
- aquarium
- simple experiments

Sensory center. When children spend time exploring sand, water, and other sensory materials, they gain small-motor coordination. They learn by experimenting with materials and by exploring the physical properties of various objects and substances.

Materials for the sensory center

- accessories for water play
  - funnels
  - eyedroppers
  - measuring cups
  - containers for pouring
  - boats
  - fish
  - people
- sand or rice tub
  - containers of all sizes
  - scoops for pouring
  - measuring cups
  - funnels

  - objects
  - plastic bugs, animals
- shaving cream
- oatmeal
- cornstarch
- sawdust
- flour
- play dough
- goop (cornstarch, water, food coloring)

Math center. Children's experiences with materials in the math center will give them the opportunity to weigh, measure, count, evaluate, calculate, and much more.

Materials for the math center

- variety of objects that can be sorted, grouped, and counted
- various types of clocks
- cash register
- counting cubes/bears
- number games
- lotto games
- abacus
- egg timer
- stopwatch
- number cards
- tactile number cards
- scale
- thermometer
- play money
- rulers
- magnetic numbers and magnet board

Large-motor center. A number of activities requiring vigorous movement can safely be brought indoors if children have a center that encourages large-muscle development. These activities are especially valuable on rainy days, giving children an active choice indoors.

Materials for the large-motor center

- beanbags
- targets (teacher-made or purchased)
- ring-toss games
- hopscotch carpets
- play tunnels
- scarves
- parachute (for a group activity)
- walking cups (small plastic cups that act like stilts)
- balance beam
- rocking boat

Although the activities listed above are safe for children when properly supervised, it is not recommended that teachers set up plastic indoor climbing equipment in the classroom. Neither carpeting nor portable mats provide sufficient cushioning to prevent injury when children fall.[15, 16]

Equipping the Indoor Environment

Important to children's learning experiences at the early education center are the quality and variety of the available materials. To make the most of children's time at school, the classroom must have ample supplies of manipulatives, puzzles, learning equipment, blocks, and so forth. When classrooms are not well stocked, children have difficulty selecting an activity, and they may begin to use the classroom equipment inappropriately or destructively. Classrooms for two-year-olds and young threes will need to have several sets of popular toys.

Along with a sufficient quantity of learning materials, programs need to have a large variety. Different types of equipment accomplish different purposes. You would never sign up for a gym that had only three types of weight machines. In the same way, children need a rich variety of equipment to exercise their mental muscles. Because children are overwhelmed by classrooms with too many items, much

of this varied equipment must be kept in a central storage area and regularly rotated into the classroom.

One way to ensure that the center is appropriately equipped is to budget for replacing and expanding classroom materials on an annual basis. It is also helpful to review a variety of catalogs for ideas on new materials that can enhance the classroom. Teachers should have a part in selecting the new materials since they are aware of the children's needs and can make informed choices about what materials would be beneficial. When teachers have input into the equipping process, they are likely to take great care in selecting items to purchase.

■ Evaluating potential equipment purchases

No early education center can afford to purchase equipment haphazardly. A baseline consideration in evaluating materials is safety for the children. For younger children, in particular, items need to be large enough so that they are not a choking hazard. Items should be tested with a choke tube.

Questions to ask when considering purchases:

- Does the item appear to be of high quality? Is it well-made? Is it constructed of durable material?

- Does it have multiple uses? Some materials are quite versatile and can be used in several different learning centers for a variety of purposes (counting bears, for example).

- Is it age appropriate? A range of difficulty in the levels of the materials will ensure that the needs of all the children will be met. Directors need to keep in mind the kinds of experiences that the typical child of each age needs to have. Equipment that is too far beyond a child's ability will be frustrating, is likely to be misused, and may even be unsafe. Materials that are too immature will not provide enough challenge.

- Will the item have value for the child's growth and development? Typically, toys that are commercially available have a single use, limiting the child's creativity and learning. These items may entertain, but they are not open-ended enough to stimulate growth.

- Can I accomplish the same purpose using a real object? For example, instead of purchasing a wooden lemon attached with Velcro for children to cut apart, using a real lemon for the same purpose will enrich the experience. Real objects often have more sensory appeal and provide the child with a deeper knowledge of the world.

- Will the materials or equipment stimulate learning? Are there pieces that can be sorted and categorized in a variety of ways? What skills will the child develop as a result of exploring the materials? Are basic concepts reinforced, such as sizes, shapes, and colors? Does the material guide children toward achieving one or more of the school's expected outcomes?

- Will it be difficult to maintain? In making larger purchases, such as classroom furniture, it is important to consider that natural wood will require less ongoing maintenance than a painted surface.

▪ Storage

Well-organized, functional storage space is vital in providing an effective early education program. How does something as simple as a cabinet or a closet impact the program? Good storage allows teachers to make the most of the program's resources. Materials that can't be found won't be used. A well-developed storage system also promotes harmony within the teaching staff, minimizing conflicts over shared materials by providing established places for them. Orderly storage of classroom materials helps children to recognize things that belong together and gives

them practice in taking responsibility for returning materials after they have used them.[17] An indirect benefit of a storage system is that it enables the teaching staff to enrich the classroom environment and supports the teachers' motivation to do so.[18]

Materials and equipment can be displayed and stored in a variety of ways. Open storage is often found in classroom interest centers, allowing children to see the available equipment, select an item, and return it after use. Learning materials displayed in open storage need to be rotated regularly to maintain children's interest. If the same materials are always displayed, the children no longer "see" any play choices, and boredom often follows. Having new and varied items to manipulate and explore stimulates children's development.

Closed storage refers to cupboards and storage areas that are not visually accessible. Items in closed storage can be forgotten if they are not regularly inventoried. Posting an inventory list on the inside of a cabinet door provides a visual reminder of what items can be found there. This procedure assists new staff members and volunteers in maintaining the classroom organization. Some storage facilities are fixed, such as a closet or a built-in cabinet, while others are portable—a rolling cart, for instance.

In planning for storage, the director should remember that effective storage is *functional*. Materials should be stored near the place where they will be used. This principle applies to both children (paper and drawing implements near the art center) and staff (resource books near the area where lesson planning is done). The amount of storage space is maximized when containers are the right shape and size for the items they contain and for the shelf where they will be placed. In addition, using clear containers that allow easy identification of the materials inside can make storage more functional.

A storage system must be easy to maintain for both the adults and the children. Items that are well labeled (both the container and the shelf where it is stored) are more apt to be returned properly. Color-coding is another way to make a storage system easy to follow.

Storage equipment can be a part of the director's overall strategy for creating beauty in the class-room. Natural baskets used to store manipulatives or polished rocks add variety and texture to the environment. Plastic trays are practical and easily cleaned, so they are well suited for messy projects, while wooden or woven trays are useful for storing and displaying materials that require less durability.

Outdoor Space

When the administrators and staff begin planning the playground, they need to know the state and local regulatory agencies' requirements for outdoor play space. Many playground manufacturing and sales companies will provide free consulting on the use of outdoor space. They will help with the planning for the immediate play areas and will keep the school's budget in mind as they identify needed and desired equipment. The consultant can also suggest play equipment to be purchased later as the budget permits. Many early education centers have parents who can make playground equipment. It is important that any parents who are involved in building equipment know the safety standards and meet them.

■ Benefits of the outdoor "classroom"

Why is it that early educators sometimes approach children's playground time with less care and planning than they invest in indoor classroom experiences? Some teachers hold an unspoken belief that outdoor play is less meaningful for children, that it represents "off-duty" time for both children and staff. Certainly, one of the great benefits of outdoor play is that it is in a setting *different* from the indoors. On the playground, children can move more freely, express themselves with exuberance, and release their energy with less restriction than they can indoors. Behavior deemed too boisterous or noisy indoors is appropriate on the playground. The expanded options for self-expression offered by outdoor play supply the young child with a needed change of pace.

Although the playground is of great value in stimu-lating children's large-motor growth, the benefit doesn't end there. In addition to the unique advan-tages noted above, the playground functions as an extension of the indoor environment. Their learn-ing and development are not put on "pause" as children exit the classroom door. In some ways, the playground may actually provide a richer learning environment because of the abundance of sensory input it offers.[19] The outdoor environment is rich with possibilities for dramatic and constructive play, which enhances children's cognitive and social development. When the weather is fair, many indoor pursuits can be brought outdoors, including circle time, meals, and art activities.

■ Role of the teacher in outdoor play

The first step in maximizing children's time on the playground is becoming aware of the elements that can be added to the environment to promote all aspects of children's development. The early educator plays an essential role in developing the outdoor environment through observing children on the playground and adding props to enrich their play and build on their interests. Children's outdoor time needs to be planned, and the teach-ing staff can divide up the work by rotating the responsibility for planning it. An attentive teacher observes the invented games that take place sponta-neously indoors and makes plans to provide those experiences on the playground. For example, when children build block structures to jump over or to launch small cars across the room, the teacher can redirect those interests to the playground, providing safe space, suitable materials, and appropriate guidelines for similar activities. Conversely, the playground setting is a great place for teachers to assess the children's cognitive and social development, discovering the skills they have already attained and planning curriculum activities to extend their learning. Teachers can carry a small clipboard or notebook to the playground as a convenient way of recording these observations. Finally, in addition to enhancing children's learning on the playground, adults play a key role in keeping children safe by carefully guiding their use of equipment.[20]

Playground Essentials

Thoughtful playground design addresses both the quantity and quality of activities that will be provided, ensuring that there is a sufficient number of play spaces and that the activities are varied and challenging enough to maintain children's interest. A crowded playground in combination with bored children greatly increases the likelihood of accidental injury. A minimum of 75 square feet of playground space per child is recommended. The playground space should be developed so as to provide five play spaces per child for the number of children in the outdoor area at any given time.[21] When children have plenty of appealing activity choices, they are less likely to wander or misbehave when they are ready to change activities.

The playground should be divided up into activity zones, including areas for climbing, dramatic play, sensory play, and wheel toys. Pathways should be developed to guide children's entrance into the zones and to minimize the potential for collisions. A variety of surfacing is needed: soft cushioning material underneath and around climbing structures, hardtop for tricycles and ball play, and grass for running, rolling, and games.

Shade must be provided, as it protects children from the sun and gives them a place to rest. Plans for the playground should include planting trees that offer shade, are safe for children, and are easy to care for. Awnings or wooden lattice coverings can be installed to supplement any existing trees or to provide shade until the newly planted trees mature.

Options for playground surfacing should be carefully researched and considered. The local licensing agency may require particular types of surfaces for various activities. Below are some suggested areas and some of their uses:

- *Grass area*: great for rolling on, sitting on, playing on, picnicking on

- *Asphalt/blacktop*: great for riding toys, playing ball, drawing on

- *Sand area*: good for using play equipment, water play, digging

- *Fibar*, a synthetic material that simulates bark

- *Pea gravel*: good to put under climbing equipment (pros: drains well in wet weather; cons: children have a tendency to throw it, and it is inaccessible for wheelchairs)

- *Poured-in-place rubber fill systems or interlocking pads*: protect children using climbing equipment (pros: requires little maintenance; cons: expensive and must be replaced after a limited number of years)

▮ Risk

Playgrounds provide safe places for children to master physical challenges. The opportunities they offer for healthy risk-taking build children's confidence and encourage them to tackle other challenges. Because children are growing and changing throughout the school year, playgrounds need to provide graduated challenges that are appropriate for the various age groups using the space as well as activities that can be made more challenging by adding materials.[22] If the playground doesn't provide sufficient challenge for children, they will create their own opportunities and will take risks through the misuse of equipment. When adults anticipate children's need for challenge and plan appropriately, there is less incidence of injury.

■ Loose parts

Playgrounds will hold children's interest when they provide plenty of materials that children can act on and manipulate to create something new. In a recent study of children's preferences in play equipment, children chose to play with loose materials twice as often as any other type of equipment.[23] Given children's innate drive to construct knowledge, it is not surprising that they prefer equipment that supports their need to explore and discover. Loose parts are creative materials that children can make an impact on. Children can "move them, build with them, stack, arrange, tear down, and rearrange them, use them as props for imaginative play, create structures for gross-motor activity, and even incorporate them into games with rules."[24] Loose parts enhance the complexity of play. For example, to the sand and water areas might be added equipment for pouring and sifting, such as scoops, funnels, and pails. Loose parts support both construction and dramatic play. Milk crates and planks, combined with large and small blocks, may be used to create any number of imaginary worlds, from an airplane to a gas station. Other loose parts are supplied by the natural world. In addition to shade, trees offer leaves and twigs that children can collect and transform into money or muffins, depending on the requirements of the play theme.

■ Functionality

If teachers are to make the most of children's outdoor time, the playground must be easy to use. Convenient storage must be available near the play area to house the loose parts, or they will be brought out only infrequently. Children can use simple tools, such as small dustpans and hand-held brooms, to sweep up sand spills. Thus they develop coordination and confidence as they enhance the safety of the environment. Easy access to bathroom facilities from the outdoor area minimizes problems of supervision. Adding child-sized tables creates space that can be used for art activities as well as for just sitting and chatting. Installing effective drainage on the playground increases opportunities to access the playground after wet weather. Even better, when the indoor and outdoor environments can be connected with covered patios, porches, or decks, children can enjoy being outdoors throughout the year.[25]

■ Safety

A number of critical safety issues must be addressed when playgrounds are designed. Extensive guidelines for regulating all components of the playground have been developed by the U.S. Consumer Product Safety Commission. These guidelines include detailed information on the appropriate dimensions for climbing equipment, spacing of equipment, surfacing beneath equipment, and specific hazards, such as head entrapment and protrusions. Because playground safety is such a complex topic, anyone who is designing a playground should access the national safety guidelines and consult playground safety experts when possible.

Playground Areas and Activities

Frances Wardle described an ideal playground as a "safe replica of the natural outdoor environment many of us enjoyed growing up—a variety of textures and materials, gardens, streams, loose parts, places to get away from the crowd, and things to create."[26] Developing a playground that re-creates the best features of the natural environment is not an easy task. However, since the beauty and variety in God's creation reflect His glory, it is definitely a worthwhile pursuit. The early educator can begin by making small improvements to enrich the various activity zones on the playground. Ideas for making the most of the playground can be generated by considering how to optimize in each activity area the potential for children's learning and development.

■ Active large-motor play

Playground equipment should give children opportunities to experience fundamental movements, such as swinging, sliding, rolling, running, jumping, throwing, kicking, bouncing, and balancing. There are multiple places on the playground that allow for these kinds of movements. A low cement divider built to retain the cushioning material under the climbing equipment can also function as a balance beam for children to walk along. Teachers maximize this opportunity by observing children and then adding a challenge, such as suggesting that they walk backwards or sideways, or by supplying a beanbag to balance on their head as they walk. While climbing equipment represents permanent challenges to children's large-muscle development, temporary opportunities for active play should also be provided. For example, teachers can create an obstacle course with spaces for children to crawl underneath, climb over, and wiggle between. Making available a variety of materials, such as balls and beanbags, enhances the developmental opportunities found on the playground. Fully inflated, hard balls are best suited for dribbling, while a stuffed cloth ball is great for catching.[27] Portable basketball hoops on the playground can stimulate the children's interest.

■ Wheel toys

Riding toys are a perennial favorite, providing young children a sense of freedom and independence while also encouraging social play. Playgrounds need to include hard surfaces for wheel toys, with well-developed paths or tracks that provide an interesting route to travel. Different styles of tricycles provide different challenges for steering and coordination, allowing children to develop a range of abilities. Providing varied types of riding toys (traditional tricycles, big-wheel-style tricycles, scooters, and two-wheelers) increases children's opportunities to grow.

Some classes of wheel toys lend themselves well to social play. Wagons and rickshaw-style tricycles give children the chance to take turns giving and taking rides. A wheelbarrow can be guided by a pair of children working together to move loose parts from one place to another, all the while developing their balance and coordination.

■ Dramatic play

Children will engage in make-believe or pretend play on the playground whether the environment encourages it or not. However, the play will be richer in its complexity when it is supported with props and open-ended play structures such as a stripped-down rowboat or a portion of an old car. Even a steering wheel mounted to a wooden box has the potential to become a plane or a bus. An open-framed small playhouse can serve as a jail, a fort, a house, or a hospital. Dress-up clothes and other playhouse props, such as pots and pans, can be brought outside, although the dramatic play area should be located at a distance from the climbing structures to discourage children from trying to climb while wearing capes or other dress-up clothes.

■ Sand play

Sand is a wonderful medium for sensory experiences, exploration of the physical world, dramatic play, and small- and large-muscle coordination. When provided with appropriate tools and accessories, children have the satisfying experiences of burying and digging, sifting, molding, pouring, and measuring. Zoo or farm animals, cardboard tubes, small zip-up plastic bags, and combs can be added to enrich such sand-play staples as scoops, buckets, and sieves. Teachers may vary the environment by maintaining two separate baskets containing different sand toys and rotating them from week to week.

■ Creative expression

Many art materials lend themselves to use in the outdoors. Chalk may be used for sidewalk drawings.

Crayons are terrific for making rubbings of natural items like bark and leaves. Children can create collages of nature materials they have collected. Paint easels can be brought outdoors, where spills can easily be hosed off. Side-by-side outdoor easels can be mounted on chain-link fences, encouraging children to converse and interact as they paint. And afterward, the chain-link fence is a convenient place to hang the paintings as they dry. Painting with water is always a popular activity, one the teacher can easily enrich by providing a variety of brushes. It is also an excellent science activity, allowing children to observe evaporation firsthand. The large, wide-open spaces provided by the hard surface on the playground are particularly convenient for activities that involve a number of children, such as painting a group mural or drawing to music.

■ Exploring nature

Perhaps the best teachable moments for encouraging children to acknowledge God as Creator come from discoveries children make in the natural world. Teachers can support the children's desire to explore by providing such props as these:

- magnifying glasses for looking at grass and leaves
- small containers for collecting and carrying bugs, small pebbles, and other treasures

When teachers and children work together to plant a vegetable or flower garden, children observe the life cycle of plants and have opportunities to develop responsibility in tending to their growth.

Guidelines for Purchasing Outdoor Equipment

Safety must be a key consideration in purchasing outdoor play equipment. Other concerns include how durable the equipment is and how it will benefit children. The early education center should purchase equipment to encourage the children's development, not just for appearance.

Designing a safe and adequate playground takes insight and careful planning. A professional consultant will assist in securing the needed fencing and equipment at a cost that is within the preschool/childcare center's budget. The following are specific types of playground equipment and the kinds of development they can enhance:

- swings: kinesthetic awareness, motor coordination
- climbing equipment: judgment of space and size, self-assurance
- wheeled toys: self-confidence, awareness of space and of other children, large-muscle coordination
- tires: sensory/motor perception, opportunity to jump, bounce, and learn balancing skills
- balls: visual/motor coordination, perceptual development
- sandbox: textures, gravity, tactile stimulation
- playhouse: cooperative play, language development
- crawl-through structures: opportunity for crawling, kinesthetic awareness, muscular coordination, quiet space for a child
- balance beam: balancing, manipulative skills, muscular coordination
- slide: sense of balance, awareness of movement through space
- playhouse: social development, representation/understanding abstractions

The playground area is greatly enhanced by landscaping, which adds color, texture, sound, and motion for children to experience. Children can also observe the changing seasons and the growing process through the trees and plants that are included in the outdoor areas.[28] The selection of trees and foliage must be carefully researched to ensure that the plant materials are nontoxic. A good resource listing poisonous plants and safe plants can be found in *Caring For Children: National Health and Safety Standards.*

Adult Space in the Early Education Center

■ Early education office

An organized, functional office plays a key role in the overall success of the director and in others' perception of the program. An office that appears professional, orderly, and aesthetically pleasing can enhance the director's credibility with parents and staff. When an office is cluttered with papers and learning equipment, stacks of files and broken toys, parents have difficulty viewing the director as competent and trustworthy. Parents can perceive the level of care the director takes in maintaining her own office as consistent with the level of care she gives to managing the program. Sometimes, a director has spent so much time in her office over the years that she doesn't notice the peeling wallpaper or the broken toys. However, ongoing attention to the care and maintenance of the office, including regular cleaning up of the inevitable messes, pays big dividends in parent and staff relations. When the office is warmly and attractively decorated, parents and staff are made to feel more comfortable, and even the director's personal outlook is more positive.

In addition to portraying a positive appearance, the director's office needs to be functional. A filing system needs to be developed and maintained so that important documents can be accessed as needed. Ideally, the director's office is located near the reception area and the classrooms. A clear view to the entrance, so that parents can be greeted as they arrive, is a valuable feature—an essential one for centers that lack a receptionist. The director's office must be large enough to accommodate such basic furnishings as a desk, a chair, two guest chairs, filing cabinets, shelving, and space for a cot for a sick child. The office area needs to be wired to allow for a computer, a printer, a phone, a fax machine, and a copier. Access to the Internet is also becoming an increasingly important tool for successful directors.

■ Staff lounge and workroom

One of the best ways to demonstrate care for the staff is to meet their need for a comfortable place to reenergize in the midst of a busy day with children. Access to a separate, private bathroom is a plus. The staff lounge is a place for teachers to take breaks, eat meals, have staff devotions, and simply relax. A mix of comfortable furnishings (such as a cozy couch) and functional furnishings (such as a table and chairs and shelves for storing resource books) should be provided. The same care used in decorating and arranging the director's office should be taken in making the lounge an attractive place. If the lounge doubles as a workroom, the space will also need to include a place for teachers to work together in planning curriculum and preparing materials. If the staff will be eating meals in the lounge, a microwave and sink are assets. To equip the lounge for its workroom functions, a computer for shared use can be provided along with necessary office supplies. Counter space and additional storage are also desirable. The staff lounge is an ideal place for a bulletin board displaying required postings, recent memos, and notices of upcoming events. A whiteboard facilitates communication and can even be a means for teachers to share Scripture verses or encouraging thoughts with their colleagues. Directors can encourage this practice by posting blank *Today, I noticed ...* forms for staff members to fill out as they see praiseworthy actions among the staff team. Posting such thoughts publicly sets a positive tone in the staff lounge.

■ Reception area for parents

Both arriving at school and picking children up each day can be hectic, stressful times for busy parents. A few comfortable adult-sized chairs placed in the reception area give parents a place to sit and collect their thoughts or share the day's experiences with their child. Making available some Christian parenting magazines or children's books allows the parents to share a story with their child or enjoy a few quiet minutes reading an article. An attractive bulletin board with parenting information and notices of church and community events is a valuable asset to the reception area. Another bulletin board with staff members' photos and brief biographies can help parents connect with the teachers on a more personal level. Having coffee and refreshments available encourages parents to linger and visit with staff and other parents. These meaningful connections are a lifeline for young families who may lack support or may feel isolated. Providing a lending library of books and videos on parenting, marriage, and topics of general Christian interest helps the early education center to fulfill its role as a resource to families. (A list of suggested books for such a library is provided in Appendix B.)

Maintaining the Environment

■ Maintenance procedures

The director must determine that all indoor and outdoor equipment is safe, in good repair, and ready for use each day. The playground should be inspected daily before children are allowed to play. This inspection should include a visual sweep of the grounds to ensure that the playing surfaces do not contain any new hazards. If toys, materials, equipment, or supplies need repair, the job should be done as soon as possible. The director needs to maintain written procedures identifying which individuals or companies to contact for maintenance of the various aspects of the facility. This document becomes a valuable reference for both the director and any staff member managing the program in her absence. A form for the staff to complete advising the director of maintenance needs provides a written record and allows such needs to be prioritized. At times, a parent or a volunteer from the church can be tapped to assist with simple projects, such as assembling bookshelves. A director can often avert a minor plumbing crisis simply by using a plunger, but it is wise to budget funds for most maintenance emergencies.

■ Custodial duties

The sights and smells of the early education center affect every child, parent, staff person, and visitor who enters. From the environment indoors and outdoors, people form conscious or subconscious attitudes about the quality of care the program provides. Dirty carpets, overflowing trash cans, and potty smells are not inviting to anyone, big or small. The director is responsible for setting the standards of cleanliness for the facility. These standards need to be clearly understood by the teaching staff and the custodial crew, who must be held accountable for meeting them every day.

Any cleaning products used in the center must meet the requirements for effectiveness set by the state and local licensing and regulatory agencies. All cleaning supplies must be kept in locked storage out of the reach of children. All spray bottles and storage containers with chemicals in them must be clearly labeled. Cleaning rags should be laundered every day, and fresh rags and cleaning supplies made available to the staff. The director needs to ensure that an adequate supply of tissues, paper towels, and toilet paper is always available and that dispensers are always full and ready for use.

It is unrealistic to think that one cleaning per day will keep the early education center in tip-top shape. In fact, all staff members, including the director, must take responsibility all day, every day, for housekeeping duties. It is important for everyone involved in the program to help keep the facilities clean. Children can be taught how to clean up after themselves, and teachers should be encouraged to do their part in keeping the facilities attractive.

FORM 9.1

Facility Components

- Parking areas for parents and staff: well lighted and secure
- Entryway or transition space: benches and awnings add comfort and appeal
- Secure entryway: visual supervision by staff, or some type of keypad entry for security
- Reception area
  * Warm, bright, welcoming, comfortable
  * Sofa, chair, coffee table, end table
  * Slotted fee box (locked) for tuition checks
  * Bulletin board for parents
  * Toys or books for children
- Classroom space
  * Divided into areas or zones
    _ Arrival: cubbies, sign-in sheets, parent bulletin board, children's take-home art projects, mailboxes for parents
    _ Interest centers
    _ Open area for group circle times (flexible space)
    _ Flexible table space for snack and lunch
  * Basic classroom equipment
    _ Small tables and chairs, sized for the age group
    _ Shelves/storage units
    _ Home-living equipment
    _ Blocks
    _ Toys
    _ Books
    _ Manipulatives
    _ Sensory table
    _ Adult chairs
    _ Easels
    _ Cubbies (coat and backpack storage units)
    _ Sink
  * Classroom storage
    _ Learning materials
    _ Cots or mats and children's bedding
  * Teacher's storage
  * Display space or bulletin boards on walls for children's artwork
  * Countertops for preparing materials
  * Intercoms to director's office
  * Doors with windows, allowing people to see in
  * Sinks: separate ones for art, food preparation, and bathroom
  * Bathrooms
    _ One toilet, one hand-washing sink, and one drinking fountain for every 12 children, all at the children's level
    _ Soap dispenser, paper towels
    _ Waste cans with lids
    _ Safety mirrors at the children's level
  * Flooring: some carpeted space, some hard surfacing for messy areas
  * Windows: at children's eye level, providing views so children can observe outdoor happenings
  * Water fountain
  * Easy access to the playground

FORM 9.1

Facility Components (Continued)

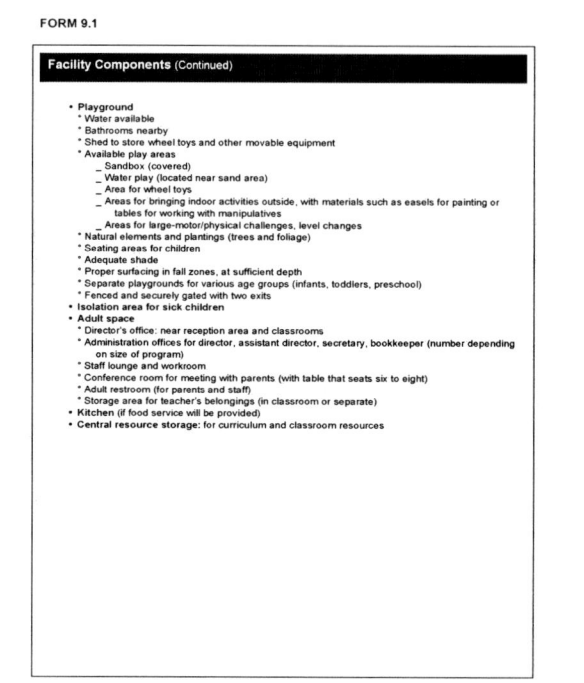

- Playground
  * Water available
  * Bathrooms nearby
  * Shed to store wheel toys and other movable equipment
  * Available play areas
    _ Sandbox (covered)
    _ Water play (located near sand area)
    _ Area for wheel toys
    _ Areas for bringing indoor activities outside, with materials such as easels for painting or tables for working with manipulatives
    _ Areas for large-motor/physical challenges, level changes
  * Natural elements and plantings (trees and foliage)
  * Seating areas for children
  * Adequate shade
  * Proper surfacing in fall zones, at sufficient depth
  * Separate playgrounds for various age groups (infants, toddlers, preschool)
  * Fenced and securely gated with two exits
- Isolation area for sick children
- Adult space
  * Director's office: near reception area and classrooms
  * Administration offices for director, assistant director, secretary, bookkeeper (number depending on size of program)
  * Staff lounge and workroom
  * Conference room for meeting with parents (with table that seats six to eight)
  * Adult restroom (for parents and staff)
  * Storage area for teacher's belongings (in classroom or separate)
- Kitchen (if food service will be provided)
- Central resource storage: for curriculum and classroom resources

RECRUITING AND ENROLLING STUDENTS

Chapter 10

So neither he who plants nor he who waters is anything, but only God, who makes things grow. (1 Corinthians 3:7)

First Impressions

To base a decision on a first impression seems unfair. However, the fact is that all of us depend on first impressions until we get more complete information. The first impressions a parent receives when visiting an early education center or telephoning for information are very important. The sights, smells, and sounds of the center will influence prospective parents before they ever meet the director or observe the program. Planning ahead with the staff can help the staff members make good first impressions. Here are a few helpful ideas:

• Staff members should use a prepared script in answering the telephone. ("Good morning, this is Westside Christian Early Education Center. How may I help you?") By instructing the staff to answer the phone in this manner, the director helps to ensure that all callers will be greeted politely. Teaching the staff to smile as they speak will improve the impression the information gives. Information about the center should be prepared and accessible, posted near the phone, so that any staff member will be able to give the basic facts to a caller. The staff should be instructed to tell only what they know. There is nothing wrong with saying, "I don't have that information, but I'll make sure the director calls you with it." Incorrect information is confusing and suggests that the center's staff members are incompetent. A telephone log or an inquiry form should be kept by the phone to ensure that the director can follow up on prospective parents. (See form 10.1 Inquiry Source Log.) The log should contain the following information:

- date and time of call
- Name and number of caller
- Nature of the call
- Further action regarding the call
- Action completed[1]

• People have different feelings about telephone answering machines, and using them can be risky. However, having an answering machine give basic information after hours is better than providing no information at all. During hours of operation, the center should never use an answering machine as a substitute for a human voice. Even if all available staff members are too busy to give detailed information, someone can still answer the telephone and take a message.

• The entrance to the center should be clean and inviting to prospective parents and children. What parents see when they enter the building will make them want to go further or turn around and leave. Uncluttered entrances, hallways, and floors tell parents that the center's staff members are well-organized and conscientious about safety. Backpacks, coats, and other items should be kept in designated places. A "Parent Messages" board lets parents know that the director and staff members care about keeping them informed.

• A sign-in roster should be placed at the entrance to the center so that visitors can register. Child safety is of utmost concern to parents. It's a good idea to show prospective parents that the center wants to know who is visiting the building at any given time. A sign-in roster also helps the director by providing an address to use in following up on the visit.

• If the center is blessed to have a receptionist on staff, the place for that person is at the building entrance. The receptionist should be prepared to greet each person and give appropriate information.

• Being real and honest about mistakes, errors in judgment, and those unprepared-for moments lets prospective parents know that the center is not perfect. A situation in which the director, staff members, and/or children work together to solve problems lets the parent see firsthand how the center handles difficult situations.

• The director should be prepared to spend time answering questions and touring the center with prospective parents. Visiting parents enjoy meeting the staff, but they are most interested in the director. They know that the director sets the tone for the center. If the director is unable to spend time with a parent, the assistant director, secretary, or another qualified staff member should be ready to answer questions and give a tour of the facility. While it is important for someone to be available to assist prospective parents, the director must always put the care of the children first. Children must never be left unattended for any reason. Parents will appreciate knowing that children are put first.

• Giving parents an information brochure to read will suffice until a staff member can give further information without interruption. The brochure and other materials about the center can be compiled and put into an introductory packet, which will often be a parent's first contact. The packet should be attractive and informative, and the information in it should make the parent want to find out more. A neat, attractive packet will say to parents that the center cares about quality. With a little time and money, the director can create a packet that will market the center effectively. The packets should always be handy and available for handing out or mailing. If someone requests that an information packet be mailed, it should be sent out as soon as possible. A follow-up call should be placed to give the prospective family a chance to ask questions.

- There is never a second chance to make a good first impression. However, if the director believes a parent's first impression of the center has been unfavorable, she should make every effort to help the parent form a new and more positive impression.

Policies and Procedures

The availability of clearly defined policies and procedures helps the director answer questions and clarify problem areas at the time of enrollment. Specific procedures for handling tuition and class placement should be clearly identified as well as charges for both late tuition and late pick-up. These policies and procedures should be given to prospective families at the time of their tour or of their child's enrollment. Some state licensing agencies require that this information be given before the child starts school. Having a signed statement clearly acknowledging that the parent has read and agreed to the school's policies can prevent potential misunderstandings at the time of enrollment. A good rule of thumb is to require that the signed statement be submitted at the time of enrollment to ensure that is collected and documented. A shortened version of the policies can be provided in the registration packet and given out as a part of the parent handbook at the beginning of the school year.

Managing Enrollment

Managing enrollment is one of the top priorities of the early education director. The future success of the program rests on the ability to maintain full enrollment, keeping up with the turnover by regularly filling the slots as they become available.

Waiting lists need to be maintained with current information to avoid time spent on outdated numbers and uninterested families. Periodically, the school should send out a form to those on the waiting list to determine their continued interest in remaining on the list. In that way the center can keep its lists up to date. To maximize available openings, programs that maintain a consistent schedule of M–F, MWF, TTH, and full or half days find it easier to identify those on the waiting list who would be interested in any available spot. Programs that allow families to enroll for the days they prefer have a more difficult time finding a match for the openings. Some centers establish a priority waiting list for families who are willing to complete all the registration forms and pay the registration fee in advance, demonstrating their intent and expediting enrollment once a slot becomes available.

Another important consideration is how long the center will wait to hear back from a family that has been contacted about an available opening. Some families place their names on several waiting lists at a time. They may not have visited every program and thus may not be ready to make a decision at the time they are called. When parents first place their name on the waiting list, they should be encouraged to visit the program for a tour. If the director indicates that they will have only a short window of time to respond after they are called about an available opening, they are more likely to be prepared to decide quickly. Waiting two weeks to hear back about a potential student will result in a significant financial loss. Giving families a short window of time to inform the center of their decision will enable the director to move on and find an interested party to fill the opening. If there are no potential students on the waiting list, the center may receive phone calls from those who are looking for an immediate spot. It is wise to let callers know of any opening immediately, while they are on the phone. Also, letting callers know that the openings will be available on a first-come-first-served basis to the family that shows an interest by touring the facility will put the center in a better position to fill the opening with the most interested family.

Facility Tours

Centers that offer tours at established times or days of the week can make the most of their time with potential families. This is not to say that those who show up unannounced should not receive a tour, but having regular tour times will help cut down the time the director spends out of the office. Typically, tours are short, and they sometimes include the child. Some parents want to see how their child responds to the program. Parents should be encouraged to bring their children, visit the classrooms with them, and enjoy the center's environment together for a short time. Teachers can inform the parents if after a few minutes their child needs to transition out of the classroom. If parents wish to arrange to make an extended stay or to allow their child to interact with the other children, arrangements can be made for them to do so at a later time.

Interview/Orientation

Most state and local regulatory agencies require that a parent interview/orientation be conducted before a child is accepted into the early education center. Typically this interview/orientation is conducted in the child's absence, and prior to or at the time of enrollment. The interview/orientation should involve both parents, and it should last no longer than one hour. The parent interview/orientation is an opportunity for the director to let the center shine. The director will want to prepare for a relaxed and comfortable environment. Arrangements should be made for another staff member to take phone calls or handle any other interruptions. The parent interview/orientation should include the following:

- Questions by the director to determine the mutual compatibility of the center and the family
- Information about parent participation in the center
- Questions by the director about the child
- Information about the program
- Information about discipline
- Information about payment
- A time for parents to ask questions
- A tour of the center and teacher introductions
- A time to go over important information about the center's policies and procedures for medication, sick children, accidents, and so forth
- All information forms and parent handbook given to parents at the end of the interview

The parent interview/orientation is an important opportunity for the director to begin building a relationship with the parents. Parents are entrusting their dearest gift from God into the care of the early education center. They need to leave the interview confident that the center takes this responsibility seriously.

Information Packet

Utmost care and thought should be given to creating an information packet. This packet should be a true reflection of the nature of the program. Attractive, informational marketing materials should be included along with basic information regarding the program. The information packet should include the following:

- *A greeting letter from the director.* The greeting letter should thank the parents for their interest in the center and invite them to come for an observation and to call with any additional questions.

- *A basic informational brochure* about the center and its programs. The information brochure should be concise and up-to-date, and it should be designed in a way that suggests the attractiveness and the inviting nature of the program. It should contain the following:

  ° Program philosophy
  ° Objectives
  ° Admission policy
  ° Staff
  ° Hours and sessions
  ° Center activities
  ° Program distinctives
  ° Tuition rates (See form 10.4 Bookkeeping Notice.)
  ° Parent communication
  ° Address and location
  ° Nondiscrimination policy
  ° Organizations the center belongs to

- *Policies and procedures booklet.* This booklet should contain the main policies and procedures of the center's program in an edited version to minimize printing costs. The major areas the booklet should cover are class placement, finances, discipline, and late charges. (See form 10.8 Early Education Center Manual.)

- *Overview of the curriculum guide.* This overview would contain a shortened version of each monthly theme as well as Bible truths, character traits, learning concepts, and a description of any resources used in the classroom to supplement the curriculum.

- *Expected outcomes.* ACSI is encouraging all member schools to develop a set of expected outcomes for their programs. These outcomes identify what the center wants the children in its program to look like when they leave the program. Each domain can be identified. ACSI has developed a

model of early education outcomes to use in beginning this process.

- *Copy of the daily schedule.* The daily schedule helps parents understand the nature of the program and know how the children will be spending their time at school.

- *Enrollment forms.* Each state has certain required forms that parents need to complete to enroll their child at the preschool/childcare level. It is important to identify which forms are required by the state and which are unique to the program. Required enrollment forms may include an application or general information form, a medical release, pick-up authorization, an agreement to abide by the policies, a tuition agreement statement, an immunization history, a physician's report, a health history, and a family questionnaire. (See forms 10.5 Enrollment Agreement, 10.6 Parental Agreement, and 10.7 Parent Questionnaire.)

Application and Enrollment Process

The center should establish a plan for giving and receiving applications for enrollment. (See form 10.2 Application for Enrollment.) Some programs have a registration process that involves first registering continuing students for the new school year and then enrolling siblings, church members, and those on the waiting list. (See form 10.3 Child Intake Checklist.) A typical process could include these elements:

- Information packet given to the parent
- Parent visit for observing the center
- Submission of the application and payment of the application fee
- Parent/director interview
- Acceptance of the child into the center
- First day of school and phasing in the child

The application form may ask for basic information about the child and the parent consistent with the center's philosophy and statement of faith. This information includes the child's name, date of birth, address, parents' phone numbers (home and work), specifics about the child's health (including any allergies and/or medications), fears, eating habits, previous early education experience, reasons for wanting the child enrolled, and other pertinent information. Questions about Christian testimony, church attendance, pastoral reference, and philosophy of Christian education can also be included. The application should help the director decide whether the preschool/childcare center and the prospective family are compatible. Admission policies should reflect the program's philosophy and its statement of faith, and the school should inform parents of the program's Christian philosophy at the beginning of the application process.

A nonrefundable registration fee should be turned in with the application along with all necessary forms. The fee need not be high, but paying it can help the parent make a firm commitment to the application process and to the center. Also, the fee will cover any administrative costs incurred. Centers should establish a strong policy that all forms need to be turned in before the child begins school. Parents should also be informed of how much time they need to allow for this process and when their child can begin school.

Publications

The time and money invested in creating high-quality publications will pay off in the long run. Brochures should be both attractive and informative, covering basic facts about the program. The selection of words and pictures communicates the school's love for children and its attention to detail. The availability of appropriate computer programs and preprinted paper make it fairly easy to create an attractive brochure at a low cost. If you as a director struggle to be creative, ask a talented staff member to help you. Printed materials provide parents with impressions that can make or break their decision to enroll. Besides being attractive, parent handbooks need to be detailed and informative about the nature of the program and the curriculum.

Discounts/Incentives

Many programs use discounts as a strategy to attract new families. Advertisements in local publications, often including coupons or offering discounts, can be useful and cost effective. Giving the center's existing families an opportunity to earn a discount for each family they bring in is another strategy. Your current families are your best advertisement.

Student Placement/Class Selection

Selecting the right child for the right class is a challenge for any director. Not knowing some of the children makes the job even harder. The center needs to establish a philosophy regarding the grouping of children. The two basic strategies for grouping children are chronological grouping and vertical grouping.[2] In chronological grouping, children of similar ages, typically within a range of one year, are placed in the same class. Vertical grouping establishes classes of mixed age ranges. Programs need to identify which strategy they will use. Here are some points for directors to remember when making class selections:

- First and foremost, pray! The director will need to depend completely on the Holy Spirit for wisdom and direction. At the beginning of the year, when many children are new and all have grown and matured over the summer, the director must depend on the Spirit of God to impart His insight for placing children in a class.

- The director should make every effort to understand the background of each child. It is helpful to reread each child's application carefully and review the interview notes. Information about the child's birth date, previous early education experience, and likes and dislikes can help immensely. If the child was enrolled in a preschool/childcare center in the preceding year, consulting the classroom teacher may be beneficial.

- Balancing a class according to birth dates and the boy-to-girl ratio is sometimes tricky, particularly if the enrollment of the entire center is not balanced in these areas. It is important, though, for each class to be as balanced as possible.

- Class size is also a concern. The effort to keep each class at or under the teacher-to-child ratio set by the center will influence class selection. These ratios need to be strictly maintained.

- Special needs of students need to be considered in class placement, with consideration given to the children's developmental age as well as their chronological age. Placing a child with a particular teacher can also be beneficial in meeting individual needs.

Determining the best group arrangement for each classroom is key to a successful program. Licensing guidelines will provide some parameters in arranging the classes. Following are some basic considerations:

- Number of children allowed based on room size
- Determining your maximum group size
- Age range of the children
- Adult/child ratios
- Qualifications of the teaching staff

Directors can also solicit information from parents to help finalize the children's placement according to the following:

- Ages of the children
- Their personality characteristics
- Developmental level of the children
- Previous early education or group experience of the children
- Special needs of the children[3]

FORM 10.1

Inquiry Source Log

Date	Name Address	How They Heard						Brochure Sent (date)	Tour Scheduled (date)
		Phone Book	Newspaper Ad	Drive By	Friend	Other			

FORM 10.2

Application for Enrollment

<Early Education Center *logo*>

Application

for

<church/school name> Early Education Center

Submit completed application to the *<church/school name>* Early Education Center office with the $*<amount of fee>* nonrefundable application fee.

Welcome!

Thank you for expressing an interest in *<church/school name>* Early Education Center. As part of the application process, we invite you to take a few moments and carefully read through this information packet. We also encourage you to come in and visit the center's facility. We feel that the best way for you to get to know us is to see us in action. Please give our office a call if you have any questions. We look forward to serving you and your family in the future.

In His service,

Director

FORM 10.2

Application for Enrollment (Continued)

For office use only	
Entered on computer	
Account number	
Registration applied	
Room assignment	

<church/school name> Early Education Center

Application for Enrollment

Current date:		Starting date:		
Child's full name:				
	Last	First	Middle	Answers to
Date of Birth	☐ Male	☐ Female		
T-shirt size:	☐ 2/4	☐ 6/8	☐ 10/12	
Toddler class (Check class appropriate for child)	☐ 3-year-old class	☐ 4-year-old class	☐ Prekindergarten	

Parent/guardian #1

Mr./Mrs./Ms.	Home phone:		
Home address:	Cell phone:		
City/state/zip:	Lives with student?	☐ Yes	☐ No
Relation to student:	Billing party?	☐ Yes	☐ No
Employer/occupation:	Work phone:		

Parent/Guardian #2

Mr./Mrs./Ms.	Home phone:		
Home address:	Cell phone:		
City/ state /zip:	Lives with student?	☐ Yes	☐ No
Relation to student:	Billing party?	☐ Yes	☐ No

Other than parents, the child will be released only to persons indicated below (must include at least two local persons to call for illness, accidents, late pick-up, or other emergency reasons). Please list them in the order of preference for us to contact.

Mr./Mrs./Ms	Home phone:		
Home address:	Cell phone:		
City/ state /zip:	Lives with student?	☐ Yes	☐ No
Relation to student:	Billing party?	☐ Yes	☐ No
Employer/occupation:	Work phone:		

FORM 10.2

Application for Enrollment (Continued)

Mr./Mrs./Ms.	Home phone:		
Home address:	Cell phone:		
City/state/zip:	Lives with student?	☐ Yes	☐ No
Relation to student:	Billing party?	☐ Yes	☐ No
Employer/occupation:	Work phone:		
Mr./Mrs./Ms.	Home phone:		
Home address:	Cell phone:		
City/state/zip:	Lives with student?	☐ Yes	☐ No
Relation to student:	Billing party?	☐ Yes	☐ No
Employer/occupation:	Work phone:		

Special physical conditions/allergies we should be aware of:

Names and ages of other children in the family:

Has your child ever been in an early education center before?	☐ Yes	☐ No

If yes, where?

Church membership or religious preference:

Medical Information

Name of child's physician or clinic:

Physician or clinic address:	Phone:

Name of medical insurance:

Date when child was last examined by a physician:

Consent to Medical Care and Treatment of Minor Child

I, *<name of natural parent or legal guardian>*, hereby give permission for my child *<name of child>* to be given emergency treatment, to include first aid and CPR by a qualified staff member of *<church/school name>* Early Education Center. I further authorize and consent to medical, surgical, and hospital care, treatment, and procedures to be performed for my child by my child's regular physician, or when that physician cannot be reached, by a licensed physician or hospital when deemed immediately necessary or advisable by the physician to safeguard my child's health if I cannot be contacted. In such a case, I waive my right of informed consent to such treatment.

FORM 10.2

Application for Enrollment (Continued)

I also give permission for my child to be transported by ambulance or aid car to an emergency center for treatment. I further authorize said center to take my child to a hospital, and I agree that I will pay all physician and hospital bills, and said center will not be responsible for them.

Signature of Parent/Guardian	Date

Photograph Release

I release <church/school name> Early Education Center to photograph and/or videotape my child participating in daily activities, and to use the photographs and/or videos in photographic displays or other publications showing these daily activities.

Signature of Parent/Guardian	Date

FORM 10.3

Child Intake Checklist

<church/school name> Early Education Center		
Child Intake Checklist		
Child's name	Birth date	Class assigned
Parent's name(s)		
Starting date		
Days of attendance		
Director's Responsibility		
• Tour of center scheduled for <date>		
• Policies and procedures of center		
• Philosophy of center		
• Fees (registration, monthly tuition, premium), number of days, finance charge, late pickup fees)		
• Forms (registration, immunization, agreement, bookkeeping)		
• Immunizations, yearly checkups		
• Sick children, medication (doctor-prescribed and over-the-counter)		
• Food program		
• Check-in and check-out procedures		
• Intake form to center office		
Bookkeeper's Responsibility		
• Registration form or fee returned		
• Student file set-up		
• Registration fee applied to account		
• First month's tuition applied to account		
• Recurring tuition schedule set-up		
• Agreement form to parent/guardian on <date>		
• Agreement form returned <date>		
Administrative Assistant's Responsibility		
• Copy of registration form to director		
• Copy of registration form to bookkeeper		
• Note to teacher		
• T-shirt to parent		
• Child's name added to class list and posting book		
• Medical information added to master list (updated copy to all teachers)		

FORM 10.4

Bookkeeping Notice

	For office use only
	Computer Adjusted
	Refund Requested

Child's name:			
☐ Toddler	☐ 3-year-old Class	☐ 4-year-old Class	☐ Prekindergarten

Account name:		
Classroom:		

Change the following (check all boxes that apply)

Classroom assignment		to	
	Effective date		
Child now reserved for:	M T W Th F (full days)	M T W Th F (half days)	
Request change to:	M T W Th F (full days)	M T W Th F (half days)	
	Effective date		
Dropping: last day			
Please send refund check to the following address:			
Would like to return, starting			
Comments:			

Parent's signature:		
☐ Approved	☐ Disapproved	☐ See comments
Date	Director's signature	

Director's comments:

New monthly tuition:

FORM 10.5

Enrollment Agreement

	For office use only
	Effective Date
	Account Number
	First Month Tuition Applied
	Recurring Tuition Setup

<church/school name> Early Education Center
Enrollment Agreement

<church/school name> Early Education Center agrees to provide qualified staff and facilities consistent with state licensing requirements for the care and education of your child.

The monthly tuition includes breakfast, hot lunch, and afternoon snack.

I, <name of parent or guardian>, agree to register my child, <name of child>, into the <name of program> at <church/school name> Early Education Center.

I am registering for (please check days):

Full days

☐ Monday	☐ Tuesday	☐ Wednesday	☐ Thursday	☐ Friday

Half days

☐ Monday	☐ Tuesday	☐ Wednesday	☐ Thursday	☐ Friday

My monthly tuition will be	$
Less the multiple child discount of	$
Total monthly tuition	$

I understand that tuition is due the last working day of the month for the following month unless a written agreement has been made with the director or bookkeeper. I also understand that I pay for the number of days reserved for my child regardless of attendance.

I agree to pay my monthly tuition by the last working day of the month for the following month, with payments made:

☐ Weekly	☐ Biweekly	☐ Monthly

A late fee of 1.5 percent per month of the past-due balance will be added to the account if not cleared by the 5th of the following month. The early education center's services may be subject to termination for unpaid balances.

Date:	Signature of parent or guardian:
First month tuition $	Signature of bookkeeper:

FORM 10.6

Parental Agreement

<church/school name> Early Education Center

We, the parents of *<name of child>*, have read the General Policy and the *Parent Handbook* and will cooperate with the policies and purposes of the school.

We as parents are aware of the requirement of our attendance at the parent workshops and will fulfill our responsibility by attending each session unless other arrangements have been made with the director.

We further understand that the Bible and religious training are a part of every aspect of the early education center's program.

Father's signature: _____

Mother's signature: _____

FORM 10.7

Parent Questionnaire

	<church/school name> Early Education Center
1.	What would you like your child to learn about God?
2.	What are your three highest priorities regarding the total education of your child?
	a.
	b.
	c.
3.	Why have you chosen *<church/school name>* Early Education Center for your child?

Please give any information concerning your child that will be helpful in his/her experience in the early education environment:

Play habits	
Likes and dislikes	
Fears	
Eating behaviors	
Home situation	
Other	

FORM 10.8

Early Education Center Manual

Early Education Center Logo

<church/school name> Early Education Center

Parent Handbook

FORM 10.8

Early Education Center Manual (Continued)

Letter of Welcome
Welcome to *<church/school name>* Early Education Center. We're glad that you are a part of our family. Clear communication is one of the keys to a successful early education program. This handbook contains specific information and requirements set forth by *<church/school name>* Early Education Center, ACSI (Association of Christian Schools International), and the State of *<name of state>*. After reading it, please sign the handbook verification stating that you have received, read, and understood this information. This verification will be kept in your child's file and must be turned in within 30 days of his/her enrollment at the center. The handbook is designed as a handy reference for you. We suggest you keep it in a convenient place for easy referral throughout the school year.

Regulations
In compliance with the State of *<name of state>* Department of Human Services, *<church/school name>* Early Education Center is required to have the following information in your child's file. It is necessary to have this information updated on an annual basis.

Health Status
A dated, written statement about the child's current health status, signed by an approved health professional, shall be obtained at least annually for each child less than seven years old, or whenever the director shall have reason to suspect that a child participating in the program may have a condition hazardous or potentially hazardous to others, or finds that the child's general condition indicates the need for such examination. The statement of health status shall be obtained at the time of admission or within 30 days after admission.

Immunization Form
Information regarding all immunizations the child has had, including the month and year when each immunization was administered. Immunizations must be recorded on the certificate of immunization form supplied by the *<name of state>* Department of Health. The immunization form shall be obtained at the time of admission or within 30 days after admission.

Emergency Form
The parents' (guardians') home and work emergency contact information, the child's known allergies to foods or medications, a release permitting emergency medical treatment, and a release for field trips shall be obtained at the time of admission or within 30 days after admission.

Authorization for Pickup
Information giving permission for person(s) other than the parents to pick up the child from the early education center. Any person other than the child's parent will be asked to show identification. It is a good practice for the parent to notify the staff or director when other person(s) are picking up the child on a given day. In emergency situations, parents sometimes need other person(s) not on the "Authorization for Pickup" form to pick up the child. In such cases, the parent must give written authorization or verbal authorization over the phone. The authorization for pickup also includes information indicating anyone who is not allowed to pick up a child. The center has specific instructions for the director and/or staff in the event an unauthorized person attempts to pick up a child. These instructions are located in the classroom.

FORM 10.8

Early Education Center Manual (Continued)

Handbook Verification
A parent/guardian-signed verification that the parent has received, read, and agrees to abide by the policies and practices in the *Parent Handbook* is kept in the child's file. This information shall be obtained at the time of admission or within 30 days after admission.

Photo Release
A parent/guardian-signed consent for your child to be photographed shall be in the child's file.

Video Release
A parent/guardian-signed consent for each child to watch center-approved videos shall be in the child's file.

Reenrollment
Held during the month of February at <church/school name> Early Education Center. During this month you will have an opportunity to enroll your child in a class for the following school year.

Sign-in/Sign-out Procedures
Each child must be signed in and out by an adult. Sign-in logs for students are located on the outside of the center classroom doors. Sign-out logs are located in the classrooms.

Adjustment Period
Starting school for the first time often causes anxiety for children. We recommend that you visit the early education center with your child before the first day of school, allowing him/her to meet some of the staff and see other children at play. We will work with you and your child to make this adjustment period a positive experience. We recommend that you give your child at least one month to adjust to the early education center experience.

PAYMENT PROCEDURES
Tuition Policy
It is the policy of <church/school name> Early Education Center that all tuition be paid on or before the 1st of the month. A rebilling fee of <amount> per month will be charged if payment is made after the 15th of the month. If an account becomes 30 days past due, the family has 10 days to bring the account within the 30-day limit. Failure to do so will result in the child's being withdrawn from the school until the account is current.

Withdrawal Notice
A two-week advance written notice is required to withdraw a child from the center or program.

Reenrollment Fee
There is an annual fee for reenrolling for the following school year.

FORM 10.8

Early Education Center Manual (Continued)

Late Pickup Fee
Parents who fail to pick their children up after school will be charged a late pickup fee of <amount>.

MEDICAL/EMERGENCY INFORMATION
Absences
We plan our programs with the assumption that every child will attend every scheduled class. If your child is unable to attend the center, please notify the office. If your child is absent because of illness with a communicable disease, please let us know as soon as possible. We are required to notify all parents of communicable diseases.

Sick Children
State regulation <number or regulation> requires that there be daily observation of each child on arrival at the center by a person capable of recognizing common signs of communicable diseases or other evidence of ill health. A child who is ill upon arrival at the center will not be admitted or will be separated from the other children until parent or guardian can pick the child up.

When children have been exposed to communicable diseases such as hepatitis, chicken pox, measles, or strep infection, all staff members and all parents or guardians of children shall be notified immediately by the center. For any infectious disease, we ask that you seek your physician's advice and always notify us of the disease.

If a child becomes ill while at the center, the parent or guardian will be contacted and expected to pick the child up as soon as possible. The child will be separated from the other children until the parent's arrival.

If a child displays any of the following symptoms, he/she must be kept at home:

fever
diarrhea
nasal secretions that are thick, yellow or green, and accompanied by a fever. Cloudy or colored nasal secretions may indicate an allergy. Please check with your doctor to rule out infection.
sore throat with fever or throat spots
cough accompanied by fever, chills, vomiting, nausea, and the coughing up of green or yellow mucus
eye drainage of any type should be checked by a doctor to rule out infection
unusual rashes should be checked by a doctor to rule out bacterial infection
child not feeling well, such as lethargic behavior and/or crying

The child may return to the center after illness when one of the following happens:

fever has broken for 24 hours
nausea, vomiting, or diarrhea has subsided for 24 hours
at least 4 doses of antibiotic have been given over a 24-hour period for any type of strep or bacterial infection
child is feeling well again and normal behavior has returned

FORM 10.8

Early Education Center Manual (Continued)

Medication
Tranquilizers and sedatives, or special medical procedures, shall be given or applied only when the child's parent(s) or guardian(s) has provided a written order or a prescription from a physician. Without a written prescription from a physician, the center will not administer over-the-counter medications to the child, including cough syrup, aspirin, and allergy medications. All prescribed medications must be in their original containers, and parents or guardians must sign the Medication Release stating the kind of medication, the amount to be given, and the time it is to be administered.

Allergies
All allergies to medication and/or other substances must be stated on the emergency and medical forms. <name of state> law requires that we have a signed note from a physician explaining any food allergies that a child may have. The physician must recommend alternate food choices for the child. Information about children with allergies will be posted in all classrooms and in the kitchen.

Accidents
All head teachers are certified in infant/child care and infant/child first aid. In the case of any accident, assessment and treatment of the injury will be given under the supervision of the teacher and/or director. If further treatment is deemed necessary, the parent, guardian, or emergency contact person will be called. All accidents are recorded on an accident report form that requires the signature of the parent.

Inclement and Excessively Hot Weather
On days of inclement or excessively hot weather, children will be kept inside the classrooms. Sunscreen is applied to all children on warm sunny days. The center uses two types of sunscreen: <name of sunscreen> and <name of sunscreen>. If you wish to provide another brand of sunscreen for your child, it must be labeled with the child's first and last names and given to the teacher. Do not send it in your child's backpack. By signing this handbook, you are giving permission to apply one of the brands named above.

Tornadoes
In the event of a tornado warning, students will be escorted to a safe shelter in one of our inner rooms (kitchen, staff bathroom, office) and instructed in proper safety procedures.

Snow Days
When severe weather conditions exist, please listen to the radio for school closings. Stations <name of station>, <name of station>, and <name of station> will carry this information. In the event of a delayed opening, please listen to the radio for specific information about the early education center classes.

Fire Drills
Fire drills are held on a monthly basis in order to familiarize the children with proper and safe procedures for exiting the building in an emergency. In the event of a fire, students will be evacuated according to plan. The school building is inspected on a regular basis by the fire marshal. The most recent inspection information is located in the school office.

FORM 10.8

Early Education Center Manual (Continued)

Child Abuse
The staff of <church/school name> Early Education Center are required by <name of state> state law to report any suspicion of child abuse.

Health
<church/school name> Early Education Center is inspected on a regular basis by the Department of Health. The most recent inspection information is located in the office.

Early Education Center Information
The center's activities revolve around a monthly theme. These themes include Bible-based character-building studies, open-ended art projects, and much more. All activities are presented in an age-appropriate manner.

Parent Involvement
We welcome parent involvement in the early education center classroom, and we feel that parent involvement benefits not only the center but the parent and child as well. Parents are encouraged to participate as classroom helpers on a regular basis. Parent participation enables the teacher to offer a variety of creative activities for students. The State of <name of state> requires that all parents who participate in the center classroom must have a current negative TB test on file. All parent volunteers must sign in when they come to work in the classroom. Some ways that parents can participate in the early education experience are driving and chaperoning on field trips, helping with special-day themed events, serving on the teacher-appreciation committee, and much more. Parents driving on field trips must have evidence of insurance in their child's file.

Field Trips
Field trips are an integral part of the early education center experience. They enhance learning by offering opportunities not available in the classroom. Parents will be notified of a forthcoming field trip at least two weeks in advance. We encourage all children going on a field trip to wear a center T-shirt. The T-shirts are sold at minimal cost throughout the year and are available in the center office.

Special Event Days
Throughout the school year the center's staff plans special activity days to enhance the monthly classroom themes. Parents are encouraged to participate by helping in the classroom or by providing special snacks or activities.

Snacks
Classroom snacks are provided by parents on a rotating basis. Parents are encouraged to provide nutritious and safe snacks. Parents supply juice, napkins, and 5-ounce cups along with the snack. Teachers may ask parents to bring a special snack that enhances the monthly theme or special activity. Parents will be notified each month of their specific snack day. All snacks are to be in their unopened original containers or individually wrapped. No homemade snack foods are allowed. Fruit or vegetables must be cut and prepared in the center's kitchen or classroom using the center's utensils. Check with the teacher if you are in doubt about a particular snack. Some suggested snacks follow:

FORM 10.8

Early Education Center Manual (Continued)

- Juice: apple, orange, mixed fruit. Please do not bring sugar-sweetened red punch or grapejuice.
  Please do not bring popcorn, nuts, or grapes.
- Other snacks: crackers, breads, pretzels, fruits, cheese, vegetables

Birthdays are very special occasions for children. We would like you to help us celebrate by bringing a special snack for your child's birthday. Cakes or cupcakes are appropriate for the occasion (must be store-bought and in their original container). The teacher will contact you in advance of your child's birthday. Summer birthdays are celebrated during the school year.

Book Clubs
Each month parents will receive a book club newsletter and order form. These books are offered at exceptional prices and allow families to build their home libraries. When you purchase books through the book clubs, the teacher receives points with which he or she can order books for the classroom free of charge. We do ask that you choose your books carefully, as we cannot endorse all the materials offered. If you have a question about a particular book or would like us to make recommendations, talk to your child's teacher. When ordering books from a particular book club, please use a check as payment and make sure your check(s) are made out to that particular club.

Supplies
Parents need to provide the following items for children enrolled in the early education center. We share the first five items among the children in the classrooms; therefore, we ask that you do not label them:

Box of 16 crayons
Set of large, washable basic-color Crayola markers
Single set of Crayola watercolors
Large box of tissue
One school-sized bottle of glue (washable)
Package of number 2 pencils (4-year-olds and up)
Full-sized backpack (please label)
Change of clothing in backpack (3-year-olds only; please label)

Parent Communication
We want to do our best to keep all our families informed about what is happening here at <church/school name> Early Education Center. Parents need to be aware of several very important forms of communication that we use.

Parent/Teacher Conferences
A parent/teacher conference will be held in January. At that time the teachers will give parents information about the child and a class recommendation for the following school year. The teachers and the director are available throughout the year for individual conferences with parents.

Early Education Center Connection
This monthly publication includes information about activities happening at <church/school name> Early Education Center as well as general early childhood news.

 purposeful design

Early Education DIRECTOR'S MANUAL

FORM 10.8

Early Education Center Manual (Continued)

Weekly Classroom Newsletter
The teachers send home a weekly newsletter containing specific class information.

Message Board
In the entrance to the center is a message board that contains FYI Today, a newsletter that is updated daily.

School Directory
A schoolwide directory is published at the beginning of each school year. The directory contains names, addresses, and phone numbers of all students enrolled at <church/school name> Early Education Center. A copy of the directory may be purchased at the center office.

Discipline
Child guidance has an important place in the program at <church/school name> Early Education Center. Parents and teachers will need to work together in order to be consistent and effective in training children to make appropriate choices in a classroom setting. We have developed a formula we feel is appropriate in shaping and encouraging responsible behavior in children. If you have any questions about our discipline procedures, please talk to your child's teacher or the director.

OTHER
School Visitors
Parents are encouraged to visit the school at any time. When you visit the center for any reason, please sign in on the guest register on the wall of the foyer.

Solicitation
The center may not be used as a setting for solicitation.

Gum/Candy
Please do not allow your child to bring candy or gum to school at any time.

Personal Hygiene
All possible provisions have been made to assure that children and teachers follow appropriate rules of personal hygiene. Antibacterial soap is used for handwashing before meals and after toilet use. Disposable paper towels are used for drying hands.

Toys
Please do not allow your child to bring toys to school except on designated share days.

 purposeful design

Early Education DIRECTOR'S MANUAL

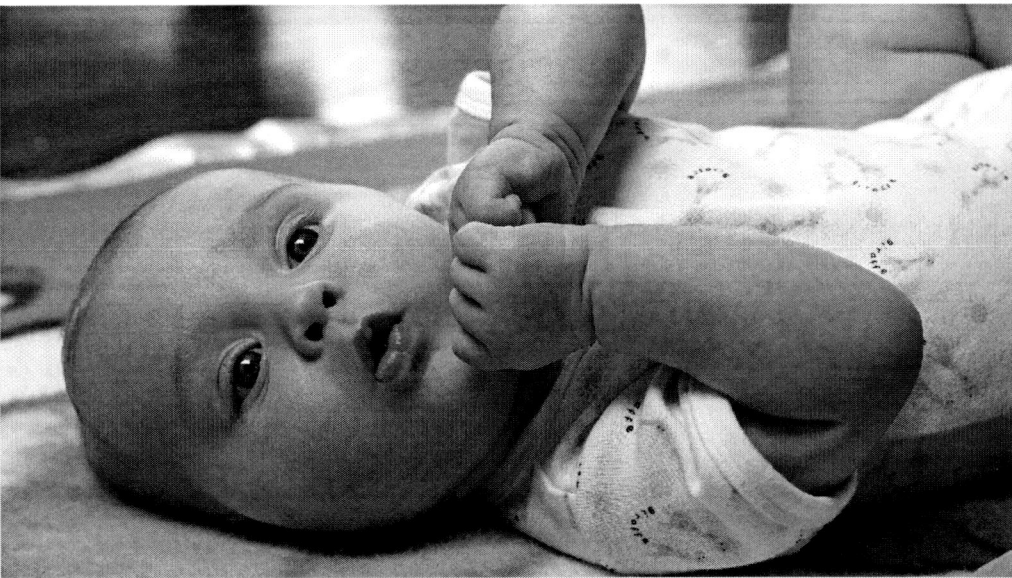

Chapter 11

Do not withhold good from those who deserve it, when it is in your power to act. (Proverbs 3:27)

Health and Safety Standards

The administrator has the responsibility of providing a safe environment for the children in the early education program. When setting specific health and safety standards, the director should seek information from health-care professionals. A wealth of resources promoting safe and healthy practices is available. Because recommendations are updated regularly, directors need to access current information. Also, they need to research the requirements of state and local regulatory agencies when creating procedures, policies, and forms to use in meeting the standards. Both the staff and parent handbooks should define all procedures, policies, and processes clearly. The health and safety standards should include the following:

- General safety procedures
- Procedures for handling accidents, illnesses, wounds requiring first aid
- Medication policies, procedures, and forms (See forms 11.1 Early Education Center Emergency Information and 11.2 Emergency Phone Numbers.)
- Current medical, immunization, and emergency forms
- Appropriate nutritional policies and practices
- Kitchen and food service policies and procedures
- Staff health and safety standards
- Rest and nap-time policies and procedures
- Evacuation procedures

It is up to the director to ensure that these standards are upheld by the teachers and parents. Children will test the standards, as will parents and staff members. Letting a child come to the center when he should stay home because of illness may not seem a big thing to some parents; however, the director and teachers must consider the possible impact on the health of the other children, not to mention the sick child. Also, the children will constantly test their teacher by not washing their hands before eating a snack or after going to the bathroom. Insisting that a sick staff member remain at home may not be easy when substitutes are difficult to find. Taking a firm stand on health and safety standards may not be easy, but in the long run staff, parents, and children will benefit.

Sick Children

Sick children are a fact of life. The issue is not *if* they will get sick but *when* they will get sick. Most teachers and parents understand that being in the early education center adds to their child's risk of catching a communicable disease. It is important for the director to let teachers and parents know what standards the center has set to minimize the risk.

■ Daily health checks

Most state and local regulatory agencies require daily observation of children entering the center. The daily health check is commonly performed by the staff person who greets the child upon his arrival. It should be conducted unobtrusively as the teacher welcomes the child into the center.[1] All staff members should be trained in recognizing the common symptoms of communicable diseases or other evidences of ill health.[2]

Successful daily health checks depend on staff members' paying close attention to what they see, hear, and feel when they greet the child. As they bend down to the child's level, they should examine her eyes, skin, and hair. They should look for signs of

lethargy or other changes in behavior from the previous day.[3] The purpose of the daily health check is to prevent an ill child from being left at the center for the day.

■ Exclusion policy

Each early education program must develop specific guidelines for excluding children from participation. Staff members need to be trained in implementing the exclusion policy, and parents need to be informed of the exclusion guidelines through the parent handbook and reminded of them as necessary.

State and local regulatory agencies may offer guidelines for developing exclusion policies. A national resource, Exclusion and Inclusion of Ill Children in Child Care Facilities, may be downloaded from the National Resource Center for Health and Safety in Child Care.[4] (This is an excerpt from the National Health and Safety Performance Standards. The excerpt includes detailed information about communicable illnesses.) It is recommended that the director confer with a health consultant in developing the center's exclusion policies. All health policies need to be updated regularly in response to ongoing developments in the field.

In general, children should stay home when they are not feeling well enough to participate fully in the day's activities or when they exhibit symptoms of illnesses for which exclusion is recommended. In Excluding Children Due to Illness, the California Childcare Health Program makes the following recommendations for symptoms or conditions for which exclusion is recommended:[5]

• Fever along with behavior change or other signs of illness such as sore throat, rash, vomiting, diarrhea, earache, etc. Fever is defined as having a temperature of 100° F or higher taken under the arm. Oral temperatures should not be taken on children younger than four years of age. Rectal temperatures are no longer recommended in the childcare setting, and mercury-containing thermometers should be avoided. *A temperature over 99° F (under the arm) in an infant under 4 months of age should be evaluated by a medical professional.*

- Symptoms and signs of possible severe illness such as unusual tiredness, uncontrolled coughing or wheezing, continuous crying, or difficulty breathing.

- Diarrhea—runny, watery, or bloody stools.

- Vomiting—more than once in a 24-hour period.

- Body rash with fever.

- Sore throat with fever and swollen glands, or mouth sores with drooling.

- Eye discharge—thick mucus or pus draining from the eye. (Viral conjunctivitis usually has a clear, watery discharge and may not require medication or exclusion.)

- Head lice.

- Severe coughing—child gets red or blue in the face, or makes high-pitched whooping sound after coughing.

- Child is irritable, continuously crying, or requires more attention and care than you can provide without compromising the health and safety of the other children in your care.

■ Onset of illness during the school day
Sometimes children appear well when they arrive at school, but they begin to show signs of illness later in the day. In this situation, children need to be separated from the rest of the group and made comfortable until someone can call for them. (See forms 11.3 Pickup Authorization and 11.4 Illness Report.) After the child has been made comfortable, a staff member should contact the parents and note in the child's file the date, symptoms, and actions taken in caring for the child.[6]

Each center should have a separate area where sick children can rest comfortably and be properly supervised. A "sick box" of toys and books can help children as they are waiting for a mom or dad to pick them up. A "surprise bag" of stickers, small books, or toys to take home can help to cheer them up. Special precautions must be taken to sanitize any cots, linens, pillows, and toys that a sick child has had contact with. Children are very sensitive when they have had a "sick" accident. Throwing up or having a bout of diarrhea can be traumatic for a young child. The director and staff need to show extra TLC (tender loving care) when a child is sick.

■ Infectious and communicable diseases
When a physician diagnoses a child as having a communicable disease, or it is known that the child was exposed to a communicable disease, all staff and parents must be notified. The director should get all the facts from the parent and/or the physician before notifying the staff in order to lessen any possibility of panic. Every director should have a medical reference book with information about communicable childhood diseases. Additionally, several national organizations provide one-page descriptions of the basic facts about common childhood illnesses (including incubation periods) that directors should access when necessary. Competent directors prepare for situations that may arise by thoroughly reviewing information about common communicable diseases beforehand. However, the director and staff should be very careful about diagnosing illnesses. It is better to provide the parents with an accurate description of the symptoms the child displays. Parents should be encouraged to seek the advice of a physician when

children are ill. Symptoms of communicable diseases common in preschool-aged children today are listed below:

Disease	First Symptoms
Chicken pox	Not feeling well; tiredness; fever; small bumps with the appearance of tiny, clear water blisters.
Pinkeye (conjunctivitis)	Pink and swollen eyelid, white of eye reddened, pus (infectious discharge from one or both eyes). May be viral or bacterial. Pinkeye caused by an allergy is not contagious.
Virus (RSV)	Stuffy nose, chronic cough, wheezing or shortness of breath, low-grade fever, blueness around mouth or in face area, loss of appetite. Common in winter.
Hand, foot, and mouth disease	Low-grade fever; soreness in mouth; small blisters in mouth, on palms of hands, on soles of feet.
Strep throat	Fever, sore throat.
Fifth disease (slap face measles)	Headache, body ache, sore throat, low-grade fever and chills, lasting two to three days; one week later, bright red rash on cheeks, which may be followed by lacy rash on arms and legs. (Adults may not have rash but develop joint pain in hands and feet.)

■ *Readmission after illness*

Guidelines for readmission should be part of the school's exclusion policy. Because of the complexity of the many illnesses affecting young children, guidelines for readmission will vary with the child's specific condition.[7] In general, the guidelines allow children to return to the center when the following are true:

- Nausea, vomiting, or diarrhea has subsided.
- For an infectious disease, at least four doses of an antibiotic have been given over a 24-hour period.
- The child is feeling well again, and normal behavior has returned.

Healthy Staff

Children are not the only people in the early education center who get sick. Staff members are exposed to the same germs and diseases as the children. Working in the early education setting is stressful and demanding, and a stressed-out staff member is susceptible to illness.

■ *Maintaining staff health*

The director should encourage the staff to do the following:

- Wash their hands, following proper guidelines.
- Take scheduled rest and lunch breaks, leaving the center if possible.

- Receive proper training and take advantage of opportunities for professional growth.
- Use nontoxic art and cleaning supplies.
- Use sunscreen when on the playground.
- Take paid vacations and sick leave.
- Stay home when sick.
- Get annual physical examinations (see state rules and regulations for staff physical-exam schedule).
- Make sure they are up-to-date with their immunizations.
- Get physical exercise.
- Follow safe procedures when lifting children and items around the center.
- Follow guidelines for handling children's body fluids and dealing with accidents or illnesses.
- Maintain a balanced and healthy diet.
- Get sufficient rest.
- Have realistic expectations for themselves, remembering that they are not perfect.

When possible, the center should provide health-care benefits for all staff members. Staff members should be allowed a certain number of days of paid sick time. When staff members get sick, they should stay home. Sick staff members spread their germs to the children, the parents, and the other staff members. Without proper rest, they recover more slowly, and they cannot be at their best in caring for young children until they are well. Even if the director has to substitute occasionally for a sick staff member, in the long run the center will benefit from providing sick leave.

■ Staff health appraisals

All newly hired staff should have a routine health examination, including an update of any needed immunization and a TB test. Periodic retests for TB are no longer recommended unless the staff person is considered at high risk.[8] However, state and local health requirements should be consulted and followed, as they reflect local circumstances and risks of exposure.

Sanitation Procedures

Recalling the saying about "an ounce of prevention," the director should invest in developing good sanitation habits among the staff and children. Following sanitary procedures for handling food, trash, toileting accidents, body fluids, and custodial duties can cut down tremendously on the amount and spread of germs. Training in *standard precautions* must be a requirement of all early education center employees. The state and local regulatory agencies will inspect the center on a regular basis. The latest inspection report must be kept on file and available to parents on request. These agencies can provide the director with information on the required sanitation procedures.

■ Cleaning

Before surfaces can be sanitized, they must be thoroughly cleaned; otherwise, efforts at sanitizing are ineffective. Illness is spread through a variety of methods: coughing, sneezing, direct skin-to-skin contact, or touching a contaminated object or surface. At times, staff members or children may be contagious before they manifest any symptoms of illness. Bodily secretions may contain viruses that may remain infectious for varying lengths of time. Therefore, staff members must be diligent in performing routine cleaning of all surfaces, toys, and other objects. This routine cleaning, which includes a thorough cleaning of all areas of the room and of all the classroom surfaces, is important in minimizing the spread of illness.

■ Sanitizing

To provide a safe environment, the director and staff should make sure that hard surfaces are cleaned and disinfected at the end of each day. These surfaces includes tabletops used for eating, other tables, rest cots or mats, and other hard surfaces that children come in contact with. If body fluid has contaminated a surface, that surface should be cleaned and disinfected before any activity is allowed to continue there. Soiled surfaces should be cleaned promptly with a sanitizer, such as a diluted bleach solution. Disposable towels or tissues should be used whenever possible, and mops should be rinsed in disinfectant. Those who are cleaning should wear gloves and other protective equipment, and they should avoid exposing open skin lesions or mucous membranes to blood or body fluids.

The following are some effective sanitizing solutions:

- A solution of bleach and water *mixed fresh daily* in the following proportions: ¼ cup household bleach to 1 gallon of water; or 1 tablespoon bleach to 1 quart of water[9]

- An industrial product that meets the Environmental Protection Agency (EPA) standards for "hospital grade" germicides

The sanitizer needs to be in contact with the surface long enough to kill germs. Two minutes is recommended as the minimum contact time for a bleach-and-water solution. When using an industrial sanitizer, the label directions should be followed. Spray bottles need to be labeled with the name of the solution (i.e., *bleach sanitizer*) and kept out of reach of the children.

The various surfaces and equipment of the early education facility require diverse schedules for cleaning and sanitizing. A helpful one-page chart detailing the frequency of cleaning and sanitizing in the different components of the facility was published in *Caring for Our Children* and can be accessed online. (See appendix A for specific instructions.)

Standard Precautions

The spread of infectious disease is of concern to all early education center governing boards, directors,

staff members, and parents. The governing board, with input from the director, should establish precautionary policies and procedures to prevent the spread of any infectious disease. The administrators, staff, and parents need to have correct information about infectious diseases. The director is responsible for making sure accurate information is available.

To protect the health of children and staff, all early education center staff must practice *universal precautions* when handling any body fluids in an early education setting. According to the Occupational Safety and Health Administration (OSHA) in its release of the *Final Rule for Occupational Exposure to Blood-Borne Pathogens* in the Federal Register on December 8, 1991, everyone needs to take precautions when exposed to blood or other body fluids. "Universal precautions" and "Universal blood and body fluid precautions" refer to the handling of body fluids from all students and not just those known to be infected with blood-borne pathogens. Universal precautions were written for staff in health-care settings and for public-safety workers. However, early education center staff members frequently come in contact with blood and other body fluids, and therefore they should exercise the same precautions. These precautions focus on preventing the transmission of blood-borne pathogens, primarily hepatitis B (HBV) and human immunodeficiency viruses (HIV). Exposure is defined as contact with blood or other body fluids through percutaneous inoculation (such as needle sticks with contaminated needles) or contact with an open wound, non-intact skin, or mucous membrane while performing normal job duties. In the occupational setting, blood is the single most important source of HIV, HBV, and other blood-borne pathogens. When staff members have been exposed to blood or other body fluids, they must be offered the opportunity to accept or decline the HBV vaccination series. Any staff member who chooses not to must sign and turn in a *declination form.* The early education center is responsible for covering the costs for those staff members who choose to have the series.

In addressing the staff members' potential exposure to blood and other potentially infectious fluids, it is now recommended that early education centers adopt a modified version of the "Standard Precautions" developed by the Center for Disease Control and Prevention for use in hospitals.[10] The publication of National Health and Safety Standards, *Caring for Our Children*, provides the following definitions:

> *Standard Precautions.* These apply to contact with non-intact skin, mucous membranes, blood, all body fluids and excretions except sweat, whether or not they contain visible blood. The general methods of infection prevention are indicated for everyone in the childcare setting and are designed to reduce the risk of transmission of microorganisms from both recognized and unrecognized sources of infection. Although standard precautions were designed to apply to hospital settings, with the exceptions detailed in this definition, they also apply in childcare settings. Standard precautions involve the use of barriers as in "Universal Precautions" as well as the cleaning and sanitizing of contaminated surfaces.

> *Child care adaptation of standard precautions* (exceptions from the use in hospital settings):

> a. In childcare settings, use of nonporous gloves is optional except when blood or blood containing body fluids may be involved.

> b. In childcare settings, gowns and masks are not required.

> c. In childcare settings, appropriate barriers include materials such as disposable diaper-

table paper, disposable towels, and surfaces that can be sanitized in childcare settings.[11]

Universal precautions apply to blood, other body fluids containing blood, semen, and vaginal secretions, but not to feces, nasal secretions, sputum, sweat, tears, urine, saliva, and vomitus unless they contain visible blood or are likely to contain blood. Universal precautions include avoiding injuries caused by sharp instruments or devices and the use of protective barriers such as gloves, gowns, aprons, masks, or protective eyewear, which can reduce the risk of exposure of the worker's skin or mucous membranes that could come in contact with materials that may contain blood-borne pathogens while the worker is providing first aid or care.[12]

Procedures for implementing standard precautions:

a. Surfaces that may come in contact with potentially infectious body fluids must be disposable or of a material that can be sanitized. Use of materials that can be sterilized is not required.

b. The staff shall use barriers and techniques that (1) minimize potential contact of mucous membranes or openings in skin to blood or other potentially infectious body fluids and tissue discharges and (2) reduce the spread of infectious material within the childcare facility. Such techniques include avoiding touching surfaces with potentially contaminated materials unless those surfaces are sanitized before further contact occurs with them by other objects or individuals.

c. When spills of body fluids, urine, feces, blood, saliva, nasal discharge, eye discharge, injury or tissue discharges, and human milk occur, these spills shall be cleaned up immediately and further managed as follows:

(1) For spills of vomit, urine, human milk, and feces, all floors, walls, bathrooms, tabletops, toys, kitchen counter tops, and

diaper-changing tables in contact shall be cleaned and sanitized as for the procedure for diaper-changing tables in Standard 3.014, Step 7: *Clean and sanitize the diaper-changing surface.*

- Dispose of the disposable paper liner used on the diaper-changing surface in a plastic-lined, hands-free covered can.

- Clean any visible soil from the changing surface with detergent and water; rinse with water.

- Wet the entire changing surface with the sanitizing solution (for example, spray a sanitizing bleach solution of 1/4 cup of household liquid chlorine bleach in one gallon of tap water, mixed fresh daily.

- Put away the spray bottle of sanitizer. If the recommended bleach dilution is sprayed as a sanitizer on the surface, leave it in contact with the surface for at least 2 minutes. The surface can be left to air dry or can be wiped dry after 2 minutes of contact with the bleach solution.

(2) For spills of blood or other potentially infectious body fluids, including injury and tissue discharges, the area shall be cleaned and sanitized. Care shall be taken to avoid splashing any contaminated materials onto any mucous membrane (eyes, nose, mouth).

(3) Blood-contaminated material and diapers shall be disposed of in a plastic bag with a secure tie.

(4) Floors, rugs, and carpeting that have been contaminated by body fluids shall be cleaned by blotting to remove the fluid as quickly as possible, then sanitized by spot-cleaning with a detergent-disinfectant, and shampooing or steam-cleaning the contaminated surface.[13]

For an in-depth discussion of these issues, see the *Fact Sheet* published by the Pennsylvania chapter of the American Academy of Pediatrics.[14]

Health and Immunization Records

Regulatory agencies require that all students in early education centers have specific health information in their file. This information may include evidence of an annual health examination by a licensed physician, a record of communicable diseases, immunization information, and information on known allergies to foods or medications (including substitutes for foods that cause allergic reactions).

Some states allow for children who are not immunized to receive an immunization waiver. The state and local regulatory agencies will have specific guidelines for accepting these children into the center. Schools should be aware that they can adopt stricter standards than the state regarding these waivers. Health and immunization forms are usually updated annually. These records contain confidential information and should be treated as such. Parents need to be informed of these requirements during the pre-enrollment process. Parents who plan to volunteer as parent helpers may also need to be up-to-date with their immunizations and have proof of a negative TB test. Centers should check the state regulations regarding parent volunteers. Those centers that serve children younger than two must develop a method for tracking the due date of each child's next immunization. A tickler system, in which parents are reminded of scheduled immunizations, is valuable in helping staff members monitor the children's ongoing immunization status.

The center should also encourage parents to establish good health and safety practices in their own families. Published information about optimum health and safety practices is a helpful resource and should be obtained and distributed on a regular basis.

Personal Care Issues

There is no more effective way to reduce the spread of disease than handwashing. According to the recommended guidelines, staff, parent helpers, and children should using the following method for washing their hands:

- Use soap and running water.
- Rub the hands together vigorously for at least ten seconds.
- Wash all parts of the hands including the back of the hands, the wrists, between fingers, and under fingernails.
- Rinse the hands well, leaving the water running.
- Dry the hands with a single-use paper towel.
- Turn off the water tap, using a paper towel instead of bare hands.

Staff and parent helpers should wash their hands at the following times:

- When they come to the center each day.
- Before and after preparing and serving food.
- After wiping a child's nose, own nose, sneezing, coughing, or using a tissue, cleaning up toileting accidents, vomit, or any accident involving body fluids (even if gloves were worn).
- After using the bathroom, helping a child with toileting, or changing diapers.
- After playground time.
- After handling a pet or any animal.

Children should wash their hands at the following times:

- When they arrive at the center.
- Before they prepare, serve, and eat food.
- After they have used the toilet or had a toileting accident.
- After they have vomited or had an accident involving body fluids.
- After they have had contact with another sick child.

- After blowing, wiping, or picking their nose or other body parts.
- After sneezing, using a tissue, drooling, sucking thumbs, and so on.
- After playing outside.
- Before and after engaging in water play.
- After handling an animal/pet.

Tissues should always be available in the classroom and on the playground for staff and children to use. Even very young children can be taught to use a tissue, throw it away, and wash their hands. Children should not share items such as hairbrushes, combs, hats, and hair clips. Personal care items brought from home must be kept in a sealed container.

Administering Medication

Most state and local regulatory agencies will provide the early education center director with specific procedures for administering medications to young children. A good policy to follow is to allow only physician-prescribed medications to be given to the children. Any medication should be brought to the center in its original container with the prescription information intact. In all cases a parent must complete and sign a medication form including the following information: name of medication, proper dosage, times of administration, other pertinent information including any unusual reactions, and a release of liability. Staff members who administer medication should receive training on topics such as dosage, measurement, documentation, and the specific policies of your center.[15] All medications must be kept in a locked area inaccessible to children. Parents should list on the child's emergency card any and all of the child's allergies to medications.

Caring for Special Needs

From time to time, there may be children enrolled in the program who have chronic health conditions (such as seizures, asthma, diabetes) requiring ongoing medical care. In such situations, the director needs to arrange for staff members to receive training from health-care providers related to the specific conditions and accompanying treatment responsibilities. (See at the end of this chapter Emergency Information Form for Children with Special Needs. This form may be photocopied, but not modified. Please make sure that the copyright line on the bottom of the second page is legible on the photocopies.) Ongoing consultation with the child's primary health-care provider should also be maintained. Of course, the director should review state and local regulatory agencies' restrictions and guidelines prior to accepting a child with a chronic health condition.

■ First aid and infant/child CPR training

Many state and local regulatory agencies require that a percentage of the early education staff be trained in first aid and infant/child CPR. Even if such training is not required in your area, it is recommended that the director and all staff members receive training annually. The American Red Cross and the American Heart Association offer classes for early education teachers, and the cost in time and money is relatively small. Recently, recommendations in this area have been adapted so that there is now a greater emphasis on the provision of first aid training and proficiency in rescue breathing. Training in infant/child CPR is recommended when the center offers swimming or wading activities or provides care for a child with a special health need that would make him more likely than the typical child to require cardiac resuscitation.[16] First aid training should prepare staff to recognize and respond to the following pediatric emergencies:

- Abrasions and lacerations
- Bleeding, including nosebleeds
- Burns
- Fainting
- Poisoning, including swallowed, contact, and inhaled

- Puncture wounds, including splinters
- Injuries, including insect, animal, and human bites
- Shock
- Convulsions or nonconvulsive seizures
- Musculoskeletal injury, such as sprains and fractures
- Dental and mouth injuries
- Head injuries
- Allergic reactions, including information about when auto-injected epinephrine might be required
- Eye injuries
- Electric shock
- Drowning
- Heat-related injuries, including heat exhaustion or heatstroke
- Cold injuries
- Moving and positioning injured or ill persons
- Management of a blocked airway and rescue breathing for infants and children, with return demonstration by the learner
- Illness-related emergencies (such as stiff neck, inexplicable confusion, sudden onset of blood-red or purple rash, severe pain, temperature of 105° F or higher, looking or acting severely ill)
- Standard precautions
- Organizing and implementing a plan to meet an emergency for any child with a special health-care need
- Addressing the needs of the other children in the group while managing emergencies in a childcare setting[17]

■ First aid kits

The center should have at least one well-stocked first aid kit. Smaller kits can be stored in a safe and appropriate location in each classroom. Additional first aid kits need to be in reach when staff members are on the playground. A first aid kit should always be taken on any field trip or other off-campus trip.

The first aid kits should include the following:
- Disposable nonporous gloves
- Band-Aids
- Sterile gauze pads
- Bandage tape
- Flexible roller gauze
- Adhesive strip bandages
- Plastic bags for cloths, gauze, and other materials used in handling blood
- Safety pins
- Triangular bandages for making a sling
- Tweezers (disinfected before and after each use)
- Scissors (disinfected before and after each use)
- Thermometer
- Cold packs
- Current American Academy of Pediatrics (AAP) standard first aid chart or equivalent first aid guide
- Any emergency medication required by child with special needs
- List of emergency phone numbers, parents' home and work phone numbers, and the Poison Control Center phone number

Storing bottles of syrup of ipecac in the center's first aid kits is no longer recommended. Any remaining bottles should be discarded.

Protecting Children from Injury and Accident

Early education directors have a serious responsibility to protect children's health and provide a safe environment. A proactive approach to preventing injury is the best way to demonstrate the center's commitment to the children's well-being. A keen awareness of potential hazards and an ongoing alertness to changes in the environment are essential. Regular communication with staff reminding them of safety issues will help encourage awareness.

■ Safety inspections

Directors need to develop a safety checklist that corresponds with the needs of their facility. It's wise to begin by performing a general safety audit of the environment. The PAAAP (the Pennsylvania Chapter of the American Academy of Pediatrics) has a comprehensive health-and-safety checklist that can be downloaded from their website.[18] A published checklist will alert you and your staff to hazards you might not have considered. The director needs to monitor the safety inspections and ensure that they are completed monthly. However, involving the staff in conducting the inspections raises their awareness of potential hazards and thus contributes to the ongoing safety of the center.

■ When accidents happen

Even when every possible precaution has been taken, accidents happen in the early education environment. Children are active and inquisitive. They will test their abilities to the limit without thinking of the consequences. When an accident happens even after every effort has been made to create a safe environment, it is the director's and staff's responsibility to ensure that the injured child is properly cared for.

It is recommended that all staff be certified in basic first aid procedures. When an accident happens, the child should be examined and the type and extent of the injury assessed. When assessing an injury to a child's genitals or buttocks, the teacher should always have a second teacher in the room. The child should not be moved if there is a chance that the neck or spinal column is injured. If the injury is life threatening, emergency medical professionals should be contacted. If the injury is not life threatening but still requires medical attention, the parent must be called to come and assess the injury. The director should always recommend that the child be seen by a physician.

The director or another appropriate staff person should call the parent immediately if there is any injury to the child's face, neck, or head, or if the injured area is bruised, swollen, red, or marked. The director needs to inform the parents of the injury and recommend that even though the child may look and act fine, the parent may want to come to assess the injury. The person who calls to inform the parent should also document the time of the phone call on the accident form.

All accidents occurring at the center need to be documented by the teacher supervising the child at the time. (See forms 11.5 Ouch Report and 11.6 Accident/Injury Report.) The parent needs to read and sign the accident report. Accident documentation should be kept on file for at least three to five years. The director should check with the state regulatory agency, the center's lawyer, and/or the center's insurance company for information on how long the center needs to keep accident records.

■ Building and playground safety

It is the responsibility of the director to ensure that each child is safe, whether in the building or on the playground. The director or other designated person should inspect the building and playground daily for potentially harmful situations. In order to protect the children, whoever does the inspection is responsible to inform the staff of any danger discovered and to see that the situation is corrected in a timely manner. Ignoring a danger will not make it go away.

The director is also responsible for developing safety procedures for the classrooms and playground, and for communicating these procedures to all staff members and to any volunteers. Safety procedures should be published in the staff handbook. The director and staff should review and update these procedures annually.

The staff must be safety conscious every second of the day. What each staff member does impacts the care and safety of the children. Carrying a steaming cup of coffee around the classroom, leaving a pair of adult scissors within a child's reach, leaving an electrical plug exposed—all are unintentional, but they can become serious dangers to a small child. And above all else the staff must realize that they are fully responsible for supervising these precious little ones at all times while they are in the care of the early education center. Human laws make the staff legally responsible, and God's law makes them morally responsible.

■ Playground safety issues

There are a number of critical safety issues to be addressed by those who design playgrounds. The U.S. Consumer Product Safety Commission has developed extensive guidelines for regulating all components of a playground. These guidelines include detailed information on the appropriate dimensions for climbing equipment, spacing of equipment, surfacing beneath equipment, and specific hazards such as head entrapment and protrusions. Because playground safety is such a complex topic, anyone designing a playground should access national safety guidelines and consult playground safety experts when possible. The following are some key issues for a center to address in order to keep children safe on its playground.

Age-appropriate equipment. Because of physical and developmental differences, separate playgrounds should be provided for infants and toddlers, two-to-five-year-olds, and five-to-twelve-year-olds. "Height limits for play equipment should generally be one foot per year of age of the intended users. In some states, height limitations for playground equipment are as follows: (a) 48 inches for young children (30 months to 5 years of age); (b) 6.5 feet for school-age children (6 through 12 years of age)."[19]

Surfacing. Falls from climbing equipment are the leading cause of playground injuries.[20] Chances of injury are greatly reduced when there is appropriate cushioning material underneath and around playground equipment. There are a number of types of surfacing materials, each having pros and cons. Loose fill materials include wood chips and sand or pea gravel. These are less costly initially, but they require more ongoing maintenance than synthetic materials such as rubber tiles, mats, and poured surfaces. Grass, dirt, and asphalt are unacceptable surfaces for climbing equipment. In order to effectively absorb the impact from a fall, cushioning material must go sufficiently deep, its depth being proportional to the height of the equipment. A depth of twelve inches is a general guideline for most loose cushioning materials,[21] but the national standard for each type of material should be consulted. Soft surfacing materials need to be raked and redistributed regularly so that they are present in the appropriate depth both directly below the equipment and in the fall zones (generally six feet in all directions beyond the equipment).[22]

Sun protection. While they are on the playground, children need to be protected from the harmful effects of exposure to the sun. Playgrounds must provide adequate shade through both portable structures such as umbrellas, tents, and tarps, and permanent structures such as awnings and fabric shade canopies. It is particularly important to provide shade for such areas as sandboxes, where children are likely to remain at play for an extended period of time.[23]

Strangulation risk. When children move from the bike area to the climbing equipment, they need to remove their helmets.[24] Injuries have happened when children's bike helmets were caught on protrusions in playground equipment. Teachers should check children's clothing carefully, ensuring that there are no drawstrings around the hood and neck of children's jackets. These drawstrings, along with strings from attached mittens and jump ropes or nametags hanging around the neck, may be caught on playground equipment, resulting in strangulation.[25]

Inspection and ongoing maintenance. Teachers need to inspect the playground daily, before children enter the area. Sandboxes need to be covered when not in use and inspected for foreign materials before each use. The sand must be replaced at least every two years. Surfacing should be checked for hazards such as broken glass, and metal climbing equipment should be examined to see if it is too hot for children to play on. In addition to daily checks, formal comprehensive inspection and maintenance of all components of the playground are essential to children's safety and should be performed according to a regular schedule. Various components of the playground will have different inspection schedules. The director should identify the kinds of playground equipment that need monthly, quarterly, and annual inspections. Newly installed playground equipment should be inspected by someone with expertise and/or certification (Certified Playground Safety Inspector, or CPSI) in playground safety.[26]

■ Water safety

Children enjoy playing in and with water, but extra caution must be used at such times. When children are playing outdoors in warm weather, there should be ample provision for drinking water and shade. Water tables, wading pools, and sprinklers provide wonderful and fun experiences for young children; however, they should be used only if the following precautions are taken:

- One or more staff members monitor the activity continuously.
- Water temperature is appropriate for young children.
- Water toys are in good repair.

- Water table or wading pool is emptied and sanitized after every use.
- Standing water is never left on the playground, in the water table, or in the wading pool.

Some state licensing regulations prohibit the use of wading pools in early education settings. Please check with your local licensing agency for such regulations.

If children are taken to a public pool for swimming lessons or free swimming activities, the state or local regulatory agency guidelines for staff-to-child ratio must be followed. Children should never be left at a public pool without the supervision of a staff person from the center, even if the pool is staffed with water safety instructors or lifeguards. A staff person trained in infant/child CPR and first aid should always be supervising children at a pool.

Rest or Nap Time

Most early childhood centers provide some type of rest or nap period during the day. Appropriate bedding must be used with proper distance between the cots or mats. The cots or mats need to be labeled with the children's names and placed so that the children are positioned alternately head to toe.[27] Placing each child's cot in the same location each day provides a sense of security. Nap time can often be a difficult transition for a young child. To minimize children's stress, teachers need to build routines and rituals into the transition to nap time. Giving children responsibilities for preparing their nap space helps structure the nap transition. Allowing children to look at books, reading stories to them, and playing quiet music are other common techniques for nap time. Mats or cots should be stored in a way that allows none of the bedding surfaces to touch each other. Bedding should be laundered weekly, and the mats or cots should be sanitized weekly. Check the state's rules and regulations for other guidelines for rest periods.

Children's Storage Space

Each child must have his or her own storage space for personal belongings. The storage spaces should be convenient and accessible to children, staff members, and parents. Cubbies need to be clearly labeled with each child's name. Parents need to be reminded to check their child's cubby each day. Keep in mind that parents often feel frustrated when they cannot find their child's belongings at the end of the day. All storage areas need to be cleaned and disinfected regularly. Cubbies may be sprayed with an approved disinfectant at the end of every day. Teachers should check cubbies for safety, looking out for potential hazards such as splintered wood and broken hooks.

Nutrition and Food Services

Good menu planning is just as important as good lesson or activity planning. Menus providing variety and vital nutrients are essential to the children's growth and development. The center's menus should list the quantities and types of food that meet children's nutritional needs. The number of meals and snacks served to children depends on the number of hours they are in attendance. The following issues must be considered when serving meals to young children:

Regulatory requirements

- State and local rules and regulations concerning food service
- Kitchen equipment for food preparation and storage
- Rules and requirements for leftovers

Food-preparation practices

- Cleaning and sanitizing food-preparation, kitchen, and eating areas and equipment
- Monitoring temperature of food; refrigeration and freezer units
- Handling of food

Menu-planning guidelines

- USDA food program requirements
- Nutritional quality and variety of menu items
- Emphasis on fresh fruit, fresh or frozen vegetables, and whole-grain products[28]
- Serving portions
- Minimal addition of fat, sugar, and sodium[29]
- Infant and toddler special needs/requirements, including identification of choking hazards
- Special diets for children
- Dietary allergies
- Visual appeal of foods served
- Picnic/sack lunches

Mealtime procedures

- The way the food is served (family style or individually)
- The attractiveness of service
- The time of day when meals and snacks are served
- Safety when eating
- Staff interaction with children during mealtimes

Characteristics of children

- The ages of the children in the center
- Social/cultural differences among children
- Children sharing food
- Furniture and eating utensils of appropriate size
- Availability of water throughout the day

Nutritional awareness and education

- Explicit instruction and play activities
- Staff modeling healthy attitudes toward food
- Cooking activities with children

■ Involving Parents

All menus should be posted and distributed to parents in advance so that parents can see the types of food their children will be served. When parents wish to provide meals or snacks for their own children, the director should share basic nutritional guidelines to guide the parents' selection of meal items. This is particularly important if parents are providing snacks for the entire group. In such an instance, the center should provide the parents specific written guidelines for the types and quantities of food that the children may have. The early education program can play a valuable role in raising parents' awareness of children's nutritional needs and providing guidance, information, and recipes that support parents in this area.

■ Choking hazards

Young children are prone to choke on certain foods, including nuts, seeds, popcorn, raw vegetables, whole grapes, peanut butter, raw carrot rounds, meat sticks, and hot dogs.[30] These foods should not be offered to children under four. Food must be cut into small bites (1/4-to-1/2-inch pieces) so that it can be easily chewed. Children must be closely supervised when eating so that adults can observe them and respond immediately to any problems.

■ Food allergies

The most common chronic disease encountered in early education programs is food allergies, which affect approximately two to eight percent of infants and children.[31] The most common food allergens are peanuts, tree nuts (such as walnuts or pecans), shellfish, fish, milk, soy, wheat, and eggs.[32] Children's reactions to the offending foods can range from mild skin reactions to shock and serious, life-threatening difficulty in breathing. Children who are enrolled in the program and have a known allergy will need a special-care plan that includes written instructions regarding the child's allergy, strategies for avoiding the food, and a treatment plan detailing the response to be taken should the child exhibit symptoms of an allergic reaction. Information about the food allergy should be posted in the classroom and in any other areas where food is served. The staff will need training in recognizing the symptoms and performing the appropriate interventions.[33]

Evacuation and Emergency Plans

Every early education center must be prepared for unexpected emergencies or disasters. Local public safety and civil defense officials will help the center develop an adequate plan. The plan should include specific courses of action to take in case of various kinds of disaster. Each staff member should be familiar with the disaster plan so that it can be carried out quickly and efficiently. Panic can be one of the greatest dangers to children. A staff prepared and trained in emergency procedures will be able to provide the assurance young children need.

The most commonly practiced emergency procedure is the fire drill. State regulatory agencies require that fire drills be held on a regular basis and may also have specific record-keeping requirements. Centers can provide any required documentation of emergency drills by maintaining a log indicating the date of each fire drill, the time it began and ended, and the number of children and adults who were evacuated.

The director will want to post a map and procedures for emergency evacuation in each classroom and hallway. All emergency fire equipment and the alarm system must be tested by a fire official or alarm specialist annually. The fire marshal will inspect the building, and all resulting information must be kept on file and made available for parental inspection.

When the director and staff are planning the year's first fire drill, it is a good idea to prepare the children. Many cities have a fire prevention program for young children. Firefighters will often visit the center to present a special program on fire safety.

Nutrition Activities for Children

The American Dietetic Association lists some exciting nutrition education activities to help teachers integrate nutrition education across the curriculum:

- Learning about food safety and good nutrition through "cup cooking" or "baggie cooking" as children make their own snacks of apple salad in a cup or vegetable salad in a bag
- Learning about size, smell, shape, color, and growth as children "explore a potato"
- Visiting the local grocery store to see the produce or a farm to see the animals and crops
- Visiting other stores, such as a fish farm or fish market, a bakery, or a cheese factory
- Sectioning fruits, counting the parts, and discussing the concepts of "whole" and "part"
- Learning about size by lining up fruits from smallest to largest
- Making geometric shapes out of frozen dough and baking for snack time
- Identifying the parts of a melon (i.e., skin, rind, meat, and seeds)
- Doing lessons on "I can make my own breakfast," "I can name foods"[34]

Sometimes they will even help prepare children for the first fire drill. Young children are frightened and bewildered by loud noises and unusual activity. Advance preparation can eliminate some of their confusion and fear.

Earthquake and tornado drills must also be practiced regularly if the center is located in a region that is prone to those threats.

Emergency Information Form for Children With Special Needs

Last name:

American College of Emergency Physicians*

American Academy of Pediatrics

Date form completed By Whom	Revised	Initials
	Revised	Initials

Name: | Birth date: | Nickname:

Home Address: | Home/Work Phone:

Parent/Guardian: | Emergency Contact Names & Relationship:

Signature/Consent*: |

Primary Language: | Phone Number(s):

Physicians:

Primary care physician:	Emergency Phone:
	Fax:
Current Specialty physician: Specialty:	Emergency Phone:
	Fax:
Current Specialty physician: Specialty:	Emergency Phone:
	Fax:
Anticipated Primary ED:	Pharmacy:
Anticipated Tertiary Care Center:	

Diagnoses/Past Procedures/Physical Exam:

1. | Baseline physical findings:

2.

3. | Baseline vital signs:

4.

Synopsis: | Baseline neurological status:

*Consent for release of this form to health care providers

Diagnoses/Past Procedures/Physical Exam continued:

Medications:

1.

2.

3.

4.

5.

6.

Significant baseline ancillary findings (lab, x-ray, ECG):

Prostheses/Appliances/Advanced Technology Devices:

Management Data:

Allergies: Medications/Foods to be avoided   and why:

1.

2.

3.

Procedures to be avoided   and why:

1.

2.

3.

Immunizations

Dates						Dates					
DPT						Hep B					
OPV						Varicella					
MMR						TB status					
HIB						Other					

Antibiotic prophylaxis: Indication: Medication and dose:

Common Presenting Problems/Findings With Specific Suggested Managements

Problem	Suggested Diagnostic Studies	Treatment Considerations

Comments on child, family, or other specific medical issues:

Physician/Provider Signature: **Print Name:**

FORM 11.1

Early Education Center Emergency Information

Child's name		
Birthdate	Age	Weight
Address		
City	State	Zip
Home phone	Cell phone	Other phone
Father's name		
Employer		Phone
Mother's name		
Employer		Phone
Emergency contact		
Person		Phone
Address		

Medical information
Known allergies to medications and other substances
Hospital preference
Insurance carrier
Group number
Policy/individual number

Child's doctor	Phone
Address	

Child's dentist	Phone
Address	

FORM 11.2

Emergency Phone Numbers

Fire	
Police Dispatch	
Poison Control	
Child Protection Agency	
Health Department	
Humane Society	
Local Hospitals	
Red Cross	

FORM 11.3

Pickup Authorization

Child's name

I give permission for my child to be picked up at <church/school name> Early Education Center at the end of the program day by either of the following:

Name	Phone
Name	Phone

I DO NOT GIVE PERMISSION TO	
Name	Phone

I agree that <name of director> may authorize the physician of his or her choice to provide emergency care in the event that neither I nor the family physician can be contacted immediately. I also give my permission for my child to go on trips from the premises of the school, whether on foot or by vehicle.

Signature of parent or guardian	Date
Director's signature	Date

FORM 11.4

Illness Report

Student's name		Date	Time

Symptoms are		
☐ Body temperature		☐ Exhibiting signs of a communicable illness
☐ Vomiting		☐ Skin condition requiring further treatment
☐ Diarrhea <number of times> in one hour		☐ Other

Report initiated by			
Were parents notified?	☐ Yes ☐ No	By whom?	
Time parents were notified		Time child departed	
With whom?			

Administrator signature

Dear Parent:

I'm sorry your child was sent home sick from school today. As noted in the *Parent Handbook*, your child will need to be away from the center until he/she

Has been free from diarrhea for 24 hours or has had a regular bowel movement
Has been fever-free for 24 hours
Has had at least 4 doses of antibiotic over a 24-hour period (for any type of strep or bacterial infection)
Is no longer vomiting and has eaten and retained a meal

Thank you for your cooperation.

Parent's signature _____

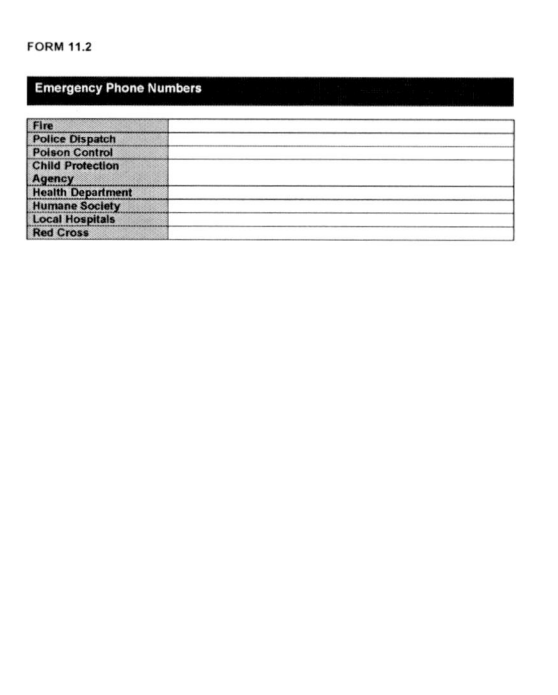
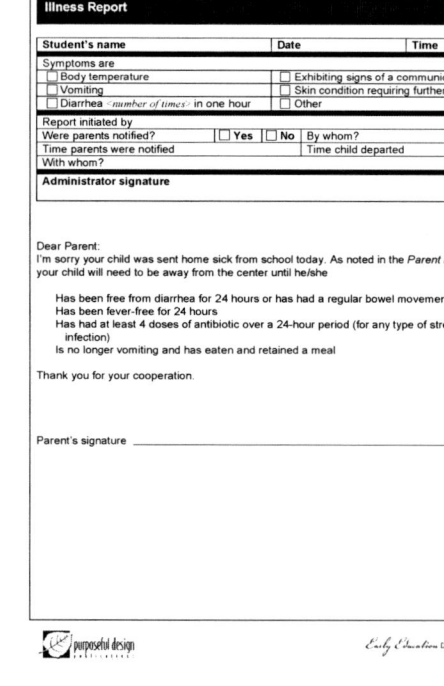

FORM 11.5

Ouch Report

Child's name

Date	Time

Today, I, *<child's name> <injury situation>*.

My hurt was treated with
- ☐ Soap and water
- ☐ Band-Aid
- ☐ Ice pack
- ☐ Other

Staff member(s) present when it happened

Teacher's signature

Parent's signature

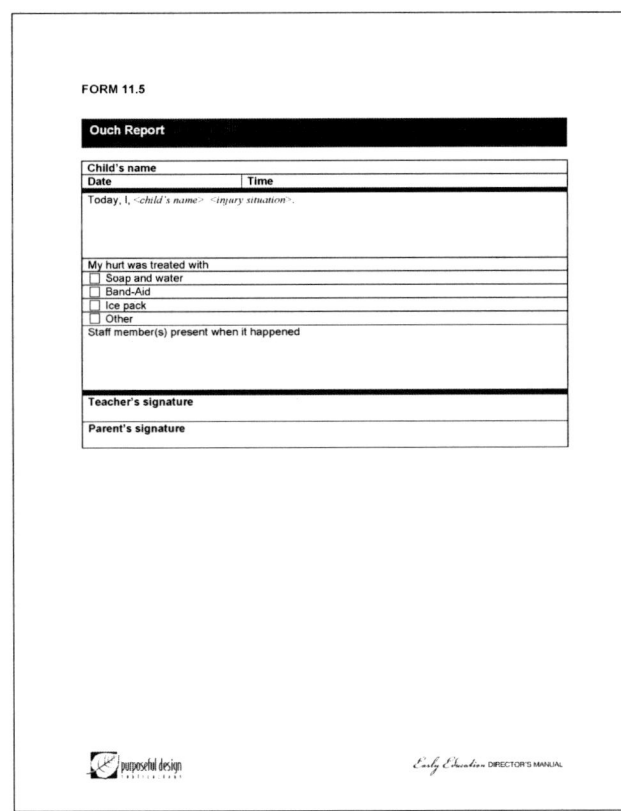

FORM 11.6

Accident/Injury Report

Student name	Date	Time

Nature and circumstances of accident or injury

Place of accident or injury

Play equipment or other items involved

Recommended follow-up treatment

	Yes	No	
Was this reported to parents?	Yes	No	Time
Was physician contacted?	Yes	No	Time
Was child picked up after injury?	Yes	No	By whom?
Witnesses			

	Yes	No	
I, *<name of parent or guardian>*, have been informed of the accident/injury.	Yes	No	

Parent's signature	Date
Teacher's signature	Date
Director's signature	Date

(Area of injury is circled)

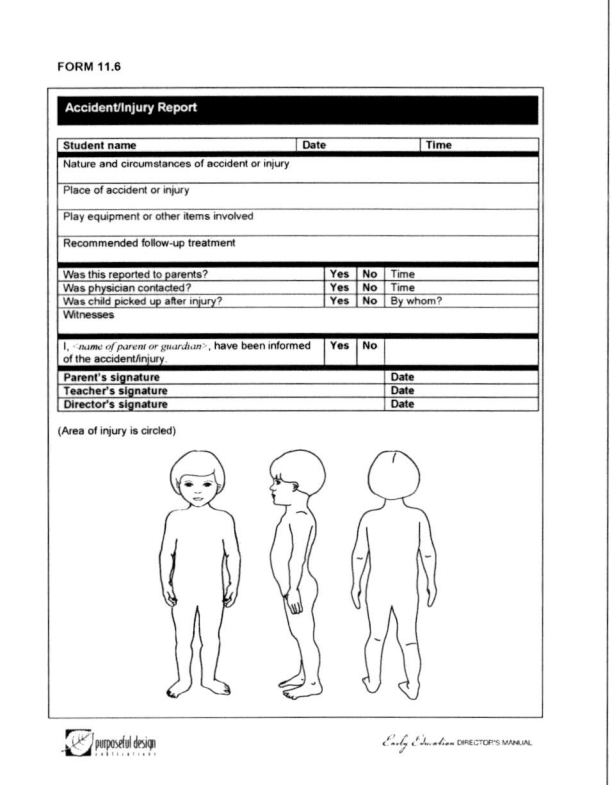

PARTNERING WITH PARENTS

Chapter 12

Train a child in the way he should go, and when he is old he will not turn from it. (Proverbs 22:6)

Building Bridges

Establishing positive relationships with parents is important in ensuring that the child will make a smooth transition between home and school. The school can develop trust by reviewing important aspects of the program with parents and helping them feel comfortable with the environment they are considering for their child. The bridge-building process also involves good communication on the part of the office during the enrollment phase as well as bringing the parent and child into the classroom environment. Once the parent and child arrive in the classroom, it is critical for the teacher to welcome them and to make them feel comfortable.

Taking the time to get to know the child and the parents will help establish a trust relationship. More than anything else, parents want to know that their child will be loved, nurtured, and taught the elements essential for school success. Staff members can develop strong relationships with families by making eye contact and greeting parents at the door, following up on their questions and concerns in a timely way, and giving ongoing positive feedback about the child. Concerns regarding the child should only be shared privately with the parent in an overall concern for the child's welfare.

Through the course of the school year, teachers can get to know their families and come to value their insights regarding their children, recognizing the resource parents provide for getting to know the children better. Parents can begin to understand that the better the school knows the child the more potential there is for learning to occur.[1]

Building bridges can take many forms. In *The Christian Preschool*, Beth Yancey highlights a few ways that teachers can connect with parents:

- See the parents as knowing their child the best and having the responsibility of raising their child.
- Pray that the parents will grow spiritually.
- Assure parents that they are doing a good job as parents.
- Encourage parents that their child has great potential.
- Discover where the child's strengths and talents lie and share these insights with parents.[2]

Parents, the Primary Educators of Their Child

As Christian educators, we recognize the important responsibility God has given to parents as the primary caretakers and educators of their children. This role is God given and assumes a huge amount of responsibility. The Bible speaks clearly about the role of the family in telling the next generation about God's blessings. (See Psalm 78:1–8.) Christian school staff should view their role as supporting parents in this responsibility by offering the child a Christian educational foundation. Scripture is clear that parents are to raise their children "in the training and instruction of the Lord" (Ephesians 6:4). Parents assume their responsibility for educating their child by

- Providing early experiences for their child to encourage growth in all areas
- Encouraging their child's language skills through modeling and literacy experiences
- Teaching early-learning concepts that prepare their child for the school experience
- Selecting the early education program that will best meet their child's needs

- Supporting their child's development by engaging their child in learning skills at home that relate to concepts taught at school
- Communicating with center staff their concerns for their own child
- Spending time at the center involved with program activities
- Volunteering to help in the classroom or on special projects

The early education program should always defer to parents in making decisions for their child. Centers that assume parental responsibilities create an unhealthy dependence. Parents have spent the most time with their children and are emotionally invested in their children's success. Parents may be tempted at times to abdicate their responsibility for educating their child and turn it over to the early education center. Programs that understand the important role of parents should think of ways to communicate this partnership concept. A partnership involves both parties working together for a common goal, the success of the child. Learning does not stop at the classroom door but takes place every moment the child is awake. One of the most important aspects of that learning is the integration of knowledge and spiritual truth.

In *Transforming Children into Spiritual Champions*, George Barna notes that 85 percent of parents believe they have the primary responsibility for the moral and spiritual development of their children, but more than two out of three leave that responsibility to the school and/or the church. Some reasons are as follows:

- Most families do not have a genuine spiritual life.
- Parents, thinking they turned out pretty well, follow the pattern their own parents set for them.

- Most parents are neither spiritually inclined nor spiritually mature.
- Parents believe they are incapable of meeting their child's spiritual needs.
- Parents seek out the best help they can find and get out of the way.[3]

Barna identifies fifteen truths in Scripture that detail the family's responsibility in raising godly children:

1. Parents should provide the primary spiritual training of children. (Ephesians 6:4)

2. The purpose of spiritual training is to instill a passion to love, obey, and serve God. (Matthew 10:37)

3. Parents must start the spiritual training of children when they are young. (Isaiah 7:15)

4. Worshipping God is one of a believer's most significant responsibilities. (1 Samuel 1:19)

5. Spiritual development is a lifelong process. (Deuteronomy 6:7)

6. Part of the parents' responsibility is to introduce appropriate discipline into children's lives and to avoid pampering them. (Proverbs 3:11–12)

7. Parents are called to introduce their children to appropriate behavior. (Numbers 18:11)

8. Spiritual transformation requires us to rely on God's grace and power; we must therefore pray for the children we seek to impact for God. (1 Samuel 1:10–16)

9. The basis for spiritual training is in the Bible. (Proverbs 30:5)

10. A family will grow in spiritual maturity through serving God and people as a family unit. (Joshua 24:15)

11. Young people will retain childish perspectives and reasoning unless their parents help them grow beyond such limited thinking. (1 Corinthians 13:11)

12. Parents are encouraged to work in tandem with reliable spiritual partners but should be sure that those partners are committed to the things of God. (Romans 14:19)

13. The worldview of children should be shaped after the worldview of their parents. (Luke 6:40)

14. The father is charged with passing spiritual blessing on to the children. (Genesis 27)

15. Before God will hand over great spiritual responsibility to an adult who has children, the person must give proof of being a dedicated and effective parent. (1 Timothy 3:4–5, 12)

■ Making a smooth transition

Children may need help in making the transition to your program, as new experiences can cause them to feel unsettled. Typically it takes an adult at least two weeks to feel comfortable in a new situation, and children can take longer because of their deep need for security. It is not uncommon for a child to display feelings of insecurity for up to a month after beginning school. At first young children may cry or cling to their parents, but both parents and staff need to be assured that the child will eventually make a successful transition. Often parents are distressed when their child expresses this kind of insecurity. Directors need to help their staff work through these issues with parents. Preparing parents ahead of time for the types of behavior a child may display during the transition period can ease parents' fears. Reassuring parents that their child is responding normally and will soon make the adjustment can provide comfort for both the parent and the child.

Centers need to make clear their expectations for this transition time. Parents may need to be guided to develop a daily routine for saying goodbye, matter-of-factly releasing the child to the teacher and then leaving. Such rituals provide the child with a sense of structure that helps her to cope with the transition. A quick follow-up call to an anxious parent to inform her that her child has settled down, including a quick description of the activity the child is currently engaged in, goes a long way toward gaining the parent's trust. Allowing sufficient time for the child to adjust and giving parents tools to help the child make the transition can shorten the adjustment period. The following are a few strategies for making transitions successful:

- Talk to the child ahead of time to prepare her for the transition.
- Arrange for a special time before the first day of attendance when the child can come with the parent to visit the classroom and can leave with the parent a short time later.
- Develop a graduated schedule by which the child is left for a short time to begin with and stays for a longer time the next day.
- Allow the child to bring a stuffed animal or something familiar from home.

■ *Open-door policy*

Establishing an open-door policy is essential in developing a trust relationship with parents. Both parents and staff members need to know that the director will address their concerns in a timely way. Directors need to balance their schedule so that they are available to address immediate concerns yet have time to focus on other matters. Being accessible during the day to answer questions can set the tone for good communication. It is also a good practice for directors to communicate when they will be available and how soon they can respond.

■ *Parent handbook*

The parent handbook is a vital tool for imparting information to parents. It should be easily and attractively formatted so that parents can find pertinent information quickly, and it should be updated annually. Both parents and staff members should be familiar with the information it contains. Many state and local regulatory agencies require parents and staff to read the parent handbook upon their child's admission into the program. To encourage this practice, many programs require parents to sign an acknowledgement that they have received a copy of the parent handbook and have read it. Parent handbooks can include an information and calendar section. Curriculum topics can also be inserted so that parents can follow up with learning at home. Parent handbooks should be comprehensive, outlining the policies of the program. The ideal time to distribute the parent handbook is during the interview/orientation prior to enrollment when the director can refer to and highlight specific information. (For a list of suggested elements to include, see form 12.2 Topics for Parent Handbook.)

Parent/Center Communication

Parents want and need to receive communication from the early education center. The easiest and most obvious way is through the written word. Regular written communication helps parents know where and when they can get specific information. When writing home to parents, teachers should check for correct spelling and grammar and for neat handwriting. Any written communication reflects directly on the person sending it and indirectly on the center. The director needs to stress to the staff the importance of quality. The following are ways of maintaining regular written parent communication:[4]

- *Daily memo or newsletter.* The early education director publishes a daily memo or newsletter. This publication is usually a one-page sheet presenting information about the events of that day or the next couple of days. It can include the day's field trip, a new-student or new-teacher welcome, a new-baby welcome, special parties and events, birthday notices for children and staff, and a short daily quip of encouragement. The memo or newsletter is posted at the entrance on a bulletin board or message board.

- *Regular teacher newsletter.* Each classroom teacher sends a newsletter to each child's home on a regular basis. Some teachers prefer to send it at the beginning or end of the center's week. The newsletter contains important information such as greetings from the teacher, news about upcoming special events, notices of coming field trips (at least two weeks in advance), a Bible story and reference, a Bible verse, the letter and/or number of the week, book order due dates, names of special helpers for the week, a note of appreciation to parent volunteers, and special messages from the director. The teacher newsletter should not be so long that parents are turned off. It should be refrigerator friendly, or small enough to post on the refrigerator.

- *Monthly newsletter.* The director publishes a monthly newsletter for parents. Its purpose is to give general information about the center and about early childhood education. It can include greetings from the director, class themes and special events for the month, a monthly calendar, parent educational information, heath tips for young children, fun recipes for parents and children, lively anecdotes involving young children, community/church events, and recommended books, videos, and toys. The monthly newsletter should come out at the same time each month. It's a great public relations and recruiting tool for new and prospective center families and staff.

- *Classroom notes.* At times the head teacher will want to send specific information to a child's parents. The director may wish to receive a copy of any written communication sent to a child's home.

- *Daily report.* The daily report is a brief review of the child's day, including whether the child napped and for how long, when and how much the child ate, and a general description of the child's mood and/or any unusual incidents. These are more typically used by teachers of very young children.

- *A family room.* A family room is a room at the entrance of the facility that has information the parents will need from time to time. A bulletin board should be provided for posting essential information along with a place for forms that parents may need to submit involving medications and vacation time. A lending library of books on parenting, attractively displayed, is also an asset. This area should be inviting and attractive, a place where children can feel comfortable.

■ Parent observation

Inviting parents to come in and observe their child during the school year can provide them with a valuable experience. (See form 12.3 Parent Observation Form.) Often, issues arise with the child that the teacher has a hard time explaining. Parents sometimes find it difficult to regard concerns about their child objectively. The classroom has a different dynamic than the home environment, and children display different behaviors there. Having parents observe their child in the classroom setting can help answer their questions and open up communication by allowing the teacher and parent to be on the same page. Observations are most effective when the parent can observe without the child's knowledge. If this is not possible, the teacher and parent need to decide when and how the child will be observed. The age and behavior of the child will determine how the observation will take place. Observations should be planned with a specific purpose in mind. To encourage a natural class setting, only one parent should be observing at any one time. Observations that require parents to observe specific areas and to respond on a written form can be very useful for making assessments and for conferencing. Questions can focus on the activities the child is engaged in, the specific behaviors that were observed, the child's interactions with peers, and the child's ability to be an independent learner.

■ Parent-teacher conferences

One of the quickest ways to send fear and dread into any teacher or parent is to say the words "parent-teacher conference." The giving and receiving of an evaluation is not always easy. However, with careful planning, practice, and prayer, the parent-teacher conference need not loom as a threat to anyone—teacher, parent, or director. Here are a few guidelines for determining when and why to schedule conferences:[5]

- Once or twice a year to discuss the child's progress
- To support parenting skills
- To discuss school readiness
- To address a significant concern
- To get to know the family

With the necessary background information and preparation, the teacher can be calm and ready. It is important for the teacher to be clearly in charge of the conference; in that way teacher and parents alike will feel more relaxed. It is important to keep in mind that the early education center and the parents are in partnership in the education and development of the child. The teacher must approach the conference with the attitude that the parents are allies, not enemies. One of the ways teachers gain parents' confidence is by sharing specific examples of the child's daily school experiences. By passing these

school scenes along all through the year, teachers assure parents that they know their child well.

Many times the teacher and the parents share the same joys, expectations, and concerns about the child. Finding this common ground will help the teacher and parents feel comfortable and will open the doors of communication. Thus the teacher will receive information and gain assistance that will prove invaluable in the development and education of the young child. Below are some practical dos and don'ts for parent-teacher conferences.

In advance of a parent-teacher conference, teachers should

- Have in mind what they want to discuss—the important areas in the child's development and early education.
- Collect specific data relating to those areas of the child's development and use the data during the conference.
- Make an honest effort to evaluate and understand the child. Several weeks before the conference, the teacher should spend some one-on-one time with the child, evaluating his emotional, cognitive, social, and spiritual development. The teacher should not guess or assume anything about the child's development.

To establish good rapport with the parents,

- Greet them in a friendly, relaxed manner.
- Be sensitive to them and their personal situations.
- Be honest but tactful.
- Let the parents know that you are a partner with them.
- Convince parents of your sincere interest in the child.

- Start and finish the conference on a positive note; prayer at the beginning and/or the end is invaluable!

During the conference, teachers should

- Be organized and prepared for the conference.
- Establish rapport with the parents; begin on a positive note.
- Know what they are saying and why they are saying it.
- Say what they mean.
- Be specific by showing examples.
- Encourage parents to be a part of the process.
- Communicate the philosophy and objectives of the early education program and of the individual class in particular.
- Be a good listener.
- Center the discussion on the child's progress; keep focused.
- Stress the child's overall development.
- Realize that the conference is time for two-way communication.
- Pray, pray, pray!

However,

- Don't overwhelm parents with too much information.
- Don't be evasive; either they know or they don't know.
- Don't use high-powered education terminology.
- Don't discuss other children, the class, or early education center problems.
- Don't try to be the whole answer for the child's success or failure.
- Don't forget to listen to the parents.
- Don't be defensive. (Teachers need to accept what they can change and give the rest to the Lord.)
- Don't forget the power of prayer!

Formal parent-teacher conferences can be held on an annual or biannual basis. The director can establish the time and date. The teacher, parents, or director can schedule other conferences as needed. Both parents should know that they are expected to attend any scheduled parent-teacher conference. The conference dates should be established at the beginning of the school year and published in the preschool/childcare center calendar. Notices about the conferences should be included in the center's daily, weekly, and/or monthly written publications. Several weeks before a conference, teachers should assign a conference time for each family or give parents the opportunity to schedule a time with the teacher. One week before the conference, the director or assistant director should send a note to the parents letting them know that the teacher is looking forward to meeting with them on the scheduled date and time. (See form 12.5 Parent Conference Letter.)

The parent-teacher conference usually lasts no longer than twenty minutes. The teacher needs to schedule more conference time if there is a particular concern about a child that cannot be expressed and answered in twenty minutes. After the conference the teacher may want to make notes for the child's file. The director should be notified if the teacher has specific concerns about the parents, the child, or the conference.

■ Parent complaints and concerns

Sooner or later, every director and/or staff member will have to deal with an unhappy parent. Instead of running for cover, the center should face the situation head-on. (See form 12.4 Parent Concern Form.) That does not mean that the director gets out the combat boots and prepares for battle, nor does it mean she lies down and lets herself be walked on for the sake of peace. A prayerful, balanced approach is preferable. Hot complaint topics are discipline and money. The director needs to communicate the center's expectations and procedures clearly. Some helpful tips for dealing with complaints are the following:

- The director listens respectfully and acknowledges the parent's concern or complaint. Sometimes just giving the parent an opportunity to talk and blow off steam will defuse the situation. Sometimes it is helpful to repeat the complaint back to the parent to make sure it is clearly understood.

- Instead of becoming defensive and combative, the director needs to investigate the concern or complaint. At such a time, the director may not be able to respond immediately and may need to tell the parents that they will be contacted just as soon as information has been gathered. Parents should not be made to feel that they are being brushed aside, but the director should indicate that time is needed for looking into the concern or complaint. Sometimes it's a good idea to give parents time to cool down. The director should be sure, however, to get back to them soon, and she should never leave a concern or complaint unresolved. It will come back later to haunt her.

- After completing the investigation, the director should share conclusions and solutions with the parent. The parent needs to be assured that whether or not the complaint is justified, the director appreciates the sharing of concerns. A director who feels the complaint is unjustified can often satisfy parents by promising to keep an eye on the situation. If the complaint is justified, the parents must be assured, through actions and words, that the situation has been dealt with.

- Sometimes the director will confront a no-win situation. It is important for the administration and the staff to know that it is impossible to please everyone and to meet everyone's expectations. The Christian early education center is a ministry first,

but it is also a service business, and an important part of any successful business is customer relations. God will honor the center that is honest and just in dealing with its customers.

■ *Parent evaluation of the center*

Parents should have the opportunity to evaluate the center on an annual basis, or when they withdraw from the program. The director should develop an evaluation tool to ensure that parents will give constructive criticism. A survey is a one way to receive feedback about the overall program. Surveys can contain a rating scale, multiple choice selections, and/or open-ended questions. Surveys need to be easy to fill out with questions that will elicit the greatest amount of information possible. While some parents have a difficult time being objective when it comes to anything about their child, most can contribute ideas and suggestions that the center will find helpful. After all, the director and staff want satisfied parents and happy children.

Parent Involvement
■ *Parent volunteers*

Parents can be a wonderful resource to the program, either using their unique talents or just spending time at school helping with various tasks. Parents of young children have an innate desire to be around their children in order to watch them grow and develop new skills. They want to enjoy this period of wonderment as their children seem to change and grow before their very eyes. Allowing parents to be involved in the program can be a wonderful way to make them a part of the growing process. Sometimes it can be intimidating for a teacher to have a parent in the classroom on a consistent basis. Every situation is unique, and teachers need to use discretion, making decisions that are in the best interest of the children. With that said, having parents in the classroom can be a great experience for both the children and the teacher. Many times Christian schools are so strapped financially that limited support staff are available to assist teachers with projects. Parents can fill in the gaps, and they become a valuable resource to the classroom and the school. (See form 12.6 Parent Volunteer Opportunities.) In order for parent volunteers to be successful, they need to attend an orientation where relevant issues are discussed for the following purposes:

- Helping parents become familiar with the early education program
- Letting them know you value their involvement
- Helping them to have a clear understanding of their role
- Providing specific instructions for classroom activities
- Introducing staff, goals, licensing
- Addressing confidentiality issues
- Letting them know the parameters of their involvement

Some parents may not be available during the school day but may still want to contribute to the center. They can be given suggestions for tasks to do at home, such as making play dough, covering paperback books with contact paper, creating classroom learning materials, and gathering items for the home-living area. When the parent involves the child in these volunteer activities, the child sees and experiences the parent's support of his early education world.

Parents can assist by helping with parties, special events, special projects, field trips, classroom time, outside activities, fundraising, and office tasks. Parents can also become a wonderful resource as they share a special talent with the class and as they acquaint the children with some who work in the community. A great way to show that you value the families' diverse cultures is to invite parents to share a special family tradition with the entire class. Regardless of whether parents volunteer or just want to hang out in the classroom, they should always feel welcome to be part of their child's school experience.

The director should be careful not to assign to volunteers tasks that require a professional level of responsibility. For example, parent volunteers should not be responsible for supervising the playground or for maintaining classroom discipline. These helpers are not in the classroom to take on the responsibilities of paid staff members or employees. Letting parents know they are appreciated when they volunteer is important. Like paid staff, the volunteers want to know that they are doing, and have done, a good job. Some ways to show them appreciation are these:

- A word of thanks from the teacher and/or director
- A note of appreciation from the teacher and/or director
- A note of appreciation to specific volunteers in the center's publications or on the message boards
- A special volunteer name tag to wear when doing volunteer tasks
- A tea or luncheon for volunteers at the end of the year
- A thank-you card handmade by the children

■ Parenting workshops and resources

Parents often need assistance in specific matters relating to their child's behavior or development. Parents do not have all the answers and need a support system to help when they get stuck. It is common for parents to mimic styles that their parents used with them, and sometimes the resulting practices are not in the best interest of the child. The Christian early education center can be a wonderful resource for building parental skills in strengthening the family and in handling situations according to the principles of grace and truth. The program can offer workshops on parenting skills as well as on specialized topics that relate to specific needs. (See form 12.1 Parent Education Survey.)

Successful workshops may involve the entire family, beginning with a meal and continuing with activities for the children to do while their parents meet for a lecture or discussion. Some programs have been successful at requiring at least one of the parents to participate in a workshop as a part of their involvement in the center's program. Having an abundance of materials available for parents, including books and tapes they can check out, can be a great way of exposing them to excellent lectures, authors, and topics presented in a variety of ways suited to different learning styles and time constraints. The director can also be a resource for parents by distributing informational literature and referring parents to special services when needed. The director and/or staff must be careful about giving specific advice in situations they are not qualified to address. There are many excellent Christian referral agencies that can help parents seeking specific counsel or information.

■ Events for parents

Back-to-School Night. Back-to-School Night can be held at the beginning of each new school year. The evening should be planned for parents only, unless there are planned activities and adequate supervision for the children. The director and teachers should be free of any responsibility for children so they can spend time imparting information to parents and answering their questions. The evening can begin or end with a social activity for the parents and staff. The main focus is the time parents spend with the teacher in their child's classroom. One hour is usually sufficient for the teacher to greet the parents and give specific classroom information. Back-to-School Night is not the time to discuss individual concerns parents may have about their child. Invite parents to make appointments to discuss such concerns later.

Suggestions for Back-to-School Night

- Open with prayer.
- Make introductions. All classroom staff members share personal background and professional preparation.
- Review the class goals for the year.
- Give specific information about classroom logistics.
  - Facility layout.
  - Procedures and location for early-morning arrivals and late-afternoon pickup.
- Explain the daily class schedule and the value of the various activities.
  - Introduce each of the classroom learning centers.
  - Allow time for parents to examine the classroom learning materials.
  - Set up a sensory-learning activity and use it to illustrate the program's educational philosophy.
  - Model a read-aloud session, using a favorite children's book. Show parents how to involve their child when reading stories at home.
- Discuss.
  - Parent/teacher communication.
  - Parent conferences.
  - Field trips and procedures.
  - Guidelines for parent volunteers.
  - Classroom discipline techniques.
- Provide time for questions and answers.

Parents' Night Out. Early education directors and teachers are regularly asking parents for help. As a refreshing change of pace, some centers provide a parent event or service as a way of expressing appreciation and support. Offering a Parents' Night Out is one way to give parents a gift of time, a chance for them to share a date night or to do some holiday shopping. During a Parents' Night Out, the program stays open for an evening session, providing a meal and special children's activities, using the current center staff. The staff must be paid accordingly for this event, which may include overtime.

Suggestions for Parents' Night Out

- Determine the best date for the event and add it to the school calendar.
- Consider adopting a theme or emphasis for the evening, such as allowing children to attend in pajamas.
- Distribute a flyer describing the event, including the procedures for signing up and the schedule of activities.
- Once you know the number of sign-ups, schedule staff members to work the event, paying careful attention to ensure that a staff member from each age group is present.
- Assign staff members to plan and prepare children's activities.
- Follow existing sign-in and sign-out procedures, ensuring children's security during the event.
- Take photographs and create a bulletin board celebrating a memorable evening.

Children's Programs. Some early education centers present an annual Christmas program, involving children in singing and dramatizing the birth of Christ. Such a program prepared for parents and grandparents can be an effective outreach tool, helping parents connect with the facility and the pastoral staff of the sponsoring church. The program can also be effective in directing the children's focus to the reason for Christmas festivities. On the down side, such programs can be taxing for children, requiring them to perform in ways that are not age-appropriate. The key to a successful Christmas program is planning with the children's needs in mind, being sensitive to their limitations and allowing them to be as actively involved as possible. It is tempting to present a program that parents will find "cute" or "entertaining," but such a program can come at the children's expense. Directors should consider ways to make the program meaningful to the children, gearing the songs and actions to children's understanding and abilities. In this way, early educators create a memorable experience for the children and their parents. The same guidelines can also be followed in planning programs for Easter, Thanksgiving, and other occasions.

FORM 12.1

Parent Education Survey

Thank you for taking the time to fill out this survey regarding parent helps that we can provide for you. We value our partnership with you in providing your child the best environment and early experiences for their development. Our desire is to support you as the primary educators of your children. We are interested in offering parenting workshops that will give you practical strategies for working with your preschool children to help prepare them for their future education. Please answer these questions to help us know how to serve you.

What are you most excited about in your role as a parent?

List two of your greatest joys as a parent.
1.

2.

What are your greatest challenges as a parent?

What areas do you feel the least prepared in?

List three topics about being a more effective parent that would be of interest to you.
1.

2.

3.

What suggestions would you make for effective workshop topics or parent helps?

FORM 12.2

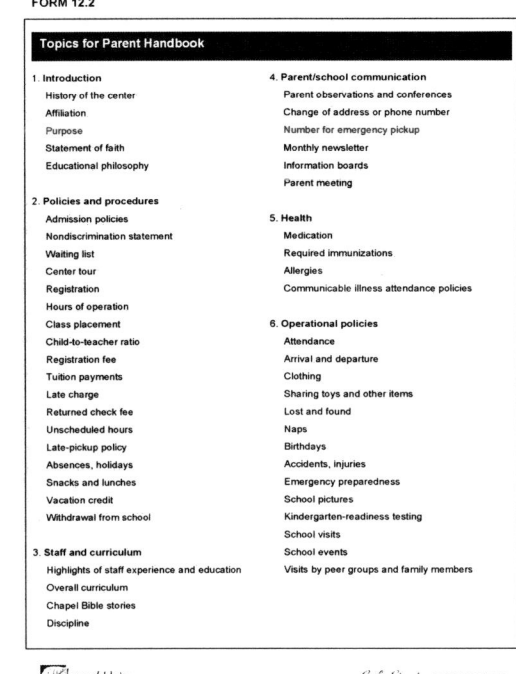

Topics for Parent Handbook

1. **Introduction**
   History of the center
   Affiliation
   Purpose
   Statement of faith
   Educational philosophy

2. **Policies and procedures**
   Admission policies
   Nondiscrimination statement
   Waiting list
   Center tour
   Registration
   Hours of operation
   Class placement
   Child-to-teacher ratio
   Registration fee
   Tuition payments
   Late charge
   Returned check fee
   Unscheduled hours
   Late-pickup policy
   Absences, holidays
   Snacks and lunches
   Vacation credit
   Withdrawal from school

3. **Staff and curriculum**
   Highlights of staff experience and education
   Overall curriculum
   Chapel Bible stories
   Discipline

4. **Parent/school communication**
   Parent observations and conferences
   Change of address or phone number
   Number for emergency pickup
   Monthly newsletter
   Information boards
   Parent meeting

5. **Health**
   Medication
   Required immunizations
   Allergies
   Communicable illness attendance policies

6. **Operational policies**
   Attendance
   Arrival and departure
   Clothing
   Sharing toys and other items
   Lost and found
   Naps
   Birthdays
   Accidents, injuries
   Emergency preparedness
   School pictures
   Kindergarten-readiness testing
   School visits
   School events
   Visits by peer groups and family members

FORM 12.3

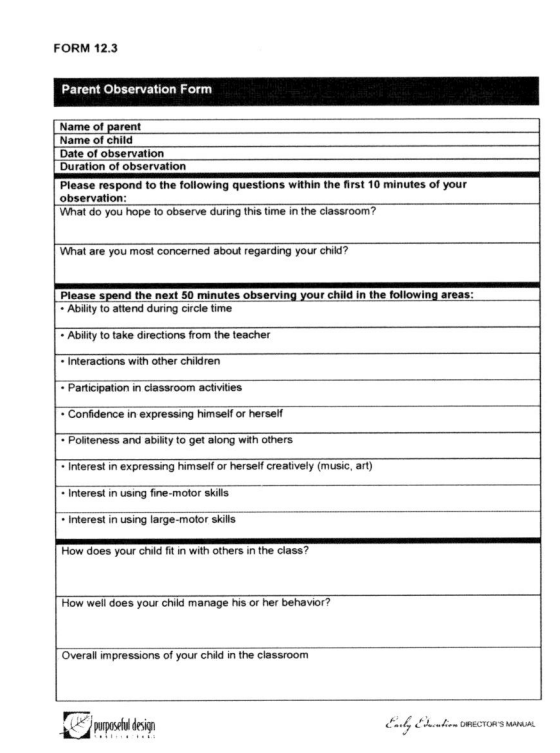

Parent Observation Form

Name of parent	
Name of child	
Date of observation	
Duration of observation	

Please respond to the following questions within the first 10 minutes of your observation:

What do you hope to observe during this time in the classroom?

What are you most concerned about regarding your child?

Please spend the next 50 minutes observing your child in the following areas:
- Ability to attend during circle time
- Ability to take directions from the teacher
- Interactions with other children
- Participation in classroom activities
- Confidence in expressing himself or herself
- Politeness and ability to get along with others
- Interest in expressing himself or herself creatively (music, art)
- Interest in using fine-motor skills
- Interest in using large-motor skills

How does your child fit in with others in the class?

How well does your child manage his or her behavior?

Overall impressions of your child in the classroom

FORM 12.4

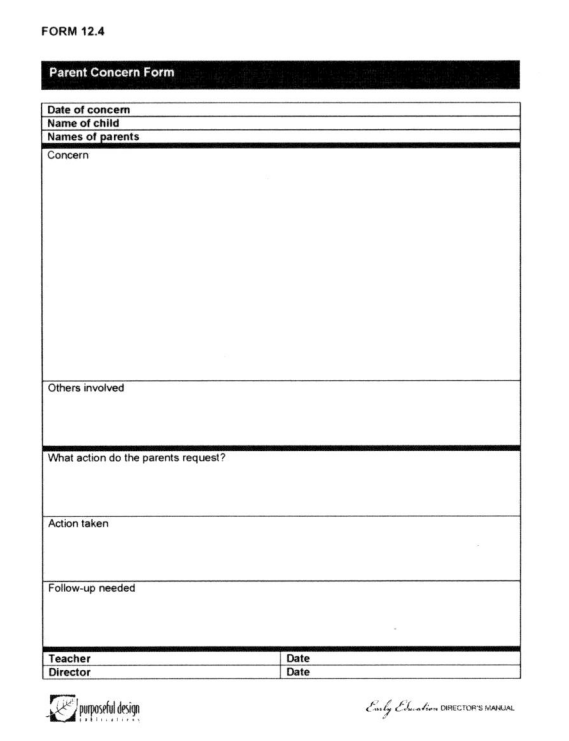

Parent Concern Form

Date of concern	
Name of child	
Names of parents	

Concern

Others involved

What action do the parents request?

Action taken

Follow-up needed

Teacher	Date
Director	Date

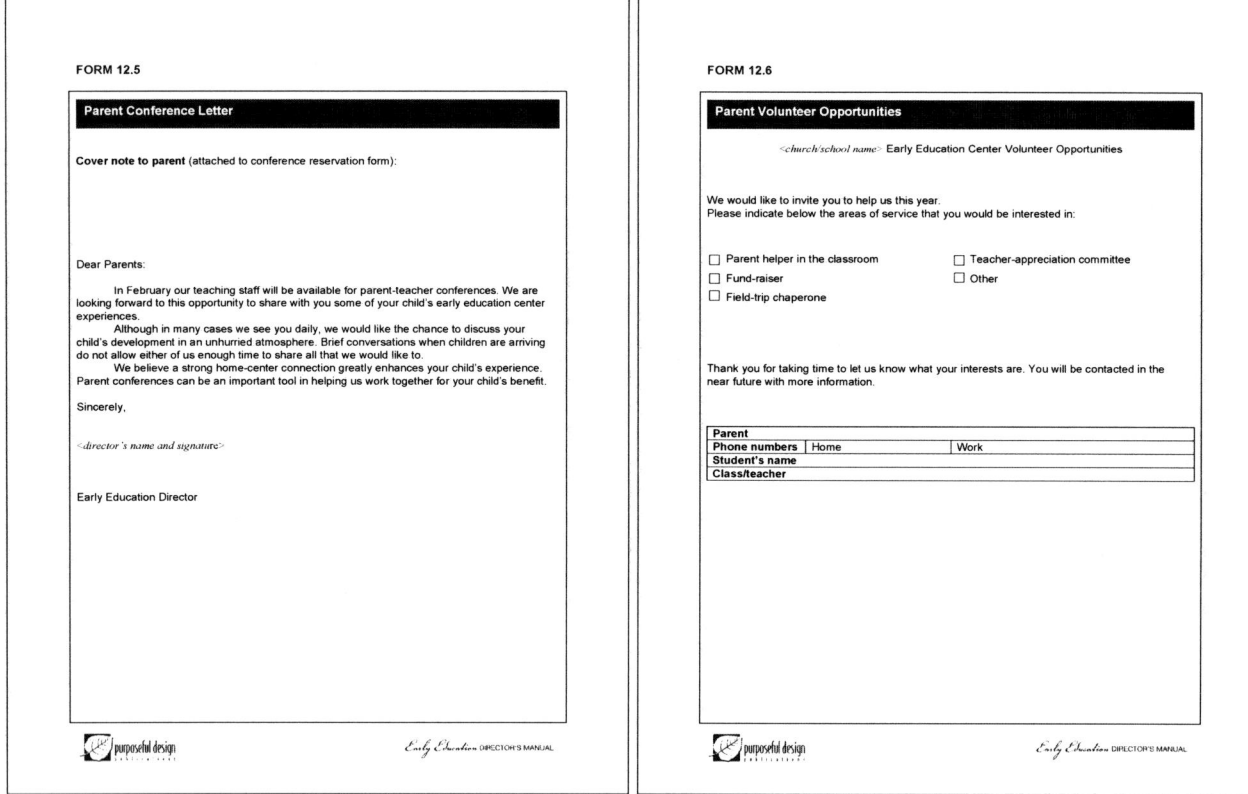

FORM 12.5

Parent Conference Letter

Cover note to parent (attached to conference reservation form):

Dear Parents:

    In February our teaching staff will be available for parent-teacher conferences. We are looking forward to this opportunity to share with you some of your child's early education center experiences.

    Although in many cases we see you daily, we would like the chance to discuss your child's development in an unhurried atmosphere. Brief conversations when children are arriving do not allow either of us enough time to share all that we would like to.

    We believe a strong home-center connection greatly enhances your child's experience. Parent conferences can be an important tool in helping us work together for your child's benefit.

Sincerely,

<director's name and signature>

Early Education Director

FORM 12.6

Parent Volunteer Opportunities

<church/school name> Early Education Center Volunteer Opportunities

We would like to invite you to help us this year.
Please indicate below the areas of service that you would be interested in:

☐ Parent helper in the classroom   ☐ Teacher-appreciation committee
☐ Fund-raiser   ☐ Other
☐ Field-trip chaperone

Thank you for taking time to let us know what your interests are. You will be contacted in the near future with more information.

Parent		
Phone numbers	Home	Work
Student's name		
Class/teacher		

PARTNERING WITH THE COMMUNITY

Chapter 13

Each of you should look not only to your own interests, but also to the interests of others. (Philippians 2:4)

Outside Connections

The director is responsible for her own personal involvement with professional organizations, referral agencies, and the community in which the early education center is located. It is not realistic to think that a director who remains isolated from the community can have a successful program. Directors need to see their role as significant but also as a small part of a larger picture. A successful center requires the support of the local church and the community in order to meet the needs of the children it serves. An early education program does not operate in isolation. Outside agencies provide the ongoing assistance necessary to keep the program functioning.

Establishing healthy relationships with those in support roles is essential and will go a long way toward creating a positive testimony. New directors must be prepared to be advocates for young children and to participate in the decision-making process in their community. These responsibilities are likely to involve time spent away from the center at meetings, forums, or training sessions. Thus school boards need to be informed about the director's outside commitments. They need to know that these commitments are part of the work of a director who takes her profession seriously. Many times decisions affecting Christian programs are made without representation from the faith-based community, and the resulting policies can limit those programs' potential ministry and enrollment. Directors should be prayerful regarding their involvement and should use their position in a positive way to effect change.

Advertising the Program

Marketing your early education program can be one of the most significant challenges you will face as a director. Building and maintaining a strong reputation in your community will take time and patience. Like the owner of any business, you must be committed to creating a distinctive program that will meet the needs of the families in the community. That part of the task includes identifying a mission and a vision that will serve as a foundation for the type of program you will offer. In addition, you will want to offer any value-added components that could make your program a good fit for the young children you hope to serve. Establishing these foundational markers allows you to move forward in marketing your program. Then you will need to convince the families in your community that you can indeed deliver on the values you've established. One way to do so is by piggy-backing on the reputation of the sponsoring church and thus attracting a core enrollment that will spread the word about your program.

Word of mouth can be the best form of advertisement when parents are pleased with what your center has to offer their children. You can reward families for spreading the word by providing a tuition credit to those who bring in a new family. First impressions also play a significant part in attracting families. Christian centers that work hard at being oriented to children and families generally have an easier time of bringing people into their programs. As Christian educators we rely primarily on the Holy Spirit to guide in this process. So many factors will be out of your control that you will need to draw strength from the knowledge that God has moved and led in the adventure.

Networking with the Community

One of the best long-term ways of building enrollment is through community involvement. This involvement can take several forms, but the goal is to network with organizations and leaders in the community. Families are much more likely to select your program if they know you are well connected and have a good reputation with those who are actively involved in community service. A good outcome of this involvement is your Christian witness. Letting others know that you care for more than the success of your own program speaks volumes about the significant contributions you want to make in other people's lives. One of the greatest shortcomings of Christian educators can be the isolated world in which we live. In our attempts to build our program and educate young children, we can easily lose sight of our responsibility for being a beacon of light in our communities. Here are a few guidelines for establishing networks in your community:

- Get familiar with community organizations that provide services to young children; attend a few of their meetings, introducing yourself and your program.
- Serve on a committee of a community organization.
- Send a letter of introduction to businesses in your area and invite them to partner with you in contributing to your center's program.
- Attend a city council meeting and get to know a few council members.
- Contact your local newspaper and invite its leaders to send a reporter to your campus for a special event.
- Invite other early education professionals to lunch and a tour of your center.
- Let others know that you care deeply about the welfare of your community's young children, and agree to partner with them to make an investment in the next generation.

■ Networking with community organizations

Community organizations have various forms and take on many roles, but typically they exist to benefit the community in some way. Some focus on volunteering to help a particular sector of the population. Others spend their resources on providing direct services, which fall into several categories of help for families and young children.

Governmental. Branches of city, state, and federal government set policy and provide services funded by tax dollars.

For-profit and nonprofit organizations. These provide medical, emotional, financial, legal, and supportive services to enhance the quality of life for young children.

Referral organizations. These provide support services for families seeking the most appropriate and cost-effective resources for their child. They are a clearinghouse for the available support services in a community.

Advocacy groups. These groups speak and act in support of the rights of young children and lobby for funding of appropriate programs.

Professional organizations. Directors frequently join one or more local, regional, or national professional organizations. Through such organizations they can accomplish several goals:

- Obtain information
- Make contacts that are personally and professionally helpful
- Effect change
- Form support groups

Those who belong to these groups have many things in common, including a strong desire to see that the rights and needs of young children are served. Some may differ in their ways of implementing these services. Relationships and partnerships with professional groups can create a strong, united voice to

represent the faith-based community. We can all do our share in accomplishing this goal.

One way to do some networking is by attending key meetings in your community. Being seen and introducing yourself at these meetings is the first step. Being prayerful about the relationships you develop can make a difference as you allow the Holy Spirit to guide you. Letting others know that you stand on common ground with them regarding certain issues builds respect and an ability to be heard at crucial times. As believers we have the opportunity to demonstrate our love for others and to be a light in our communities as we rub shoulders with others and serve along with them.

■ Building community partnerships

Partnerships are typically built through relationships. Establishing strong relationships with businesses and other resources in your community is the first step. You will want to brainstorm as a staff about which direction to go in this area and what it is you want to do together to benefit the families and the larger community you serve. You may also want to survey your center's parents for their ideas and take advantage of existing relationships. You may decide to sponsor a community event at your school to expose other community members to your program. Here are a few tips to keep things moving forward:

- Be intentional about what you want to accomplish
- Make contact with individuals for follow-up
- Be consistent with meetings and phone calls
- Be prepared with ideas
- Be clear about what you expect to accomplish and how you will move forward with any action items
- Come to an agreement
- Write an implementation plan
- Evaluate together the effectiveness of what you've done

■ Creating community awareness

In addition to parents, another valuable resource is the larger community in which your facility is located. It is vital that the community be aware of your facility and your program. Getting such knowledge out requires more than the standard phone listing, the occasional flyer, or a newspaper ad. It is important to draw positive attention to your facility throughout the community. The following strategies may give you some ideas on how to broaden community awareness of your facility and its programs.

You can promote your facility and its programs by providing short presentations at special times of the year in malls and other shopping areas. Malls are often looking for groups to perform during the Christmas and Easter seasons. Get in touch with the public-relations manager at a local mall, and ask for a calendar of planned event days. If you get your center's event on the calendar well in advance, your teachers and students will have time to plan, practice, and present a short program.

Another way to promote your facility and its programs is to create displays. The local library and other public organizations are often looking for colorful displays of children's work. You can contact one or more of them to inquire about scheduling a display or exhibition. If a large display is too difficult, have the children design their own T-shirts and add the name and location of the facility to their original design. As they wear their shirts around town, people will notice. Even posters are a good idea. If you know of a special event being held by another group—the local Women's Club for example—offer to have the children design posters for the event. Have your name and address on the bottom of each poster. Not only is this project a good method of advertising; it also creates good relations with another community group.

Some convalescent hospitals and retirement homes welcome small groups to sing favorite carols at Christmastime. You can pass out flyers or ask to leave a few at the facility when your program is finished. Although many of these people will not have young children themselves, some will have relatives that do. Set an example by volunteering to be on the staff of an organization or by having your families participate in a community activity. Hosting a community event related to children, such as a toy exchange or a children's concert, is another way to increase your center's visibility. Contact local real-estate agents, who are continually providing information about local early education centers to the families moving into the area, and offer to provide them with your school's brochures. Or invite several agents to a small reception or children's event so that they can see the program.

Women's ministries of churches are often looking for speakers with expertise in children's issues. When a local early education director gives a presentation on parenting, discipline, or understanding children's temperaments, the parents' needs are met and the center is positioned as a leader in the field and a caring contributor to the community. Another way to identify your program as having authority in early education issues is to write articles for community newspapers or company newsletters, or to offer parenting seminars to the community at large as well as to your school family.

■ Tapping into local resources

There are a number of ways you can become familiar with local resources. Each city has a chamber of commerce that can give you a broad overview of the city's organizations. You can then identify the ones that may assist you with your program in some way. You may want to contact them to allow them to become familiar with your program, or you may prefer to send them some information. Another great source is your community's resource and referral agency. Typically this agency will be the clearing house for your area to identify childcare programs and groups that serve young children in some capacity. Visiting the agency and setting up a few appointments will help you to become familiar with each other's services. Meeting face to face can help make you more visible. Taking advantage of training workshops that are already taking place helps you not to duplicate efforts.

Developing a Public Relations Plan

The center's image is an important consideration in all aspects of the public information and public relations efforts. Developing an official public relations plan helps identify the activities and the overall direction for publicizing the program in the community. (See form 13.1 Public Relations Plan Worksheet.) Often a school already engages in activities to attract families, but there is sometimes a lack of intentionality in the way these activities are conducted and coordinated. Implementing a plan will help ensure the success and viability of the program for years to come. A public relations plan can be enhanced through advertising, publicity, community involvement, referrals, and special events.

> Truth should always be the first requirement for any public relations effort. Have your people tell the truth, tell it well, and in a timely way.
>
> Bob Briner in
> *The Management Methods of Jesus*

As part of your plan, you can select the strategies that you will use for marketing your program in the upcoming year. (See form 13.2 Early Education Development Plan.) Also, you can identify contacts and create a timeline for when the events in the plan will take place. You will also need to decide how the necessary funds will be provided. Media avenues for

advertising and/or publicity include the following:

- Magazines
- Business journals
- Websites
- Radio
- Television
- Fliers
- Posters
- Neighborhood papers
- Church bulletins
- Newspapers

■ Advertising

Advertising is the most direct way of informing the community about your services. It can also be the most costly. Because advertising is paid promotion, the school controls the timing and the content of your message. The largest source of referrals not generated by word of mouth is often thought to be the phone book, followed by a sign on the premises announcing that the program is enrolling children. Often a local community newspaper can be more cost effective than a large metropolitan one because the community newspaper targets the message to the people in your immediate area. Direct mail has only a one- to two- percent return rate, but it can be cost effective if you purchase a mailing list of families who have children in the ages you serve and if you send your message by bulk mail. For direct mail to be effective, the promotional piece must be sent out multiple times, spaced a few weeks apart.

■ Referrals

The single most common reason a parent will choose a particular early education program is that a close friend, coworker, or family member recommended it. Matthew 12:34 declares, "For out of the overflow of the heart the mouth speaks." Parents who are excited about how their child is learning and growing in their program can't help telling others. Their positive comments about the program influence their coworkers, neighbors, and friends from church. Their words may even bear fruit years later, as some of those who hear may not be parents now but will be one day. There are several ways to generate positive word-of-mouth referrals among the parents, the main one being the high quality of the program. Next are daily interactions of the staff, the parents, and the children, demonstrating the director's and the center's care and respect for the family.

Word of Mouth: The Most Effective Promotion
According to the National Center for Education Statistics, parents get information about early education programs in their community in the following ways: [1]

59%	friends, neighbors, relatives, coworkers
16%	other
10%	advertisement
6%	school
5%	church
4%	employer
4%	welfare or social service agency
2%	referral service

Before families can begin to refer others to your program, you must gain their trust. A tremendous amount of energy has been expended in reaching out to a new family and encouraging them to enroll in your program. Those efforts are ultimately fruitless if your program is unable to retain the family for the entire school year and beyond. The highest rate of withdrawal occurs just six to eight weeks after enrollment. Even though the parents have made their decision and selected your center, in the following two months they will be watching for signs confirm-

ing that they made the right decision. There are a few key ways for your center to establish a strong relationship with the family from the very beginning. Before the child even starts school, a welcome call from the teacher gives the parents a chance to ask questions, calming their fears. Another idea is to send a photo of the child's first day at the center in a cardboard frame titled "My First Day at _____ Early Education Center." If you can mail this photo to the parents' workplace, you will maximize the exposure. Make sure parents receive feedback from the teachers about their child's activities and accomplishments in the first few weeks. These small efforts in communicating with families from the beginning will yield great benefits in building parents' trust and loyalty.

■ Publicity

Publicity, or media promotion that you receive free, allows the community to hear about your program from several sources. This type of promotion is particularly valuable and carries more credibility as it is considered endorsement by a third party, one that is not biased toward your program. There are a variety of forms that publicity can take, such as press releases sent to newspapers and to television stations when noteworthy events occur in the life of your center. For example, if your center earns accreditation or receives some form of local recognition, be sure to photograph any awards ceremonies and send the photos to local news outlets. If your program hosts a community event, or involves the children in public service such as visiting a hospital or retirement center at holiday time, send a photograph along with the press release. Informing the media about your program can be time consuming and may not yield immediate results. Be patient and recognize that you are making an investment. If you do get an article or photograph published, you can maximize the impact by obtaining reprints and including them with the promotional information you send to inquiring families.

The content and appearance of your center's promotional materials make a statement to parents. The text of brochures and fliers should be informative and should spell out the philosophy of the center's program. The quality of any photographs or artwork should convey the message that the staff members of the center are professional and creative. There should be consistency in design elements, including logos and colors, in all printed materials distributed to the public. As you write promotional materials for the center, it is important to consider the ethnic and cultural makeup of your audience, as well as their reading and language skills.

Promotional materials should cover all the services that are available at the center. The public-relations plan should identify which promotional materials will be used, how often they will be updated, and what new elements will be included. Another consideration is where these materials will be distributed and how much money will be needed to cover their printing and distribution. Promotional materials should include such basic information as the following:[2]

- Age range of the children
- Location of the center
- Phone number, website, and email contact information
- Philosophy, mission, and vision
- Specialized services the school provides
- Qualifications of the staff

■ Community involvement
Another part of a public relations plan is the center's interaction with the larger community. As stated above, this interaction can be accomplished through networking, volunteering, or serving on a committee. Typically, the director is involved in some kind of community effort and provides the leadership in representing the school. Directors should decide at the beginning of each year how they want to be involved, and they should make time for such an activity in their schedule. The benefits of community involvement are the following:

- Developing friendships with those outside the school
- Being in a position to represent Christ
- Representing your center's program
- Being involved in making decisions that could impact your program
- Providing leadership within your field

■ Special events
The center can host events that provide service to families. A workshop for parents, a community fair, and a silent auction are some of the possible events. Typically, a program will have several activities that highlight the students in some way such as a Christmas program, an open house, a back-to-school night, or a family night. Making these events available to those in the larger community can provide a positive experience for prospective students and their families.

■ Components of a written public relations plan
Developing a public relations plan will take time, but the investment is necessary for the overall success of the program. The plan can be developed over months and years, with the information being revised from year to year to meet the current needs of the center. Sometimes new priorities will surface and new ideas will be formulated to improve the center's record in realizing the stated outcomes. There are four crucial steps involved in the process:

Assessing the current state. Reviewing parent surveys, staff input, and community feedback will help the director make an honest appraisal of the program's current strengths and weaknesses. The director should write a summary of the findings and make it available to the staff and families. This process will send a positive message that you have taken the time to assess their input and develop some strong conclusions.

Summarizing your outcomes. The director should articulate what he or she wants to accomplish for the upcoming year by way of making the program attractive and relevant, able to meet student and family needs. These elements can be summarized in the center's overall philosophy, mission, and vision statements, along with specific direction from the Holy Spirit about the next few years. Identifying whom you want to impact will be key to making this happen.

Setting goals and objectives. Once you have defined your overall direction, it will be helpful to formulate a few goals to help you to begin moving in that direction. Keep in mind that goals are very general and are typically not easy to measure. This step will refine even further the direction to take. Goals can then be broken down into objectives that are very specific, defining what will be accomplished, who will be responsible, and when it will take place. It is important to start simply so that you set your program up for success.

Developing strategies. Once you have identified your goals and objectives, you will need to break them down even further to help ensure that they will be achieved. The objectives will include the *who*, *what*, and *when*; the strategies tell *how* the objectives will be reached. You should create action items that identify priorities, a timeline or calendar that puts a time limit on the various steps, a list of needed resources, and any financial impact.

In order for this plan to be effective, all the key players will need to be informed and trained in their roles and responsibilities. There will also need to be follow-up to monitor progress toward the stated objectives. A successful plan will result in a higher profile in the community and a greater sense of purpose for the staff.

Evaluating Effectiveness in the Community

Programs that operate on a year-round basis sometimes fall into the trap of not spending adequate time evaluating their effectiveness in meeting the needs of the families and communities. Some indicators to consider are a drop in enrollment and a higher turnover in staff. It is wise to spend time each year asking a few questions to see whether changes are needed.

1. Are the families pleased with the content and the priorities of our program?
2. Are the families pleased with the hours of operation of our program?
3. Are there additional services we could be providing to our families?
4. Is our program meeting a unique need in our community?
5. How are children's lives being changed through our program?
6. Are we accomplishing our spiritual mission?

> Our good name matters only if it is under your great name, Lord. By your providence may we have the image in the market of being the best at what we are trying to do, and by your grace may that image be accurate.
>
> From *Leadership Prayers*
> by Richard Kriegbaum

FORM 13.1

Public Relations Plan Worksheet

1. Assessing the current state

Strengths of the current program:

Areas of growth for the current program:

2. Summarizing your outcomes

What do you want to accomplish in the coming year?

What activities will support this effort?

How will this process impact your families and community?

3. Setting goals and objectives

Goal	Objective	Outcome	Activity

4. Developing strategies

Action	Plan	Timeline	Resources

purposeful design

Early Education DIRECTOR'S MANUAL

FORM 13.2

Early Education Development Plan

Program Quality: *Reputation in the Community*
Annual assessment of strengths and weaknesses
Evaluate staff, facility, education program
Survey staff and parents
Pursue accreditation
Developing New Markets: *Community Awareness*
Reaching families geographically (rotate signs)
Print ads
Direct mail
Parent-generated publicity
Successful Recruitment: *Converting Inquiries to Enrollment*
Guidelines and procedures for staff
Handling initial phone calls
Conducting tours
Special Events: *Maximize Potential for Recruitment*
Aggressively promote annual events (Back-to-School Night, Christmas program, open house, etc.)
Develop parent education evenings for the community

purposeful design

Early Education DIRECTOR'S MANUAL

Resources

Chapter 1
GETTING STARTED

Available from ACSI

Association of Christian Schools International. 1998. *Preschool accreditation manual.* Colorado Springs, CO: Association of Christian Schools International.

Braley, James W., ed. 1998. *How to start a Christian school.* Colorado Springs, CO: Association of Christian Schools International.

Available Online

U.S. Department of Health and Human Services. 2005. Individual states' child care licensure regulations. National Resource Center for Health and Safety in Child Care. http://nrc.uchsc.edu/STATES/states.htm.

U.S. Department of Health and Human Services. n.d. What congregations should know about federal funding for child care. Child Care Bureau. http://www.acf.hhs.gov/programs/ccb/providers/faithbased.pdf.

Organizations

Child Care Bureau
Administration on Children, Youth and Families
U.S. Department of Health and Human Services
Aerospace Building
370 L'Enfant Promenade SW
Washington, DC 20447
Phone: 202-690-6782
Email: ccb@acf.dhhs.gov
http://www.acf.hhs.gov/programs/ccb

National Association of Child Care Resource and Referral Agencies
3101 Wilson Boulevard, Suite 350
Arlington, VA 22201
Phone: 703-341-4100
Email: info@naccrra.org
http://www.naccrra.org
[This site provides information on your community's childcare resource and referral agency.]

National Child Care Information Center
10530 Rosehaven Street, Suite 400
Fairfax, VA 22030
Phone: 800-616-2242
Email: info@nccic.org
http://nccic.org

Chapter 2
PHILOSOPHY AND MISSION OF CHRISTIAN EARLY EDUCATION

Available from ACSI

Blamires, Harry. 2005. *The Christian mind: How should a Christian think?* Colorado Springs, CO: Purposeful Design Publications. (Orig. pub. 1963.)

Braley, James, Jack Layman, and Ray White, eds. 2003. *Foundations of Christian school education.* Colorado Springs, CO: Purposeful Design Publications.

Gaebelein, Frank E. 1968. *The pattern of God's truth: Problems of integration in Christian education.* Whittier, CA: Association of Christian Schools International.

Greene, Albert E. 2003. *Reclaiming the future of Christian education: A transforming vision.* Colorado Springs, CO: Purposeful Design Publications.

Layman, Jack. 2003. *The philosophical basis of a Christian education: A biblical foundation for Christian schooling.* VHS, series. Colorado Springs, CO: Purposeful Design Publications.

Moreland, J. P. 1997. *Love your God with all your mind: The role of reason in the life of the soul.* Colorado Springs, CO: NavPress.

Willard, Dallas. 2002. *Renovation of the heart: Putting on the character of Christ.* Colorado Springs, CO: NavPress.

Available from Other Publishers

Barna, George. 2002. *A fish out of water.* Brentwood, TN: Integrity.

Schultz, Glen. 1998. *Kingdom education: God's plan for educating future generations.* Nashville, TN: LifeWay.

Available Online

Bodrova, Elena, Deborah Leong, and Rima Shore. 2004. Child outcome standards in pre-K programs: What are standards; what is needed to make them work? Policy brief. *Preschool Policy Matters* (National Institute for Early Education Research), no. 5 (March). http://nieer.org/resources/policybriefs/5.pdf.

Espinosa, Linda. 2002. High quality preschool: Why we need it and what it looks like. Policy brief. *Preschool Policy Matters* (National Institute for Early Education Research), no. 1 (November). http://nieer.org/resources/policybriefs/1.pdf.

Fiene, Richard. 2002. 13 Indicators of quality child care: Research update. http://aspe.hhs.gov/hsp/ccquality-ind02/index.htm.

Trust for Early Education. n.d. The foundations for high quality pre-kindergarten: What all children need. http://www.trustforearlyed.org/docs/TEEvisionfinal.pdf.

U.S. Department of Education. 1999. How are the children? Report on early childhood development and learning. http://www.ed.gov/pubs/How_Children.

Chapter 3
GOD'S DESIGN FOR GROWTH

Available from ACSI

Carpenter, Darlene. 1999. *Spiritual nurturing: How to help your child grow spiritually.* Lewisville, TX: Carpenter Shop Resources.

Fuller, Cheri. 2001. *Opening your child's nine learning windows.* Grand Rapids, MI: Zondervan.

Henley, Karyn. 2002. *Child-sensitive teaching: Helping children grow a living faith in a loving God.* Rev. ed. Nashville, TN: Child Sensitive Communication.

Martin, Grant. 2004. *Help! for teachers: Strategies for reaching all students.* 2nd ed. Colorado Springs, CO: Purposeful Design Publications.

Available from Other Publishers

Boucher, Pamela K., comp. 1999. *Teaching in Christian weekday early education.* Nashville, TN: LifeWay Christian Resources.

Brazelton, T. Berry, and Stanley I. Greenspan. 2001. *The irreducible needs of children: What every child must have to grow, learn, and flourish.* New York: Perseus Publishing.

Cloud, Henry, and John Townsend. 2000. *Raising great kids: Parenting with grace and truth.* Grand Rapids, MI: Zondervan.

Dobson, James. 1990. *Children at risk: The battle for the hearts and minds of our kids.* Nashville, TN: Word.

Elkind, David. 1987. *Miseducation: Preschoolers at risk.* New York: Knopf.

———. 2001. *The hurried child: Growing up too fast too soon.* 3rd ed. Cambridge, MA: Perseus Books.

Gelber, A., S. Begley, G. Cowley, and B. Kantrowitz, eds. 2000. Your child: From birth to three. *Newsweek,* special edition (Fall/Winter): 1–88.

Greenspan, Stanley I. 2000. *Building healthy minds: The six experiences that create intelligence and emotional growth in babies and young children.* With Nancy Breslau Lewis. New York: Perseus Publishing.

Healy, Jane. 1991. *Endangered minds: Why children don't think—and what we can do about it.* New York: Simon & Schuster.

Herschkowitz, Norbert, and Elinore Chapman Herschkowitz. 2004. *A good start in life: Understanding your child's brain and behavior from birth to age 6.* 2nd ed. Washington, DC: Dana Press.

Phillips, Deborah A., and Jack P. Shonkoff, eds. 2000. *From neurons to neighborhoods: The science of early childhood development.* National Research Council. Washington, DC: National Academies Press.

Pierson, Jim. 2002. *Exceptional teaching: A comprehensive guide for including students with disabilities.* Cincinnati, OH: Standard.

Shore, Rima. 1997. *Rethinking the brain: New insights into early development.* New York: Families and Work Institute.

Zuck, Roy B. 1998. *Spirit-filled teaching: The power of the Holy Spirit in your ministry.* Ed. Charles R. Swindoll. Nashville, TN: Word.

Available Online

Council for Exceptional Children. http://www.cec.sped.org. [This international organization dedicates itself to improving the educational development of children with disabilities, children who are gifted, and those with other exceptionalities.]

National Dissemination Center for Children with Disabilities. http://www.nichcy.org.

Ounce of Prevention Fund. n.d. Ready to succeed: The lasting effects of early relationships. http://www.ounceofprevention.org/downloads/publications/OPF_Ready_To_Succeed.pdf.

University of Colorado Health Sciences Center. n.d. First start: Birth to five. http://www.uchsc.edu/firststart. [This program provides training for paraprofessionals and other caregivers working with infants, toddlers, and young children with disabilities or chronic conditions.]

Organizations

American Speech-Language-Hearing Association
10801 Rockville Pike
Rockville, MD 20852

Phone: 800-498-2071
Email: actioncenter@asha.org
http://www.asha.org
[Available information includes a chart of developmental milestones for language development, suggestions for activities to encourage language development, free information packets, and referrals to qualified speech-language pathologists.]

The Gesell Institute of Human Development
310 Prospect Street
New Haven, CT 06511
Phone: 203-777-3481
Email: Gesell.Inst@att.net
http://www.gesellinstitute.org

National Dissemination Center for Children with Disabilities
PO Box 1492
Washington, DC 20013
Phone: 800-695-0285
Email: nichcy@aed.org
http://www.nichcy.org

Program for Infant/Toddler Care
WestEd PITC
180 Harbor Drive, Suite 112
Sausalito, CA 94965-1410
Phone: 415-289-2300
http://www.pitc.org

Zero to Three:
National Center for Infants, Toddlers, and Families
2000 M Street, NW, Suite 200
Washington, DC 20036
Phone: 202-638-1144
http://www.zerotothree.org
[This resource provides articles on a variety of professional issues and downloadable handouts on child development issues for specific age ranges to share with parents and staff.]

Chapter 4
SPONSORSHIP AND GOVERNANCE

Available from ACSI

Carney, Burt, ed. n.d. *Christian school legal and administrative issues: A practical guide for Christian school leaders.* Enabling Leadership Series. Colorado Springs, CO: Association of Christian Schools International.

Carver, John. 1997. *Boards that make a difference: A new design for leadership in nonprofit and public organizations.* 2nd ed. San Francisco, CA: Jossey-Bass.

Carver, John, and Miriam Mayhew Carver. 1996. *Basic principles of policy governance.* San Francisco, CA: Jossey-Bass.

Mawdsley, Ralph D. 1995. *Legal problems of religious and private schools.* 3rd ed. Topeka, KS: National Organization on Legal Problems of Education.

Plan It. 1999. *Christian school strategic planning: Plan it—a framework for effective strategic planning.* Enabling Leadership Series. Colorado Springs, CO: Association of Christian Schools International.

Young, Paul E., comp. 1999. *Christian school board leadership: A framework for effective governance.* Enabling Leadership Series. Colorado Springs, CO: Association of Christian Schools International.

Available from Other Publishers

Andringa, Robert C., and Ted W. Engstrom. 2001. *Nonprofit board answer book: Practical guidelines for board members and chief executives.* 2nd. ed. Washington, DC: National Center for Nonprofit Boards.

Carver, John. 1992. *Empowering boards for leadership: Redefining excellence in governance.* Audiocassette. San Francisco, CA: Jossey-Bass.

Carver, John, and Miriam Mayhew Carver. 1997. *Reinventing your board: A step-by-step guide to implementing policy governance.* San Francisco, CA: Jossey-Bass.

Gangel, Kenneth O. 1997. *Team leadership in Christian ministry: Using multiple gifts to build a unified vision.* Revised ed. Chicago, IL: Moody.

Harms, Thelma, Richard M. Clifford, and Debby Cryer. 2004. *Early childhood environment rating scale.* Revised ed. New York: Teachers College Press. [Available at http://www.teacherscollegepress.org.]

———. 2006. *Infant/toddler environment rating scale.* Revised ed. New York: Teachers College Press. [Available at http://www.teacherscollegepress.org.]

Nelson, Linda S., and Alan E. Nelson. 2000. *Child care administration: Planning quality programs for young children.* Tinley Park, IL: Goodheart-Wilcox.

Sciarra, Dorothy June, and Anne G. Dorsey. 2003. *Developing and administering a child care center.* 5th ed. Clifton Park, NY: Delmar Learning.

Available Online

BoardSource (formerly the National Center for Nonprofit Boards). http://www.boardsource.org. [This organization provides resources for nonprofit boards.]

The Foundation Center. 2006. Establishing a nonprofit organization. http://fdncenter.org/learn/classroom/establish/index.html.

McNamara, Carter. 1999. Starting a nonprofit organization. http://www.managementhelp.org/strt_org/strt_np/strt_np.htm.

Organizations

International Association of Christian School Board Members (IACSB)
Association of Christian Schools International
PO Box 65130
Colorado Springs, CO 80962-5130
Phone: 719-528-6906
http://www.acsi.org

Chapter 5
MANAGING FINANCES

Available from Other Publishers

Morgan, Gwen G. 1999. *The bottom line for children's programs.* N.p.: Steam Press. [Distributed by Gryphon House, http://www.gryphonhouse.com.]

Neugebauer, Bonnie, and Roger Neugebauer. 1997. *Managing money: A center director's guidebook.* N.p. [Available through Child Care Information Exchange, http://www.ccie.com.]

Twombly, Gerald. 2000. *Funding your vision: New hope for non-profits.* Winona Lake, IN: BMH Books.

Available Online

Oesterreich, Lesia. 1998. Child care: Financial basics. Pm-1751. Ames, IA: Iowa State University Extension. http://www.extension.iastate.edu/Publications/PM1751.pdf.

Patapoff, Larry. n.d. Checklist of financial safeguards that can protect your school. http://www.acsi.org-legal.

Organizations

Church Mutual Insurance Company
PO Box 357
3000 Schuster Lane
Merrill, WI 54452-0357
Phone: 800-554-2642
http://www.churchmutual.com/

Evangelical Christian Credit Union
9240 Explorer Drive, Suite 101
Colorado Springs, CO 80920-5001
Phone: 800-634-3228
http://www.eccu.org

Evangelical Council for Financial Accountability
440 West Jubal Early Drive, Suite 130
Winchester, VA 22601
Phone: 800-323-9473
http://www.ecfa.org

Facts Management Company
PO Box 67037
Lincoln, NE 68506
Phone: 800-624-7092
Email: info@factsmgt.com
http://www.factsmgt.com

Family Financial Needs Assessment
PO Box 488
2022 Oak Tree Cove, Suite 3

Hernando, MS 38632
Phone: 662-429-3473
http://www.ffna1.com/
[This organization assists with financial aid programs.]

Chapter 6
THE ROLE OF THE DIRECTOR

Available from ACSI

Carney, Burt. 2001. *Christian school personnel forms: A resource for interviewing, contracting, and evaluating school personnel.* Enabling Leadership Series. Colorado Springs, CO: Association of Christian Schools International.

————, ed. 2005. *The best of "Legal/Legislative Update."* CD. Colorado Springs, CO: Purposeful Design Publications.

Gangel, Kenneth O. 2002. *Called to lead: Understanding and fulfilling your role as an educational leader.* Colorado Springs, CO: Purposeful Design Publications.

Available from Other Publishers

Briner, Bob. 1996. *The management methods of Jesus: Ancient wisdom for modern business.* Nashville, TN: Thomas Nelson.

Gunderson, Denny. 1997. *The leadership paradox.* Seattle, WA: YWAM Publishing.

Maxwell, John C. 1998. *The 21 irrefutable laws of leadership: Follow them and people will follow you.* Nashville, TN: Thomas Nelson.

Rinehart, Stacy T. 1998. *Upside down: The paradox of servant leadership.* Colorado Springs, CO: NavPress.

Rush, Myron. 2002. *Management: A biblical approach.* Colorado Springs, CO: Victor.

Tobias, Cynthia.1995. *The way we work: A practical approach for dealing with people on the job.* Colorado Springs, CO: Focus on the Family.

Management Books for Early Education

Bloom, Paula Jorde. 1982. *Avoiding burnout: Strategies for managing time, space, and people in early childhood education.* New York: Acropolis Books.

————. 2000. *Circle of influence: Implementing shared decision making and participative management.* St. Paul, MN: New Horizons.

————. 2002. *Making the most of meetings: A practical guide.* St. Paul, MN: New Horizons.

————. 2003. *Leadership in action: How effective directors get things done.* St. Paul, MN: New Horizons. [Available from Redleaf Press, http://www.redleafpress.org.]

Cherry, Clare, Barbara Harkness, and Kay Kuzma. n.d. *The child care center management guide: A hands-on resource.* 3rd ed. St. Paul, MN: New Horizons. [Available at Redleaf Press, http://www.redleafpress.org.]

Kriegbaum, Richard. 1998. *Leadership prayers.* Wheaton, IL: Tyndale.

Lee, Kathy H. 2003. *Solutions for early childhood directors: Real answers to everyday challenges.* Beltsville, MD: Gryphon House.

Available Online

Injoy. http://www.injoy.com/newsletters/. [Site provides free newsletters on leadership issues.]

LeadershipJournal.net by *Christianity Today.* http://www.leadershipjournal.net. [Site is geared primarily for church ministry. The section on Building Leaders includes articles on mentoring, working with volunteers, etc. Resources have more relevance for church-sponsored programs.]

Catalogs for Early Education Resource Publications

Gryphon House
Phone: 800-638-0928
http://www.gryphonhouse.com

Redleaf Press
Phone: 800-423-8309
http://www.redleafpress.org

Teachers College Press
Phone: 800-575-6566
http://www.teacherscollegepress.com

Professional Development Resources for Directors

Child Trends. http://www.childtrends.org.

Earlychildhood.com. http://www.earlychildhood.com. [This resource offers articles on a variety of topics including administration/leadership, infant/toddlers, professional development.]

NACCRRA Resource Exchange. http://www.nrex.org. [Included are basic resources for a variety of topics, including environmental health, special needs, and physical health.]

National Center for Early Development and Learning (NCEDL). http://www.fpg.unc.edu/~ncedl/index.cfm.

National Institute for Early Education Research (NIEER). http://nieer.org.

National Network for Child Care. http://www.nncc.org. [Site offers resource articles on a wide range of early education issues.]

Professional Publications for Early Education

Childhood Education. Association for Childhood Education International (ACEI). http://www.acei.org.

EarlyChildhood NEWS. http://www.earlychildhoodnews.com.

Early Childhood Research and Practice. http://ecrp.uiuc.edu.

Early Childhood Research Quarterly. http://www.sciencedirect.com/science/journal/08852006.

Exchange. Child Care Information Exchange. http://www.ccie.com. [*Exchange* is a magazine for preschool directors.]

Journal of Research in Childhood Education (JRCE). Association for Childhood Education International (ACEI). http://www.acei.org.

Organizations

(For Americans with Disabilities Act Accessibility Guidelines)
U.S. Department of Justice
Civil Rights Division
Disability Rights Section
950 Pennsylvania Avenue NW
Washington, DC 20530
Phone: 800-514-0301
http://www.usdoj.gov/crt/ada/adahom1.htm

Child Care Law Center
221 Pine Street, 3rd Floor

San Francisco, CA 94104
Phone: 415-394-7144
Email: info@childcarelaw.org
http://www.childcarelaw.org

Christian Management Association
PO Box 4090
San Clemente, CA 92674-4090
Phone: 800-727-4262
Email: CMA@CMAonline.org
http://www.christianity.com/cma

INJOY
PO Box 7700
Atlanta, GA 30357-0700
Phone: 800-333-6506
http://www.injoy.com

McCormick Tribune Center for Early Childhood Leadership
National-Louis University
6310 Capitol Drive
Wheeling, IL 60090
Phone: 800-443-5522, ext. 5056
http://cecl.nl.edu

National After School Association
(formerly National School-Age Care Alliance)
529 Main Street, Suite 214
Charlestown, MA 02129
Phone: 800-617-8242
http://www.naaweb.org

National Association of Child Care Professionals (NACCP)
PO Box 90723
Austin, TX 78709
Phone: 800-537-1118
Email: admin@naccp.org
http://www.naccp.org

Occupational Health & Safety Administration (OSHA)
U.S. Department of Labor
200 Constitution Avenue
Washington, DC 20210
Phone: 800-321-6742
http://www.osha.gov

Wheelock College Institute for Leadership and Career Initiatives
200 The Riverway
Boston, MA 02215
Phone: 617-879-2000
http://www.wheelock.edu

Chapter 7
SELECTING AND WORKING WITH STAFF

Available from ACSI

Brown, Gordon B. 2002. *Guiding faculty to excellence: Instructional supervision in the Christian school.* 2nd ed. Colorado Springs, CO: Purposeful Design Publications.

Carney, Burt. 2001. *Christian school personnel forms: A resource for interviewing, contracting, and evaluating school personnel.* Enabling Leadership Series. Colorado Springs, CO: Association of Christian Schools International.

———, ed. 2005. *The best of "Legal/Legislative Update."* CD. Colorado Springs, CO: Purposeful Design Publications.

Institute for Christian Conciliation. 2001. *Guidelines for Christian conciliation,* version 4.5. Billings, MT: Peacemaker Ministries.

Available from Other Publishers

Child Guidance

Cloud, Henry, and John Townsend. 1998. *Boundaries with kids: When to say yes, when to say no to help your children gain control of their lives.* Grand Rapids, MI: Zondervan.

Nelson, Jane, Cheryl Erwin, and Roslyn Duffy. 1998. *Positive discipline for preschoolers: For their early years—raising children who are responsible, respectful, and resourceful.* 2nd rev. ed. New York: Three Rivers Press.

Working with Staff

Albrecht, Kay. 2002. *The right fit: Recruiting, selecting, and orienting staff.* St. Paul, MN: New Horizons.

Bloom, Paula Jorde, Marilyn Sheerer, and Joan Britz. 1991. *Blueprint for action: Achieving center-based change through staff development.* Beltsville, MD: Gryphon House. [This is a source for surveys for gathering feedback from staff.]

Caruso, Joseph J., and M. Temple Fawcett. 1999. *Supervision in early childhood education: A developmental perspective.* 2nd ed. New York: Teachers College Press.

Center for the Child Care Workforce. 1999. *Creating better child care jobs: Model work standards for teaching staff in center-based child care.* Washington, DC: Center for the Child Care Workforce.

Required labor law postings

Department of Labor. http://www.dol.gov/osbp/sbrefa/poster/main.htm. [Electronic copies are available through this website.]

G. Neil. Phone: 877-968-7471. http://www.gneil.com. [This vendor sells federal and state charts.]

HR Direct. Phone: 800-346-1231. http://www.hrdirect.com. [This vendor sells federal and state charts.]

Personnel Concepts. Phone: 800-333-3795. http://www.personnelconcepts.com. [This vendor sells federal and state charts.]

Available Online

American Academy of Pediatrics, American Public Health Association, and National Resource Center for Health and Safety in Child Care. 2004. Child care providers' health and well being. http://nrc.uchsc.edu/SPINOFF/PROV/Providers.pdf.

U.S. Department of Labor. n.d. Fact sheet no. 46: Daycare centers and preschools under the Fair Labor Standards Act (FLSA). http://www.dol.gov/esa/fact-sheets-index.htm.

U.S. Department of Labor, Employment Standards Administration, Wage and Hour Division. http://www.dol.gov/esa/whd.

APPENDIX A

Chapter 8
CURRICULUM DESIGN AND IMPLEMENTATION

Available from ACSI

Bruinsma, Robert. 2003. *The joy of language: A Christian framework for language arts instruction.* Colorado Springs, CO: Purposeful Design Publications.

Graham, Donovan L. 2003. *Teaching redemptively: Bringing grace and truth into your classroom.* Colorado Springs, CO: Purposeful Design Publications.

Haycock, Ruth C. 1993. *Encyclopedia of Bible truths.* Encyclopedia of Bible Truths Series. Colorado Springs, CO: Association of Christian Schools International.

Marsden, Dorothea B. n.d. *The work sampling system.* New York: Pearson Early Learning. [This series provides performance assessment for preschool-age children.]

Meisels, Samuel J., Dorothea B. Marsden, Amy Laura Dombro, Donna R. Weston, and Abigail M. Jewkes. n.d. *The Ounce Scale.* New York: Pearson Early Learning. [This resource provides observational assessment for infants and toddlers.]

Van Brummelen, Harro. 2002. *Steppingstones to curriculum: A biblical path.* 2nd ed. Colorado Springs, CO: Purposeful Design Publications.

Available from Other Publishers

Smith, Daniel H. 1987. *How to lead a child to Christ.* Chicago, IL: Moody Press.

Early Literacy

Burns, M. Susan, Peg Griffin, and Catherine E. Snow, eds. 1999. *Starting out right: A guide to promoting children's reading success.* National Research Council. Washington, DC: National Academies Press.

Neuman, Susan B., Carol Copple, and Sue Bredekamp. 2000. *Learning to read and write: Developmentally appropriate practices for young children.* Washington, DC: National Association for the Education of Young Children.

Schickendanz, Judith A. 1999. *Much more than the ABCs: The early stages of reading and writing.* Washington, DC: National Association for the Education of Young Children.

Observation and Assessment

Curtis, Deb, and Margie Carter. 2000. *The art of awareness: How observation can transform your teaching.* St Paul, MN: Redleaf Press.

Helm, Judy Harris, Sallee Beneke, and Kathy Steinheimer. 1997. *Windows on learning: Documenting young children's work.* New York: Teachers College Press.

Leonard, Ann Marie. 1997. *I spy something! A practical guide for using observation tools in the preschool classroom.* Little Rock, AR: Southern Association on Children Under Six.

Mindes, Gayle, Harold Ireton, and Carol Mardell-Czudnowski. 1995. *Assessing young children.* Albany, NY: Delmar Publishers.

Nilsen, Barbara A. 1997. *Week by week: Plans for observing and recording young children.* Albany, NY: Delmar Publishers.

Science

Harlan, Jean D., and Mary S. Rivkin. 2003. *Science experiences for the early childhood years: An integrated affective approach.* 8th ed. Upper Saddle River, NJ: Prentice Hall.

Lind, Karen K. 1999. *Exploring science in early childhood education: A developmental approach.* Clifton Park, NY: Delmar Learning.

Seefeldt, Carol, and Alice Galper. 2006. *Active experiences for active children: Science.* 2nd ed. Upper Saddle River, NJ: Prentice Hall.

Available Online

Bowman, Barbara T., M. Suzanne Donovan, and M. Susan Burns, eds. 2000. Eager to learn: Educating our preschoolers. Commission on Behavioral and Social Sciences and Education. National Research Council. http://www.nap.edu/openbook/0309068363/html/185.html.

CTB/McGraw-Hill. 2002. Pre-kindergarten standards: Guidelines for teaching and learning. Executive summary (October). http://www.ctb.com.

Dwyer, M. Christine, Robin Chait, and Patricia McKee. 2000. Building strong foundations for early learning: The U.S. Department of Education's guide to high-quality early childhood education programs. U.S. Department of Education. http://www.ed.gov/offices/OUS/PES/early_learning/Foundations.pdf.

Ewing Marion Kauffman Foundation. 2002. Set for success: Building a strong foundation for school readiness based on the social-emotional development of young children. http://www.emkf.org [no longer available].

Helm, Judy Harris, and Gaye Gronlund. 2000. Linking standards and engaged learning in the early years. *Early Childhood Research and Practice* 2, no. 1. http://ecrp.uiuc.edu/v2n1/helm.html.

Scott-Little, Catherine, Sharon Lynn Kagan, and Victoria Stebbins Frelow. 2003. Standards for preschool children's learning and development: Who has standards, how were they developed, and how are they used? SERVE's Expanded Learning Opportunities: National Leadership Area Research Report (June). http://www.serve.org/_downloads/publications/Standards2003.pdf.

Shepard, Lorrie, Sharon Kagan, and Emily Wurtz. 1998. Public Policy Report: Goal 1 Early childhood assessments resource group recommendations. National Association for the Education of Young Children. *Young Children* 53, no. 3:52–54. [Available at http://www.journal.naeyc.org.]

Organizations

National Institute for Early Education Research
Rutgers, The State University of New Jersey
120 Albany Street, Suite 500
New Brunswick, New Jersey 08901
Phone: 732-932-4350
http://www.nieer.org

Chapter 9
ESTABLISHING APPROPRIATE ENVIRONMENTS

Available from Other Publishers

Curtis, Deb, and Margie Carter. 2003. *Designs for living and learning: Transforming early childhood environments.* St. Paul, MN: Redleaf Press.

Dodge, Diane Trister, and Bonnie Kittredge. 2003. *Room arrangement as a teaching strategy.* VHS. Washington, DC: Teaching Strategies.

Exelby, Betty, and Rebecca Isbell. 2001. *Early learning environments that work.* Beltsville, MD: Gryphon House.

Greenman, Jim. 1988. Caring spaces, learning places: Early learning environments that work. Redmond, WA: Exchange. [Available at http://www.ccie.com.]

Isbell, Rebecca. 1995. *The complete learning center book.* Beltsville, MD: Gryphon House.

Isbell, Rebecca, and Christy Isbell Gamble. 2003. *The complete learning spaces book for infants and toddlers: 54 integrated areas with play experiences.* Beltsville, MD: Gryphon House.

Olds, Anita Rui. 2000. *Child care design guide.* New York: McGraw-Hill.

Ruth, Linda Cain. 1999. *Design standards for children's environments.* New York: McGraw-Hill.

Seefeldt, Carol, and Joan Waites. 2002. *Creating rooms of wonder: Valuing and displaying children's work to enhance the learning process.* Beltsville, MD: Gryphon House.

Theemes, Tracy, and High/Scope Educational Foundation Staff. 1999. *Let's go outside: Designing the early childhood playground.* Albany, NY: Delmar.

Vogel, Nancy. 1999. *Getting started: Materials and equipment for active learning preschools.* Albany, NY: Delmar.

Wellhousen, Karyn. 2002. *Outdoor play every day: Innovative play concepts for early childhood.* Albany, NY: Delmar.

Available Online

Butin, Dan. 2000. Early childhood centers. National Clearinghouse for Educational Facilities. http://www.edfacilities .org/pubs/childcare.html. [This article provides a brief exploration of research and trends in center design.]

Fingersafe. http://www.fingersafe.com/usa/linktous.html. [This resource offers protective door devices.]

Grounds for Play. http://www.groundsforplay.com. [This resource assists in outdoor environment planning.]

Kaboom. http://www.kaboom.org. [This site offers playground planning resources.]

National Clearinghouse for Educational Facilities. http://www.edfacilities.org/rl/earlychildcenters.cfm. [This site provides lists of links, books, and journal articles providing extensive resources on design guidelines, quality indicators, and safety requirements for early childhood centers.]

National Program for Playground Safety. http://www.uni.edu/playground.

Spaces for Children. http://www.spacesforchildren.com. [This site contains resources for all aspects of designing childcare facilities, and it includes downloadable articles.]

U.S. Consumer Product Safety Commission. n.d. Handbook for public playground safety. http://www.cpsc.gov/cpscpub/pubs/playpubs.html.

U.S. General Services Administration. 2003. Child care center design guide. http://www.gsa.gov. [Although designed to be used when developing a center that has a federal government contract, this guide is a valuable review of best practices in design, including detailed architectural guidance.]

Organizations

Equipment/Classroom Materials Suppliers

ABC School Supply
Phone: 800-669-4222
Email: service@abcschoolsupply.com
http://www.abcschoolsupply.com

Childcraft
Phone: 800-631-5652
Email: service@childcrafteducation.com
http://www.childcraft.com

Community Playthings
Phone: 800-777-4244
Email: sales@communityplaythings.com
http://www.communityplaythings.com

Constructive Playthings
Phone: 800-448-7830
Email: custservice@ustoyco.com
http://www.constplay.com

Environments
Phone: 800-342-4453
Email: environments@eichild.com
http://www.environments.com

Kaplan Early Learning Company
Phone: 800-334-2014
Email: info@kaplanco.com
http://www.kaplanco.com

Lakeshore Learning Materials
Phone: 800-428-4414
http://www.lakeshorelearning.com

Nasco
Phone: 800-558-9595
Email: custserv@eNASCO.com
http://www.nascofa.com

Nursery Maid (Torelli/Durrett)
Phone: 800-443-8773
Email: service2@nurserymaid.com
http://www.nurserymaid.com

School Specialty
Phone: 888-388-3224
Email: info@schoolspecialty.com
http://www.schoolspecialty.com

Teachers' School Supply
Phone: 800-477-7745
http://www.teacherssupply.com

Chapter 10
RECRUITING AND ENROLLING STUDENTS

Available from Other Publishers

Montanari, Ellen Orton. 1992. *101 ways to build enrollment in your early childhood program.* Phoenix, AZ: CPG Publishing.

Available Online

Demuth, Dennis M., and Carol M. Demuth. 1992. Recruiting strategies for Christian schools: How to recruit and retain students. http://www.delpublications.com.

On-Target Marketing. 800-221-2864. http://www.childcareexchange.com. [This site offers a collection of articles reprinted from the Child Care Information Exchange.]

Chapter 11
CARING FOR THE NEEDS OF CHILDREN

Available from Other Publishers

American Academy of Pediatrics, American Public Health Association, and National Resource Center for Health and Safety in Child Care. 2002. Caring for our children: National health and safety performance standards. 2nd ed. http://nrc.uchsc.edu.

Aronson, Susan S. 2002. *Model child care health policies.* 4th ed. Washington, DC: NAEYC.

Healthy Childcare magazine. http://www.healthychild.net. [This bimonthly publication focuses on childcare programs devoted to health and safety issues.]

Available Online

American Academy of Pediatrics, American Public Health Association, and National Resource Center for Health and Safety in Child Care. 2002. Caring for our children: National health and safety performance standards. 2nd ed. http://nrc.uchsc.edu/CFOC. [This resource includes a chart detailing frequency of cleaning and sanitizing equipment and surfaces. Download the pdf file and find chart on page 106; the online version of the document does not contain the chart.]

American Red Cross. http://www.redcross.org.

California childcare health program. http://www.ucsfchildcarehealth.org. [Resources include *Health Notes*—two-page reviews of significant topics such as illness and injury prevention—and newsletters with topical information.]

The Food Allergy & Anaphylaxis Network. http://www.foodallergy.org. [Resources include a downloadable Food Allergy Action Plan that outlines what actions a caregiver should take in the event of an emergency (http://www.foodallergy.org/actionplan.pdf); and information on common food allergens (http://www.foodallergy.org/allergens/index.html).]

Medline Plus. U.S. National Library of Medicine and the National Institutes of Health. http://www.nlm.nih.gov/medlineplus/childdaycare.html. [This site includes links to reference articles.]

U.S. Department of Agriculture. 1999. Keeping kids safe: A guide to safe food handling and sanitation. http://schoolmeals.nal.usda.gov/Safety/KidsSafedit.pdf.

Emergency Plan Resources

Pennsylvania Emergency Management Agency. 2003. Day care planning tool kit. http://www.pema.state.pa.us/pema/cwp/view.asp?A=566&Q=254999. [The kit includes a three-part plan (basic plan, checklists, and supporting documents), a PowerPoint presentation to use in introducing the planning process, and a Daycare Facilities Planning Guide that helps fill in the blanks to complete the plan.]

Nutrition

Graves, D. E., C. W. Suitor, and K. A. Holt, eds. 1997. Making food healthy and safe for children: How to meet the national health and safety performance standards—guidelines for out-of-home child care programs. http://www

.ncemch.org/pubs/PDFs/Nutrition_Stnd/Nutrition_1_2.pdf.

National Food Service Management Institute. 2000–2006. Mealtime memo for child care. http://www.nfsmi.org/Infor mation/Newsletters/Mealtime_memo_index.html#2002. [These are pdf files of newsletters regarding nutrition.]

Organizations

American Academy of Pediatrics (AAP)
141 Northwest Point Boulevard
Elk Grove Village, IL 60007-1098
Phone: 847-434-4000
http://www.aap.org

Early Childhood Education Linkage System (ECELS)
Healthy Child Care America Pennsylvania
Pennsylvania Chapter, American Academy of Pediatrics
Rose Tree Corporate Center II, Suite 3007
1400 N. Conestoga Rd
Media, PA 19063
Phone: 484-446-3003
http://www.paaap.org
[This resource includes sample policies and forms, and fact sheets on communicable illnesses.]

The Healthy Child Care America Campaign
American Academy of Pediatrics (AAP)
141 Northwest Point Boulevard
Elk Grove Village, IL 60007
Phone: 888-227-5409
Email: childcare@aap.org
http://healthychildcare.org

National Institute of Health
National Institute of Child Health and Human Development
PO Box 3006
Rockville, MD 20847
Phone: 800-370-2943
Email: nichdinformationresourcecenter@mail.nih.gov
http://www.nichd.nih.gov

National Resource Center for Health and Safety in Child Care and Early Education
University of Colorado Health Sciences Center at Fitzsimons
Campus Mail Stop F541
PO Box 6508
Aurora, CO 80045-0508
Phone: 800-598-5437
http://nrc.uchsc.edu

National Safety Council (NSC)
1121 Spring Lake Drive
Itasca, IL 60143-3201
Phone: 630-285-1121
http://www.nsc.org

U.S. Consumer Product Safety Commission
4330 East West Highway
Bethesda, MD 20814
Phone: 800-638-2772
Email: info@cpsc.gov
http://www.cpsc.gov
[Call this toll-free consumer hotline to obtain product safety information (as well as other agency information) and to report unsafe products.]

Nutrition

Center for Nutrition Policy and Promotion
3101 Park Center Drive, Room 1034
Alexandria, VA 22302-1594
Phone: 703-305-7600
http://www.usda.gov/cnpp/index.html

Child Care Nutrition Resource System
Food and Nutrition Information Center
National Agricultural Library
10301 Baltimore Avenue
Beltsville, MD 20705-2351
Phone: 301-504-5719
http://www.nal.usda.gov/childcare

USDA Food and Nutrition Service
3101 Park Center Drive, Room 926
Alexandria, VA 22302
Phone: 703-305-2062
http://www.fns.usda.gov

Chapter 12
PARTNERING WITH PARENTS

Available Online

Healthy Start, Grow Smart Series. 2002. http://www.ed.gov/parents/earlychild/ready/healthystart/index.html. [These publications were developed by First Lady Laura Bush for distribution to parents.]

Information on brain development. http://www.serve.org/ELO/profdev.php#school.

Lerner, Claire, with Amy Dombro and Karen Levine. 2000. The magic of everyday moments series. Booklets.

http://www.zerotothree.org/magic. [These downloadable guides, published by Zero to Three, describe children's development from birth to fifteen months and offer ideas for how parents can enrich everyday moments with their child.]

National Parent Information Network. http://npin.org.

Organizations

Center for SPFM (Single-Parent Family Ministry)
PO Box 6020
Woodland Park, CO 80866
Phone: 719-687-0515
Email: info@spfm.org
http://www.spfm.org

Focus on the Family
Colorado Springs, CO 80995
Phone: 800-232-6459
http://www.family.org

Chapter 13
PARTNERING WITH THE COMMUNITY

Available from Other Organizations

Montanari, Ellen Orton. 1992. *101 ways to build enrollment in your early childhood program.* Phoenix, AZ: CPG Publishing.

Available Online

Carlsmith, Laura, and Jennifer Railsback. 2001. Designing a public relations plan. In *The power of public relations in schools.* Booklet. http://www.nwrel.org/request/feb01/designing.html.

Child Care Information Exchange. n.d. Exchange articles on CD: Marketing. http://www.childcareexchange.com. [This site offers a collection of 20 articles on the topic of marketing.]

Dolak, Dave. 2001. An example of a public relations plan. http://www.davedolak.com/prplan.htm.

Federal agency resources. http://www.childcare.gov. [Links are included to all the federal agency resources, grouped by categories.]

Books For Parent Lending Library

And Then I Had Kids by Susan Alexander Yates

Angry Kids by Richard L. Berry

The Blessing by Gary Smalley and John Trent

Boundaries with Kids by Henry Cloud and John Townsend

Bringing Up Boys by James Dobson

Building Faith: One Child at a Time by Becky Schuricht Peters

The Christian Babysitter's Handbook by Sarah Fletcher

Christian Child-Rearing and Personality Development by Paul D. Meier

Complete Marriage and Family Home Reference Guide by James Dobson

Creative Correction by Lisa Whelchel

Different Children, Different Needs by Charles F. Boyd

Discipline: 101 Alternatives to Nagging, Yelling, and Spanking by Alvin Price and Jay A. Parry

Every Child Is a Winner by Caz McCaslin and Bobb Biehl

Family Traditions by J. Otis Ledbetter and Tim Smith

501 Practical Ways to Teach Your Children Values by Bobbie Reed

The Focus on the Family Complete Book of Baby and Child Care by Paul C. Reisser

For Fathers Who Aren't in Heaven by Ron Rand

For the Family's Sake by Susan Schaeffer Macaulay

Growing a Healthy Home by Mike Yorkey

Growing Wise in Family Life by Charles R. Swindoll

Honey for a Child's Heart by Gladys Hunt

How to Be a Hero to Your Kids by Josh McDowell and Dick Day

How to Keep Your Kids on Your Team by Charles Stanley

Keeping Your Family Close When Frequent Travels Pull You Apart by Elizabeth M. Hoekstra

Little House on the Freeway: Help for the Hurried Home by Tim Kimmel

Make Room for Daddy by Elisa Morgan and Carol Kuykendall

Making Children Mind Without Losing Yours by Kevin Leman

The Media-Wise Family by Ted Baehr

Miseducation: Preschoolers at Risk by David Elkind

Motivating Your Kids: From Crayons to Career by Cheri Fuller

The Mystery of Children: What Our Kids Teach Us About Childlike Faith by Mike Mason

The New Dare to Discipline by James Dobson

The New Hide or Seek by James Dobson

The New Read-Aloud Handbook by Jim Trelease

The New Strong-Willed Child by James Dobson

Parenting Isn't for Cowards by James Dobson

Parenting with Love and Limits by Bruce Narramore

Parenting with Scripture by Kara Durbin

Parents' Guide to the Spiritual Growth of Children edited by John Trent, Rick Osborne, and Kurt Bruner.

The Power of a Praying Parent by Stormie Omartian

Quiet Times for Parents by H. Norman Wright

Raising Great Kids by Henry Cloud and John Townsend

Right from Wrong: What You Need to Know to Help Youth Make Right Choices by Josh McDowell

Shepherding a Child's Heart by Tedd Tripp

Solid Answers by James Dobson

Taming the Family Zoo: Maximizing Harmony and Minimizing Family Stress by Jim Brawner and Suzette Brawner

Teaching Your Child About God by Wes Haystead

Temper Your Child's Tantrums by James Dobson

Traveling with Kids: 101 Tips for a Great Trip by Jay A. Parry

A Very Practical Guide to Discipline with Young Children by Grace Mitchell

What Kids Need Most in a Dad by Tim Hansel

NOTES

Chapter 1 GETTING STARTED

1. Robert Couch and Lois Gamble. 2000. *Weekday early education administrative guide*. Nashville, TN: LifeWay Church Resources. (Available from http://www.lifeway.com.)

2. Kathleen Seaton and Linda Rothaar. 1991. *Early childhood ministry and your church: How to start and maintain an early childhood center*. Minneapolis, MN: Augsburg Fortress.

3. Education Commission of the States. 2000. Quick facts: Early childhood. http://www.ecs.org.

4. Eugene Smolensky and Jennifer Appleton Gootman, eds. 2003. *Working families and growing kids: Caring for children and adolescents*. Washington, DC: National Academies Press. http://www.nap.edu.

Chapter 2 PHILOSOPHY AND MISSION OF CHRISTIAN EARLY EDUCATION

1. Paul A. Kienel. 1980. *The philosophy of Christian school education*. 3rd ed. Whittier, CA: Association of Christian Schools International, 44–46.

2. George Barna. 2002. *A fish out of water: 9 Strategies effective leaders use to help you get back into the flow*. Brentwood, TN: Integrity.

3. Elena Bodrova, Deborah Leong, and Rima Shore. 2004. Child outcome standards in pre-K programs: What are standards; what is needed to make them work? Policy brief. *Preschool Policy Matters* (National Institute for Early Education Research), no. 5 (March): 4.

Chapter 3 GOD'S DESIGN FOR GROWTH

1. David Elkind. 1987. *Miseducation: Preschoolers at risk*. New York: Knopf.

2. Lorrie Shepard, Sharon Kagan, and Emily Wurtz. 1998. Public policy report: Goal 1 Early childhood assessments resource group recommendations. National Association for the Education of Young Children. *Young Children* 53, no. 3:52–54.

3. Elena Bodrova, Deborah Leong, and Diane Paynter. 1999. Literacy standards for preschool learners. ASCD. *Educational Leadership* 57, no. 2:42–46.

4. David Elkind. 2002. The connection between play and character. *Child Care Information Exchange* 184 (November/December), 41.

Chapter 4 SPONSORSHIP AND GOVERNANCE

1. Lesia Oesterreich. 1998. Child care: Financial basics. Pm-1751. Ames, IA: Iowa State University Extension. http://www.extension.iastate.edu/Publications/PM1751.pdf.

2. Roy W. Lowrie Jr. 1998. *Serving God on the Christian school board*. 2nd ed. Colorado Springs, CO: Association of Christian Schools International, 58–68.

3. Dorothy June Sciarra and Anne G. Dorsey. 2002. *Developing and administering an early childhood center*. 5th ed. Clifton Park, NY: Delmar Learning.

4. Burt Carney, ed. 2003. Your school must meet several IRS nondiscrimination requirements to keep its tax exemption. *Legal/Legislative Update* (Association of Christian Schools International) 13, no. 4 (summer): 52.

5. Linda S. Nelson and Alan E. Nelson. 2003. *Child care administration: Planning quality programs for young children*. Tinley Park, IL: Goodheart-Wilcox, 231–49.

Chapter 5 MANAGING FINANCES

1. Burt Carney. 2002/2003. Providing tax-free tuition discounts for school employees. *Legal/Legislative Update* (Association of Christian Schools International) 13, no. 2:22–23.

2. R. A. Whitehead. 2003. Budgeting for quality and survival in the 21st century. *Child Care Exchange* 153:7–11.

3. Lesia Oesterreich. 1998. Child care: Financial basics. Pm-1751. Ames, IA: Iowa State University Extension. http://www.extension.iastate.edu/Publications/PM1751.pdf.

4. Linda S. Nelson and Alan E. Nelson. 2003. *Child care administration: Planning quality programs for young children.* Tinley Park, IL: Goodheart-Wilcox.

Chapter 6 THE ROLE OF THE DIRECTOR

1. George Barna. 2002. *A fish out of water.* Brentwood, TN: Integrity, 5–7.

2. Ibid., 7.

3. Ibid., 7–8.

4. Linda S. Nelson and Alan E. Nelson. 2003. *Child care administration: Planning quality programs for young children.* Tinley Park, IL: Goodheart-Wilcox.

5. Myron Rush. 2002. *Management: A biblical approach.* Colorado Springs, CO: Victor, 126.

6. Community Care Licensing Division. 2004. Mission statement. California Department of Social Services. http://ccld.ca.gov/MissionSta_1811.htm.

Chapter 7 SELECTING AND WORKING WITH STAFF

1. American Academy of Pediatrics, American Public Health Association, and National Resource Center for Health and Safety in Child Care. 2002. Caring for our children: National health and safety performance standards. 2nd ed. http://nrc.uchsc.edu/CFOC.

2. Gordon B. Brown. 2002. *Guiding faculty to excellence: Instructional supervision in the Christian school.* 2nd ed. Colorado Springs, CO: Purposeful Design Publications.

3. John Cooley. n.d. Employment practices under the Americans with Disabilities Act. In *Christian school legal and administrative issues.* CD. Colorado Springs, CO: Association of Christian Schools International. (Also available at http://www.acsi.org.)

4. Ibid.

5. Ibid.

6. U.S. Department of Labor. n.d. Fact sheet no. 46: Daycare centers and preschools under the Fair Labor Standards Act (FLSA). http://www.dol.gov/esa/fact-sheets-index.htm.

7. Ibid.

8. Charles Pekow. n.d. Do child care centers have to pay staff for time spent in training? *Early Childhood News.* http://www.earlychildhood.com/Articles/index.cfm?FuseAction=Article&A=143.

9. Burt Carney. 2005. Responding to OSHA's final rule for "occupational exposure to bloodborne pathogens." In *The best of "Legal/Legislative Update."* Colorado Springs, CO: Purposeful Design Publications. (Also available at http://www.acsi.org/~924.)

10. Burt Carney. 2006. ACSI legal compliance checklist—January 2006. http://www.acsi.org/~legal.

11. Henry Cloud and John Townsend. 1998. *Boundaries with kids: When to say yes, when to say no to help your children gain control of their lives.* Grand Rapids, MI: Zondervan, 17.

12. Ibid.

13. Jane Nelson, Cheryl Erwin, and Roslyn Duffy. 1998. *Positive discipline for preschoolers: For their early years—raising children who are responsible, respectful, and resourceful.* 2nd rev. ed. New York: Three Rivers Press, 170.

14. Paul Kienel. n.d. *The Matthew 18 principle for solving school problems.* http://www.acsi.org/~924.

15. Linda Lumsden. 1998. Teacher morale. *ERIC Digest,* no. 120 (March).

16. Ibid.

17. Paula Jorde Bloom. 1988. Closing the gap: An analysis of teacher and administrator perceptions of organizational

climate in the early childhood setting. *Teaching and Teacher Education* 4, no. 2:111–20.

18. Joseph J. Caruso and M. Temple Fawcett. 1999. *Supervision in early childhood education: A developmental perspective.* 2nd ed. New York: Teachers College Press.

Chapter 8 CURRICULUM DESIGN AND IMPLEMENTATION

1. Joanne Hendrick. 1990. *Total learning: Developmental curriculum for the young child.* 3rd ed. Columbus, OH: Merrill, 2.

2. George Barna. 2003. *Transforming children into spiritual champions.* Ventura, CA: Regal Books.

3. Mark Eckel. 2003. *The whole truth.* Longwood, FL: Xulon Press, 64.

4. Karyn Henley. 1997. *Child-sensitive teaching: Helping children grow a living faith in a loving God.* Cincinnati, OH: Standard, 81–82.

5. California Department of Education. 2000. *Prekindergarten learning development guidelines,* 84.

6. Barbara T. Bowman, M. Suzanne Donovan, and M. Susan Burns, eds. 2000. *Eager to learn: Educating our preschoolers.* Commission on Behavioral and Social Sciences and Education. National Research Council. Washington, DC: National Academy Press. (Available at http://www.nap.edu/openbook/0309068363/html/185.html.)

7. Kathy Ralston. 2002. Developing curriculum: Traveling the road to excellence. In *Called to lead: Understanding and fulfilling your role as an educational leader,* ed. Kenneth Gangel, 147–60. Colorado Springs, CO: Purposeful Design Publications.

8. Lilian Katz. 1999. Another look at what young children should be learning. *ERIC Digest* ED430735 (June).

9. Rima Shore. 2004. Child outcome standards in preK programs. *Preschool Policy Matters,* NIEER, no. 5 (March): 5.

10. Harro Van Brummelen. 2002. *Steppingstones to curriculum: A biblical path.* 2nd ed. Colorado Springs, CO: Purposeful Design Publications, 95.

11. Hendrick.

12. Bowman, Donovan, and Burns, 185.

13. Bowman, Donovan, and Burns.

14. Ibid.

Chapter 9 ESTABLISHING APPROPRIATE ENVIRONMENTS

1. Jim Greenman. 1988. *Caring spaces, learning places: Children's environments that work.* Redmond, WA: Exchange Press, 38.

2. Rochelle Bunnett and Diane Kroll. 2000. Transforming spaces: Rethinking the possibilities—Turning design challenges into opportunities. *Child Care Information Exchange* 131 (January/February): 29.

3. Greenman, 74.

4. Jeanne Vergeront. 1987. *Places and spaces for preschool and primary indoors.* Washington, DC: NAEYC, 15.

5. Cosby S. Rogers and Janet K. Sawyers. 1988. *Play in the lives of children.* American Series in Mathematical and Management Sciences. Washington, DC: NAEYC.

6. Doris Bergen. 2002. The role of pretend play in children's cognitive development. *Early Childhood Research and Practice* 4, no. 1.

7. Dan Butin. 2000. Early childhood centers. National Clearinghouse for Educational Facilities. http://www.edfacilities.org/pubs/childcare.html.

8. Greenman, 61.

9. Vergeront.

10. Gary T. Moore. 1998. Image and scale: Child care facility design. *Child Care Information Exchange* 120 (March/April): 97–101.

11. Sybil Kritchevsky, Elizabeth Prescott, and Lee Walling. 1977. *Planning environments for young children: Physical space.* 2nd ed. Washington, DC: NAEYC.

12. Rebecca Isbell. 1995. *The complete learning center book: An illustrated guide for 32 different early childhood learning centers.* Beltsville, MD: Gryphon House.

13. Ibid.

14. Rebecca Isbell and Betty Exelby. 2001. *Early learning environments that work.* Beltsville, MD: Gryphon House.

15. National Program for Playground Safety. 2004. Child care alert: Testing results released about surfacing used under indoor playground equipment. http://www.playgroundsafety.org/safety/indoor_mats.htm.

16. U.S. Consumer Product Safety Commission. n.d. Never put children's climbing gyms on hard surfaces, indoors or outdoors. Consumer products safety alert. http://www.cpsc.gov/cpscpub/pubs/5119.pdf.

17. Greenman.

18. Kay Cutler. 2000. Organizing the curriculum storage in a preschool/child care environment. *Young Children* 55, no. 3 (May): 88–92.

19. V. Harris. 1991. Open-air learning experiences. *Extensions* 5, no. 6 (May/June).

20. Greenman.

21. Ibid.

22. Michael Henniger. 1994. Planning for outdoor play. *Young Children* 49, no. 4 (May): 10–15.

23. H. Ihn. 1998. Analysis of preschool children's equipment choices and play behaviors in outdoor environments. *Early Childhood News* 10, no. 4:20–25.

24. Ibid.

25. L. Schmidt, ed. 1995. *Child care by design: Resource guide.* Toronto, Canada: University of Toronto.

26. Frances Wardle. 1997. Outdoor play: Designing, building, and remodeling playgrounds for young children. *Early Childhood News* 9, no. 2 (March/April): 36–40, 42.

27. Harris, 1–3.

28. U.S. General Services Administration. 2003. Child care center design guide. PBS-100 (July). http://www.gsa.gov.

Chapter 10 RECRUITING AND ENROLLING STUDENTS

1. Linda S. Nelson and Alan E. Nelson. 2003. *Child care administration: Planning quality programs for young children.* Tinley Park, IL: Goodheart-Wilcox, 193, 200–01.

2. Dorothy June Sciarra and Anne G. Dorsey. 2003. *Developing and administering a child care center.* 5th ed. Clifton Park, NY: Delmar Learning, 331, 336.

3. Nelson and Nelson.

Chapter 11 CARING FOR THE NEEDS OF CHILDREN

1. American Academy of Pediatrics, American Public Health Association, and National Resource Center for Health and Safety in Child Care. 2002. Caring for our children: National health and safety performance standards: Guidelines for out-of-home child care programs, 2nd ed. http://nrc.uchsc.edu/CFOC, Standard 3.001, 85.

2. Ibid., Standard 1.009, 8.

3. Ibid., Standard 3.065, 124–28.

4. American Academy of Pediatrics, American Public Health Association, and National Resource Center for Health and Safety in Child Care. 2002. Exclusion and inclusion of ill children in child care facilities and care of ill children in child care. http://nrc.uchsc.edu/SPINOFF/IE/ExcInc.htm. [This resource is adapted from *Caring for our children: National health and safety performance standards.*]

5. Lyn Dailey. 2003. Health and safety notes: Excluding children due to illness. California Childcare Health

Program. http://www.ucsfchildcarehealth.org/.

6. Ibid.

7. American Academy of Pediatrics, American Public Health Association, and National Resource Center for Health and Safety in Child Care. 2002. Caring for our children: National health and safety performance standards. 2nd ed. http://nrc.uchsc.edu/CFOC, Standard 3.065, 126.

8. Ibid., Standard 1.045, 36.

9. Ibid., Appendix I: Selecting an appropriate sanitizer, 417–18.

10. Ibid., Standard 3.026, 101.

11. Ibid., Glossary, 492.

12. Ibid., 493.

13. Ibid., Standard 3.026, 101.

14. Susan S. Aronson. 2001. Fact sheet: Universal, standard, and transmission-based precautions as they apply to child care settings. American Academy of Pediatrics, Pennyslvania Chapter. http://www.paaap.org [article no longer available online].

15. American Academy of Pediatrics, American Public Health Association, and National Resource Center for Health and Safety in Child Care. 2002. Caring for our children: National health and safety performance standards. 2nd ed. http://nrc.uchsc.edu/CFOC, Standard 3.083, 138.

16. Ibid., Standard 1.026, 21–22.

17. Ibid., Standard 1.027, 23.

18. Susan S. Aronson. 2002. *Model child care health policies.* 4th ed. Washington, DC: NAEYC.

19. American Academy of Pediatrics, American Public Health Association, and National Resource Center for Health and Safety in Child Care. 2002. 2nd ed. http://nrc.uchsc.edu/CFOC, Standard 5.085, 222.

20. National Safety Council. 2004. Playground safety. Fact sheet. http://www.nsc.org.

21. California Childcare Health Program. 1999. Child Care Health Connections (University of California, San Francisco School of Nursing) (November–December): 5.

22. National Safety Council.

23. California Childcare Health Program. 2004. Summer safety. Health and safety notes. http://www.ucsfchildcarehealth.org.

24. Consumer Product Safety Commission. n.d. Wear bike helmets on bicycles—not on playgrounds. Safety alert. CPSC Document #5121. http://www.cpsc.gov/cpscpub/pubs/5121.html.

25. Consumer Product Safety Commission. n.d. Strings can strangle children on playground equipment. Safety alert. CPSC Document #5094. http://www.cpsc.gov/cpscpub/pubs/5094.html.

26. American Academy of Pediatrics, American Public Health Association, and National Resource Center for Health and Safety in Child Care. 2002. Caring for our children: National health and safety performance standards. 2nd ed. http://nrc.uchsc.edu/CFOC, Standard 5.085, 222.

27. Herberta Smith. 2001. FactsSheet: Preventing the spread of infectious disease in childcare. Pennsylvania Chapter American Academy of Pediatrics. http://www.paaap.org [article no longer available online].

28. Margaret E. Briley and Cindy Roberts-Gray. 1999. Position of the American Dietetic Association: Nutrition standards for child-care programs. *Journal of the American Dietetic Association* 99 (August): 981–88.

29. Ibid.

30. Susan Jensen and Mardi Lucich. 2003. Healthy snacks for toddlers and preschoolers. Rev. ed. Health and safety notes. California Childcare Health Program. http://www.ucsfchildcarehealth.org.

31. Terry Holybee. 2001. Food allergies. Fact sheets for families. California Childcare Health Program. http://www.ucsfchildcarehealth.org.

32. Jensen and Lucich.

33. American Academy of Pediatrics, American Public Health Association, and National Resource Center for Health and Safety in Child Care. 2002. *Caring for our children: National health and safety performance standards.* 2nd ed. http://nrc.uchsc.edu/CFOC, Standard 4.010, 154.

34. Briley and Roberts-Gray.

Chapter 12 PARTNERING WITH PARENTS

1. Beth Yancey. 1989. *The Christian preschool: A strategy for parents and teachers.* La Habra, CA: Association of Christian Schools International, 44–45.

2. Ibid.

3. George Barna. 2003. *Transforming children into spiritual champions.* Ventura, CA: Regal Books, 77–83.

4. Pamela K. Boucher, comp. 1999. *Teaching in Christian weekday early education.* Nashville, TN: LifeWay Christian Resources.

5. Kathleen Watkins and Lucius Durant Jr. 1990. *Complete book of forms for managing the early childhood program.* New York: Center for Applied Research in Education.

Chapter 13 PARTNERING WITH THE COMMUNITY

1. National Center for Education Statistics. 1998. *Characteristics of children's early care and education programs: Data from the 1995 National Household Education Survey.* NCES 98–128, 66.

2. Linda S. Nelson and Alan E. Nelson. 2003. *Child care administration: Planning quality programs for young children.* Tinley Park, IL: Goodheart-Wilcox.

ABOUT THE AUTHORS

Leanne Leak, B.A.

As assistant director for early education services for the Association of Christian Schools International (ACSI) Northern California/Hawaii region, Leanne Leak supports early education leaders through conferences, director networking, and preschool accreditation. Leanne has written articles for *Christian Early Education* magazine and *Early Education Leaders Report*. She holds a degree in child development from California State University, Sacramento and has completed coursework toward a master's degree in early childhood education at the same university. Prior to working for ACSI, Leanne directed a church-sponsored preschool and childcare center that served 150 children. Leanne was a contributing author to the ACSI's *Preschool Accreditation Manual* and to the *Principles and Practices of Christian Early Education* course. Leanne's interest in international education has allowed her to spend time in early education programs in Scotland and South Africa.

Debbi Keeler, M.S.

Ms. Keeler serves as the assistant director of early education for ACSI in Southern California and has been involved in Christian early education since 1980 as a teacher assistant, teacher, director, and educational leader. She earned her bachelor of arts degree in home economics from California State University, Los Angeles, and a master of science degree in educational administration from National University, San Diego, California. Debbi has taught on-campus and online courses in early education at National University, Vanguard University, and Santa Ana Community College. Her desire is for early educators to be fully equipped with the practical tools that will enable them to be spiritually and professionally effective for the kingdom of God.

Debi Lydic, B.A.

Ms. Lydic has been in the early education profession since 1978. According to Debi, "early education is a great vehicle to expand God's territory. Nurturing a young child opens the door to relationships with the entire family." She is currently serving as the executive director of Handprints Early Education Centers, based in Colorado Spring, CO. With a mission statement of "reaching the world through the heart of a child," the center aims to leave the handprints of Christ on the lives of children and families. Debi has taught and led early education programs in Florida, California, and Colorado, and currently resides in Iowa.